W9-BZC-886

Rebellion, Racism
& Religion

AMERICAN
MILITIAS

Richard Abanes

Foreword by Roy Innis
Chairman, Congress of Racial Equality (C.O.R.E.)

IVP

InterVarsity Press
Downers Grove, Illinois

InterVarsity Press® is the book-publishing division of InterVarsity Christian Fellowship®, a student movement active on campus at hundreds of universities, colleges and schools of nursing in the United States of America, and a member movement of the International Fellowship of Evangelical Students. For information about local and regional activities, write Public Relations Dept., InterVarsity Christian Fellowship, 6400 Schroeder Rd., P.O. Box 7895, Madison, WI 53707-7895.

All Scripture quotations, unless otherwise indicated, are taken from the HOLY BIBLE, NEW INTERNATIONAL VERSION®. NIV®. Copyright ©1973, 1978, 1984 by International Bible Society. Used by permission of Zondervan Publishing House. All rights reserved.

Cover photograph: David York

ISBN 0-8308-1368-3

Library of Congress Catalog Card Number: 96-77058

Printed in the United States of America ♾

21	20	19	18	17	16	15	14	13	12	11	10	9	8	7	6	5	4	3	2	1
13	12	11	10	09	08	07	06	05	04	03	02	01	00	99	98	97	96			

To my mother and father, who raised me in the heartland of America. They taught me the real meaning of patriotism—love of country, respect for authority, and obedience to the laws of the land. They, and others like them, are this nation's true patriots.

Acknowledgments

There are a number of individuals without whose help I would not have been able to complete this project. My good friend Hank Kitchen, for instance, greatly assisted me by tracking down many crucial pieces of information. Unfortunately, I cannot give several other researchers the public recognition they deserve. They have asked to remain anonymous due to the book's subject matter. I must, therefore, be content with saying that my greatest appreciation goes to all of those persons who made this work possible through their research assistance.

Further gratitude belongs to numerous friends—V, W and E—who must also remain anonymous. Their prayers and support have been invaluable to me over the last year.

A special word of indebtedness goes to Johnny Lee Clary, former Imperial Wizard of the White Knights of the Ku Klux Klan. He has left the racist road of hatred and is now traveling on a pathway of peace. Johnny, you are a brave man, and I rejoice in your freedom. You opened my eyes to a very dark corner of humanity and have proven to me that there is hope for everyone.

I also wish to acknowledge InterVarsity Press for handling this book, especially Rodney Clapp and Jim Hoover, who gave special attention to the project. A commitment to publishing truth will always be rewarded.

Last, but certainly not least, I must express loving thanks to my precious and beautiful wife, Bri. Despite her own trials and tribulations in life, she somehow manages to provide me with unending love, support and encouragement. She is my dearest friend, toughest critic and best editor.

Foreword

In antebellum America, extremist political passions were consistently fueled by racism and religion. Those passions, catalyzed by the media and exploited by politicians, increased exponentially until an explosive mixture of racial hatred and religious zeal had been created. This volatile brew eventually ignited the Civil War and produced an era of death and devastation. A number of recent events, most notably the 1995 Oklahoma City bombing, indicate that Americans are once again being confronted by individuals whose political views and religious ideologies threaten the peace and tranquility of our nation.

Richard Abanes's *American Militias: Rebellion, Racism and Religion* provides a reliable analysis of these persons and the patriot/militia movement in which they flourish. Abanes has produced a powerful, dramatic summary of the burning domestic issue of the day—as did Harriet Beecher Stowe, in the middle of the nineteenth century, with her novel *Uncle Tom's Cabin*. In fact, *American Militias* could become the *Uncle Tom's Cabin* of the late twentieth and early twenty-first centuries.

Unlike the press, prosecutors and politicians (including President Clinton)—many of whom have exploited the high profile domestic terrorism cases—Abanes does not paint with a broad brush. He does not lump together all defenders of the Second Amendment with the militias and patriot movement. He does not demonize the NRA and other legitimate gun rights groups, whether he agrees with them or not. He also does not ignore the mistakes that have been made by law enforcement authorities in confrontations with militia/patriot types, but discusses them in a balanced and insightful manner.

American Militias reveals that the patriot movement is not, as some in the media have suggested, a monolithic subculture of Johnnies-come-lately. It is a complex network of extremists who have historical roots and analogues. Some of the variants of today's militia members and patriots were early Klansmen, the antebellum proslavery gangs and the John Brown-type abolitionists. Like these mid-nineteenth century extremists, modern day patriots and militia members have wrapped their political views in religion and apocalyptic pronouncements. Furthermore, many of today's most violent patriots present themselves as martyrs when apprehended for serious violations of law. This is reflective of John Brown, who was hanged in 1859 for murder and rebellion.

Adding to the seriousness of the current situation is the fact that many naive and decent young people are getting involved with political/religious extremists due to feelings of alienation and sincere patriotism. Aggravating this problem has been the media's hype, oversimplifications and inaccuracies regarding groups like the militias. Censorship of opposing views and eloquent voices debating national issues has also heightened young people's frustrations and their sense of alienation—making them prey for dangerous fringe organizations, such as those found within the patriot movement.

I pray that the media would not add to the polarization in our country, but instead adopt the investigative and analytical approach taken by Abanes in this book. Some readers might prematurely conclude that they will reject the analyses and conclusions of Abanes. This impulse should be resisted! Richard Abanes's *American Militias* must be read.

Roy Innis
Chairman, Congress of Racial Equality (C.O.R.E)

Introduction

What is it going to take to open up the eyes of our elected officials? AMERICA IS IN SERIOUS DECLINE. We have no proverbial tea to dump; should we instead sink a ship full of Japanese imports? Is a civil war imminent? Do we have to shed blood to reform the current system? I hope it doesn't come to that! But it might.

Timothy McVeigh (February 11, 1992)
Oklahoma bombing suspect[1]

t 9:02 A.M. on April 19, 1995, Americans were stunned by the worst domestic terrorist attack in United States history—the bombing of the Alfred P. Murrah Federal Building in Oklahoma City, Oklahoma. The blast killed 169 people, including nineteen children in the America's Kids day-care center located on the structure's second floor. Approximately 600 persons were injured.[2] Terrorist experts were quickly called upon to analyze the horrific event. "Who would have done this?" asked reporters. "Are there any similarities between this bombing and the World Trade Center disaster?" "What about Arab extremists?" Within hours, irresponsible speculations about militant Muslims and Islamic fundamentalists had fanned the flames of prejudice,[3] leading to a number of attacks against inno foreign refugees and American citizens of Middle Eastern descent.[4] B promptly silenced the emotionally charged accusations when tw twenty-seven-year-old Gulf War veteran Timothy McVeigh a army buddy Terry Nichols—were arrested in connectio possible that Americans had actually targeted fe motivate a person to kill defenseless men, women commit such a "crime against humanity," as FBI Dir Disturbing answers to these and other questions surf McVeigh and Nichols' involvement in the patriot movem community of individuals from a broad cross-section of so

On the movement's moderate side are conservative Christians dissatisfied by the current state of American politics. Their primary concern is changing the government through political activism. More radical participants include both Christians and non-Christians who deny their U.S. citizenship, drive without licenses, and refuse to pay income taxes in an effort to live outside "the system." Interspersed among these two groups are the most dangerous and unpredictable "patriots"—Klansmen, neo-Nazis, and Christian Identity believers. These persons are extremely difficult to detect among mainstream conservative Christians because they blend their white supremacist views with pseudo-Christian thought.

This loosely knit network of perhaps 5 to 12 million people may be one of the most diverse movements our nation has ever seen.[6] Within its ranks are college students, the unemployed, farmers, manual laborers, professionals, law enforcement personnel and members of the military. Men and women of all ages may join, and involvement is not limited to persons of one particular religion or race (excluding the racist groups). Interestingly, patriots have no single leader. The glue binding them together is a noxious compound of four ingredients: (1) an obsessive suspicion of the government; (2) belief in anti-government conspiracy theories; (3) a deep-seated hatred of government officials; and (4) a feeling that the United States Constitution, for all intents and purposes, has been discarded by Washington bureaucrats.

Most patriots also harbor the notion that America rests in the hands of an illegitimate government. Consider the words of Mark Koernke, an influential disseminator of patriot beliefs:

> The usurpation of power on the part of the regime—not a government—but the regime that is in place . . . is about to unfold into a very evil flower. . . . It is the ambition of our enemy and in fact it is their sworn oath, to destroy the Constitution and the Bill of Rights.[7]

Koernke made this remark during a 1993 speech entitled "A Call to Arms." During the same lecture, he quoted Revolutionary War hero Patrick Henry: "If we wish to be free, we must fight. We must fight. An appeal to arms and God is all that is left to us. All that is left." Koernke then commented, "The time is the same as we see now." He went on to declare that patriots were one day closer to victory in the "occupied" states.

Like most individuals in America's new anti-government subculture, Koernke believes that there is sort of a cold war being waged between freedom-loving patriots and federal authorities. Indiana attorney Linda Thompson, a well-known personality within the patriot movement, has plainly stated, "The war is on."[8]

The chances of this war escalating into armed conflict is so great that vast numbers of patriots have formed hundreds of "unorganized" militias throughout the country. Each group of heavily armed "freedom fighters" regularly holds military training exercises in preparation for what many patriots see as an inevitable showdown with the regime now controlling the nation. Militia members view themselves as the last defenders of the Constitution, modern-day minutemen who will one day have to fight to keep the U.S. from becoming a totalitarian police state.

To complicate matters, large segments of the patriot/militia movement are being driven by religious beliefs and/or racism, two powerful forces that historically have often led to episodes of violence. This raises another disturbing issue: the unholy alliance that has formed between racists and anti-Semites on the one hand, and some conservative Christians on the other. The common ground between these two groups is apocalypticism (i.e., a belief that at some divinely appointed time in the future, the world as we know it will end through a cataclysmic confrontation between the forces of good and evil, out of which will emerge the righteous kingdom of God).

Many Christian patriots believe the end is near and view Washington politicians as evil conspirators laying the foundation for the soon-to-be-revealed Antichrist, whose reign of terror will end only when Jesus Christ returns to earth in glory. Many white supremacists also feel the end is approaching. They, however, see the government as a Jewish pawn that must be destroyed in preparation for an Armageddon-like race war.[9] In *this* last days scenario, whites emerge victorious from the battle to establish an Aryan republic in America.

A preoccupation with the end-times is shared by Christians and white suprema-cists because many white supremacists emerged from mainstream Christian de-nominations. Unfortunately, these non-Christian defectors from the faith have borrowed heavily from their Christian roots, picking those doctrines that are most appealing—especially beliefs associated with the end-times—and blending them with racial prejudice.

The reason many Christians are re-establishing links with non-Christian racists is twofold: (1) rhetoric denouncing the government has recently become wide-spread within the evangelical community; and (2) some Christian leaders are accepting without hesitation anyone who appears to be a like-minded government-basher. As a result, evangelicals—who profess a faith free of prejudice—are often endorsing and sharing public platforms with neo-Nazis, former Ku Klux Klan leaders and other racists.

The picture grows more troubling when one takes into account the high levels of paranoia that abound in the patriot/militia movement. An ocean of pamphlets, newsletters, videotapes, audiocassettes, and computer files have flooded patriot minds with farfetched conspiratorial plots the likes of which have previously been confined to bad spy novels. Most patriots, for example, believe that nearly everyone in the government is out to enslave U.S. citizens as part of an insidious scheme hatched long ago by a secret cabal of behind-the-scenes "internationalists" whose ultimate goal is world domination. Most of humanity's woes (e.g., economic trouble, wars, natural disasters, various diseases, etc.) have been caused by this clandestine brotherhood of foreign conspirators, who are often referred to as "they," "them" or "you know who."

Making the current situation even worse has been the government's refusal to ease the justifiable fears and frustrations of patriots. In fact, on more than one occasion federal behavior has only increased tensions. Consider the 1992 incident involving Randy Weaver, a Northern Idaho white supremacist charged with selling two sawed-off shotguns to undercover FBI agents. Weaver failed to show up for trial, which prompted authorities to conduct surveillance on his property. When the intruding lawmen were discovered, a gun battle ensued during which Weaver's teenage son and a federal marshall were killed. The prolonged siege that followed ended with Weaver surrendering after seeing his wife shot in the face while holding her baby in the doorway of their home. Weaver was eventually convicted of failing to appear in court, but was acquitted of the original weapons violation and the marshal's murder.[10]

The Weaver shootings were followed within six months by the government's botched raid on the Branch Davidian compound in Waco, Texas. The siege that followed this unfortunate episode ended with the fiery deaths of nearly 100 Davidians, including two dozen children. Throughout the incident, government officials regularly responded with ridicule and sarcasm to legitimate criticisms from responsible sources. It was later discovered that some law enforcement personnel had actually "engaged in a concerted effort to conceal their errors in judgment."[11]

These events and a host of other government mishandlings have served to inflame an already smoldering anger in the hearts of many Americans who are sick and tired of being abused by big government. The recent passage of "oppressive" gun-control legislation (the Brady Law and the Assault Weapons Ban), the approval of two extremely unpopular trade agreements (GATT and NAFTA) and the 1995 Mexican "bailout" have also aroused patriot tempers.[12]

Before law enforcement authorities, politicians and other concerned parties attempt to deal with the dangers inherent in the patriot/militia subculture, its members must be understood. This can be achieved only by exploring their religious beliefs, examining their psychological makeup and analyzing the deceptive information being disseminated by their leaders. *American Militias* details in a straightforward and easy-to-understand fashion the complexities of a volatile movement that threatens to disrupt the future stability of America.

Professor Phil Agre in the communication department of the University of California, San Diego, has rightly noted that the concepts expressed by the militias are so bizarre that they are "hard to even think about."[13] But think about them we must, as the Oklahoma City bombing has so clearly proven.

PART 1

Sounds of Sedition

[M]aybe we can get this out in the open and have things resolved because I feel . . . the only thing standing between some of the current legislation being contemplated and armed conflict is time.

James Johnson
Ohio Unorganized Militia[1]

The only way we'll get our country back is not at the voting booth. . . . The only way to get them to do what's right is to force them to do it.

Steve Hance
Citizens for the Reinstatement of Constitutional Government[2]

Go up and look legislators in the face, because some day you may have to blow it off.

Samuel Sherwood
United States Militia Association[3]

This is our land. And we're the ones trying to bring it back to the Constitution. And if the government doesn't come with us, then there probably will be bloodshed.

Linda Sanders
Anti-government patriot[4]

We're trying to take back the freedom God gave us. Take back our inalienable rights. God didn't give us these rights to negotiate [them] away. . . . The Patriots are not going to put up with it any longer. . . . We're ready to go to war—now!

Marvin McCormick
California patriot[5]

1

Rise of the Patriots

I want you to get mad. I don't want you to protest. I don't
want you to riot. I don't want you to write to your
Congressman because I wouldn't know what to tell you to
write. I don't know what to do about the depression, and the
inflation, and the Russians and the crime in the street. All I
know is that first you've got to get mad. You've got to say, I'm
a human being . . . . My life has value. . . . I'M NOT GOING
TO TAKE THIS ANYMORE!

Howard Beale
Fictional news anchorman (*Network*)[1]

The 1976 movie *Network* tells the fictional tale of television newsman Howard
Beale, an aging and divorced alcoholic whose decline in viewer popularity
gets him the dreaded pink slip. Beale goes over the emotional edge, but no
one notices until he makes a startling announcement during a final program: "I've
decided to kill myself. I'm going to blow my brains out right on this program, a
week from today." After the show, network officials agree that their anchorman
has made his final announcement.

But the next day, a sympathetic news executive decides to let Beale do one more
broadcast in order to say good-bye to his fans. Unfortunately, the deranged
journalist ends up bidding farewell to the television audience via a profanity-laced,
rambling dissertation on the garbage that is foisted daily upon society. Station
managers, corporate sponsors and producers are infuriated. Beale is finished!

The following morning, however, the network's ambitious female vice president
of programming pitches a wild idea to her boss: Keep Beale on the show and let
him spout his impromptu anger. The reason? Results from the previous night's
ratings indicated that Beale's popularity rose by five points:

The American people have been clobbered on all sides by Vietnam, Watergate,
the inflation, the depression. They've turned off, shot up, and . . . nothing
helps. . . . Howard Beale went out there last night and said what *every*

American feels. . . . He's articulating the popular rage.

The risky scheme is approved and Beale is turned loose on an embittered America. As the Mad Prophet of the Airwaves he soon becomes "a latter-day prophet denouncing the hypocrisies of our time."

1976 Meets 1996

The outrage voiced in *Network* bears an uncanny resemblance to the frustrations that were actually being felt throughout our country in 1976. Sadly, Beale's rantings still reflect the mood of many Americans. Consider the following monologue from *Network*:

> Everybody knows thing are bad. . . . Everybody's out of work, or scared of losing their job. A dollar buys a nickel's worth, banks are going bust, shop-keepers keep a gun under the counter, punks are running wild in the streets, and there's nobody anywhere who seems to know what to do about it. And there's no end to it. . . . [T]he air is unfit to breathe, and our food is unfit to eat. And we sit watching our TVs while some local newscaster tells us that today we had fifteen homicides and sixty-three violent crimes—as if that's the way it's supposed to be! We *know* things are bad; *worse* than bad. *They're crazy!* It's like everything, everywhere is going crazy. So we don't go out anywhere. We sit in the house, and slowly the world we're living in is getting smaller, and all we say is *please* at least leave us alone in our living rooms. Let me have my toaster, and my TV, and my steel-belted radials and I won't say anything. *Just leave us alone!*

These words could have come from the lips of anyone in the patriot movement. In fact, at a 1995 gun rally in Washington, D.C., patriot convert and prominent Watergate figure G. Gordon Liddy stated: "[Militias] are not organizing pro-actively to go after the government, they are organizing to try to get the government to leave them alone. That's what the American people want from government—Leave us alone."[2]

Exactly who are America's angry patriots? A 1995 *Insight on the News* magazine article entitled "Fringe Groups and Militias Aim to 'Restore' Constitution" describes them as participants in "a growing coalition of groups whose members share a common belief—that individual action by informed citizens is the only protection against the erosion of their constitutional rights."[3] From this perspective, patriots appear to be no different than most other Americans who are tired of getting pushed and pulled by a federal government rife with red tape, two-faced bureaucrats and out-of-touch legislation.

Insight does not present an inaccurate picture. Many patriots want only to return to a simpler era, one in which big government interfered very little in citizens' lives. Unfortunately, the world is no longer a simple place. *That* is the problem, especially for middle-class Americans who make up a majority of the patriot community. Center for Democratic Renewal researcher Noah Chandler explains:

With all these economic agreements—GATT, NAFTA, and European economic boundaries coming down—things are moving very fast. These are people who are in rural areas, they are less educated, and they have romantic ideas of the good old days. They want states' rights. The sheriff is the highest law of the land. They are close to the Constitution. They want a "well-regulated militia."[4] But the patriot movement is far more than just an expression of nostalgia. Its definition is broadened by James Ridgeway and James Zeskind, two nationally recognized experts on racism:

This is a violent revolutionary movement aimed at creating an alternative society for white men, a white, patriarchal society in which government is decentralized and kept to an absolute minimum. Its strength lies in the Midwestern heartland and in the intermountain areas of western Montana and Idaho. . . . In some states it has meshed with antiabortion forces, and everywhere it is allied to the gun lobby. It is deeply racist.[5]

Ridgeway and Zeskind are commenting on what has often been referred to in national news stories as the "angry white male" segment of the anti-government community. Although applicable, this description does not adequately account for the many non-racists in the movement. A more comprehensive listing of individuals united under the patriot banner has been compiled by political analyst Chip Berlet:

☐ Militant right-wing gun-rights advocates, anti-tax protesters, survivalists, far right libertarians

☐ Pre-existing elements of racist, anti-Semitic or neo-Nazi movements

☐ Advocates of "sovereign" citizenship

☐ The confrontational wing of the anti-abortion movement

☐ Apocalyptic millenialists, including zealous Christians, who believe we are in the "End Times" and facing the "Mark of the Beast," which may be supermarket bar codes, proposed paper currency designs or implantable computer chips

☐ The most militant wing of the anti-environmentalist movement[6]

In a 1995 article co-authored with historian Matthew Lyons, Berlet summarizes the patriot subculture as a "diverse right-wing populist movement . . . composed of independent groups in many states, unified around the idea that the government is increasingly tyrannical."[7] Herein lies the movement's cohesive thread: a negative, often hateful, attitude toward our federal government. This "soft umbrella of anger" covers loggers who feel besieged by environmentalists, ranchers angry over land- and water-use policies, and the underemployed who blame their plight on NAFTA and GATT.[8]

Mike McKinzey, a self-proclaimed lieutenant in Missouri's 51st Militia, puts it this way: "Nothing is going right. It's not any [single] thing, it's everything."[9] McKinzey is not saying he no longer loves America. He just sees it going in a different direction: down. California patriot Doug Fales expresses this sentiment in succinct terms: "I love my country—it's the government I hate." [10] When patriots are asked why they hate their government, four answers regularly surface in varying combinations: (1) declining economic conditions; (2) unwanted social change; (3) imposition of federal authority over states' rights; and (4) environmental legislation that imposes strict regulations on what land owners can do with their property. These are the grievances that form the foundation upon which the patriot movement is built. Consequently, each one must be explored.

Death of the Good Old Days

According to Rick Donaldson, the patriot movement to which he belongs consists primarily of "middle class regulars . . . whose eyes mist up when they see the American flag." [11] These people simply want to understand why they can no longer maintain a comfortable standard of living. Their financial security has somehow disappeared overnight, along with any hope of enjoying the reward that every red-blooded American envisions: twilight years of bliss and contentment earned by a life of honest, hard work.

Shedding light on this aspect of the movement are economic reports indicating that "the vast majority of Americans either tread water economically or grow poorer." [12] One study notes that "the working farmer or the average employee has seen his standard of living drift downward since the 1970s. Americans are working harder for less, and know it." [13] Berlet feels there is a whole generation for whom the American Dream has not come true:

> They bought into the American Dream, fought in the war, sent their kids to college so they'd have a better life—that was the social contract. Now they realize their children will have a lower economic status than they do, they see their pension eroding into a meaningless amount of money, and a lot of them have been downsized or moved into the service economy. [14]

The increasing disparity between social classes only magnifies this problem. Recent studies on wealth concentration show beyond doubt that the rich are getting richer and the poor are getting poorer. [15] Ed Wolff, a New York University economist who tracks wealth, reveals that 39.3 percent of *all* American assets (stocks, bonds, cash life insurance policies, jewelry, etc.) are owned by 500,000 U.S. households, or one-half of one percent of the population. Although the Reagan years saw America's net worth increase from $13.5 trillion to $20.2 trillion, $3.9 trillion of the $6.7 trillion boon was sucked up by the aforementioned top one-half of one percent of the population. [16] Consequently, the U.S. is first among prosperous nations in income inequality.

The rich are now spreading out to enjoy (patriots would say take over) what remains. Throughout the western states, invading hordes of designer-clad yuppies are making it increasingly difficult for financially strained locals to ignore their hardships. Migrating city slickers are tangible reminders that everything is changing:

Traditional industries—mining, ranching and logging—are clear losers in the new order. That old economy, based on "extracting" wealth from rocks, grass, and trees, is dying . . . [and being] replaced by high-skilled workers in high-tech companies. . . . [T]he region's most rapidly expanding employers are museums, amusement parks and fitness clubs. . . . [C]owpats and coal mining are out; cappuccino and cilantro are in. . . . [I]n the New Mexico mining town of Silver City, the A.I.R. Expresso Bar and Gallery says it all: "A.I.R." stands for "artist in residence."[17]

Putting up with a few outsiders sporting newfangled ideas and liberal values would perhaps be tolerable, but old homestead sites have been deluged by unconventional masses. Nevada's population grew by 198 percent between 1970 and 1994. Arizona's population leaped by 130 percent. The number of Utah residents jumped eighty percent and Colorado's rose sixty-five percent.[18] The era of quiet western towns is over. A way of life is dying, and it is being killed by wild, disrespectful newcomers.

Consider the fate of Moab, Utah. Uranium excavation kept it thriving until its 2,000 mining jobs were terminated when the 1979 Three Mile Island disaster shattered visions of a nuclear powered America. Fortunately, mountain bikers began flocking to Moab every tourist season and now swell the population from 6,800 to 16,000 yearly. The town's economy would collapse without them, but it is a bittersweet blessing:

Each year, 100,000 cyclists try the roller-coaster-like Slickrock Trail, parts of which have turned black from the rubber residue of the bikes' tires. And spring break turns Moab into Daytona West, with boozed-up tourists surfing big four-wheel-drive vehicles along the rocks up into the hills.[19]

Of course, the patriot movement includes more than a few thousand discontented inhabitants of the far west. There are the unemployed masses of the Midwest. Autoworkers, for instance, have experienced several cutbacks over the years. In 1980, the patriot stronghold of Michigan was home to 600,000 auto industry employees. As of 1995, they numbered 300,000.[20] The economy has dealt even harsher blows to farmers.

Crisis in the Heartland

The farmer's plight began in the 1980s when the world experienced a staggering recession, and the money that underdeveloped countries had been using to buy U.S. grain was needed to pay back international loans. A surplus of American produce resulted, which in turn sent crop prices and land values plummeting. Farmland once valued at $2,100 an acre crashed to less than $700 an acre.[21]

The situation worsened when inflation increased the cost of supplies needed to plant crops. Farmers were soon forced to borrow, which put them even deeper into debt. A mid-1980s survey conducted by the American Banker's Association "revealed that nearly one-third of the country's farms—many of them midsize family farms—were deteriorating seriously. Another one-third . . . could be pushed into serious problems by interest rate increases or weather setbacks."[22]

Cautious bankers eventually began giving loans based on "what a farmer's land and machinery were worth: they valued it with an eye to what it would bring at an auction sale."[23] When a money lender was presented with an opportunity to make a profit, he rarely hesitated to act on it. This was both a prudent and financially strategic move for everyone, except the farmer:

> [F]armers who were either behind on their payments or viewed by the bankers as a poor risk, received official-looking documents that notified them that their repayment schedules had been accelerated. They had ninety days—in some cases no more than thirty days—to make good on their outstanding loans. . . . Even the family homestead, which had been inherited free and clear, was not safe. . . . Liens were placed against living and operating expenses, and bank accounts were frozen. . . . [P]ersonal checks were no longer honored. . . . [F]armers were now required to get the bank to cosign checks for the purchase of seed, fertilizer, and even food. Farmers unable to satisfy their lenders were forced to quit: to sell off their land, their machinery, their home.[24]

Only a few families were able to retain their property through long work days and complicated court battles. The rest fell prey to foreclosure and bankruptcy. Thirty-two-year-old Roger Drevlow and his wife, Joanne, lost their 200-acre dream to the auctioneer's gavel on September 20, 1984, ten miles southeast of Maddock, North Dakota. That day was the final tragedy in a series of catastrophes that included an almost worthless, drought-stunted crop of 160 bales of hay (1977), a fire that destroyed their hog operation (1978), a hailstorm that wiped out their crop (1979), and a fire that burned down their home (1979). By 1984, the couple was $200,000 in debt.[25]

There was also the fifty-four-year-old farmer's wife in Chattanooga, Oklahoma, who could no longer watch debt bury her family's 1,280-acre wheat farm. She "climbed atop a barrel of burning trash and killed herself." In Hills, Iowa, sixty-four-year-old Dale Burr, more than $800,000 in debt, murdered his wife, a banker and a neighbor before turning the shotgun on himself.[26] In Ruthton, Minnesota, forty-six-year-old Jim Jenkins and his eighteen-year-old son Steve, who had lost their ten-acre dairy operation to foreclosure, gunned down a banker and his chief loan officer. Jim subsequently committed suicide and Steve went to jail.[27]

All of these tragedies are relevant to today's patriot movement because the federal government was, to some degree, indirectly responsible for the economic disasters that befell many farmers. During the 1970s, Secretary of Agriculture Earl Butz and the U.S. Department of Agriculture exhorted farmers to take out large expansion loans. According to federal officials, those who took the advice would reap a bountiful harvest by purchasing more land and planting fence to fence.

The world food crises, plus a U.S.-Soviet grain deal, was supposed to send corn, wheat and soybean prices through the roof. A pot of gold at the end of the rainbow awaited farmers courageous enough to seize the day. Many farmers trusted Uncle Sam, and against their better judgment buried themselves in debt, believing that bumper crops would more than lift them into profits. [28]

Everything worked out fine for a few years. In fact, by 1980 North Dakota had the second highest number of millionaires per capita in the United States. [29] Butz and his successors continued to push landowners to expand—and they did. New tractors were snatched up daily, along with new irrigation equipment, new combines, new everything. Land was being purchased in huge 640-acre lots, sometimes three at a time. [30]

Then the recession hit, the Soviet deal fell through, and farmers were left holding the bag. A congressional report "estimated that more than 1 million of the nation's 2.2 million farmers would be driven off the land by the year 2000." [31] Farmers clearly needed mercy, but they were shown none. The very same people who had urged the expansions turned a deaf ear to cries for help. Requests for just a little more time through temporary moratoriums on the foreclosures were denied. By 1983, disaster had struck:

> North Dakota alone was losing three farmers a day, as its farm debt nearly doubled from $2.5 billion to $4.9 billion. . . . Foreclosure or debt reduction accounted for nearly 40 percent of all land sales. Other states in the farm belt were harder hit, losing ten, twelve, up to fifteen farmers a day. . . . [By 1987] nearly 17 percent of rural Americans lived below the poverty line. [32]

Rural America is still struggling financially, which makes the sentiments of Missouri militiaman Mike McKinzey understandable: "The traditional thing about liberals is that you're supposed to care. I'm tired of caring. I want to make my house payment and I'm not ashamed of it. I care about us. I couldn't care less about Mexico." [33]

Against the Feds

Economic decline can account for only a portion of the anger patriots feel toward the government. Federal restrictions that affect individual state and county issues are another source of irritation. In 1992, for instance, Washington, D.C., passed "1,397 federal laws and resolutions to generate 62,928 pages of regulations," which, among other things, protects us from making "a bad deal on a nectarine."

> It is a federal crime to sell a peach in California smaller than two and three-eighths inches in diameter. Nectarines are covered, too. But nectarines have no fuzz and are therefore legal down to a diameter of two and five-sixteenths inches. [34]

Patriots view these bothersome and meaningless additions to the original U.S. Constitution as nothing more than illegal intrusions into their private lives. They believe the government, originally designed to secure rights, has become a regime that grants, rations and prioritizes rights.[35] Objective researchers of the patriot movement are sympathetic. "The grievances are real," says Chip Berlet. "A lot of these people have correctly noted that government has distanced itself from the people, that regulations don't make sense for people who have to apply them."[36]

There is, for example, the experience of Darlene Donaldson and her forty-year-old son Rick, who wanted to grow some organic fruit on their twenty-acre spread outside of Dallas. In order for them to get a little sticker certifying that their produce was indeed organic, countless hurdles needed to be cleared. The whole incident turned out to be a time-wasting, energy-consuming nightmare. Rather than deal with the continuing hassle, they ended up calling their fruit "naturally" grown.[37]

Sometimes federal regulations can not only be irritating, but deadly. In 1995, Montana loggers lodged a seemingly unimportant complaint: the Occupational Safety and Health Administration had ordered them to use steel-toed, chain-saw resistant boots for work. "They had two weeks [sic] grace period, and after that it was no boots, no work."[38] Only Montana Senator Max Baucas seemed to understand the problem:

> Steel-toed boots may sound good to someone in Washington, D.C., but in Montana they can make the job more dangerous. On a cold day, they make your feet go numb and that makes it easier to slip on a steep hill, and that is no joke when you are holding a live chain saw. . . . [N]obody at a desk in Washington, D.C., should be telling people in the Flathead what kind of shoes to wear. You can expect people rightfully to be mad about that.[39]

The patriot's solution to the whole dilemma is to get the federal government out of the states and counties and let locals decide what is best for them. To patriots, the situation is not complex: "Whatever the federal government is doing, we can do better ourselves."[40] New Mexico's Otero County Commissioner Ronny Rardin agrees: "We've been pushed so far by rules and regulations, the feds are in our pockets so deep, people are outraged."[41] Bluntly put, the widespread feeling throughout the nation seems to be that Washington's "public servants" have mutated into America's "public masters."[42]

Curse Those Environmentalists

Some of the most violent outbursts from the patriot movement have been provoked by the government's stand on environmental protection issues. According to a *Los Angeles Times* piece by journalist Gary Andrew Poole, each piece of eco-friendly legislation that is approved by federal authorities sends a loud and clear message that is unconscionable to patriots: grizzly bears, wolves, flytale fish and other endangered non-humans are more important than people.[43]

Dean Compton, co-founder the National Alliance of Christian Militia in Northern California, complains that in his local area three lumber mills were closed within one year thanks to the spotted owl. He additionally notes that because of environmental statutes he cannot even dig up the manzanita bushes on his own property. "But," he adds cynically, "you sure better pay taxes on it, or they'll take it all away from you."[44]

John P. Andrist of the Okanogan County Citizen's Coalition in Washington believes the environmental mind-set "misses the importance of these peoples' lives. . . . The prevailing attitude is, 'I have an idea of what is good for the planet and I have some science to back it up. And I'm sorry, but you don't fit into that.'"[45] Laird Wilcox, who has been studying extremist groups for more than thirty years, observes that many patriots have "bought property for investment reasons, and now they cannot do anything on it." Wilcox asks, "How would you like to have a 200-acre farm, then find out that 150 acres of it is a (protected) wetland you cannot use?"[46]

These are especially sensitive issues for persons living in the West, Northwest and Southwest, where anyone who is anti-farming, anti-grazing, anti-logging and anti-ranching is a sworn enemy. In these parts of the country, preservationists and environmentalists are commonly viewed as nothing more than "eco-terrorists" who threaten the survival of a lifestyle that residents have been enjoying for generations.[47]

Patriot attitudes toward environmentalism were clearly articulated in a letter sent by Charles Shumway of Arizona to the U.S. Fish and Wildlife Service. He warned that "unless the 'curse' of the Endangered Species Act was repealed, there would be 'rioting, bloodshed, rebellion and conflict that will make the Serbian-Bosnia affair look like a Sunday picnic.'"[48]

Encouraging this kind of rhetoric has been an extremely antagonistic conglomeration of anti-environmentalists who call themselves "Wise Use." They began emerging throughout the West, Southwest and Northwest in the late 1980s and early 1990s as a network of "lobbying groups, conservatives, and grassroots activists."[49] Environmentalists find Wise Use organizations especially difficult to work with because they seem to have an affinity for vigilantism, lawlessness and confrontation rather than civilized discourse on issues.

Observers have described Wise Use members as ruthless individuals who use "intimidation, threats and demonization of the opposition" to achieve their goals.[50] The Wise Use movement's Sahara Club, for example, has reportedly advocated various actions against its opponents, including "letting air out of tires, squeezing hot pepper in someone's face and getting large and aggressive people to follow, confront, and intimidate people in dark parking lots."[51]

According to Ken Toole, president of the Montana Human Rights Network, the economic upheaval in the West, coupled with struggles over natural resources and the organizing efforts of groups like Wise Use, have created a political climate of fear, anger and distrust. "The result," Toole says, "is that people are becoming more inclined to reject our traditional methods of resolving political differences . . . i.e., civil discourse and compromise."[52]

As of early 1996, a number of locations around the country had become hotbeds of angry words, death threats and violence. Author David Helvarg, in his 1994 book *The War Against the Greens*, discusses "hundreds of instances of harassment and physical violence in the last few years" against environmentalists.[53] Sheila O'Donnell, a California-based private investigator who tracks harassment of environmentalists, concurs that intimidation is on the rise.[54]

Washington's Okanogan County is typical of the rural communities being affected by the growing animosity between environmentalists and persons living in the West, Southwest and Northwest. The county is a sparsely populated region where crime is low and everyone knows everyone else. Things, however, are changing rapidly. Methow Valley's cross-country ski trails have become a winter haven for vacationers. The city of Oroville is developing the county's first industrial park and luring shoppers from nearby Canada. In the Omak-Okanogan area, a new Wal-Mart as well as several fast-food restaurants and convenience stores are popping up like wild weeds.

Future proposals for the area include two casinos, a lumber mill, a recreational houseboat operation and a natural gas pipeline that will link the county to British Columbia. County Commissioner Ed Thiele complains that these progressive steps are bringing newcomers who disrupt the political climate. Commissioner Ron Weeks claims the outsiders are "trying to change our way of life."[55]

Tensions increased in 1995 when the federal government proposed the creation of a wildlife park at the sacrifice of an open pit gold mine. The mine was slated to provide at least 120 local jobs for 8 to 10 years. Environmentalists applauded the wildlife park idea, warning that the mine would "destroy a forested mountain popular with hikers and local hunters."[56] But ranchers felt that creating a self-sustaining population of wolves and grizzlies in the county would make livestock easy prey. Area landowners also feared that they would one day "lose all right to manage their property."[57]

Then Wise Use activist Chuck "rent-a-riot" Cushman entered the picture. He warned that the park proposal was really a plot by the National Park Service and preservationists to make the county "part of a vast wilderness playground, where private property will be appropriated for wildlife through land-use restrictions." President Clinton—allegedly in cahoots with Canada to make a "land grab"—was scheming to create an elitist recreational region, thereby canceling "United States sovereignty, control, and traditional uses in the North Cascades ecosystem." Cushman said millions of acres of private timber and farmland would be in jeopardy of seizure.[58]

This was all Washingtonians needed to hear in order for long-simmering grievances to boil over. During a July 1994 meeting in Chelan, "400 hostile farmers, orchard owners, ranchers, and timber workers railed against . . . state enforcement of pesticide rules, delays in applications for new state water rights, and state standards for farmworker housing."[59]

These angry complaints were soon replaced by open threats of physical harm and acts of violence. Department of Ecology employees in Yakima had their car windows broken. Okanogan County residents blocked environmentalists from meeting in public buildings. An environmentalist in a neighboring county received a threat: "Watch your lug nuts." Before leaving on a trip, the environmentalist discovered that the lug nuts on his vehicle had been loosened.[60] By 1995, tensions in Riverside, Washington, were so great that the city council passed an ordinance "requiring every citizen to own a gun."[61]

Signs of similar trouble appeared in New Mexico in 1993 when a threatening letter was sent to the *Silver City Daily Press*. The angry note advocated shooting spotted owls and poisoning the Gila River to kill endangered fish. Most disconcerting was the letter's "recipe" for how to murder environmentalists:

> We might utilize some heavy wire and a few large, heavy rocks. We could attach the wire securely to the rocks on one end. The other end could be attached securely, very securely, to the arm, leg or other body extremity of an eco-pornographer. Deposit all three objects in one of the deep pools in the river and presto! Or adios, or something.[62]

Tensions continue to rise in New Mexico, Washington, Nevada, Idaho, Montana and other states in the west, northwest and southwest. During 1995 alone, Forest Service employees in western states endured thirty-four incidents of harrassment and violence that include several bombings and acts of vandalism against federal property.[63]

Fighting Government Tyranny

There is clearly a feeling permeating America that citizens' desires are no longer being represented by elected officials. James Johnson of the Ohio Unorganized Militia explained this issue before a 1995 Senate subcommittee on the militias:

> [W]e seem to have a problem here during these campaigns when all of these wonderful politicians, God love them, say whatever they are going to say and [then] they get inside the Beltway and everything is, how do we say, politics as usual. Now, what is going on? As this trend continues—and you guys have to listen to this—you are pushing people's backs against the wall out there.[64]

Interestingly, a 1994 national survey found an eleven percent increase from the previous year in persons who were "very angry" about people in positions of power who "say one thing and do another."[65] Bill Johnson of the 10th Amendment Coalition says "people do not feel like they can change the government in a political fashion any longer. Or, if they do act in a political manner, it doesn't seem to make any difference to the bureaucracies under [the elected officials], or to what's happening in their communities."[66] Nevada patriot Dick Carver concludes:

> The problem everywhere is that we're not governed by elected officials anymore—we're governed by bureaucrats who take laws passed by Congress, then adopt 26 feet of regulations based on their own interpretations.[67]

Political analysts agree that there is a rising number of "disaffected middle-class and working-class people with a strong sense of grievance" that none of the major parties are addressing.[68] In support of this observation are the results of a recent national poll in which fifty-eight percent of the respondents said people who run the country "are not very much or not at all like themselves."[69]

There is also a fear factor. Patriot John Harrell states, "We actually fear our government more than the drug cartels and the Mafia."[70] Harold Sheil, a Missouri militia member, feels the same way:

> One of the things that the people really fear from the government is the idea [that] the government can ruin your life, totally destroy your life. I don't mean kill you. But they can totally destroy your life, split your family up, do the whole thing and walk off like you're a discarded banana peel, and with a ho-hum attitude.[71]

On this point, patriots are not alone. An April 1995 Gallup Poll found that thirty-nine percent of Americans think the federal government "poses an immediate threat to the rights and freedoms of ordinary Americans."[72] Syndicated radio talk show host Armstrong Williams articulates why many Americans, not just patriots, have grown so afraid of law enforcement authorities:

> Both the Drug Enforcement Administration and the Bureau of Alcohol, Tobacco, and Firearms . . . have broken into houses without warrants or explanation, trashed property and caused bodily injuries. Sometimes, finding nothing, they have left abruptly without apology. . . . A series of irresponsible and aggressive federal actions under [Clinton's] administration has instilled a deep and legitimate concern among many decent Americans.[73]

Why are flagrant attacks on constitutionally protected rights continuing to occur with alarming regularity? Why does it seem that law enforcement personnel are rarely punished for their "mistakes"? Much of the American public has had its fill of the standard answers given by officials—e.g., poor intelligence reports, bad planning, improper judgment and neglect of duty.[74] There is an old saying: *What goes around, comes around.* It now appears that what has been going around for far too long is coming back to haunt the government.

Social and political upheavals, of course, are nothing new. They have occurred intermittently throughout history: the French Revolution, the American Revolution, the Civil War, Nazi Germany, the 1960s. Political analyst Kevin Phillips believes that there again exists the conditions necessary for creating such events:

> All the ingredients of the past surges are present again. . . . Economic anguish and populist resentment; mild-to-serious class rhetoric aimed at the rich and fashionable; exaltation of the ordinary American against abusive, affluent and educated elites; contempt for Washington; rising ethnic, racial and religious animosities; fear of immigrants and foreigners, and a desire to turn away from internationalism and concentrate on rebuilding America and American lives.[75]

The patriot movement consists largely of Americans who have simply reached the end of their rope. The message they are attempting to send to the government is simple: no more can, or will, be endured. Militia leader James Johnson comments:

> We have got people out there hungry . . . people out there starving, and people tired of getting terrorized by law enforcement. . . . They are getting outright economically terrorized, socially terrorized. I mean the political correctness is getting out of hand. . . . It [the patriot movement] is people sitting there with "don't tread on me" stamped across their foreheads. There are people drawing a line in the sand.[76]

Most patriots begin drawing their line in the sand by learning exactly where and how their liberties are being "stolen." They voraciously read patriot literature on constitutional law, attend patriot-sponsored seminars on everything from avoiding taxes to preparing for armed conflict with the feds, and watch videos that provide "the truth" about instances of governmental abuse (popular titles include *Waco: The Big Lie*, *Atrocities of Ruby Ridge*, and *Breaking the Law in the Name of the Law: The BATF Story*). Some patriots have gone one step further by banding together into paramilitary units called militias.

2

A Call to Arms

The militias are the real power behind the Patriot Movement.
Clayton Douglas
Patriot publisher, *The Free American*[1]

The militias are the last line of defense against annihilation of
the people.
Ross Hullett
State Commander, Oklahoma Citizens Militia[2]

Nearly everyone has been talking about the militias since the national news media began running stories about them in the early 1990s. Several headlines have been most disturbing: CITIZENS MILITIAS DRAWING CONCERN; SOME MILITIA MANUALS URGE ATTACKS; MILITIA MEMBERS' THREATS, ATTACKS ON OFFICIALS ESCALATE.[3]

A number of individuals wholeheartedly endorse these paramilitary units as constitutionally protected expressions of freedom. Others see the armed bands of government protesters as illegally formed private armies functioning as a breeding ground for hate. Many people simply dismiss the militias as ragtag troops of middle-aged, gun-toting boy scouts. In reality, militias are far more complex than any of these characterizations.

A Movement Is Born
The numerous militias now holding paramilitary exercises throughout this country's pine-scented forests and picturesque glens were not formed in isolation from political, social or economic factors. They are the patriot movement's militant wing, and as such, represent the ultimate implementation of patriot attitudes and sentiments—i.e., violent resistance to the allegedly tyrannical regime destroying our American way of life. Analysts of political trends in this nation agree that the rise of the patriot movement and the emergence of the militias are inseparably interwoven.

Agricultural expert A.V. Krebs sees militia growth as a response to the "permanent agricultural crisis that has created a fault line separating rural and urban America."[4] Laird Wilcox, a researcher specializing in extremist groups, cites the job market shift as an additional reason for the current militia mania. As Wilcox says, the most profitable working class job at one time was fixing cars, a trade that middle class men usually learned early in life from their fathers, or by repairing cars with friends while growing up. Now the most sought after occupation is fixing computers, a skill that usually requires higher education.[5]

This directional change in employment opportunities is just one more indication to middle-class Americans that their way of life is becoming extinct. The signs are everywhere, especially in the country's heartland, where militias are most popular:

> Corporations are buying out the small farms, and this has had an impact on hunters. Used to be you could go down the road and say, 'Ma'am, may we hunt deer on your property?' and the woman would say sure. Now farmers say, 'We don't own, we just manage this. So send a postcard to Farmland Industries in New York.[6]

Militia members, like many other patriots, are being emotionally charged by an electrifying current of anti-governmentalism wrought by the crushing weight of federal regulations. Florida militia leader Henry McClain says the government "has taken it upon themselves to regulate everything you can think or touch or smell."[7] Militias appear to be a kind of last resort for patriots. Note the tone of Jim Barnett, another Florida militia leader:

> The low-life scum that are supposedly representing us in Washington, D.C., don't care about the people back home anymore. We're grasping at straws here trying to figure out what we can do to get representation, and this is our answer.[8]

According to National Rifle Association board member T. J. Johnston, a driving force behind the militias is a widespread feeling that "people are no longer secure. The government they elected is no longer the government they control."[9] Political science professor Michael Barkun of Syracuse University echoes Johnston's view, but uses stronger terms. He says that throughout the militia world, the government is seen as: "a devious and dangerous force, the enemy of its own population."[10]

Barkun's view may be more accurate than Johnston's given the contents of a 1995 article entitled "Fight Against Police State Escalates," which appeared in the patriot publication *Freedom Network News*. It declares that militias are a "major element in the reaction to out-of-control government in America today." The article continues:

> The Feds, seeing in the militias a serious challenge to their grab for absolute power, have been desperately trying to . . . smear and marginalize all of them as lunatic-fringe malcontents—white supremacists, vile anti-semites, etc.[11]

Although militias in America have a long history stretching back to the Revolutionary War, the recent militia movement was indeed begun by racist leaders from within the white supremacist community. This does not mean *all* militias are racist. It does mean, however, that today's paramilitary groups are far from innocent of all the accusations being leveled against them.

Racist Roots

Serious thoughts concerning the formation of today's popular militias initially grew out of the August 1992 Ruby Ridge shootings involving white supremacist Randy Weaver. After the siege ended, between 150 and 175 "Christian men" hastily convened on October 23, 24 and 25, 1992, in Estes Park, Colorado, to discuss "how to respond to the Weaver killings."[12] Presiding over this "Rocky Mountain Rendezvous" was Pastor Pete Peters, a well-known white supremacist leader.[13] Other high profile racists in attendance included former Ku Klux Klan Grand Dragon Louis Beam, Aryan Nations founder Richard Butler, Montana anti-Semitic tax-protester M. J. "Red" Beckman and Charles Weisman, author of *America: Free, White and Christian.*[14]

Retired Virginia legislator Larry Pratt, who now heads Gun Owners of America, was present as well. He seems to have been the first individual to publicly suggest that citizens no longer rely on traditional lobbying techniques to change governmental policy, but form local, armed militias. In his lecture, Pratt urged American patriots to follow the example set by Guatemalan and Filipino freedom fighters, who had formed armed militia units of volunteer soldiers in order to resist communist death squads that had been terrorizing the local populace.[15]

Pratt's words did not begin to take a firm hold in the American psyche until the infamous 1993 raid by the Bureau of Alcohol, Tobacco and Firearms (BATF) against the Branch Davidians in Waco, Texas. The fifty-one-day siege that followed the botched assault ended with the fiery deaths of nearly 100 men, women and children. Although a few militias had already formed before the horrors of that last day in Waco, militia growth rate dramatically increased after the tragedy.

An additional push for the militia movement came in the summer of 1993 when President Clinton began campaigning for tighter gun control laws. The tenuous peace between federal authorities and patriots suffered even further erosion with the February 1994 passage of the Brady Law, which placed a five-day waiting period on all handgun purchases and required buyers to undergo a background check. Enraged gun owners now joined the swelling ranks of the militia movement.

Before the year's end, patriots were again protesting government oppression. Their voices were raised in response to enactment of the Crime Bill. Its apparent purpose, the outlawing of nineteen kinds of semi-automatic assault rifles and accessories was, in their viewpoint, bad enough. But after its passage, gun owners learned that "the prohibition actually applied to more than 185 different types of semiauto firearms."[16] It quickly became a widespread belief among patriots that the deceptive tyrants controlling America were making final preparations for transforming the country into a totalitarian police state. Militia growth exploded.

Accurate estimates reflecting the total number of militias, the number of specific states involved and the total militia membership nationwide are unavailable for two reasons: (1) new militias are forming weekly; and (2) federal law enforcement agencies do not collect such intelligence information.[17] Educated guesses made throughout 1995 placed militia membership at ten, twenty, forty and fifty thousand.[18] A significantly higher figure was given on May 11, 1995, in a *Gannett News Service* article, which estimated that militias in 30 states had as many as 100,000 followers. This figure was taken from a report released by the Center for Democratic Renewal, a private Atlanta group that monitors militias.[19] In June 1995, the BATF stated that militias had been activated in at least forty states, and that membership was continuing to grow rapidly.[20]

By November 1995, militia leaders were claiming to have well-armed groups in all fifty states. Dean Compton, leader of the California-based National Alliance of Christian Militia, places the membership figure at 10 million.[21] This figure may sound grossly inflated, but Compton is not alone in his claim. James L. Brown, Deputy Associate Director for Criminal Enforcement of BATF, admits that militia membership could indeed number in the millions.[22]

Modern-day Minutemen

Federal restriction of gun rights is only one complaint on a growing list of grievances that "prove" to militia members that the government is tyrannical. According to one widely circulated militia manual, gun control is nothing but an attempt by federal authorities to satiate their continuing lust for more control over the populace.[23] Jon Roland, founding member of the Texas Militia Correspondence Committee, explains:

> This Crime Bill is only the latest move in what people perceive as a progressive overthrow of the Constitution by a conspiracy of special interests that are not accountable to the people and which operate above the law. Patriotic Americans don't just want to hang on to such rights as they have left, but to roll back this growth of tyranny. They have lost confidence in the integrity of our legal institutions, including courts and elections.[24]

As with persons in the broader patriot movement, militia members' lives are primarily wrapped around a single emotion: anger. News reporter Marc Cooper discovered this as he was researching a story for *The Nation*:

> Pick just about any pocket of economic and social distress—Arizona and Montana communities suffering from a decline in the mining or timber industries, Michigan or New Hampshire mill towns where heavy industry has fled to Mexico, California edge cities where the cold war aerospace subsidy has vanished—and you will find thousands of Americans who spent part of last year dressing up in camouflage, undergoing automatic weapons training and preparing for final battle with what they consider to be an enemy federal government.[25]

John Snyder, chief Washington lobbyist for the Citizens Committee for the Right to Keep and Bear Arms, says the militias are "popping up all over the place as manifestations of grass-roots outrage at what politicians are doing."[26] Missouri's 51st Militia, for instance, was started by a small group of friends in response to several issues that irritated them: cuts in the military budget, rampant crime, gun control that seemingly effects only law-abiding citizens, a school system in shambles and a sea of welfare recipients.[27]

Of course, one does not create a militia in order to lower taxes or reform welfare. A much greater threat exists in the minds of militia members: aggressive military action by the federal government against citizens who are attempting to live within their constitutional rights. This fear is closely tied to numerous incidents that have involved the trampling of constitutional rights by law enforcement personnel.

Soldier of Fortune magazine—a military-oriented periodical that monitors combat and war related events as well as gun rights and law enforcement issues—notes that there have been scores of "outrageous, illegal and murderous actions by federal agents from the FBI, ATF, DEA, INS and U.S. Customs Service against innocent citizen's [sic]."[28] Law enforcement abuses have become so common that the American Civil Liberties Union and the NRA appealed to President Clinton to appoint a committee to investigate "lawlessness in law enforcement."[29]

Patriot Robert Higgs, in an article written for the *Freedom Network News*, offers a glimpse at the rising anger over governmental abuses of authority:

America is becoming a police state. Each year, more and more actions become either officially forbidden or officially required. The scope of individuals to decide how to live their own lives grows steadily narrower. The list of crimes grows longer and longer, and any deviance may subject the citizen to the wrath of the police, the courts, and the prisons—not to mention the fiery violence of the Federal Bureau of Investigation [FBI], the Bureau of Alcohol, Tobacco and Firearms [BATF], and the Drug Enforcement Administration [DEA].[30]

Militia members claim that their movement is a kind of "constitutional safety net."[31] In the words of Militia of Montana leader John Trochmann, it is a giant "neighborhood watch, watching out for problems" and alerting proper officials when they perceive "threats to a peaceful society."[32] All of this sounds well within the bounds of the First Amendment, which guarantees the right of the people to free speech and peaceful assembly. Unfortunately, militias often push the outside edges of constitutional liberties and regularly go well beyond its borders.

Don't Tread on Me

On June 15, 1995, Senate hearings were held to discover: (1) whether the militias posed a threat to either public safety or the federal government; and (2) to what extent Americans are joining the militia because they feel the federal government poses a threat to their constitutional rights.[33] Militia members who testified swore that militias are nonaggressive and law-abiding. Michigan militia spokesperson Ken Adams stated that most people in the militias are "certainly totally against violence."[34] Norm Olson, former Commander of the Michigan Militia, told listeners that militia members just want to be "ready" should the worst happen.

Olson added that vigilance and preparation is their motto and their posture is defensive rather than offensive.[35]

Militiamen throughout the country concur with Adams and Olson. "We're not trying to overthrow a government," they say. "Defend ourselves from a government, yes. . . . We want to keep our families safe."[36] Bob Wright, commander of the 1st New Mexico Militia, claims that militias "are about re-establishing certain constitutional guarantees, and trying to bring a federal government back into its Constitutional boundaries. There's no talk in this movement about overthrowing the government."[37]

James L. Brown, deputy associate director for criminal enforcement from the BATF, agrees that there are indeed some members of militia groups who are outstanding, law-abiding citizens."[38] This position is supported by a limited study conducted by sociologist James Aho of Idaho State University. After interviewing 368 persons associated with the patriot movement, Aho found that "the vast majority of people in the militias are not violent or dangerous.[39]

Some militias actually resemble public service groups more than anything else. New Hampshire's Hillsborough County Dragoons, for example, include shoveling snow for the elderly in their list of good works for the community.[40] Missouri's 51st Militia makes disaster relief part of its mission, and has publicly declared its willingness to cooperate with law enforcement during floods or tornadoes. The 51st has even purchased tents, first aid supplies and stretchers and, according to a 1995 article in the *Kansas City News Times*, has started a "road assistance service for motorists" traveling during holidays on a stretch of highway in their territory. Many persons involved with the militias, says Bob Gurski of the 51st, "just want to feel useful again."[41] Harold Sheil, also of the 51st, paints what is perhaps the most peaceful picture of militias ever given:

> You can take a look at the militia, and we're grown up Boy Scouts. We enjoy the camaraderie of one another. This is something that nobody wants to hear. They don't wanna believe that we're that benign. But we actually are. The thing is, it's not retaliation. It's total, totally the idea of being able to defend yourself.[42]

If every militia were as benevolent as either the 51st or the Dragoons, America would probably be a much nicer place to live. In reality, however, there is an undercurrent of violence running beneath the surface of the entire militia movement. A few leaks have already sprung loose. In September 1994, for instance, three Michigan Militia members dressed in camouflage clothing were stopped by police in Fowlerville. The vehicle contained a deadly arsenal of significant proportions:

□ six loaded, semi-automatic weapons: three 9mm pistols, an AK-47 assault rifle, an M-1 rifle and an M-14 rifle

□ three revolvers, including a .357 magnum

□ 700 rounds of ammunition, including armor-piercing ammo and tracer rounds

- □ night vision goggles
- □ gas masks, knives and bayonets
- □ two-way radios and notes indicating that the men were conducting night surveillance of law enforcement officials.[43]

The men were arrested on weapons charges and released until their trial. None of them showed up. Instead, about forty militia members arrived at the Livingston County courthouse, calling police "punks with badges." The angry crowd then threatened to shoot and kill law enforcement officers if they tried to seize militia-owned guns.[44]

The year 1994 also saw four members of a Virginia's Blue Ridge Hunt Club (BRHC) militia charged with stockpiling machine guns and planning to raid a nearby National Guard armory. BRHC leader James Roy Mullins—arrested on July 27, 1994—was charged "with possession and sale of a short-barreled rifle and unregistered silencers, and with facilitating the unlawful purchase of a firearm." A computer disk found by federal investigators contained chilling information:

> We will destroy targets such as telephone relay centers, bridges, fuel storage tanks, communications towers, radio stations, airports, et cetera. . . . Human targets will be engaged when it is beneficial to the cause to eliminate particular individuals who oppose us like troops, police, political figures, snitches, et cetera.[45]

Within six months of Mullins's arrest, another group—the North American Volunteer Militia—sent a Hamilton, Montana, judge a message that threatened "open warfare" against game control agents. "We number in the thousands in your area and everywhere else," the letter read. "How many of your agents will be sent home in body bags before you hear the pleas of the people?"[46]

Such extreme actions are clearly contradictory to the words of many militia leaders and militia participants who maintain that violence is not part of their behavioral code. Michigan Militia spokesperson Ken Adams makes it seem as if militia members want nothing to do with violence:

> There is no time for any people to go against the laws of their government and to take those laws into their own hands. That is totally unacceptable in any society, and we certainly fully agree with that. . . . [W]e must be law-abiding. The only exception to that, which I believe has already been stated, is for self-preservation and self-defense of our persons and family if an unlawful act were being perpetrated against us.[47]

This statement, although an apparent denial of violence, contains a massive qualifier. Notice that the "exception," or the condition wherein violence is justifiable, centers around "an unlawful act" perpetrated against patriots. An obvious question must be asked: What is an unlawful act? The answer: Anything a patriot determines to be unlawful, anything that contradicts their interpretation of the Constitution.

Another expression of this loophole can be found in a 1995 *Esquire* magazine interview with a militiaman named "Max," who said people have nothing to fear unless they try to force patriots "to do something that's unconstitutional, illegal, or immoral."[48] Again, it must be asked: Who decides what is unconstitutional or illegal? The answer, of course, is patriots.

This justification for violence can usually be found in the oath most militias require new members to take. It often includes: (1) a vow of allegiance to the Constitution; (2) a promise to protect and defend America from all enemies foreign or domestic; (3) a pledge to abide by the constitution of their individual states; and (4) an agreement to obey all *legal* laws—federal, state and local.[49]

Point number four can always be cited to legitimize violence because it indirectly allows anything a patriot deems illegal to be disobeyed. James Johnson of the Ohio Unorganized Militia makes a clear reference to this point when explaining why and when force can be used against law enforcement personnel:

> I don't see a reason for using any kind of force to justify your actions. Of course, once again, you suspend the Constitution. For that reason, I don't have to recognize anybody in Federal law enforcement.[50]

In essence, Johnson is saying that if patriots believe the Constitution and their interpretation of it has somehow been superceded by what they see as unconstitutional laws, then they have every right to disobey any authority attempting to enforce those "unconstitutional" regulations. According to this ideology, resistance through violent means would be acceptable since such actions would amount to defending one's liberty.

This excuse for violence is especially disturbing when one considers an interesting tactic patriots are using to escape the oppression of the federal government. They are renouncing their citizenship and declaring themselves to be "sovereign" citizens who are bound by no federal or state laws. They support their alleged sovereignty through a combination of legal acrobatics, convoluted reasoning, ignorance of the law, and novel interpretations of the Constitution.

Patriots claim they are simply getting out of "the system." But countless confrontations have resulted between patriots *out* of the system and law enforcement personnel/private citizens still *in* the system. In the patriot mind, persons *in* the system keep committing unconstitutional, or unlawful, acts against them. When law enforcement attempts to intervene, then heavily armed defenders of liberty and freedom are justified in holding authorities at bay. Montana county attorney John Bolman is extremely frustrated: "We have people who are saying, 'You cannot arrest us because we out-gun you.' "[51]

Dangerous Times Ahead

There is no doubt that some militias are composed of peaceful citizens whose only desire is to see America become a better place to live. They have legitimate grievances, as well as justifiable concerns about federal abuses of authority and excessive governmental interference in state and local issues. Unfortunately, there are just as many, if not more, militia members who are seriously preparing for war with the U.S. government. Some in this latter group have already taken it upon themselves to begin the fight. They are resolute in their belief that full-scale war looms on the horizon.

The *U.S. Militiaman's Handbook* by Dan Shoemaker, for example, is being used to spread instructions that can be described only as protocols of war. Among these protocols is a suggested course of action to be taken after launching an attack against an enemy: "A public-relations announcement may be necessary after an assassination or failed attempt."[52] This same book contains some frightening words that are intended to be read on an occasion that many militia members long to see:

> You (call the prisoner by name, if you know his name) have committed treason against the United States Constitution and against your fellow citizens and members of the United States Militia. You are executed.[53]

In attempting to justify their calls for war and their acts of civil disobedience, patriots have articulated some of the most unusual legal views ever to be voiced in American courts. Strange ideas about flags, citizenship, the Civil War and driver's licenses are now being heard regularly by dismayed judges. The next chapter will examine the patriot movement's views of law and order. Ironically, their beliefs lead in the very opposite direction, toward lawlessness and disorder.

3

Sovereign
Citizen
Rebellion

No longer believing in the positive role of government, the
new populist anger distills into a sour cry for personal armed
sovereignty. The bullet replaces the vote, gun ownership
becomes the litmus issue and federal agencies the targets of
choice.
Robert Scheer
Former *Los Angeles Times* correspondent[1]

[W]e want a bloodless revolution, but if the bureaucrats won't
listen, we'll give them a civil war to think about. We're ready
to look the federal government in the eye.
Samuel Sherwood
United States Unorganized Militia[2]

hristians revere the Old and New Testaments, Jews honor the Torah, and
Muslims respect the Koran. In like fashion, patriots venerate the Constitution. There is a slight difference, though, between the way religious persons
interpret their sacred writings and the manner in which patriots read the Constitution. Most followers of a particular faith agree that their scriptures contain
metaphors, similes and other figures of speech. Patriots, on the other hand,
interpret all provisions in the Constitution literally and rigidly. Each word and
phrase of America's founding document means neither more, nor less, than its
precise dictionary meaning. No judge, government official or politician may place
any restriction upon, or make any addition to, the document's simplest reading.
Patriots believe this was the intent of the Founding Fathers.

Accompanying their "legal fundamentalism" is an insatiable appetite for
literature explaining the ins and outs of the legal system. Paul Glastris of the
Washington Monthly notes that for "every camouflage-wearing amateur soldier

drilling on weekends there are several amateur lawyers sitting at home reading federal statutes."[3]

For patriots, learning about the laws of the land and discovering how to discern the constitutionality or unconstitutionality of those laws is more of a holy crusade than a conscientious effort to become informed. Patriot Lynne Meredith writes in a tone typical of the movement in which she has become a well-known tax protester:

> It was corrupt legislation and engineered ignorance that got America into this financial abyss and good legislation and education will set us free from the foreign monetary vultures! We will wage a fearless, intellectual war with our own silent weapons; weapons that are more powerful than all of theirs combined! They are our Constitution, the Higher Laws and the Truth that will set us free! We will go as "sheep among wolves," as "doves among vultures" and as a nation under God, the Supreme Commander of the Universe! We will re-educate America, reclaim our Rights, re-exert our Sovereignty and take back our precious America for ourselves and for our posterity, so help us God![4]

Private study of Constitutional law has created a growing mass of patriots who regularly serve as their own legal counsel. They need no lawyers, they say, because everything in the Constitution and Bill of Rights is in plain English. Unfortunately, many of these self-taught law experts have ended up with a skewed view of legal realities, which in turn has landed them in jail on charges ranging from failure to pay income taxes to traffic violations. Do such setbacks cause patriots to pause and reconsider the accuracy of their knowledge? Hardly. The "persecution" only reinforces their belief that a tyrannical regime is running our nation.

The most common court battles involving patriots have come from their unwillingness to abide by numerous state and federal regulations. They drive without licenses, operate unregistered cars, and refuse to pay income taxes. Their convoluted arguments reveal a peculiar obsession with the 14th Amendment, which granted citizenship to former slaves.

Rebels with a Cause

Who is entitled to the rights guaranteed by the U.S. Constitution? The 14th Amendment, ratified in 1868, answered this question by granting full citizenship to newly freed slaves, thus extending to them constitutional protection. The 14th Amendment prohibited states from depriving "any person of life, liberty, or property, without due process of law." This amendment is of pivotal importance to patriots, who claim that it created a second type of citizenship.

The first type of citizenship, which patriots call "state" citizenship, is said to have existed prior to the 14th Amendment. It is considered a "natural" citizenship conferred upon persons when they are born in America. Each individual is a "sovereign" citizen of that state, or republic, in which they are born. These citizens are supposedly not bound by the laws of the United States government.

The second type of citizenship, allegedly created by the 14th Amendment, applies to all individuals who agree to receive from the federal government the "benefits" contained in the Bill of Rights. Persons gaining Constitutional rights in this manner are looked upon by patriots as having an inferior citizenship, one that was granted to them. They are second-class citizens subject to all statutory laws passed by the power that gave them their citizenship, meaning the federal government located in Washington, D.C. As citizens of *that* government, or *U.S.* citizens, they must obey federal rules and regulations, such as paying taxes, following speed limits, obeying gun laws, etc.

According to patriots, nearly all Americans have been duped into rejecting their sovereign status and opting for second-class U.S. citizenship. How so? By unknowingly placing themselves under federal jurisdiction through "illegal contracts" with the government such as driver's licenses, birth certificates, marriage licenses, etc. These documents allegedly make someone a U.S. citizen and void his state citizenship. This, in turn, causes him to become a subject of federal authority and federal rules. As one publication states: "If you have ever signed a document claiming to be a 'U.S. Citizen,' you are *presumptively* one of these 'subject' citizens."[5]

This interpretation of the Constitution culminates in the notion that people can free themselves from federal subjugation by choosing to live as a state citizen, rather than as a citizen of the United States. It is argued that one can "legally" obtain this preferred status by: (1) breaking all existing contracts with the federal government; (2) renouncing federal or 14th Amendment citizenship; and (3) claiming only state or sovereign citizenship. Persons who take these steps and become state citizens are supposedly no longer subject to *any* federal laws.

Most patriots begin their walk to "freedom" by breaking (i.e., physically destroying) the "unlawful contracts" that have been thrust upon them by the government. These include birth certificates, Social Security cards, driver's licenses, marriage licenses, car registrations, and other legal documents. Patriot Stewart Balint proudly declares, "I've gotten rid of all my contracts with government. . . . rescinded them—Social Security, birth certificate, driving license, hunting license. I know the law, and it's not a losing battle for me."[6]

Steve Hance, a carpenter from Charlotte, North Carolina, also embraces this belief. His homemade identification card, which replaced the driver's license he threw away, reads: "I have taken legal steps to remove myself from the foreign jurisdiction of the Motor Vehicle code and all of its regulations."[7] In patriot Jim LeValley's words, "If you are not part of the corporate entity of the United States you don't have to worry about the laws set forth by the United States. . . . It makes life a whole lot easier."[8]

Sovereign citizens do not claim immunity from all laws. They recognize common law, which is "an unwritten set of laws that get their binding force from age-old usage and acceptance."[9] For example, everyone knows that stealing is wrong. Therefore, a patriot cannot steal. Murder also has been historically unacceptable, so a sovereign citizen cannot kill (except in self-defense).

Allegiance to common law is one reason why patriots view the American justice system as invalid. This has led to the formation of a network of illegal "citizen courts" convening nationwide in a variety of locations, such as hotel rooms, private homes and banquet halls. Sixty-one-year-old William Earl O'Brien of Waynesville, North Carolina, explains the merits of these courts:

> The criminal attitude will be vastly different when this is not a revolving door. . . . We won't have the same level of crime. If someone steals from you he'll have to pay you double of whatever he stole. If he steals from you again, he'll have to pay you three times. For violent offenders, the jury [citizens] will tell the [patriot-appointed] constable to find a tall tree and a short rope. It worked before and it will work in any age. [10]

Most patriots also ignore the authority of state and federal courts because such courts allegedly function under military rule with no jurisdiction over civil matters. This idea comes from the notion that 14th Amendment citizens—besides being "federally-made" citizens—are products of "admiralty" (military rule) granted by occupying forces during the Civil War. Consequently, patriots usually refuse to pledge allegiance to an American flag with gold fringe on it. The fringe supposedly signifies admiralty law. Hence, as *non*-admiralty citizens, they will not pledge allegiance to a foreign (i.e., federal) flag.

Perhaps the greatest federal burden that patriots believe they can escape by rejecting federal citizenship is taxation. "Why <u>fight</u> the IRS?" reads one patriot magazine. "Become <u>sovereign</u> instead. A sovereign is not liable for income or property taxes. He has no government intrusion in his life." [11]

Paul Machalek, chief of the IRS criminal investigation division in Greensboro, North Carolina, says the arguments patriots use to get out of paying taxes have two things in common: (1) they place patriots in danger of facing IRS enforcement action; and (2) they are consistently rejected by the courts. [12] An apparent verification of Machalek's warning is an interesting qualifier sometimes found in advertisements for a highly popular patriot publication, Lynne Meredith's *Vultures in Eagles Clothing*, a book that purports to teach people how to avoid taxes. The qualifier is simple and straightforward: "[W]e do not necessarily recommend the use of any forms contained in this book." [13] Despite this caveat, Meredith's book sells for forty dollars.

I Wish I Were in Dixie

Patriot beliefs concerning the 14th Amendment clearly promote a superior citizenship (Constitutionally secured) over a *second-class* citizenship (Congressionally granted). [14] Lynne Meredith writes: "[T]here are two classes of citizens, one class who is protected by the Constitution and one class who is not." [15]

Meredith's assertion reveals one of the clearest links between the patriot movement and racism. White supremacists believe that white people are state, or "organic," citizens with inalienable (irrevocable) rights, while African-Americans, along with other people of color, are only 14th amendment or "federal" citizens with alienable rights granted by Congress and subject to revocation.[16]

This view dates back to just after the Civil War. White supremacists have always "distinguished carefully between 'White Common Law Citizens of the State' and inferior Americans whose citizenship was conferred upon them by the 14th Amendment."[17] A sampling of quotations from patriot sources shows that this post–Civil War mindset is still very much alive:

- With the unlawful passage of the 14th Amendment, a second class citizenship was established for blacks and those unsuspecting Citizens of Freeman character who unknowingly, unwillingly or unintentionally volunteered to give up their Constitutional [organic] protections for corporate State Privileges (birth certificate, marriage license, driver's license, banking account #, social security #, etc. . . .), moving them under the jurisdiction of Admiralty Law.[18]

- This amendment [14th] is only of admiralty or equity jurisdiction, and these de facto citizens [blacks] are not [citizens] under Common Law. They do not have unalienable rights, only limited statutory "civil rights," that Congress has seen fit to grant them.[19]

- There is only one race that founded this country and that is the White Race. The Constitution recognizes this and clearly states that only white people can be citizens of this country. The 14th Amendment changed all that, but we feel it became law illegally and as such is not binding. . . . Blacks really wouldn't care if they lost their rights. I mean look at the L.A. riots. Now can you really say that those people that burned the city down are capable of governing themselves? If the Blacks don't like it here they should leave.[20]

- The Constitution of the United States of America (1787), which is available only to White Common Law State Citizens. . . . [A]re you a White Common Law Citizen of the State or a federal citizen of the District of Columbia?"[21]

In 1995, Richard McDonald, whom many patriots view as the father of the modern sovereignty movement, made a interesting comment about flags in America:

The U.S. government hasn't flown the civil flag since the Civil War, as that war is still going on. Peace has never been declared, nor have hostilities against the people ended. The government is still operating under quasi-military rule.[22]

This is a blatant expression of what many patriots harbor in their hearts: a feeling that the war between the states is still raging. They are angry over the expanded federal powers contained in the 14th Amendment and hold a deep-seated grudge over the citizenship granted to non-whites. Predictably, McDonald feels he belongs to the "free born white sovereign state citizen" class of citizens.[23]

McDonald claims he uses the term "white" only because that is the word used in the "original laws." But anti-discrimination organizations point to other statements McDonald has made in his newsletter the *Patriot.* In one issue, he writes: "[F]orced integration is destroying the White Political Cultural group known as State Citizens in all the States."[24]

Setting the Record Straight

In seeking to reclaim their sovereignty, patriots file impressive sounding documents renouncing their citizenship from "the foreign jurisdiction known as the municipal corporation of the District of Columbia."[25] The documents, however, are legally meaningless because the entire theory is flawed. In fact, constitutional scholars scoff at patriot assertions about sovereignty as "outdated and uninformed."[26]

Jonathan D. Varat, professor of constitutional law at the University of California, Los Angeles, says "the 14th Amendment and subsequent Supreme Court rulings settled the question of whether federal authority prevails." Even if someone is a "state" citizen, that does not mean he is immune from federal taxation and regulation because he is also a U.S. citizen.[27] Erwin Chemerinsky, a constitutional law professor at the University of Southern California, says patriots like McDonald are "trying to prove the unprovable":

> No court has ever held there are two classes of citizens, one held over the other. It is equivalent in science if someone spent their life trying to prove the earth was flat. And they got fancy science books, and they pulled out this scientific fact and that scientific fact and strung them together with the appropriate citations—and said this is why the earth is flat.[28]

Patriots build their theory on the erroneous assumption that until the 14th Amendment there were no federal citizens, only state citizens. In reality, the 14th Amendment did not create federal citizens, the *Constitution* did! This was accomplished so that persons traveling from one state to another would have equal rights and protection under an umbrella union: the federal United States.

Before the Constitution's ratification, both the states and the *United* States existed, but persons were not assured the rights of one state while journeying into another state.[29] Consequently, the Constitution was adopted "in order to form a more perfect union" wherein colonists would enjoy the same rights in every state.[30] Colonists became citizens of the federal United States, as well as citizens of their respective states.[31] The document further determined that the posterity of colonists would also be state *and* federal citizens.

Even before the Civil War, courts recognized that this was how the Constitution affected citizenship. The ruling that emerged from the *Dred Scott v. Sanford* case explained that colonists and their posterity became United States citizens through the Constitution:

> [E]very person, and every class and description of persons, who were at the time of the adoption of the Constitution recognized as citizens in the several States, became also citizens of this new political body. . . . [I]t was formed by them, and for them and their posterity. . . . [T]he personal rights and privileges

guarantied [sic] to citizens of this new sovereignty were intended to embrace those only who were then members of the several state communities, or who should afterwards, by birthright or otherwise, become members. . . . It was the union of those who were at that time members of distinct and separate political communities into one political family, whose power, for certain specified purposes, was to extend over the whole territory of the United States. And it gave to each citizen rights and privileges outside of his State which he did not before possess, and placed him in every other State upon a perfect equality with its own citizens as to rights of person and rights of property; it made him a citizen of the United States.[32]

The 14th Amendment did not make blacks second-class citizens of the federal United States. It guaranteed them equal footing with other Americans by declaring them legitimate citizens of the United States *and* citizens of each state in which they resided. This was how whites were already classified by the Constitution.

Contrary to what patriots believe, it was the Constitution that placed everyone under federal authority. In *Lane County v. Oregon*, the court ruled that the Constitution established a more perfect union by granting the national government power to act *"directly upon the citizens."*[33] This ruling said nothing new. Alexander Hamilton expressed the same thing in *The Federalist No. 15*: "[W]e must extend the authority of the Union to the persons of the citizens—the only proper objects of government." This, Hamilton wrote, was one of the "ingredients" that formed a "characteristic difference between a league and a government."[34]

Some patriots understand the weaknesses of "sovereign" arguments. Southern California patriot Peyman Mottahedeh, for instance, has produced an information package entitled "State vs. U.S. Citizenship Theory Debunked." He writes: "Almost everyone in America is a State citizen and a U.S. citizen at the same time."[35] Even Kirk Lyons, a well-known patriot attorney from North Carolina, agrees that it is counterproductive to worry about state citizenship:

That view of government is based on theory, not fact. It's not based in reality. Trying to argue states rights is not going to work; that was decided by the bayonets of the Union army. It's the same thing with not paying taxes. You're not going to get away with it.[36]

Unfortunately, most patriots remain woefully ignorant of these facts and continue to cause trouble for themselves, as well as for others.

Courtroom Cases

One of the most talked-about cases involving personal sovereignty took place in 1993 when James Nichols, brother of Oklahoma bombing suspect Terry Nichols, was stopped by police for driving nearly 70 mph on a Michigan country road. Nichols was ticketed for speeding and driving without a license. When he appeared in court, Nichols gave rambling legal arguments about his right to travel guaranteed by the Constitution.

Judge James A. Marcus remembers Nichols bolstering his position by citing one Supreme Court case after another. Judge Marcus recalls how Nichols would "lift a sentence or phrase that he thought was applicable, but he'd do so out of context so that the meaning was completely incorrect or nonsensical."[37]

The Michigan judge attempted to explain to Nichols that the Constitution does indeed protect a private citizen's right to travel, but that the federal government can regulate how individuals exercise that freedom. Nichols would hear none of it. Judge Marcus comments: "You can't follow their arguments because they're listening to a different music no one else hears."[38]

James Nichols also appeared in court for failure to pay child support. According to presiding Judge Donald Teeple, Nichols claimed that "the court didn't have any jurisdiction [over him]." The irate patriot further maintained that he did not have to pay child support because "he wasn't a citizen." He felt he had "revoked his acceptance of the marriage license" by proclaiming himself a sovereign in 1992.[39]

James' brother, Terry, also has appeared in court. He argued legalities after refusing to repay approximately $31,000 that he had charged on a credit card. Terry said he did not have to repay the debt since the bank had lent him "credit" rather than "legal tender." He did, however, offer to settle the dispute "with what he called a certified fractional reserve check—a worthless piece of paper." [40]

During another case, Terry attempted to convince the court that he did not have to repay a $13,691.64 loan acquired from a bank. He petitioned the Sanilac County court in writing to "revoke, cancel, annul, repeal, dismiss, discharge, extract, withdraw, abrogate, recant, negate, obliterate, delete, nullify, efface, erase, expunge, excise, delete, strike, repudiate, wipe out, disavow, recall and renounce, destroy, adjure, blot, disclaim, disown, reject, give up, abandon, surrender and relinquish all signatures and powers of attorney." When he appeared before the judge, Terry said he "did not recognize the authority of the court."[41]

Patriot arguments in the courtroom often make little sense because they commonly employ a logical fallacy known as "making a distinction without a difference." This happens when a particular issue is being discussed, and then that same issue is identified as something entirely different by making a meaningless distinction. Tax protesters, for example, admit that United States citizens do indeed have to pay taxes on income, but that they, as sovereigns, do not earn income. They receive wages. Consequently, patriots do not have to pay taxes.[42]

This kind of twisted logic can also be found in a standard objection to driver's licenses. Richard McDonald contends he needs no driver's license because God's common law gives him the inalienable right to unregulated *travel*. Federal laws, he argues, apply only to *driving*. "See, 'drive' is another key word," McDonald says. "Under the state Constitution, I am allowed to travel." Although McDonald regularly drives a 1972 white BMW Bavari, he still declares: "I don't drive; I travel."[43]

Judges have persistently thrown out such arguments. McDonald himself spent nine months and twenty days in a federal prison in 1988 for failing to file income taxes. In December 1994, patriot David Sanders of Sylmar, California, was sentenced to six months in jail for driving without a license. Sanders defended himself by stating that the law did not apply to "white, common law citizens of California." [44]

Another "sovereign citizen" of California, thirty-seven-year-old Alan Bird, was convicted of driving without license plates. He, however, was acquitted of charges that he drove his vintage Mustang without a license or vehicle registration. [45] This partial victory was hailed by patriots as an example of how their arguments can work. But the Ventura County District Attorney's office reveals that the outcome had nothing to do with Bird's arguments. He was acquitted on a technicality when the prosecutor failed to get Department of Motor Vehicles documents to court in time for the trial. [46]

Sovereign Terrorism

In a 1995 interview with *The Nation*, Montana attorney Dusty Deschamps reported that an increasing number of patriots are defying federal regulations and posing "a serious law-enforcement problem." [47] Several violent clashes have already occurred between patriots who have defied the authority of courts, disobeyed gun laws, refused to pay their taxes and failed to register their cars. Such acts are to be expected, given the mindset of most patriots regarding their sovereign status. Peter Coppelman, the Justice Department's Deputy Assistant Attorney General for environment and natural resources, summarizes the problem:

> Whenever you have an enforcement officer confronted by a citizen who refuses to comply with legal requirements, you have the potential for violence. So this is definitely a very volatile issue. [48]

Consider the attitude of Andy Mill, who heads Constitutional Revival in Connecticut: "Every one of us is sovereign. Every one of us has the absolute right to do anything that is not a provable threat to others." [49] Notice, again, the qualifier: "provable." In other words, even if federal law prohibits going 85 mph on a country road because it is a threat to others, patriots may not accept such a ruling because: (1) they do not personally see speeding as a legitimate threat; and (2) their interpretation of the Constitution allows them free, unencumbered "travel."

This line of reasoning also is employed by patriots when they refuse to pay taxes. Federal officials who demand payment of taxes from a "sovereign" are viewed as acting "illegally," which in turn justifies resistance. One form of resistance used by tax protesters is filing common law liens (claims against property for debts) against government personnel. These bogus documents are designed to do one thing: harass public officials. Although illegal, they are often placed in the record by busy clerks who do not have time to verify them. If recorded, the fraudulent liens can, among other things, confound efforts to sell or finance property. They are eventually discovered and nullified, but only after complex paperwork is filed and expensive court time is wasted.[50] The tactic has effectively bogged down many courts throughout the country.

The entire sovereignty issue rests on who has the power to govern citizens' lives. Steve Hance, of Citizens for the Reinstatement of Constitutional Government, points out in no uncertain terms *exactly* who has the power:

We've got to let the people who think they're in power know that we are in power and that they serve at our will. We the people own this country. . . . It doesn't matter who we elect. We need to start hanging a few, or throwing a few in jail.[51]

Recently, threatening rhetoric has given way to violent physical expression. In 1994, three patriots in northern California were arrested for hiring a thug to assault Stanislaus County Clerk Recorder Karen Matthews, who had refused to remove an IRS lien on the home of a local tax protester. Matthews also had refused to record phony patriot liens that this same tax protester wanted filed against IRS employees.

During the assault, Matthews was severely beaten and knifed. Her assailant then dry-fired a gun at her head several times. "He told me why he was there," remembers Matthews. "[He said] that I'd better start to record the documents they were giving to me, and do my job. That I was a messenger to other recorders."[52]

The most notorious users of terrorist tactics are Freemen, who reside primarily in Montana. Freemen have taken sovereignty to an extreme by creating a private kingdom called Justus Township in Garfield County, Montana. The small cluster of houses and other buildings rests on a 960-acre wheat farm that was seized by the IRS due to failure of its former owner—Freeman Richard Clark—to pay his back taxes. The Township has its own laws, currency and system of government based on teachings from the Bible, the Magna Carta, common law, the U.S. Constitution, parts of the Montana Constitution and sections of the Uniform Commercial Code."[53]

Justus Township Freemen even set up their own common law courts in which they convicted and sentenced enemies dwelling in the outside world. Throughout 1994 and 1995 they placed several $1 million bounties on law enforcement officials. The sentence passed against these lawyers, judges and sheriffs was consistent: hanging. The Freemen also "placed phony liens on property, floated bogus money orders, and declared war in general on civil society."[54]

In 1995, numerous conflicts arose between Freemen and law enforcement officials. One Freeman, William Stanton, was convicted for his participation in a false money-order scheme. He wrote a worthless $25,000 check against equally bogus money orders totaling $3.8 million.[55] Stanton also was sentenced for his role as a Freeman "constable" in issuing a $1 million bounty for the local sheriff, the county attorney and a judge. According to Stanton, Sheriff Charles Phipps was scheduled to be "tried in a common law court and hanged by a rope from a bridge."[56]

This same year, a clerk and county recorder in Garfield County was confronted by several Freemen who wanted bogus liens to be filed. After being denied the request, these patriots threatened to kidnap the female clerk. They subsequently ordered her to appear before their Freeman Court. Failure to appear, they said, "would be contempt of court and she would be guilty of official misconduct."[57] This prompted Montana representative Deb Kottel to introduce state legislation making it a felony to threaten public officials. For Kottel's efforts, she received phone calls from persons threatening to kidnap her seven-year-old child.[58]

Problems with the Freemen climaxed in early 1996 when two Freemen leaders— fifty-seven-year-old LeRoy Schweitzer and fifty-three-year-old Daniel Peterson—were arrested on March 25 in Jordan, Montana, located thirty miles southeast of Justus Township. Law enforcement moved against the Freeman the day after the anti-government rebels held a videotaped meeting at which Schweitzer outlined a plan to kidnap local government officials: "We'll travel in units of about 10 outfits, four men to an outfit, most of them with automatic weapons, whatever else we got—shotguns, you name it. . . . Anyone obstructing justice, the order is shoot to kill."[59]

When the two Freemen appeared in court for their arraignment, both shouted objections and protests at the magistrate. "I don't have to listen to the court,' Peterson yelled. Scwheitzer shouted, "I object to any arraignment. This court lacks jurisdiction. You're without power to go on."[60] Despite their protests, the two men, along with eight other Freemen who were not apprehended, were charged with crimes stemming from schemes involving $19.5 million in phony checks and money orders.[61] The indictments also listed charges of criminal syndicalism, or advocating violence for political aims. Schweitzer and Peterson were additionally charged with making death threats against U.S. District Judge Jack Shanstrom.[62]

On the same day as their arrests, a prolonged siege began at Justus Township after 100 FBI agents surrounded the property. Inside the compound, several women and children, along with nearly two dozen heavily armed Freemen—many of them with outstanding arrest warrants—remained, watching and waiting. As of May 1996, there was no foreseeable end to the siege.

A Growing Menace

Violence associated with patriots, Freemen, sovereign citizens and militia members has increased greatly since the early 1990s. The underlying reason for their actions is clear: an unwillingness on their part to obey federal authority:

- □ In southern California, members of the Citizens Rights Task Force attempted to arrest IRS agents who were trying to seize a local antique mall for unpaid taxes.[63]
- □ In Denver, a self-described militia member threatened board members of the Northwest Coalition Against Malicious Harassment who had scheduled a meeting at the Sheraton Inn. Newspapers referred to the event as an upcoming

"anti-militia group" meeting. The anonymous militia member stated: "We'll be there, we'll be armed and someone is going to get hurt." The meeting took place without incident.[64]

☐ A seventy-four-year-old tax protester in San Antonio was arrested and charged with attempting to "hire an assassin to kill the mayor in the belief that the Constitution gives citizens the right to remove public officials—if necessary, by execution."[65]

One of the most frightening incidents of 1994 involved Duane Baker and Leroy Wheeler of the Patriots Council, a Minnesota-based tax-protest group. They were arrested on August 4 for manufacturing ricin, "a highly toxic derivative of the castor bean. They planned to use ricin to kill a police officer who had served eviction papers on one of the group's members."[66]

The two men were subsequently indicted on "conspiracy charges for planning to use the lethal poison to kill Federal employees and law enforcement agents." In March 1995, both Baker and Wheeler were convicted of violating the 1989 U.S. Biological Weapons Anti-Terrorist Act.[67] It was the first prosecution in America under the six-year-old federal act.[68]

The threats, intimidation and violence coming from various patriot groups, especially the militias, has now begun to stifle the freedom of others. People in small communities are no longer running for public office "because they do not want to submit themselves and their families to the intimidation." Some federal workers have been forced to use their personal vehicles on the job and not wear uniforms "in order to avoid identification as a federal employee."[69]

Richard M. Romley, a Maricopa County attorney from Phoenix, Arizona, observes that patriots refuse to bring their grievances to the ballot box or the courts, and instead have chosen to challenge laws by insurrection:

> In their quest for notoriety, power, and financial gain, these fanatical individuals shroud their insurrection in patriotism. . . . They have literally declared war on the very system that guarantees them the freedoms that they demand. It is as if, in the absence of a real threat or enemy, they have turned inward against their own government.[70]

If patriots have declared war on the government, they have done so only because in their minds the government declared war on them first. As patriot leader Linda Thompson writes, "They have declared war. We are prepared to wage a defense."[71] To patriots, federal authorities have declared war not once, not twice, but three times.

The government's initial declaration of hostilities was made during the deadly siege on the hills of Ruby Ridge in Idaho. Next came the disastrous federal actions in Waco. A third proclamation of war was made in Washington, D.C., when a number of gun control measures sailed through Congress.[72] The importance of these events to patriots cannot be overstated. Consequently, each must be reviewed.

PART 2

Enough Is Enough

To: The Honorable Arlen Specter
From: Bob Worn
Dear Senator Specter . . . I have seen my government turn
from a fully functional government of the people, by the
people and for the people . . . to a regime of self-serving
politicians and bureaucrats who think law enforcement has to
destroy the Constitution. . . . Recently we have seen
governmental agencies completely out of control . . . in
incidents such as the murder of the wife and son of Randy
Weaver at Ruby Ridge . . . and the completely barbaric,
senseless slaughter of innocent adults and children at Waco.
. . . I feel I must prepare to defend myself and my loved ones,
should this government perpetrate unlawful, unconstitutional
acts against any member of my family. . . . [T]here is a great
number of American citizens who are firmly convinced that
the blood of those killed and injured at the Murrah Federal
Building bombing are on the hands of you and the rest of
Congress for your complacent inaction to hideous crimes
against American citizens perpetrated by harsh and tyrannical
agents of their government. . . . [N]othing will change until
Congress is awakened from their "politically-correct" slumber.
Bob Worn
Concerned patriot, *USA Patriot Magazine*[1]

4

The Saga of Ruby Ridge

Americans are demonstrably fearful of their government, and
the government's criminal malfeasance seems bent on
validating the wildest prognostications of the fearful far right.
Soldier of Fortune[1]

There is no doubt that there are government abuses. I think
the government behaved badly in the case of the Weaver
shoot-out.
Daniel Junas
Political researcher[2]

atriots see the Ruby Ridge and Waco tragedies as calculated "practice runs"
launched by political forces bent on stripping Americans of life, liberty and
the pursuit of happiness. Less conspiratorially minded individuals believe
the catastrophes were little more than predictable by-products of an out-of-control
government. Others say the disasters resulted from bureaucratic bungling, faulty
planning and criminal negligence.

Federal authorities argue that "the popular accounts of Weaver and Waco are
grossly exaggerated."[3] Investigations have been done. Fault has been found. Such
officials argue that it's time to stop dwelling on the past and look forward to the
future. Only in this way can the wounds from these terrible events be healed.

Who is telling the truth? We may never know. But this should not stop concerned
citizens from taking a look at the two cases. This chapter contains the documentable
facts surrounding the Ruby Ridge shootings. Chapter five will cover the Waco raid
and subsequent siege. My hope is to give an accurate account of these tragic
episodes and also to dispel some of the myths and rumors they have spawned.

A Man Named Randy

In 1983, Randy and Vicki Weaver, along with their three small children—Sara,
Sammy and Rachel—moved from Cedar Falls, Iowa, to the rustic hills of Northern

Idaho. They were an old-fashioned family, cut from the backwoods of the Midwest, with views shaped by years of primitive country living. The couple settled on a small tract of land 4,000 feet up in the Selkirk Mountains, where Randy built a ramshackle cabin that included a big, open room with a sleeping loft, and a "birthing shed" nearby where Vicki and the girls went when they were menstruating.[4]

The Weavers had always been fiercely religious, but wanted no part of traditional denominations in Iowa. They chose, instead, to hold home Bible studies and debate Scripture with like-minded born-agains in coffee shops and restaurants.[5] The family eventually joined the Christian Identity movement, a loosely connected network of white supremacists who blend Christian doctrine with anti-Semitic views.

Identity believers, who see themselves as God's chosen people, are vehemently anti-government and live in a world of hate constantly overshadowed by the looming specter of civilization's collapse. Many adherents are survivalists who stockpile weapons and food in preparation for a future time of unparalleled world turmoil when they will have to fend off government forces and marauding bands of non-whites.

Three times during the 1980s, Randy and Vicki attended the annual congress of the Aryan Nations in nearby Hayden Lake. During the meetings, which had the atmosphere of a county fair, their children played on "Whites Only" campgrounds while men wandered about in Nazi regalia. Aryan Nations founder Richard Butler "gave out leaflets for 'a nig—r shoot' and hawked pamphlets about how Jews were plotting to enslave the white man."[6]

But not all was well with the Weaver clan. By 1989, just two years before Vicki gave birth to Elisheba, financial difficulties plagued the family. Randy had no steady employment, nor did he see prospects of long-term work. All of his income came from odd jobs like cutting wood for area farmers, and the struggle had become tiresome.

A helping hand came from Gus Magisono, a six-foot, 245-pound biker whom Randy had met at an Aryan Nations gathering in 1986. "I can get you some cash from dealin' guns," Magisono promised. "What I need from you are some sawed-off shotguns." Weaver was desperate and ended up agreeing to deliver the goods.[7]

A week later, Randy gave two illegally shortened shotguns to Magisono in exchange for $300. Magisono promised that another $100 was on its way. The money, however, never came. Gus Magisono was actually Kenneth Fadeley, a gunrunner whom the government had talked into mounting a sting against Weaver. The FBI hoped that once Randy faced prosecution, he would go undercover among white supremacists, specifically, the Aryan Nations.[8] Weaver refused. In response, the Feds charged him with firearms violations.

Gunfight in the Hills

Randy was arraigned on weapons charges in January 1991, and was told to appear again in court on February 19. The date was subsequently changed to February 20, but when the U.S. probation office sent Weaver a confirmation letter, it read *March* 20. This clerical error meant little, however, since Weaver failed to show up on either date. A bench warrant was issued for him, and marshals began formulating an arrest plan.

For 18 months, Randy remained holed up in his cabin. This rebellious act reflected the feelings that Vicki had articulated in a confrontational letter written to the government near the beginning of their legal ordeal: "My husband was setup for a fall because of his religious and political beliefs. There is nothing to discuss. He doesn't have to prove he is innocent. Nor refute your slander."[9]

On August 21, 1992, at about 11:30 A.M., six deputies were conducting surveillance on Weaver's property. They might have gone unnoticed in the dense foliage of Ruby Ridge had not the Weaver's yellow Labrador, Striker, picked up their scent. The agitated canine alerted everyone on the property. Randy, his fourteen-year-old son Sammy, and twenty-four-year-old Kevin Harris (a friend who lived with the Weavers) went to investigate the dog's beckoning yelps. All were armed.

Randy split off from the group, trying to head off what he thought was a deer in the brush. Unexpectedly, he found himself face to face with a camouflaged deputy who ordered him to freeze. Weaver turned and ran as he yelled instructions to Sammy and Kevin to get back home. But it was too late. They had discovered three lawmen: William Degan, Larry Cooper and Arthur Roderick.

Because of contradicting testimony, objective investigators have never determined with absolute certainty who shot first. Circumstantial evidence suggests that the gunfire may have started when Roderick—slightly further down the trail from Cooper and Degan—shot the Weaver's dog to silence it. Sammy then appeared from out of nowhere and screamed, "You killed my dog, you son of a bitch."[10] He subsequently fired his .223 assault-style rifle twice at the deputy, who dove for cover just in time. Only his shirt was pierced. Bullet casings strewn across twenty-two feet of dirt and grass indicate that Degan was probably moving when he fired. At some point early in this confrontation, Harris raised his 30.06 and blew away a large chunk of Degan's chest. Cooper fired a barrage as he threw himself over some brush, landing next to Degan.[11]

Randy continued running back to the cabin, all the while hearing gunshots echoing in the hills around him. He fired his shotgun into the air twice in an attempt to draw attention away from his son, but his efforts failed.[12] Suddenly, the gunfire stopped. Degan was dead. Striker was dead. And Sammy, shot in the back and arm, was dead.

Harris ran for the cabin to get Randy and Vicki. Upon arriving, he confirmed their worst fears. "Sammy's dead," he said. When Vicki and Randy went to their son, they found him face down in the dirt. The Weavers carried Sammy back to the birthing shed, where Vicki washed her boy's lifeless body and covered it with a sheet. An eleven-day siege had begun.

A Fatal Decision

The message sent from Idaho to the marshall's headquarters in Washington, D.C., was blunt: "This is Operation Northern Exposure. We got one dead, others stuck on the mountain." Within hours, the Justice Department had been notified. Unfortunately, federal agents misunderstood "stuck on the mountain" to mean "still trapped under fire." Consequently, when Henry Hudson, director of the U.S. Marshals Service, met with FBI planners, he stated that deputies were "pinned down."

This confusion continued even after Idaho law enforcement officials tried making it clear that all shooting had ceased. Hours into the situation, the word inside top-level Justice Department meetings was that officers were "still pinned down by gunfire." Equally flawed information circulated about Weaver being "a combat-trained Vietnam veteran who might have booby-trapped his mountain with bombs and grenades." A "bureaucratic frenzy" resulted. [13]

The misinformation, along with other factors, ultimately led to a tactical change in the FBI's standard rules of engagement. The elite Hostage Rescue Team (HRT) deployed around the cabin was given unprecedented shoot-on-sight orders: "If any adult in the compound is observed with weapons after the surrender announcement is made [to the Weavers], deadly force can and should be used to neutralize this individual." [14]

Most HRT agents wondered whether these instructions were legitimate. [15] In fact, every sniper team surrounding the Weaver cabin chose to ignore them. Every sniper team, that is, except that of Lon Horiuchi and his spotter, FBI Special Agent Dale Monroe. [16] This proved deadly at 6:00 P.M. on the day after the initial gun battle, when Randy had decided to go see his son's body. Upon reaching the door of the shed, a sharp crack split the frigid mountain air and a burning pain ripped through his upper arm. Horiuchi had hit his target. [17] Kevin Harris and nineteen-year-old Sara Weaver, both of whom were armed, happened to be outside at that same moment. "Get to the house!" cried Sara as she ran to her father. [18]

Randy sprinted as best he could for the cabin, followed by Sara and Kevin. Vicki, meanwhile, heard the shot and went to the door with ten-month-old Elisheba in her arms. In a rage she shouted at the invisible agents: "Bastards! Murderers!" [19] She saw her husband running toward her and threw open the door. Vicki stepped back just as Randy, Sara and Kevin crossed the threshold. Horiuchi, hidden in thick brush approximately 646 feet north of the cabin, fired again.

A split second later, Harris landed on the floor with a silver dollar-sized hole in his left upper arm. Tragically, Vicki had not stepped back far enough and was struck first by the bullet. It tore through her face, entering near the temple and exiting through her upper neck. She died instantly.[20] "Her hands were still cradling Elisheba so tightly they had to pry the baby out of her grasp."[21] Weaver and Harris surrendered ten days later.

Martyrs, Myths and Militias

Weaver and Harris were charged with several crimes, including murder, conspiracy and assault. But for twelve weeks in 1993, it seemed the government was more on trial than the defendants.[22] A Boise, Idaho, jury "acquitted Harris of all charges and convicted Weaver only of failing to appear on the original firearms charge."[23] Furthermore, the government received a $10,000 fine during the trial for misconduct after it admitted staging photographic evidence of bullets found on Weaver's land.[24] Federal prosecutors also failed repeatedly to get crucial documents to defense attorneys on time. For this, Judge Edward Lodge slapped a $1,920 fine on the government, declaring that the FBI had shown a complete lack of respect for the court, and a callous disregard for the defendants' rights and the interests of justice.[25]

The government's actions at Ruby Ridge and in court were reprehensible, but the persistent falsehoods surrounding the incident only obscure the real problems that need to be addressed. For example, many patriots allege that the charges of racism which have been leveled against Randy Weaver are nothing more than government and media lies designed to smear Weaver's character.[26] But Randy's white supremacist beliefs have been confirmed in numerous interviews with neighbors and close friends. His ties to the Aryan Nations have also been confirmed.

Moreover, a 1989 family portrait of Weaver shows him wearing a T-shirt that reads: "Just Say 'No' To Z.O.G." The term Z.O.G. stands for Zionist Occupational Government. In white supremacist literature, it is another name for the U.S. government, which is supposedly under the control of Jews. According to most Christian Identity believers, Jews are the literal descendants of Satan.

Another myth concerns Vicki Weaver. She has been painted by the militia movement as a defenseless mother cowering in the cabin's corner with her children. This is untrue. Vicki was an anti-government racist with a gun strapped to her hip.[27] On more than one occasion, Vicki expressed a deep hatred for Z.O.G. In a February 3, 1991 letter sent to the U.S. Attorney's office in Boise, Vicki delivered a scathing message addressed to the "Servant of Queen of Babylon." She claimed that "the stink of lawless government had reached 'Yahweh' [God] and 'Yashua' [Jesus]." It continued: "Whether we live or whether we die, we will not bow to your evil commandments."[28]

Still, these facts do not justify the FBI's actions. I agree with reporter Tom Morganthau of *Newsweek*, who called the Weaver incident "one of the most shameful episodes in the history of American law enforcement."[29] Federal behavior during the siege demonstrated an "outrageously arrogant abuse of power."[30] When

Randy Weaver appeared before the Senate Judiciary Subcommittee on Terrorism, Technology and Government Information in 1995, he stated: "If I had it to do over again . . . I would make different choices."[31] One can only hope the government feels the same way.

Federal Fallout

Three years after the Weaver shootings, FBI Director Louis Freeh admitted that the bureau's actions were "tragically flawed."[32] The FBI's standard rules of engagement, which "forbid the use of deadly force except in instances of imminent threat to human life and safety," were wrongfully replaced by shoot-on-sight orders that Justice Department officials now say "contravened the Constitution of the United States."[33] In other words, the orders were illegal and unconstitutional.[34]

On December 21, 1995, members of the Senate subcommittee that held hearings on the Ruby Ridge incident released their final report. Although it blamed the three deaths that occurred during the episode primarily on Randy Weaver, there was "substantial fault" placed on the performance of the Bureau of Alcohol, Tobacco and Firearms, the FBI, the U.S. Marshals Service and the Idaho U.S. Attorney's Office.[35]

In response to the information obtained by investigators, Attorney General Janet Reno imposed new rules of engagement that instruct all federal law enforcers "on when they may—and may not—use deadly force in seeking to apprehend or question suspects."[36] These directives, signed in October 1995, prohibit deadly force from being employed if it appears an alternative course of action can reasonably accomplish law enforcement purposes. Furthermore, senior managers of federal police agencies can no longer adapt rules of engagement to specific situations.[37]

Regarding Vicki Weaver's death, Freeh says it was a "constitutional shot," meaning that Horiuchi was following orders. At the same time, Freeh does not believe it was a "good shot," since the rules of engagement given to Horiuchi were unconstitutional. "There were mistakes that were made," he says. "[T]here were errors of judgment; there were severe lapses in our administrative procedure. More importantly, I don't think we were equipped, in 1992, to handle a Ruby Ridge situation."[38]

Despite Freeh's admission, controversy continues to surround several events that began when Larry Potts, the top FBI official involved in overseeing the siege, was promoted to the FBI's number two position. The decision understandably angered many Americans, especially when a subsequent Justice Department investigation "uncovered evidence that documents were shredded to protect Potts and others."[39] This information surfaced after Eugene Glenn, the Ruby Ridge on-scene commander, wrote a blistering letter to FBI headquarters charging that the first Justice Department review of the case "had been inaccurate, incomplete and designed 'to create scapegoats and false impressions.' "[40]

When a second probe was finally launched focusing on E. Michael Kahoe, the Washington head of the FBI's violent crime section who supervised the Ruby Ridge siege, an overlooked fact emerged: Kahoe also oversaw the shooting incident review team that justified the government's actions. Kahoe was eventually polygraphed. He failed. Only then did he admit to destroying important documents relating to who approved the unconstitutional shoot-on-sight orders.

Freeh has since acknowledged making a "grave error" in promoting his long time friend Larry Potts, and has also expressed regret over relying on the first investigation by the Justice Department, which he now admits was flawed.[41] Potts has since been removed as deputy director and suspended along with several other FBI officials. In August 1995, the Justice Department agreed to pay $3.1 million to Randy and his three surviving children for Vicki's death.[42]

Further investigations into the Weaver case were ongoing as of May 1996, with criminal charges against FBI officials pending the investigation results.[43] Allegations against federal officials include obstruction of justice, perjury, making false statements and shredding documents.[44] One of the most significant documents that appears to have been shredded was a "line-of-sight report by Horiuchi."[45]

Horiuchi claims he shot Vicki Weaver accidentally by discharging his rifle while "leading" Kevin Harris (i.e., aiming in front of Kevin Harris to compensate for his forward movement). The missing document may have been shredded because it contained information indicating that Horiuchi "lied when he said he was leading Kevin Harris before squeezing off the second and fatal shots—and that he definitely saw the mother, babe in arms."[46] According to the March 1996 issue of *Soldier of Fortune* magazine, there exists significant evidence, including statements from FBI agents and several independent witnesses, "that Horiuchi shot Vicki Weaver deliberately."[47]

Despite these troubling aspects of the case, most observers doubt that any charges will ever be brought against FBI authorities. Perhaps even more frustrating to patriots is the probability that no criminal charges will ever be filed against law enforcement officials involved in an even deadlier showdown between American citizens and the government: the Branch Davidian tragedy. It is to this disastrous event that our attention now turns.

5

Waco
Revisited

Operation Waco was the beginning of religious persecution
of unpopular, non-mainstream religious groups in America.
Since the American people (including Christians) did not
protest one peep over the destruction of the Branch Davidian
sect, the attacks will now begin to accelerate.
Don McAlvany
Christian "economist"[1]

ew Americans have been able to erase from their memory the destruction of
the Branch Davidian religious commune just east of Waco, Texas. When the
billowing black smoke from that fiery episode cleared, cult leader David
Koresh and more than eighty of his followers, including two dozen children, were
dead.

The religious sect first grabbed media attention on February 28, 1993, when
100 federal agents from the Bureau of Alcohol, Tobacco and Firearms (BATF)
attempted to serve a search warrant at the isolated fortress. Their plan was to
surprise the Davidians, who had stockpiled a massive cache of legal and illegal
weapons in preparation for Armageddon, which Koresh saw as being very near.
It would later be discovered that the group had more than one million rounds of
ammunition.[2]

That day's ninety-minute gunbattle left four agents dead and twenty wounded.
Six Davidians also had been killed. The ensuing standoff under FBI jurisdiction
lasted fifty-one days. Then, in the early morning of April 19, the FBI mobilized
several tank-like Combat Engineering Vehicles (CEVs) to punch huge holes into
the walls of the Davidian's poorly constructed domicile. Tear gas was subsequently
injected through the gaps in hopes of forcing the cultists from their stronghold.

In deciding to launch the assault, FBI planners failed to adequately consider
the Davidian's religious fervor and its influence on the situation's outcome.
Officials realized this miscalculation six hours into the operation, when tiny puffs

of white smoke began to escape from the building. Within minutes, fire had engulfed the entire structure and the world watched in horror as the Davidian's home burst into a city block-sized funeral pyre.

The flames that devoured the Davidians have long since been extinguished, but the images of that deadly blaze continue to sear the consciences of men and women throughout the country. Many Americans have allowed the tragedy to kindle within them a burning hatred of the government. Some patriots, like Jeffrey Rudd, psychologically placed themselves in the Davidian's position, and now feel as if they have an obligation to speak for those who died: "I watched that place burn to the ground, killing everyone inside. I thought, that could be me, with my house burning to the ground."[3]

According to Ted Daniels, director of the Millennial Watch Institute, Waco fed "right into the way people were feeling about the Federal Government."[4] Amo Roden, a long time Davidian who now lives in a dilapidated shack on the barren property, says people visit the site daily:

They come through to see just what the Government did—Constitutionalists, tax-protesters, religious people—I see them all. And they're all angry and frustrated about how they're being treated by the Government.[5]

Patriots have every right to be angry about Waco. But some of their anger is based on false accusations, misleading information and conspiratorial theories. Much of their inaccurate data can be found in two influential videos: *Waco: The Big Lie* (also known as *Waco I*) and *Waco II: The Big Lie Continues*. These anti-government tapes were produced by Indiana attorney Linda Thompson, who chairs the American Justice Federation (AJF), an organization allegedly "dedicated to providing educational services to the public concerning current issues of Constitutional law and individual Constitutional rights."[6]

It is widely acknowledged that Thompson has "done more than any other single person to stoke the fires of rage and paranoia about Waco."[7] She first grabbed newspaper headlines after pronouncing herself the "Acting Adjutant General of the Unorganized Militia of the United States of America." Her claim to this grandiose title coincided with a March 28, 1993, call to arms she posted on her computer bulletin board service:

COME TO WACO SATURDAY, APRIL 3! . . . We simply must take a stand now. There is no other choice, except to be slaves, living in fear of our own government. . . . The Unorganized Militia of the United States of America [1] will assemble [2], with long arms, vehicles . . . aircraft, and any available gear . . . [3], at 9:00 A.M. on Saturday, April 3, 1993, on Northcrest Drive . . . off the interstate in Waco, Texas.[8]

A motley crew of only about twenty persons showed up.[9] This, however, did not discourage the tenacious lawyer, who began waging a highly successful propaganda war against the government. Although her videos are filled with little more than erroneous conclusions, groundless speculations and outright lies, they have succeeded in making Koresh a folk hero of sorts to patriots. They have also provoked in patriots an ardent hatred for the government. Journalist Adam Parfry has dubbed the videos "get-the-bastards motivational tapes."[10] Thompson's influence has indeed been tremendous.

The Big Lie

Waco: The Big Lie appeared shortly after the Davidian siege ended. Even the most basic information it contains about the group is erroneous. It states: "Former leader George Roden's wife gave leadership of the group to Koresh." In reality, George Roden never led the Davidians. He was Koresh's archrival who attempted to gain control of the group, but failed.[11] For that matter, George Roden's wife, Amo, never led the Davidians either. It was George's *mother*, Lois Roden, who held the reins of power prior to Koresh. Moreover, no one *gave* leadership to Koresh. He seized it from Lois over the course of several years as followers switched their allegiance to him.[12]

Thompson further maintains that Koresh was not a polygamist. Her "proof " is a 1991 film clip of an interview between Koresh and Australian reporter Martin King, who asks Koresh, "How many wives do you have?"

The Davidian prophet replies, "One."

"One?" King asks again.

"One wife," Koresh repeats.[13]

An obvious question arises: If Koresh had only one wife, where did all of the polygamy charges come from? According to Thompson, the stories were vicious lies the government spread in order to make Koresh look bad. Thompson completely dismisses eyewitness accounts of several former Davidians as unreliable testimony from "disgruntled" and "vengeful" defectors, who, in cooperation with Big Brother, helped destroy the group.

To discover the truth about Koresh's marital status, I telephoned his mother and father. During a March 28, 1993, taped interview, I asked Bonnie Haldeman if her son ever had more than one wife at the same time. She responded honestly: "I do know that there are *several* wives, other ones that he has. . . . It bothered me at first. . . . I'm not sayin' it's the ideal situation, but you know . . . I've seen it all over."[14] On April 25, 1993, I posed the same question to Koresh's father, Bobby Howell. He gave an equally candid reply: "I know that he had a lot of wives."[15]

Besides historical inaccuracies, *Waco I* contains serious accusations that are not only false, but finally unsupportable. One of the most extreme allegations made is that the government murdered the Davidians by deliberately torching their compound. The film shows a CEV ramming the structure as the narrator explains what is happening: "You can see that this tank has a gas jet on the front that shoots fire. You can also see the fire quite plainly."

At first glance, the CEV does seem to have flames coming from its front end.

This scene confirmed widespread fears that the FBI had cruelly immolated the Davidians. Then, Mike McNulty—head of the California Organization of Public Safety (COPS), a privately funded grassroots thinktank—obtained the original, uncut footage that Thompson used. McNulty forwarded the clip to *Machine Gun News* columnist Ken Carter, who in a February 1994 issue of that magazine, described what Thompson had edited out:

> [I]n the COPS version, rather than stopping the video at the point where the illusion of flame is most apparent, as in the AJF tape, the camera continues to follow the vehicle as it backs clear of the building. . . . As [the] tank turns away from [the] camera, [the] reflection spreads to reveal what appears to be a large section of tan wallboard leaning against the turret.[16]

Carter, who originally believed Thompson's story, commented: "As certain as I previously was that the tank was spewing fire, I am now more convinced that what appeared to be flame was nothing more than an optical illusion created by reflector sunlight."[17] One month prior to the release of the *Machine Gun News* article, Carter was interviewed by *Gun Week* for a January 21, 1994, piece entitled " 'Waco: The Big Lie' Revealed As A Hoax." The story quotes an embarrassed Carter:

> Linda Thompson suckered all of us with that one. And she had to have known exactly what she was doing, since the videotape sequence was edited a split second before the vehicle pulls back and executes a hard turn which clearly shows the 'flame' image stabilize and turn(ed) out to be a piece of wallboard.[18]

In a 1994 feature article, *Soldier of Fortune* magazine also spoke out against Thompson: "What appears to be flames in the Thompson video is actually a visual trick. . . . The apparent fire at the end of the CEV gas induction tube is actually wallboard and other construction debris knocked loose by the CS [gas] sprayer boom."[19]

The Big Lie Continues

One would think that after being found out, so to speak, Thompson would discontinue her accusations. Instead, she produced *Waco II: The Big Lie Continues*, which alleges that the government "not only had flame throwing tanks, but flame throwing backpacks and incendiary bombs" the day of the fire. It also claims that agents fired first, even though no one has been able to prove the accusation. The video additionally charges agents with killing "children the day of the raid" and alleges that "ATF agents were executed by [other] government agents (not accidentally)."[20] *Waco II* further implies that non-lethal weapons such as laser guns, low-level sound and microwaves may have been used on the Davidians.

This second video begins with a still photo of the cult compound during the BATF raid. Attention is drawn to a little yellow blur located in the foreground. The narrator, in a speculative style Thompson is known for, identifies the smudge for viewers: "If you examine it carefully, you can see there was a child outside as the ATF began firing wildly." The spot, however, looks nothing like a child. In fact, it appears to be a splash of paint on the building. This difficulty, of course, can be explained: "The features of the child in the photograph were deliberately blurred by someone to prevent recognition." The narration continues: "The child has been identified as probably being Cyrus Koresh, David Koresh's eight-year-old little boy."

How could anyone have identified the blurred object as Cyrus if the entire face is blurred? Thompson never answers this question. Viewers are again simply expected to believe the assertion. The video goes on to imply that little Cyrus fell victim to bloodthirsty BATF killers. In reality, Cyrus was not killed by out-of-control agents. A homemade video recorded by sect members during the standoff shows a wounded David Koresh sitting next to Cyrus, very much alive.[21]

The rest of *Waco II* continues in a similar fashion, showing innocuous film footage to which is added unsubstantiated descriptions of what is *really* happening. Both tapes use a typical propaganda technique: present video clips (which in and of themselves mean little) followed by narration that *tells* a viewer what is occurring. The credulous will take care of the rest by convincing themselves that what they are being *told* is what they are being *shown*. Note the following examples from *Waco II*:

Image: The burning compound is shown while pops are heard in the background.
False conclusion: The FBI is shooting at the burning building.
Reality: There is no way to know that these are shots. It could be crackling wood.

Image: BATF agents are shown climbing ladders while rapid-fire machine guns can be heard.
False conclusion: It is the BATF firing fully automatic weapons at non-aggressive Davidians.
Reality: The shots might be the Davidians since no BATF agents can actually be seen shooting.

Image: A barely visible and blurry black figure is seen on the roof of the burning compound.
False conclusion: It is an FBI agent who has just helped set the Davidian building on fire.
Reality: It could be anyone. No features or physical characteristics are discernible from the video.

When faced with tangible evidence, Thompson prefers her own version of reality, even if it means misrepresenting documentation. Consider this *Waco II* quotation:

The overall perspective for the raid was spelled out in an internal Treasury Department memorandum from Christopher Cuyler to Michael Langan before the raid in which Cuyler matter-of-factly says that agents will be raiding a Branch Davidian Seventh-day Adventist Church. It doesn't get any plainer than this. They've spelled it out for us. The government set out to conduct a military assault on a church.

The Treasury Department's memorandum actually states that the BATF "will be executing both arrest warrants and search warrants on Sunday, February 28, 1993, at the compound of the Branch Davidian Seventh-day Adventists, a religious cult near Waco, Texas."[22] The word "church" is found nowhere in the document. Nor does Cuyler's letter refer to the Davidian sect as part of the Seventh-day Adventist denomination. The government clearly viewed the Davidians as an Adventist-related "cult" that had broken away from mainstream Christianity.

Perhaps the most self-defeating portion of *Waco II* contains Thompson's unconvincing attempt at explaining away McNulty's tape. She cannot get around the fact that her "fire" in *Waco I* is wallboard. Consequently, she tries to discredit the COPS video by noting that it had been digitally enhanced. Exactly how digitization, which simply improves a film's clarity, affected the validity of McNulty's tape is never made clear.

Thompson also re-identifies the "flames" pictured in her first video. She originally said they were a huge glow at one end of the CEV. But in *Waco II*, the "flames" are suddenly pointed out as fleeting and barely visible flickers of light—which are obviously just more reflections—some five to twenty feet *beyond* the glow she originally identified as fire in *Waco I*. What does Thompson say about that huge glimmer of "fire" in *Waco I* that turned out to be wallboard? Absolutely nothing.

In a computer bulletin board message, Thompson sought to cast additional doubt on the COPS tape by painting McNulty as some kind of anti-patriot con man:

> McNulty, the 'insurance salesman,' supposedly 'expert investigator' with the 'bonafide' office, seems to have folded up shop; the general public was never able to obtain copies of this tape, which seemed to have as its sole purpose, to attack the Waco tape.[23]

My investigation revealed that McNulty is indeed an insurance salesman, and also has an office. In fact, I called him several times throughout 1993 and 1994. For a fee of $25, I was able to obtain a copy of the allegedly unobtainable tape.

The Firestarters

Who started the fire? This question remains unanswered for many people. Thompson and her band of loyalists stand behind the *Big Lie* tapes. Others, like McNulty, believe FBI tanks accidentally started the fire by knocking over kerosene lanterns.[24] The government, as well as several outside arson investigators, feel that the fire was probably set by the cultists themselves.[25]

I must agree that the Davidians likely started the blaze. My position is based in part on recorded conversations obtained with listening devices hidden by the FBI in the Davidian's wooden structure. Several cultists made comments about pouring fuel, spreading it around and lighting a fire.[26] Why would the Davidians do such a thing? Because fire played a major role in their eschatology—beliefs about the "last things," or more specifically, the end of the world.

I learned of their doctrines regarding "the end" by reading a Bible owned by Robyn Bunds, one of Koresh's many wives. The text contains notes written by her during the years she studied with Koresh. One notation in the Bible's margin linked Armageddon—which Koresh believed would be a confrontation with the government—to the sixth seal of Revelation 6:12, 17.[27] Several verses she had cross-referenced involve fire:

- ☐ Is 13:6–9, "[T]he day of the LORD is at hand. . . . Every man's heart shall melt. . . . their faces shall be as flames" (KJV).
- ☐ Dan 7:9–10, "[H]is throne was like the fiery flame, and his wheels as burning fire. A fiery stream issued and came forth before him" (KJV).
- ☐ Nah 1:6, "Who can stand before His indignation? And who can abide in the fierceness of His anger? His fury is poured out like fire and the rocks are thrown down by him" (KJV).

Robyn also had referenced Jeremiah 50 to the sixth seal passage. This is noteworthy in that Koresh quoted Jeremiah 50:22 to the FBI in a letter sent from the compound.[28] Verses 24 and 32 of that prophetic section read as follows:

I have laid a snare for thee. . . . Thou hast striven against the LORD. The LORD hath opened his armoury. . . . I will kindle a fire to his cities, and it shall devour all round about him." (KJV)

In an April 13 interview, FBI agent Bob Ricks revealed that Koresh had warned them that they might be "devoured by fire."[29] Could Koresh have thought that fire would somehow act as a defensive weapon against the unholy invaders? Yes, according to several other passages in Robyn's Bible that had been highlighted. Consider Amos 1:2-7: "The LORD will roar from Zion . . . and the top of Carmel shall wither. . . . I will send fire" (KJV). Interestingly, the Davidians called their home Mt. Carmel. Next to verse 7, Robyn had scribbled: "The fire that will cleanse."

Even more significant is a cross-reference Robyn makes from the Amos passage to Isaiah 4:4-5, which says:

The LORD shall have washed away the filth of the daughters of Zion, and shall have purged the blood of Jerusalem . . . by the spirit of judgment, and by the spirit of burning. And the LORD will create upon every dwelling place of mount Zion. . . a cloud and smoke by day, and a shining of flaming fire by night: for upon all the glory shall be a defence. (KJV)

Next to "washed away the filth of the daughters of Zion," Robyn had penned a fascinating message: CHANGE THE DNA. Beside the phrase, "a cloud and smoke by day, and the shining of a flaming fire by night," she had written an even more cryptic reminder: FACES OF FLAME.

Other notes in Robyn's Bible, when compared with information contained in teaching tapes by Koresh, indicate that he and his followers expected some type of genetic mutation to occur. As God's representative on earth, Koresh would be the one to loose fire upon the faithful, thereby killing off their old nature and transforming them into flaming entities of divine judgment that would smite the enemy.

Adding support to this theory are six words in Robyn Bunds' Bible that are written next to Isaiah 34:2. The passage reads: "For the indignation of the LORD is upon all the nations, and his fury upon all their armies: he hath utterly destroyed them, he hath delivered them to the slaughter." Here, Robyn had scrawled "Because we're cloven tongues of fire."

Another relevant passage is Nahum 2:3-4. It explains exactly what might have prompted the Davidians to light the fires on April 19:

The shield of his mighty men is made red . . . the chariots shall be with flaming torches in the day of his preparation . . . .The chariots shall rage in the streets . . . . they shall seem like torches, they shall run like lightnings. (KJV)

Above this verse's reference to "chariots," Robyn had written the word TANKS. The implication is clear. When the government's "chariots" (i.e., tanks) attacked the compound, the Davidians believed that Nahum's prophecy was unfolding before their eyes. It was time to unleash the fire: "Behold, I am against thee, saith the LORD of Hosts, and I will burn her chariots in the smoke." (Nah 2:13 KJV)

During a January 10, 1987, recorded study, the Davidian prophet tests his class with a penetrating question: "[T]hose who dwell in the land during this time shall be what?"

A lone voice responds: "Consumed."

Koresh reacts to the unsatisfactory answer: "Burned!" He continues: "[T]he whole land shall be devoured by the fire of his jealousy: for he shall make a speedy riddance of all them that dwell in the land." Wanting to make sure his flock got the message, Koresh again prods them for an answer: "Going to be devoured by what?"

The class replies with one voice: "The fire of his jealousy."[30]

A final question needs answering. The FBI's assault started at 6:00 A.M., but the fires did not begin until between 11:55 A.M. and 12:07 P.M. Why? The mystery is possibly solved by Amos 8:9, which states: "And it shall come to pass in that day, saith the LORD God, that I will cause the sun to go down at noon and I will darken the earth in the clear day" (KJV). Next to the words "at noon," Robyn had transcribed Koresh's final prophecy: DEATH OF CYRUS. Cyrus was a regal title Koresh applied to himself.

The adults at Ranch Apocalypse were not the only ones who understood prophecy. Eleven-year-old Scott Mabb and his nine-year-old brother Jake knew the future too. They sat unmoved in front of the television on April 19 and watched their former home go up in flames. The boys had been among the twenty-one children released midway through the siege. After the fire died down, the two lads looked up at their father, and with eerie calm responded: "Mom said a year ago they might have to burn it down."[31]

Rumors, Rumors, Rumors

Several rumors about Koresh and his followers continue to circulate among rank-and-file patriots thanks to anti-government propagandists, uninformed academicians and cult sympathizers obsessed with guaranteeing "freedom of religion" at any expense. One rumor about the Davidian tragedy involves the purpose of the BATF's initial raid on the sect's compound: to conduct a search for illegal weapons. Patriots and cult sympathizers mistakenly believe that "[no] illegal firearms have turned up."[32] This is simply untrue. A review of the evidence by the Texas Rangers "found that the compound contained 48 illegal machine guns and four illegal hand grenades."[33] These weapons were listed by Ken Carter in the March 1994 issue of *Machine Gun News*.[34]

Patriots also object to the child abuse allegations that have been directed against Koresh. Davidian supporters say the group "was completely exonerated" by Child Protective Services, which found "no evidence of child abuse" during a 1992 investigation.[35] Davidian attorney Kirk Lyons calls the child abuse charges "old and bogus information that was used to inflame Attorney General Janet Reno and get her to order the attack."[36]

But historical documents and eyewitness testimony indicate that the Davidians were not "completely exonerated" of child abuse charges. Officials were *forced* to close the 1992 probe due to uncooperative Davidians and legal red tape. According to Joyce Sparks, former Children Protection Services investigative supervisor of the Davidian case in Waco, the Sheriff's Department may have deliberately sabotaged the investigation. "I had one conversation with (Sheriff) Jack Harwell," recalls Sparks. "He said, 'Whatever those people are doing, if they're doing it inside the compound, it's none of your business, and you don't need to go out there.' "[37]

Sparks further maintains that she and other caseworkers were denied access to the children they needed to verify allegations of physical and sexual abuse.[38] No children at the compound were ever examined, or spoken to, without adult Davidians present, and many of the children were never even seen. Koresh had so many wives, no official knew exactly how many children lived at Mt. Carmel.[39] The adults denied all charges of abuse.

Unhindered access to the cult's underage members was not possible until several children were released during the siege. Dr. Bruce Perry of Baylor College of Medicine was one of the first individuals to interview them. Patriot supporter Don McAlvany quotes Dr. Perry as saying, "*none of the 21 children had been sexually abused or molested.*"[40]

But according to Perry, who headed the trauma assessment team that examined the Davidian children, the youngsters were definitely "being raised in an abusive setting. Ranch Apocalypse, by 1992 and through 1993, was clearly a psychologically destructive environment for children."[41] The children's stories leave no doubt that child abuse was, in fact, occurring within the Davidian sect:

- The children described urinating and defecating in pots they were made to empty daily.
- Food was withheld from them for sometimes as long as a full day as punishment.
- Only Koresh could be called father. Children were made to call their biological parents dogs.
- From a very early age, girls were groomed for becoming Koresh's mate. Once a girl had been made "ready," she received a little plastic Star of David.
- For infractions as minor as spilling milk, children were beaten with "the helper," an instrument variously described as the broken paddle end of an oar or a rice stirrer. Several young girls had circular lesions on their buttocks, presumably from "the helper."
- Koresh's sermons, which children were allowed to hear, included graphic descriptions of sexual acts.[42]

Some of the worst child abuse involved harsh corporal punishment inflicted on children as young as eight months old. The beatings sometimes continued for up to forty-five minutes, or until the child's bottom bled. Several witnesses have come forth to confirm this abuse. Lonnie Little, a Michigan man whose thirty-two-year-old son died in the fire, saw a child beaten with a stick for fifteen minutes nonstop in 1990.[43] Former Davidian Michelle Tom states in a signed affidavit that she watched Koresh beat her eight-month-old daughter "for forty minutes because she did not sit on his lap."[44] Debbie Bunds, an ex-Davidian who witnessed this beating, describes what she saw:

> He [Koresh] took the baby . . . and pulled down her diaper and started beating her with a wooden spoon. He beat that baby for forty minutes. He kept saying, "I'm not going to stop 'til you stop cryin." . . . I mean he put his hand way up in the air and he came down as hard as he could. . . . You try to imagine enduring that for forty minutes.[45]

A Waco Whitewash?

Nine Davidians survived the fire. Five of them—along with six other cult members taken into custody during and after the siege—stood trial on a variety of charges, including murder, conspiracy and weapons violations. Three of them were acquitted of all charges. Five of the defendants were given forty years, and the remaining Davidians received lesser sentences, ranging from three to twenty years. Despite the prosecution's successes, many complaints about the government's actions in Waco remain unresolved.

It is now known that the BATF's element of surprise, a crucial factor to the mission's success, had been lost through a chance meeting between KWTX cameraman Jim Peeler and a Davidian postal worker making his morning rounds. The mailman just happened to be David Jones, Koresh's brother-in-law. After learning of the raid, Jones quickly returned to the cult's commune.

Koresh was in the middle of a Bible study when he was interrupted by Perry Jones, David Jones' father. Koresh left the room, but returned a few minutes later. He was visibly upset and walked over to the window. Among the students watching him was BATF undercover agent Robert Rodriguez. The Davidian leader paused as he looked out the window. "They're coming, Robert," Koresh said. "The time has come."[46]

Rodriguez left the compound to inform BATF supervisors of the security leak. They ignored him.[47] This was a final blunder in a series mistakes that had doomed the entire operation almost from its inception:

☐ Koresh knew his group had been infiltrated. The eight BATF agents who took up residence at an undercover house adjacent to the Davidian property posed as college students attending Texas State Technical College. But the agents were hardly typical college students: all were more than forty-years-old, carried briefcases and drove new cars. Koresh confirmed his suspicions by running checks on the cars: three of the four had no credit liens outstanding.

☐ BATF believed Koresh never left the compound. Consequently, he could be arrested only through a direct frontal assault on the compound. In reality, Koresh often left the commune, and did so in late 1992, as well as just a few weeks before the raid.

☐ BATF intelligence information indicated that the Davidians kept their weapons "under lock and key in a central location." The guns were actually distributed and readily available.

☐ Surveillance ended eleven days before the raid, but the BATF's tactical planners thought it was ongoing up until the raid.

☐ The raid's planners thought the compound housed 75 Davidians when 125 actually lived there.[48]

Problems plagued the extended siege as well. Confusion reigned as FBI negotiators continually clashed with FBI tacticians.[49] Negotiators wanted to resolve the situation using diplomacy. Tacticians chose psychological terrorism, which included shining powerful spotlights into the compound at night and blasting the cult with loud music, Tibetan chanting, sirens and rabbits being slaughtered.[50] This tactic only strengthened the Davidian's us-against-them mentality and bolstered their view that the government, along with the entire outside world, was utterly evil and untrustworthy.

Retired FBI agent Peter Smerick, who advised the FBI high command in Waco, says he "warned that getting tough could lead to fatalities—and that he was pressured to adopt a harder line."[51] Smerick's testimony is supported by Dr. Alan Stone, a Harvard professor retained by the government to review the tear gas assault. In November 1993, Stone concluded that during the standoff, FBI commanders had ignored their own behavioral experts and instead "embarked on a misguided and punishing law-enforcement strategy that contributed to the tragic end at Waco."[52]

Stone further revealed that a preassault assessment compiled by behavioral experts described Koresh as "a religious fanatic who was likely to fulfill his apocalyptic visions." FBI leaders ignored this review, choosing instead to characterize Koresh as "a petty con artist who would not likely commit suicide."[53]

It seems government leaders simply could not, or would not, understand Koresh's mindset. They became irritated, lost patience and eventually threw caution to the wind. One of the last FBI announcements made prior to the fire has a decidedly sarcastic and taunting tone, indicating just how out of touch officials were with the seriousness of the situation:

> David, we are facilitating your leaving the compound by enlarging the door. David, you have had your 15 minutes of fame. . . . Vernon [Vernon Howell, Koresh's original name until he changed it in 1990] is no longer the Messiah. Leave the building now.[54]

Several months after the siege's end, repercussions began hitting law enforcement personnel. BATF Director Stephen Higgins was forced into early retirement after it was discovered that top officials lied to the public about the initial raid. Higgins himself stated that the BATF "would not have executed the plan" if supervisors felt like surprise had been lost. He assured everyone: "[W]e did not believe that we had lost that element of surprise."[55]

Five other BATF supervisors were fired for their roles in the initial raid, but two of them—Charles Sarabyn and Philip Chojnacki—were later reinstated with back pay.[56] James Jorgenson of the National Association of Treasury Agents denounced the rehiring: "This most recent callous action by the government is disgraceful. It defiles the memory of the brave ATF agents who gave their lives doing their duty."[57]

A Justice Department review of the FBI, which is itself part of the Justice Department, found "no fault during the standoff and the tear-gas assault."[58] Janet Reno, who ordered the attack on the siege's last day, has repeatedly lashed out at FBI critics: "It is unfair, it is unreasonable, it is a lie to spread the poison that the government was responsible at Waco for the murder of innocents."[59]

FBI Director Louis Freeh has at least recognized that the procedures and structures that the FBI relied on to do the job in Waco were "inadequate."[60] Many Americans, patriot and non-patriot alike, are convinced "that those responsible for the debacle are not telling all they know."[61]

Civil War II

Ruby Ridge and Waco have no doubt contributed to the widespread anger this country is feeling toward federal authorities. Patriot Clayton Douglas asks: "How long will it be before Montana, Idaho, Wyoming or Texas have had enough of the government's excesses and secede [from the Union]?"[62] Douglas's comment suggests that the recent rebellion and violence originating from within the patriot movement may be precursors to something far more terrible: revolution.

There are some signs that conflict is indeed on the horizon. In 1994, Arizona patriot David Espy—leader of the Association of the Sons of Liberty and the Volunteer Militia—publicly called for "the legal cessation [sic] of Arizona from these federal United States."[63] Also in 1994, Linda Thompson sent a "Declaration of Independence" to Congress:

> [E]ach of the sovereign citizens undersigned are . . . [f]ree and independent Sovereign Citizens . . . they are absolved from all Allegiance to the federal government of the United States of America, and all political Connection between them and the federal government . . . is and ought to be dissolved; and that as free and Independent Sovereign Citizens, each has the full Power to levy War, conclude Peace, contract Alliances, establish Commerce, and to do all other Acts and Things which an Independent Sovereign may of right do.[64]

Within months of Thompson's declaration, the Montana Shooting Sports Association drafted a constitutional initiative to "repeal Article I of the Montana Constitution and replace that article with a new Article I giving state government sufficient power to operate Montana as a sovereign nation."[65]

To some patriots, the future is all too clear. What supposedly lies ahead was articulated to me on November 7, 1995, by Steven Hempling, director of the patriot movement's Free Enterprise Society. "We're headed for civil war," Hempling said. "That's what we're headed for."[66]

6

Guns,
Government
and Glory

From Ruby Ridge mountains . . . [to the] Waco plains of
Texas . . . the sky is red from the blood of those that savored
Freedom. . . . So rises up the men and women that will be
persecuted and prosecuted to let it be known that they will
regain what has been lost, FREEDOM. The common-name for
these brave men and women will be MILITIAMAN.
Thomas Posey[1]
American's Bulletin

The militias have threatened widespread insurrection if Washington politicians do not repeal "oppressive" legislation and stop law enforcement abuses.[2] Their warnings raise three fundamental questions: Is armed rebellion a constitutionally guaranteed option for those disagreeing with federal policies? Are we facing a degree of tyranny that justifies revolution? Do today's militias conform to the structure and purpose of the colonial militias that fought during the American Revolution?

These questions involve two issues that regularly spark debate: (1) the right to bear arms; and (2) the legal definition of the militia. Both issues are linked to the Second Amendment. According to Wayne LaPierre, chief executive officer of the National Rifle Association (NRA), the battle over the Second Amendment is "a battle to retake the most precious, most sacred ground on earth. . . . This is the battle for freedom."[3]

Guns, Guns, Guns

"America was born with a rifle in its hand." A 1624 survey in Jamestown, Virginia, counted one firearm for every colonist.[4] Of course, guns were viewed differently four hundred years ago. No one thought of their weapon as a luxury item, or as a piece of recreational equipment. The gun was an "an essential tool of survival."[3] In fact, this nation never would have been born without firearms.

Our Founding Fathers understood the importance of guns to maintaining freedom. Consequently, they sought to protect the liberty of future generations by guaranteeing them the right to bear arms via the Second Amendment: "A well-regulated Militia, being necessary to the security of a free State, the right of the people to keep and bear Arms, shall not be infringed."

In 1791, everyone understood the meaning of these words. But times change. People change. Expressions change. That which was once obvious becomes obscure. As a result, heated debate now rages over the intent of the Second Amendment. The main point of contention is whether the right to bear arms is a *collective* right of the states or an *individual* right of the people. The position one takes often depends on the political camp into which one happens to fall. Both sides have good arguments.

The Liberal Viewpoint

Citizens favoring tight gun control laws argue that Americans should stop complaining about gun restrictions and be grateful that they have any guns at all. To these "liberals," the Second Amendment protects only the collective right of states to maintain militias (such as the National Guard), "while it does not protect the right of 'the people' to keep and bear arms."[6] There are two basic arguments in support of this view.

First, it is maintained that the Second Amendment's meaning must be gleaned from its opening words: "A well-regulated Militia." It is asserted that these words place the rest of the amendment in the context of militia formation. The right to bear arms, then, is only a state's right to keep its citizens armed as a means of protection against the possibility that the new national government would "use its power to establish a powerful standing army and eliminate the state militias."[7] Such a reading, which eradicates an *individual's* right to bear arms, is supported by the American Civil Liberties Union (ACLU):

> [T]he individual's right to bear arms applies only to the preservation or efficiency of a well-regulated [state] militia. . . . The possession of weapons by individuals is not constitutionally protected.[8]

Another argument against an individual's right to bear arms stems from the advancement of technology. Liberal scholars contend that even if "the people" mentioned in the amendment does indeed apply to individual citizens, the development of powerful modern armies and police forces renders the right to bear arms "anachronistic and dangerous."[9]

Liberal politicians and their supporters believe that gun ownership may be legitimately restricted since Americans possess guns only because the federal government is affording them the privilege of even having guns. Such individuals see gun control as a primary means of securing a safe society. Some political left-wingers feel that the "privilege" of gun ownership should actually be taken away, given the level of crime in America. Their reasoning is straightforward: Guns mean violence. Get rid of the guns and you get rid of violence. Their conclusion is understandable given several alarming statistics:

- There are 1.1 million crimes committed with handguns annually.
- Two of every three homicide victims are killed by guns.
- A child is killed by a gun every two hours.
- An estimated 100,000 students carry a gun to school each day.
- By the year 2003, the annual number of gun-related deaths will surpass the number of people killed in motor vehicle accidents, thus becoming the leading cause of injury-related deaths.[10]

Pro-gun advocates often counter such statistics with a well-worn cliché: "Guns don't kill people; people kill people." Liberals respond by citing psychological studies indicating that guns can actually incite people to kill. According to Leonard Berkowitz, emeritus professor of psychology at the University of Wisconsin, "The finger pulls the trigger. But the trigger may also pull the finger."[11] For 40 years, Berkowitz has studied the "weapons effect." He claims his conclusions are indisputable:

Even the sight of guns, which people think of as objects that can hurt others, can induce aggressive ideas. A weapon can function as a conditioned stimulus, eliciting both the thoughts and motor responses associated with its use.[12]

Various psychological experiments lend support to Berkowitz's theory. In one behavioral test, subjects were instructed to throw wet sponges at a carnival clown. Some players had a rifle situated in their visual field at the booth's front end. Others played without a firearm present. Researchers found that those exposed to the rifle threw more sponges. Interestingly, other objects did not elicit similar responses. Even when the clown insulted participants, there was no discernible increase in player aggression. Only the rifle's presence seemed to have that effect.[13]

In an experiment where teenagers were instructed to electrically shock fellow high school students, psychology professor Ann Frodi found that teens "administered more and longer electric shocks to other students when a weapon was present." Frodi concludes that objects "with clear aggressive connotations can trigger violent acts." She also says parents know that "kids who play with toy guns can become more aggressive. It's the same with adults, and it's provable."[14] How can guns drive someone toward violence? Berkowitz explains:

[A gun's] presence increases the chance that something bad will happen, and not just because they have the power to cause injury. . . . People disposed to aggression because of their perception of the world feel powerful around guns, and those guns can prime their aggressive ideas. Weapons may not be a precipitating influence, but they are likely a reinforcing factor. Guns aren't neutral. They create aggression that wouldn't exist in the absence of guns.[15]

Other studies suggest that outlawing guns, or at least imposing a severe restriction of guns, would indeed reduce violent crime. Two 1969 Chicago studies on assaults, as well as a 1969 report by the National Commission on the Causes and Prevention of Violence Task Force, found that firearms "are not only the most deadly instrument of attack but also the most versatile." Firearms also help criminals by enabling them to overpower physically stronger persons who would otherwise have been left alone.[16]

Some researchers hypothesize that guns may even "facilitate attacks by persons too squeamish to come into physical contact with their victims or to use messier methods to injure them." For those psychologically unable to knife someone, the gun provides "a more impersonal, emotionally remote, and even antiseptic way of attacking others."[17]

As convincing as these arguments may sound, gun control opponents have powerful rebuttals, especially about the "collective" right to bear arms interpretation of the Second Amendment.

The Conservative Outlook

Conservatives believe the Second Amendment protects the *individual's* right to bear arms. According to the results of a 1995 *U.S. News & World Report* survey, seventy-five percent of all American voters believe the Constitution guarantees them the right to own a gun.[18] Such a feeling is no doubt accentuated by law enforcement's inability to adequately protect citizens. A 1993 article in *The Public Interest*, a quarterly journal of opinion, quotes some disturbing Justice Department statistics for 1991: "[F]or all crimes of violence, only twenty-eight percent of calls are responded to within five minutes." Gun owners understandably mock police claims of timely service. "Call for a cop, call for an ambulance, and call for a pizza," they quip. "See who shows up first."[19]

Self-protection is of primary importance to gun-rights advocates. Although firearms are indeed used in many crimes every year, there is an interesting fact that casts severe doubt on arguments for stricter gun control:

> [G]un restrictions appear to exert no significant negative effect on total violence rates. . . . Not only did [statistical] results rarely indicate that gun laws reduce total rates of violence, they also indicate that most laws do not even seem to reduce the use of guns or induce people to substitute other weapons in acts of violence.[20]

The apparent failure of gun laws to curtail crime may be a result of the fact that law-abiding citizens are the only ones who obey firearms regulations. Criminals are not going to comply with gun laws. This was confirmed in a 1983 prison survey:

> Among the "hardened criminals" who reported previous gun possession when questioned in a recent prison survey, only 15 percent claimed to have ever even applied for a permit to purchase or carry any of the guns, even though about 91 percent of the sample were imprisoned in states with provisions for one or the other permit and 32 percent were in states with both.[21]

Eighty-two percent of the prisoners polled agreed with the statement that gun laws "affect only law-abiding citizens; criminals will always be able to get guns."[22] This finding indicates that there is apparently some degree of truth behind the pro-gun slogan, "When guns are outlawed, only outlaws will have guns."

Aside from the pros and cons of gun control, a more important issue is whether the Constitution protects the *individual's* right to bear arms. It appears that this was indeed the intent of the Founding Fathers. In 1776, Thomas Jefferson wrote that no free man "shall be debarred the use of arms within his own land."[23] Patrick Henry echoed this sentiment: "The great object is that every man be armed."[24]

James Madison agreed that the advantage of being armed was possessed by Americans "over the people of almost every other nation . . . [where] governments are afraid to trust the people with arms."[25] Samuel Adams urged that the "Constitution be never construed to authorize Congress to . . . prevent the people of the United States, who are peaceable citizens, from keeping their own arms."[26]

Most constitutional scholars side with the individual-ownership view of the Second Amendment. An article in the *Encyclopedia of the American Constitution* summarizes the Second Amendment literature produced in 1986: "[O]f the thirty-six review articles published since 1980, only four support the anti-gun position, while thirty-two articles support the individual right position."[27]

Political historian Joyce Malcolm—a professor whose work as been underwritten by the American Bar Foundation, Harvard Law School and the National Endowment for the Humanities—writes that the Second Amendment "was meant to guarantee the individual's right to have arms for self-defense and self-preservation." Like many scholars, Malcolm also recognizes that the Constitution guarantees personal ownership of firearms for a much broader purpose—militia service.[28] This brings us to an extremely relevant question: What is the Constitutional definition of the militia?

A Well-regulated Militia

The position of modern-day patriots is that the militia, as defined by the Constitution, is the citizenry at large. They are absolutely correct. Title 10 of the U.S. Code, section 311 reads:

> The militia of the United States consists of *all* able-bodied males at least 17 years of age and . . . under 45 years of age who are . . . citizens of the United States and of female citizens of the United States who are commissioned officers of the National Guard.

The militia is further divided into the organized and unorganized militia. The former is composed of persons called into service. The latter consists of individuals held in reserve. The Founding Fathers clearly advocated this position. Samuel Adams stated, "The militia is composed of free Citizens."[29] George Mason felt the same way: "I ask, sir, what is the militia? It is the whole people, except for a few public officials."[30]

James Madison did not fear oppression by a federal army because the troops would be outnumbered by "a militia amounting to near half a million of citizens with arms in their hands."[31] Since the population in 1790 was only 800,000, Madison was obviously referring to every man capable of bearing arms.[32]

Constitutional scholars agree that the totality of American citizens are the militia. Consider the authoritative words of Yale law Professor Akhil Amar:

> The ultimate right to keep and bear arms belongs to the "people," not the "states." . . . Nowadays, it is quite common to speak loosely of the National Guard as "the state militia," but [when the Second Amendment was written] . . . "the militia" referred to all Citizens capable of bearing arms. [Thus] "the militia" is identical to "the people."[33]

Although patriots may be correct in identifying the nature of the militia, they are mistaken as to how the militia is to be activated. As Karen L. MacNutt accurately notes in a 1995 article for *Women & Guns*, there is a big difference between *the* militia and being part of *a* militia: "*The* militia is all citizens capable of bearing arms. *A* militia is an organization of citizen soldiers."[34]

The crucial point involves the means by which ordinary citizens, who are *the* militia, may organize and participate in *a* militia. The United States Supreme Court has limited "the right to raise a militia *to States*" rather than private citizens (*Presser v. Illinois*). In other words, only State authorities can call citizens into a militia in order to protect that state from enemies both foreign and domestic.

Alexander Hamilton made this clear in *Federalist No. 28* by declaring that "uniformity in the organization and discipline of the militia would be attended with the most beneficial effects, whenever they *were called* into service for the public defense" [emphasis added]. Hamilton then proposed that the states alone would be responsible for "the appointment of the officers, and the authority of training the militia according to the discipline prescribed by Congress."[35]

Private citizens cannot simply band together, saying, "Okay, we're a militia. We're here to protect our rights against what we believe is a tyrannical federal government." The militias of today's patriot movement are functioning outside constitutional boundaries. They are *unconstitutional* militias. The Constitution stipulates, "Congress shall have the power . . . To provide for calling forth the militia . . . To provide for organizing, arming, and disciplining the militia . . . reserving to the states respectively, the appointment of officers, and the authority of training the militia."

According to Daniel Levitas, cofounder of the Institute for Research and Education on Human Rights, the language of the Second Amendment "in no way authorizes or justifies the existence of the private gangs of paramilitary vigilantes that make up the militia movement."[36] Patriot movement militias do not have any standing under the Constitution since constitutional militias can be authorized only "by federal or state governments."[37] Even the decidedly pro-gun periodical *Soldier of Fortune* magazine has leveled a serious charge against patriots: "These militias that . . . have appointed their own officers and conduct training without authority from the state, are therefore in apparent violation of Article 1, Section 8, Subsection 16 of the U.S. Constitution."[38]

Several militias are currently acting "in violation of laws against paramilitary activity."[39] Forty-one states have statutes "banning either private militias or paramilitary activity or outlawing the existence of private militias."[40] Oregon, for instance, has a law that explicitly prohibits the forming of militias. Idaho and California have forbidden paramilitary training by civilians.[41] Despite these restrictions, militias continue to function as private armies generally without police interference.

Uncle Sam Is not King George

Militia leader John Trochmann, who heads the Militia of Montana, maintains that the militias have a singular mandate: "Return to the Constitution of the United States." He also proclaims that the Declaration of Independence is again speaking "as it did over 200 years ago when flagrant injustice continued out of control by oppressive public servants."[42] Trochmann is obviously making a comparison between today's militias and those of 1776. Rhetoric like this is common among today's patriots, who fancy themselves modern-day counterparts to the patriots who founded America. Richard McDonald states, "I consider myself a patriot, in the same way Benjamin Franklin and George Washington were. They were for America, and that's what I am about."[43]

But unlike modern-day militias, which assemble independently, without the consent of state and local officials, colonial patriots were summoned into service by "the selectmen, mayors, constables, wardens, and other representatives of local government."[44] In 1775, militia members had to sign a muster roll (official member- ship list), which bound them to the articles of war. They were also paid for their services from the public treasury. Furthermore, they "were chartered by the states, swore allegiance to the state, and were a part of the state's military forces."[45]

Many observers feel that the modern militia movement is nothing but a perversion of an honorable calling heeded long ago by honorable men who knew their place as soldiers under authority:

To Sam Adams, April 19, 1775, was a glorious day because local government committed itself to American independence, not because a mob of radicals attacked the British Army. Until called into service by civilian authorities, the militia had no legal authority to act.[46]

It is noteworthy that our twentieth century patriots also compare the "oppression" they now endure to the tyrannical domination the colonists suffered under the British Crown.[47] Note the following endorsement for the militias that appeared in an October 1994 patriot newsletter:

At no time in our history since the colonies declared their independence from the long train of abuses of King George has our country needed a network of active militias across America to protect us from the monster we have allowed our federal government to become. Long Live the Militia! Long Live Freedom! Long live government that fear [sic] the people![48]

James Johnson of the Ohio Unorganized Militia states essentially the same thing: "[S]ome of the legislation that has been coming out of Washington . . . ladies and gentlemen, these things started the revolution 200 years ago."[49]

But Glenn Reynolds, associate professor of law at the University of Tennessee, believes that modern-day militia members "sort of lose the thread" by not realizing that the framers had "a very exacting definition of what a tyrannical government was, and when it was appropriate to start thinking about revolting against it." He explains:

> If you apply the test the framers had of what constituted a legitimate revolution, like the American Revolution, rather than a mere insurrection or rebellion, which they regarded as just other varieties of crime, you can't really find any justification for armed revolt today.[50]

Only persons who are woefully ignorant of history would think for a moment that today's legislative irritations and federal abuses of authority are in any way comparable to the sufferings our colonial forebearers endured. It is almost an insult to the memory of America's founders to suggest otherwise. American colonists were ruled by a king living 3,000 miles across the Atlantic. The British troops occupying the colonies not only used, but abused, the citizens. They were often slaughtered openly in the streets. For example, on March 5, 1770, unarmed residents of Boston who were pelting soldiers with snowballs and insults were shot. Five died.[51]

The British Crown also issued Writs of Assistance, which were virtual blank-check search warrants allowing soldiers to go into any house, anywhere, at any time.[52] At one point, colonists were not allowed to leave their city "unless they turned in their arms."[53] A Quartering Act, passed in 1765, authorized officials "to hire public houses and vacant buildings to house the troops . . . and directed officials to procure supplies at the expense of the colonists."[54]

The complaints being voiced by today's patriots pale in comparison to those raised by America's eighteenth-century colonists. Many modern militia members often cannot even detail the ways their liberty has been encroached. They often bring up minor irritations that are insufficient reason to take up arms against the federal government. Consider this PBS interview with Jim McKinzey of Missouri's 51st Militia:

MacNeil/Lehrer: "Where do you believe your liberties have been impinged upon by the federal government?"

McKinzey: "There's literally *thousands* of things that my liberties have been infringed upon. One item is just going out and buying a firearm. The Bill of Rights gives us the right to be armed, but yet you have to go out and fill out paperwork, both state and federal, in order for a law-abiding citizen to own this weapon."

MacNeil/Lehrer: "Are there other examples?"

McKinzey: "Uh. [long pause] There are [pause] yeah, like I said, there's countless examples. Uh, uh, if you read the Constitution [pause], you'll find that the federal government is very limited on what they can do within the bounds of the Constitution. Uh, some of these, uh [pause] items are requiring that on our highways we only drive fifty-five miles an hour. Uh, I read nothing in the Constitution that says that the federal government can tell me how fast I can drive my automobile. Uh, carrying a social security card. . . . I don't read that in the Constitution anywhere."[55]

It is true that the our nation's leaders have instituted a few restrictions that make some aspects of life inconvenient. Many Americans might even agree that "the government is too big and bloated, that federal agencies sometimes overstep their bounds, that citizens pay too much taxes, etc."[56] But not everyone runs around in the woods with AK-47s rehearsing for a day when they will have to fight the feds. Why? Because the real motivation behind the patriot movement is much more complex than all of the complaints and irritations that have been discussed thus far.

Unlike most Americans, who are simply tired of our government's problems, patriots cling to an elaborate conspiratorial theory that the ongoing economic and political events are part of a much larger plan to "enslave Americans by disarming the population and making the currency worthless. The eventual result . . . will be the New World Order—a one-world government administered by the United Nations."[57]

PART 3

Conspiracies Unlimited

Let us imagine a person healthy in body and strong, talented and not unkind. . . . We know that this person (or people) is now in a very sorry state. If we want to help him, we have first to understand what is wrong with him. Thus we learn that he is not really mad, his mind is merely afflicted to a considerable extent by false ideas approaching folie de granduer and a hostility toward everyone and everything. . . . [H]e imagines dangers that do not exist, and builds upon this the most absurd propositions. It seems to him that all his neighbors offend him . . . and in every way want to harm him. He accuses everyone in his family of damaging and deserting him, or crossing over to the enemy camp. He imagines that his neighbors want to undermine his house and even to launch an armed attack. Therefore he will spend enormous sums on the purchase of guns, revolvers, and iron locks. If he has any time left, he will turn against his family. We shall not, of course, give him money, even though we are eager to help him, but will try to persuade him that this ideas are wrong and unjustified. If he will still not be convinced and if he perseveres in his mania, neither money nor drugs will help.
Vladimir Solovyov
Russian philosopher, 1892[1]

7

Operation Enslavement

There exists a subterranean world where pathological
fantasies disguised as ideas are churned out by crooks and
half-educated fanatics for the benefit of the ignorant and
superstitious. There are times when this underworld emerges
from the depths and suddenly fascinates, captures, and
dominates multitudes of usually sane and responsible
people, who thereupon take leave of sanity and
responsibility. And it occasionally happens that this
underworld becomes a political power and changes the
course of history.
Norman Cohn
Author and scholar[1]

Wake up America! This nation "is in its death throes as the final assaults
are made on the freedoms that all of mankind throughout history have
cherished, fought and died for."[2] An unparalleled horror approaches: the
New World Order (NWO), a system that "pretends to care for the masses but
actually controls them for the benefit of unseen, unelected masters."[3] It is nothing
but "a new name for Communism"[4] and will bring about "dictatorial enslavement
and control over the entire planet."[5]

Through ignorance and complacency, so this conspiracy goes, most Americans
are blithefully marching into an NWO global community wherein all international
borders and national sovereignty will be destroyed. The coming totalitarian regime
allegedly will reduce humanity to slaves whose sole purpose will be to serve the
"international bankers, wealthy elite, socialists and liberals."[6] These evil "one-
worlders" apparently have been conspiring for decades "to destroy America's
independence and throw our nation into a melting pot of United Nations, a New
World Order—a one world government."[7] Patriot Jim Keith warns that "the time
is ripe to implement plans that will turn America into a socialist slave state in
everything but name."[8]

From a patriot's perspective, the NWO is a cross between Communist Russia and a society reminiscent of the one depicted in the 1976 sci-fi movie *Logan's Run.* In this film's twenty-third century world, no one has a family, all persons are property of the state, people have numbers rather than names, and life ends at thirty after an age-sensitive crystal inserted into one's palm at birth turns black.[9] Some patriot versions of the NWO sound remarkably like the sci-fi thriller:

> What the Elite plan for us, and are putting into effect . . . is a technologized future of biobehavioral controls. No responsibilities, no decisions to make, no fears of the unknown; a planned existence, from before conception, to death. It will be a heavily structured authoritarian society. Prior to conception, there will be isolation of "smart" genes, elimination of "negative" genes and total genetic manipulation. Oxygenation of the fetus, mega-protein feeding to the mother, scientific conditioning of the child, positive drug therapy for memory. . . . [G]enetics, drugs, diet, conditioning will be some of the manipulative tools of the 21st Century Global Rulers. We will have a total class society based on Genetic Ratings (A, B, C, etc.). . . . Genetic manipulation, psychological conditioning, molecular biology, psychoneorology [sic], computer technology, psychopharmacology, neurophysiology, etc., will all be utilized.[10]

Patriots say this futuristic nightmare will be implemented after the globe is partitioned into three main regions of power: a European Union; a North American region merging the U.S., Canada and Mexico; and Pacific Rim countries. Border redefinition will lead to regional governments that will subjugate the sovereignty, constitutions, and heritage of all countries. America itself will be divided into ten regions governed by men directly assigned by the president, "kind of like in *Star Wars.*"[11]

One-World Government

If the phrase New World Order sounds familiar, it should. President Bush used it on September 11, 1990, before a joint session of Congress. It was the end of the Cold War, in the midst of the Gulf crisis, and shortly before the reunification of Germany:

> We stand today at a unique and extraordinary moment. . . . Out of these troubled times, . . . a new world order can emerge; a new era—freer from the threat of terror, stronger in the pursuit of justice, and more secure in the quest for peace, an era in which the nations of the world, East and West, North and South, can prosper and live in harmony.[12]

Bush was speaking of "a reinvigorating of the system of collective security envisioned by the drafters of the United Nations Charter."[13] The ultimate goal, of course, is to usher in an era "where diverse nations are drawn together in common cause [i.e., peace]."[14] Many individuals view the NWO as "a noble and vitally necessary condition for the future."[15] Caspar W. Weinberger, U.S. Defense Secretary from 1981 to 1987, explains:

[The NWO] means that the U.S. and other democratic nations agree to be governed by a rule of law whereby any country breaking that law is treated much as criminals are in each country. They are tried and, if found guilty, punished. The process will be carried out in the same manner that police and courts enforce local laws.[16]

Responsible political opponents of the NWO fear that U.N. policies may set up our country as "the world's policeman trying to impose a Pax Americana on the rest of the world."[17] Patriots, however, voice an entirely different complaint. They believe communists, socialists and international elitists "intend to eliminate U.S. sovereignty and independence and merge us into a world government."[18] Bush's comment is seen as a blatant attempt to indoctrinate the masses. Consider the following advertisement placed in the *USA Patriot Magazine*:

As corrupt politicians disarm you, sell out your birthright, your posterity and your country, the rest of the world goosesteps into a "New World Order," as lemmings off a cliff. . . . DEPROGRAM YOURSELF, discover your AMERICAN SPIRIT, 'n shove serfdom back up the **New World Order** keister![19]

According to influential patriot Jack McLamb, the NWO will be "an oligarchy of the world's richest families who will place one half of the masses of the earth in servitude under their complete control, administered from behind the false front of the United Nations."[20] Well-known patriot sympathizer Don McAlvany warns, "This is not the America we grew up in. Welcome to the USSA, a branch of the New World Order."[21]

Our Invisible National Police

The New World Order envisioned by patriots supposedly will be brought about through strategic maneuvers made by the numerous evil conspirators now covertly manipulating America. One of the first steps taken involves the creation of a Multi-Jurisdictional Task Force (MJTF), a national police force. This belief can be traced to the late 1980s, when a Michigan janitor named Mark Koernke began lecturing about the NWO.

Koernke asserts that the MJTF is a product of various legislative moves that have authorized the use of federal funding "to convert local and State forces into national police forces."[22] Patriots conclude that this MJTF will be "the umbrella group that will make up the national police force in the United States."[23] All local law enforcement agencies will be replaced, or at the very least completely controlled, by the MJTF. After all, a country cannot be a totalitarian police state unless it has a unified police.

Forming a national police was one of the steps Hitler took in unifying Germany and consolidating his power. According to William F. Shirer, author of *The Rise and Fall of the Third Reich*, it was on June 16, 1936, that the *Führer* created what had never before existed in Germany: a "unified police" for the whole of the Reich:

[P]reviously the police had been organized separately by each of the states.

. . . [now there was] the German Police. . . . The Third Reich, as is inevitable in the development of all totalitarian dictatorships, had become a police state.[24] Although a large number of patriots have neo-Nazi sympathies and even idolize Hitler (see chapters twelve and thirteen), *most* patriots not only despise Hitlerian methods of rule, but fear that his dictatorial tactics may soon be used by our federal government. This phobia is due, in part, to the final report of the National Performance Review (NPR) headed by Vice President Al Gore. It recommended that the attorney general be designated Director of Law Enforcement to coordinate federal law enforcement efforts. Patriots contend "this scheme would actually create a national police force for the first time in our history."[25]

In reality, there is no MJTF. There are, however, a number of ways local police and federal authorities work together. In a few cases, local officers are even "federalized" in order to assist federal authorities in certain law enforcement actions. But this is a far cry from having a national police force. Policy analyst Craig Hulet notes that for many years various law enforcement agencies have been joining forces in order to overcome jurisdictional impairments. These joint efforts, however, belie nothing sinister.[26]

No documentation whatsoever exists to substantiate patriot allegations about an MJTF, yet they insist it is somewhere, and will eventually consist of local police, federal law enforcement personnel, the military, and oddly enough, street gangs:

> [A] full agreement has been signed in Los Angeles, and both the Bloods and the Crips are now being trained, equipped, and uniformed with federal funding through California. . . . Their mission is to be the forefront, the master forces, to come through the door.[27]

Claiming that street gangs are being recruited by the government is groundless rumor. Hulet feels the problem centers on the fact that "in the crazy, convoluted world of conspiracists every 'thing' is suspect, especially those things not understood."[28] This observation holds especially true when it comes to the United Nations.

The Devil's Headquarters

Another dark vision patriots have of the NWO involves merging of the MJTF with foreign troops to form an occupying army that will be this nation's "Multinational Peacekeeping force."[29] Here is where the "true" purpose of the United Nations' blue-helmeted army fits into patriot ideas. The NWO crowd is allegedly going to use these troops to patrol America.

The stated purpose of U.N. peacekeeping forces is to help keep peace in countries where the government cannot do so for itself. What does this have to do with the United States? Plenty. The global conspirators supposedly are causing a systematic breakdown of our society so peacekeepers can be called in to rescue us from ourselves. "With just the 'right' manipulation, they have been successfully conditioning our people to see **all** our societal problems—government, political,

educational, penal, ecological, etc.—as completely **out of control**."[30] The goal is
to have U.N. forces invade America:

> This is the coming of the "New World Order." A one world government where,
> in order to put the new government in place, we must all be disarmed first. To
> do that, the government is deliberately creating schizms [sic] in our society,
> funding both the anti-abortion and pro-choice sides, the anti-gun/pro-gun
> issues, black-white race riots, gay/anti-gay hysteria, trying to provoke a riot
> that will allow martial law to be implemented and all the weapons seized, while
> "dissidents" are put safely away.[31]

Unseen manipulators, "along with thousands of their world government 'comrades' in the U.S. have been deliberately whipping the American public into a
fearful frenzy."[32] Americans will soon be *wanting* peacekeepers to come and
restore order. Then the United Nations—a political body that "ignores God and
was founded for the purpose of Global Socialism"—will invade the country to
"eliminate U.S. sovereignty and independence and merge us into a world government."[33] According to patriot Vernon Weckner, U.N. troops are already stationed
here and waiting to attack:

> If Clinton declares a national emergency, he has this big multinational force, a
> United Nations force, made up of German, Dutch, French and Gurkha
> [Chinese] soldiers. There's a bunch of them out at the air base and a bunch
> more right across the border in Canada."[34]

Jack McLamb warns, "[W]hen America, the last 'holdout,' is brought to its knees,
the American sheep will **beg their new god (GOVERNMENT) to save them!**
The 'salvation' they are being tricked into demanding will be the merging together
of all nations under that great 'bastion of peace and freedom,' the **United
Nations.**"[35]

To patriots, then, calling U.N. forces peacekeepers is a ruse. It is all part of a
master plan by elitists who will use the organization's international troops to
subjugate Americans. The federal government is not going to stand in the way
because it, too, is "under the direct control of the bankers through the IMF
[International Monetary Fund] and the U.N.[36] There is no doubt in patriot minds
regarding this matter:

> It is not a matter of conjecture anymore. The plan of the owners of the world
> is to institute a New World Order—in essence just the consolidation of world
> control into fewer hands. When the U.N. has a "peacekeeping" force superior
> to that of the U.S. military (or perhaps before that) there is no doubt, no
> argument, that U.N. forces will be used to subjugate the U.S. The forces who
> intend to implement the New World Order (and they include the politicians who
> currently rule the roost in the United States) simply will not take no for an
> answer.[37]

"Be warned," says former Militia of Montana (MOM) representative Bob Fletcher.
"The United Nations one world government will not take the United States of

America, they will not take the American patriots. And you better watch out, because we're not going to put up with it any longer."[38] According to MOM, the game is already over: "[T]he **UN** is **NOW** in **CONTROL** of America!"[39] Mark Koernke agrees:

> All of the [law enforcement] agencies are overlapping and under the general authority of the United Nations. . . . [W]e are now an international organization, not the United States.[40]

Conspiratorial theories involving the establishment of a one-world government are not new. The John Birch Society (founded in 1958) has "always argued that behind communism is the secret elite."[41] But with the collapse of the Soviet Union, Birchers and other communist fighters have had to transform "the dysfunctional scapegoat of the 'red menace conspiracy' into the 'one-world government, new-world order conspiracy.' The government itself has become the new subversive collectivist enemy."[42]

The demons guiding humanity toward one-world communism are no longer slithering about in the USSR. They have wormed their way into institutions such as the Council on Foreign Relations, the Trilateral Commission, and the U.N., which secretly call the shots.[43] Changing world conditions means that "right-wing ideologues have had to improvise."[44] But patriot identification of the U.N. as some sort of insidious, freedom-destroying communist monster is far from probable.

First, the U.N.'s ineptitude since its creation has been well documented. U.N. operations are still hampered by poor planning, incompetent forces and politics. As one Marine Corps sergeant wrote in a letter to *Soldier of Fortune*, "the United Nations is a nutless bureaucracy that carries no weight with its title and serves the sole purpose of wasting money and the lives of troopers from all nations."[45] Another letter sent to the popular publication paints a similar picture of U.N. forces:

> These crazies who are paranoid about the U.N. 'taking over' America . . . seem to have missed the point. The U.N. 'Farces' in what used to be Yugoslavia can't even drive to the newsstand for a smut book without getting their asses kicked.[46]

Second, the U.N is constantly on the brink of insolvency and chronically facing delays and logistical restraints.[47] This hindrance is due largely to America's failure to pay its portion of the world organization's operating costs. In 1992, the United States' delinquent dues to the U.N. totaled $380 million.[48] By 1996, the U.N. was owed more than $2.3 billion from its member nations, while America's debt had risen to more than $1 billion "for peacekeeping and regular dues."[49] U.N. Secretary General Boutros-Boutros Ghali mentioned this problem during a 1995 speech before the U.N. General Assembly:

> [T]he United Nations have not been given the resources required to accomplish the tasks imposed. The financial crisis is a symptom of a deeper problem: Member States simply do not regard the United Nations as a priority. . . . I

appeal to you to give the United Nations a firm financial base. If steps towards this cannot be set in motion . . . I urge you to give serious consideration to calling a special session of the General Assembly to deal with the financial crisis of the organization.[50]

Finally, although it is true that the U.N. has increased its level of influence over U.S. *foreign* policy, it is not true that the U.N. has any control over *domestic* policy. According to Martin Sorensen, an American undersecretary general to the U.N., the organization's power "is given to it by its member states. It is not a world government. These critics completely misunderstand the function, role and limits of the U.N. and the U.S. relation to the U.N."[51]

Patriots turn a deaf ear to such explanations, convinced that the U.N. is presently setting up a strike force in this country. At some point in the near future, the president will declare martial law in response to a trumped up national emergency.[52] Then, U.N. "peacekeepers" will emerge. This infamous day will also see the U.S. government replaced by the agency patriots fear and hate the most: FEMA.

America's Shadow Government

In 1978 President Jimmy Carter organized the Federal Emergency Management Agency (FEMA) as an agency that would "plan for emergencies—natural, manmade, and nuclear." Its original purpose was to function as a back-up system for the government should a nuclear war occur. Consequently, FEMA developed "a shelter program, a defense against chemical, biological, and radiological weapons, a warning system, and measures to be undertaken following an attack."[53]

Under President Reagan, FEMA's powers were greatly expanded.[54] But with the end of the Cold War and the collapse of the Soviet Union, those powers became unnecessary. FEMA has since become "deeply involved in disaster relief."[55] Its continued existence, however, has produced pandemic fear in the militia community. The agency is viewed as a "shadow government" ready to assume control of America. A 1994 National Federal Lands Conference newsletter ran the following warning:

> When the federal government decides to enact martial law; and they will; the Director of FEMA becomes a virtual DICTATOR. . . . The American people will be held in bondage and can be killed on the spot with impunity: even if they are in the right. . . . Don't be misled, there is a war going on between our heritage of freedom and our subservience.[56]

Although there is no real evidence to support such wild accusations, patriots insist that they do indeed have proof of their conspiracy theories involving FEMA, the U.N, and the NWO: black helicopters.

Demons of the Dark

The bane of the patriot movement has been mysterious, unmarked black helicopters allegedly "flying over our land in violation of all local and federal laws, carrying on their secret business, and taunting and terrifying the populace."[57] They swoop down from the night skies without a moment's notice, and are forever appearing at low altitudes in no-fly-zones, especially above patriot houses and meeting areas.

"What's happened is that the military have painted all of their helicopters black and the government is run by FEMA," explains Vernon Weckner.[58] Patriot Ken Gomes recounts a story that typifies the kind of tales being told throughout the country:

> My sister and family were visiting my parents when a black helicopter circled my parent's house then flew off but while still in view came back and circled again, it flew off again and did the same thing a third time. Then it flew to the back yard, my family was standing next to the house, and the copter hovered over them for about three minutes with its side to them, then it turned its nose toward them and then took off.[59]

Black helicopter stories, like most other patriot rumors, contain both truth and error. Strictly speaking, black helicopters do exist. Most military helicopters are dark green, but over the last few years they have received "a special chemical-resistant coating that substantially darkens the olive drab making it appear black."[60] Several types of these helicopters (Hueys, Cobras, Apaches) belonging to the Army and the Army National Guard are stationed at Aurora's Buckley Air National Guard Base in Colorado.

The aircraft are flown to assist in law enforcement operations such as stopping drug trade, fighting fires, conducting training flights, and providing additional security for visiting dignitaries. None of the helicopters are _truly_ black. Nor are they unmarked. They are dark green with black lettering. Maj. Tom Schultz, a public affairs officer for the Colorado National Guard, admits that they may appear black and unmarked to casual observers because anyone further than one hundred yards from the aircraft is not going to see the markings.[61]

According to Sgt. 1st Class Kiki Bryant of Corps Public Affairs at Fort Bragg, _all_ U.S. Army choppers are marked with a serial number and the words "U.S. Army." Bryant theorizes that the mysterious black helicopters seen by patriots may be darkly painted Apaches. Their black markings would be difficult to see even in daylight and nearly invisible at night, which coincidentally is when most black helicopter sightings occur.[62]

Appearance is only part of the "black helo myth" that has evolved.[63] These choppers have been given a personality all their own. _Spotlight_, a widely read patriot newspaper, reports that the demon-like specters "have been chasing people, hovering over houses, following cars on the roads, killing birds and cattle, and pointing what appeared to be guns at people."[64] Linda Thompson has made similar reports:

> [They] have spotted them practicing "strafing" patterns over suburban areas. . . . [T]he storage locations for them are secret. They are frequently spotted over the homes of persons targeted by the government as "dissidents."[65]

Even the copters' occupants have found their way into patriot mythology as aggressive, black-suited foreigners. Without giving any references or documentation, Don McAlvany states the following in his widely read *McAlvany Intelligence Advisor*:

> These black chopper crews are occasionally sighted on the ground and reports filtering in indicate that they are very unfriendly, that they seldom speak, that many do not speak English, and that some appear to be Oriental and of East European descent.[66]

Some critics of the patriot movement have observed that black helicopters display the same characteristics as elusive UFOs: "They shy away from us. They become aggressive if we draw too close. They don't want us to know where they come from so they have no markings, etc."[67] This may be because one of the patriot movement's leading "experts" on black helicopters is Jim Keith, a renowned UFO chaser.

Keith's book, *Black Helicopters Over America: Strikeforce for the New World Order*, is manna from heaven to conspiracy-hungry minds foraging for food in the patriot movement. The "veteran researcher" claims his work is based on "hundreds of reports from all over the land of these ominous black craft."[68] He allegedly "cracks the case of the mysterious black choppers and the sinister forces who control them" by drawing "on a wide variety of sources."[69]

In reality, the book merely rehashes allegations previously made by various patriot sources, such as the *Patriot Report*, *Spotlight*, and Mark Koernke.[70] The bulk of these accounts come from anonymous witnesses whose stories cannot be verified. Witnesses include "girls on horseback"; "two girls out walking"; "a family"; "a man driving a pickup truck"; "a rancher"; "a state trooper"; "a hunter."[71]

Sometimes Keith does identify an eyewitness by name. But whenever he does so, only the county in which they live is usually is given: "in Jersey County, Illinois . . . Mrs. Phylis Beutell"; "in Wood County, Texas, Mrs. A.D. Cruse"; "in Franklin County, Kansas, Virginia Burkdoll."[72] This, again, makes each story difficult to trace. On rare occasions when an actual city is given, the individual either remains nameless, or only their initials are provided, which once more makes the person difficult to trace: "a man in St. Maries, Idaho."[73]

Keith tries to sound as if he is an objective observer, but his obsession with UFOs often surfaces. In fact, it is difficult at times to tell whether a UFO or a helicopter is being discussed. The text breezily slips back and forth between its intended subject and alien spacecrafts, such as the one he mentions on page twenty-five: "It was an orange, wedge-shaped object. . . . The tapered end had a bright red light. . . . It was making sudden, jerky 'Z' movements, very fast, I thought."[74] Keith admits, "this is an example of a mystery helicopter sighting which also conforms to more classic 'UFO' sightings."

Why are these types of stories included in a book about black copters? It may be due to Keith's unwillingness to "absolutely rule out the possibility that some of these sightings of black helicopters might have something to do with UFOs of the truly alien variety, as many researchers have suggested." [75]

Readers of *Black Helicopters* are assured that reports of America's high-tech demons in the sky "are not easily-dismissed occurrences linked to the lunatic fringe, but are often solid reports sometimes backed up by photos which cannot be disputed." [76] But then we are "treated," as *Soldier of Fortune* sarcastically comments, to what amounts to "the worst insult to rational intelligence: Photographic 'evidence,' 'which cannot be disputed,' of black helicopters—using black and white pictures!" [77]

Patriots believe black helicopters are by far the most visible manifestation of the evil government preparing to close in on America. They are allegedly being used to monitor patriot activities in preparation for a massive airlift of "dissidents" to secret detention centers located in several locations throughout the country. [78]

An American Gulag

The full spectrum of bizarre patriot theories concerning the NWO can be seen in the widespread belief that when the U.S. government finally falls, loyal patriots will be herded off to concentration camps operated by FEMA. The prisoners either will be forced into slave labor or exterminated. [79] The Environmental Protection Agency "will be responsible for reprocessing the corpses." [80] Most patriots contend that the camps are already built nationwide. [81] A publication distributed by the Wolverine Brigade of the Southern Michigan Regional Militia gives an ominous report:

> There are four massive crematoriums in the USA now complete with gas chambers and guillotines . . . more than 130 concentration camps already set up from Florida to Alaska . . . more than two million of us are already on computer lists for "detention" and "liquidation." [82]

It may be surprising to some people that there are indeed detention centers in America, as well as government policies relating to procedures for arresting large numbers of citizens. But these centers and plans are not connected to a U.N./NWO takeover through an invasion of foreign armies. The federal government simply has "contingency plans for rounding up people in times of civil unrest." [83]

This may seem like an overly simplistic explanation, especially for those who find patriot conspiracies emotionally satisfying. For such individuals, everything must be part of a grander scheme. Patriot George Eaton, for example, believes the introduction of fluoride into America's drinking system and the Environmental Protection Agency's approval of oxygenated gasoline usage fit into the NWO. Eaton says fumes from the gasoline "creates malaise" and that fluoridated water "creates docile behavior." He concludes: "The conspirators who are trying to brainwash America into accepting a one-world government are working to produce a state of lethargy in the people so they will not be capable of resistance." [84]

Environmentalism has even been linked to the NWO as being part of a plot to steal land away from patriotic Americans. According to this twist on the one world takeover, eco-management is designed to leave citizens homeless and landless, which will in turn make them vulnerable to the enslavement planned by invading U.N. troops. Don McAlvany says environmental regulations "are to be the vehicle for socialism, and they're a major part of moving us toward world government."[85]

This enviro-paranoia has served as a bridge between the militias and anti-environmentalists, especially those within the militant Wise Use movement. Eric Ward, who works for the Northwest Coalition Against Malicious Harassment—a Seattle-based human rights organization formed in 1986 to oppose racism—says he is seeing "incredible crossover of people and materials between Wise Use and the militias from Washington to western Montana, eastern Oregon and northern Idaho."[86]

For a brief period of time, "General" Linda Thompson pointed to another means of controlling citizens: Hillary Clinton's healthcare plan. In a February 1994 computer message sent to her BBS users, Thompson suggested that the government "might be planning to release nationwide contaminants" in order to create a "real 'need' for 'Hillary's Healthcare plan'" while helping to depopulate the U.S."[87] Of course, Thompson's theory fell through when the healthcare plan was shelved.

Gaining Perspective

How should the patriot movement's New World Order conspiracies be described? "It's all bull," answers Robert Brown, editor and publisher of *Soldier of Fortune*. "But [they] don't want reasonable explanations . . . because they don't fit their preconceived notions."[88] But a reasonable explanation must be given. America is not losing its sovereignty. Nor is it on its way to becoming a totalitarian police state under control of the U.N. government. Military leaders actually see a *sovereign* United States participating in the NWO as a leader of various nations trying to create a peaceful environment.

The idea of a NWO is not new: "In the wake of almost every upheaval, a new generation hoped to be able to create a new international system to obtain everlasting peace and stability—peace in our time."[89] After every major war, men and women have tried to find a way to prevent further clashes. The end of the Napoleonic Wars saw the major states of that era meet at the Congress of Vienna (1815) in hopes of creating a new "balance of power that would preserve the peace" in war-torn Europe.[90]

A similar attempt was made after World War I when Woodrow Wilson proposed the ill-fated League of Nations. Although it was only Wilson's hope to stop future wars, he is often vilified by patriots as one of the early ring leaders of the accursed New World Order. But Wilson based his position on the phrase "every people has a right to choose the *sovereignty* under which they shall live" [emphasis added].[91]

This is exactly what the United States and other free countries are trying to now do through the U.N.

According to a 1992 report prepared for the U.S. Army by the federally funded RAND Institute, "President Bush's articulation of a 'New World Order' suggests that the United States will become more involved in promoting stability and security in and among developing nations."[92] Notice that the U.S. is spoken of as the "United States" rather than some ten-region, non-sovereign entity under the authority of a U.N.–backed, one-world government.

The U.S. Army, according to the RAND report, is going to be a key player in the new effort at global cooperation. This "requires a doctrinal overhaul, changing focus of doctrine from the conventional battlefield to emphasize flexibility across environments, whether peacetime, conflict or war."[93] In other words, a number of changes in the military currently are taking place and will continue to do so in order to secure peace.

The RAND document's research was undertaken within the strategy and doctrine Program of RAND's Arroyo Center for the deputy chief of staff for operations and plans, U.S. Army. The booklet clearly states that the Army is to remain an essential tool of *U.S.* foreign policy in the 'New World Order' "[emphasis added].[94] Again, there is no talk of dissolving the U.S. armed forces into a multinational peacekeeping police.

The reality of America's future role is found on page one of the RAND Institute's report. The New World Order will be an era "in which the United States, to guarantee *its own* stability and security, must promote international stability and security as well."[emphasis added][95] During his January 29, 1991 State of the Union Address, President Bush declared: "It is a big idea—a new world order, where diverse nations are drawn together in common cause to achieve the universal aspirations of mankind: peace and security, freedom, and the rule of law."[96]

If patriots would only engage in more open, fact-based discourse, they might see that many of their fears are unfounded. But intellectual bantering is not very important to a majority of patriots. They feel their version of the future *must* be true because their information allegedly comes directly from God, through the Bible. These spiritual underpinnings of the movement cannot, and must not, be ignored. They shall be explored in the following chapter.

8

Antichrists & Microchips

Enemies of America have been at work for many decades. . . .
to replace the U.S. Constitution with a United Nations
Constitution and neutralize Christianity.
George Eaton
Patriot Report[1]

When you hear the term New World Order, it's not new, it's
old. Pick up your Bible. . . . It goes back to the Tower of
Babel and the worship of Baal. . . . God says there is a
conspiracy!
Dean Compton
North American Alliance of Christian Militia[2]

A clear majority of patriots hold to some form of conservative Protestantism. "There is a huge overlap between militias and Christian fundamentalists," contends Charles Strozier of John Jay College's Center on Violence and Human Survival.[3] This overlap has prompted some observers to label the anti-government subculture the Christian Patriot movement.[4] Militia leader Dean Compton agrees. "Most of the people of the patriot movement are born-again believers," he says. The movement is "closely interwoven with mainstream Christianity."[5]

Christians are especially susceptible to the conspiracy theories circulating in patriot/militia circles because such explanations of world events seem to fit well with selected biblical passages that allegedly outline the chronology of the "last days," a period believed by many Christians to be those years just prior to the world's end. One important segment of this age is its final seven years, known as the tribulation. During these closing years of history "a world dictatorship under the influence of the antichrist . . . will be established—enslaving all nations and destroying individual freedoms."[6] This time period will also see unparalleled global turmoil, culminating in the battle of Armageddon, which will in turn lead to the Second Coming of Christ.

Many conservative churchgoers believe the tribulation will be precipitated by "the rapture," an event wherein Christians are miraculously transformed into glorified physical beings and transported to heaven.[7] Then, after seven years, all Christians return to earth with Christ, who will overthrow the Antichrist and set up the Millennium, a thousand-year era during which Jesus will rule from Jerusalem.[8] When that golden age of peace expires, Jesus will judge humanity and establish a glorious eternity. Although this scenario (called pretribulational, dispensational premillenialism) is embraced by a large number of patriots, most patriots subscribe to a self-styled, extremist version of an eschatological position known as *historic* premillennialism.

Like dispensationalists, historic premillennialists believe that during the tribulation the Antichrist (sometimes called the Beast) will halt all normal means of purchasing food, acquiring housing, and obtaining employment. Only by receiving the Antichrist's mark (666) will anyone be able to function normally in society:

There is a plan to enslave the entire world by forcing them to take an economic mark on their right hand or forehead, and without that mark no one will buy or sell, or own a home, or pay property taxes, or use the freeway, purchase anything anywhere, because the whole world will have been taken cashless. . . . [I]t will be a crime to have any method with which you can circumvent this debit and credit system that's coming.[9]

But unlike pretribulational dispensationalists, historic premillennialists believe Christians will not be rescued from the tribulation. They will instead be forced to endure the Antichrist's reign. Christians are understandably worried about facing life where daily living depends on accepting a satanic mark. In some premillennialist believers, this fear has fostered a survivalist mindset: "If we do not accept the Mark [of the Beast], we're going to have to take care of ourselves," says Mark Koernke.[10]

Many patriots have responded to this looming threat of the Antichrist by retreating to isolated regions of America with large quantities of food and weapons. Their hope is to live as quietly as possible during the seven-year reign of the Antichrist, who will rule earth through a one-world government—the New World Order. Such actions clearly separate these extremists from others who may hold to historic premillennialism, but have nothing to do with either survivalism or the patriot movement.

Influential Christian and patriot sympathizer Don McAlvany asserts that there are "powerful forces at work in America today which have a well-strategized design to move America into a socialist police state and a globalist New World Order . . . to control and subjugate the American people . . . by the year 2000.[11] It is all part of a grand satanic finale:

The New World Order has a target date for its establishment (i.e., the year 2000). . . . [T]his concurs with the target date of the year 2000 articulated by many New Age leaders for the establishment of a world government and the "dawning of the age of Aquarius." . . . And it also coincides with the time frame which many students of Bible prophecy believe will see the rise of the biblical anti-christ . . . and the Second Coming of Jesus Christ.[12]

Militia News, published by the Christian Civil Liberties Association of Afton, Tennessee, states, "The time is at hand when men and women must decide whether they are on the side of freedom and justice, the American republic and Almighty God, or if they are on the side of tyranny and oppression, the New World Order and Satan."[13] Like non-Christian patriots, Christian patriots also think that the U.N. is the instrument through which American sovereignty will be destroyed.[14]

Beliefs concerning less significant details of the tribulation may vary slightly, but nearly all Christian patriots agree on at least three things: the Antichrist is now alive,[15] the mark of the Beast is about to be introduced to society,[16] and the end of the world as we know it is imminent.[17] In reference to apocalyptic obsession, John Hegeland, professor of Religious Studies at North Dakota State University, observes:

As one can see from the history of it, it nearly always arises in times of suppression, chaos, fear, or disadvantage. As such, its first appearances are a register of the degree of social and psychological pain people are suffering. We are dealing with frightened people caught in the jaws of history, not kooks.[18]

Renowned scholar Norman Cohn notes that obsession with the end of the world has historically occurred "not when times are merely bad, but when they are *unprecedentedly* bad, when people are being uprooted and their traditional ways of life—however unpleasant they may have been—are being destroyed."[19]

This is clearly the state of American society. According to a Time/CNN poll released on January 17, 1996, half of all Americans believe the country "is in deep and serious trouble," and sixty-three percent said "the American dream of security and prosperity had become impossible for most people to achieve."[20]

Many Christians do not realize that people have been proclaiming the imminent end of the world since the earliest centuries after Christ. Each appearance of a new year containing multiple zeroes has enlivened populations with an end-time lunacy that has resulted only in misery and disappointment. This has been most apparent in the endless efforts that have been made at identifying the Antichrist.

Antichrist Grab Bag

"The Antichrist is not coming—he's here!" reads one Militia of Montana publication.[21] But exactly who, or what, is the Antichrist? This has been a source of debate for years and has led to an extensive list of candidates for "the cruelest dictator of all time."[22] Stalin, Mussolini, Hitler, King Juan Carlos of Spain, Anwar Sadat, Pope John Paul II, Henry Kissinger, Ayatollah Khomeini, Muammar Gadhafi, Saddam Hussein, Jimmy Carter, Ronald Reagan, Mikhail Gorbachev and a host of other religious and political personalities have at various times been identified as the Antichrist.[23]

No one is immune from being labeled the Beast. In 1985, for instance, a zealous conspiracy-believer named Constance Cumbey pointed an accusatory finger at Pat Robertson, who himself had announced in 1980 that the Antichrist was at that time "approximately 27-years-old . . . [and] being groomed to be the Satanic messiah."[24] When Robertson threatened to sue Cumbey, she dropped the charge.[25]

Many patriots are certain that the Antichrist "is alive today—alive and waiting to come forth."[26] They are not alone in their belief. Numerous mainstream Christian prophecy teachers such as Dave Hunt claim the same thing:

> Somewhere, at this very moment, on planet Earth, the Antichrist is almost certainly alive—biding his time, awaiting his cue. . . . Already a mature man, he is probably active in politics, perhaps even an admired world leader whose name is on everyone's lips.[27]

Another prophecy interpreter, Saint Martin of Tours, believed the Antichrist existed in his day. Martin died in A.D. 397:

> *Non est dubium, quin antichristus.* . . . There is no doubt that the Antichrist has already been born. Firmly established already in his early years, he will, after reaching maturity, achieve supreme power.[28]

The coming of the Antichrist was also predicted in Western Europe "for the year 1000, and later on for 1184, 1186, 1229, 1345, 1385, 1516, and other dates in-between."[29] All of these erroneous identifications were built on the presupposition that the Antichrist is a real personality. Such a view has not always been so popular. In fact, even among conservative Christians there are those who disagree with premillennialists. They stress that "the modern doctrine of the Antichrist is an amalgamation of biblical concepts and events that either are unrelated or find their fulfillment in past events. . . . Modern Antichrist hunters are pursuing a figure who does not exist."[30]

A close examination of several biblical verses lends support to this contention. The word "antichrist" appears only in two books of the Bible's sixty-six books: 1 and 2 John. The term is used to describe *anyone* who denies that Jesus is the Christ (1 Jn 2:22), rejects the Father and the Son (1 Jn 2:23), refuses to profess faith in Jesus (1 Jn 4:3), and disbelieves that Jesus the Christ came in human flesh (2 Jn 7). The apostle John was obviously not referring to a particular leader, but rather to individuals who preached a Jesus different from the one described in Scripture. Hence, an anti-Christ. This fits well with Paul the apostle's warning to the Corinthians:

> But I am afraid that . . . your minds may somehow be led astray from your sincere and pure devotion to Christ. For if someone comes to you and preaches a Jesus other than the Jesus we preached . . . you put up with it easily enough." (2 Cor 11:3-4)

Many Christians believe the term Antichrist simply means anyone who denies the Christian doctrine that God took on human flesh in the historical person of Jesus. The apostle John plainly stated that during his time "many" antichrists had already risen (1 Jn 2:18b). Influential evangelical theologian Benjamin Warfield (1851–1921) wrote: "To deny that Jesus is Christ come—or is the coming Christ—in flesh, was again just to refuse to recognize in Jesus Incarnate God. Whosoever, says John, takes up this attitude toward Jesus is Antichrist."[31]

In all fairness, it must be noted that there are a few biblical passages which suggest that a specific individual may one day epitomize all antichrist attitudes. He is described as *the* "antichrist that is coming" (1 Jn 2:18a) and *the* "man of lawlessness" who is to be revealed (2 Thess 2:3). Even so, it is foolishness to play pin the tail on the Antichrist, so to speak. The folly of attempting to name this dark figure is perhaps best illustrated by an incident involving prophecy peddler Colin Deal.

In his 1979 book *Christ Returns by 1988—101 Reasons Why*, Deal identified a computer in Belgium, reportedly called the Beast, as the Antichrist. This high-tech brain allegedly contained "all the basic information about every human on earth":[32]

Common Market leaders during a crisis meeting in Brussels, Belgium, were introduced to the "Beast," a gigantic computer that occupies three floors of the Administration Building at the Common Market Headquarters. The computer is capable of assigning a number to every person on earth in the form of a laser tatoo. Then, through infrared scanners, this invisible tatoo would appear on a screen.[33]

A 1979 *Awakeners Newsletter* repeated the rumor, but added its own colorful embellishments:

The European Common Market Computer at Brussels, Belgium . . . [is] prefixed by the numbers 666. It is called the Beast by those who built it and work on it. . . . The Beast has many tentacles in the Mafia, the CIA, the Knights of Malta and other sinister organizations which have been working for many years together to bring this enslavement about. Those who accept the "Mark of the Beast" will spend time in Hades after passing over in death. This alone is worth thinking about. In January of 1979 we were told that the current Pope in Rome is an actor, a look-alike for the real Pope who was murdered in this World-Wide conspiracy. Also recently Jimmy Carter was injected with cancer [leukemia] by agents of the Beast who need him replaced by one more obedient in this world-wide plan to enslave humanity.[34]

This particular rumor grew out of an August 1976 *Christian Life* magazine story. Apparently, the article's author was unaware that the computer was only a fictional creation from the novel *Behold a Pale Horse* by Joe Musser. In a letter to *Christian Life*, Musser expressed his irritation:

The item referring to a computer "Beast," a confederacy of Common Market nations, and a laser tattooing for a world-wide numbering system (*People and Events*, August) is based on fictional portrayals of end time events, drawing from my novel, *Behold a Pale Horse* (Zondervan), and a screenplay I wrote for the David Wilkerson film, *The Rapture*. For more than three years I have heard my army ideas circulated as fact. Perhaps, in light of what's happening in the world today, items such as the one printed seem quite plausible. However, for the moment, they are fiction.[35]

Regarding Christian preoccupation with the Antichrist, biblical scholar Robert Mounce observes, "almost eighteen hundred years of conjecture have not brought us any closer to an answer."[36] Christians would do well to heed a wise saying often repeated by responsible biblical teachers: *Where Scripture is silent, I too must be silent.*

The Mark of the Beast: 666

Revelation, the last book of the Bible, has been the source of countless speculations about the end times. Verses sixteen to eighteen of that book's thirteenth chapter have drawn perhaps the most attention:

He [the Antichrist] also forced everyone, small and great, rich and poor, free and slave, to receive a mark on his right hand or on his forehead, so that no one could buy or sell unless he had the mark, which is the name of the beast or the number of his name. This calls for wisdom. If anyone has insight let him calculate the number of the beast, for it is man's number. His number is 666.

Some theorize that the dreaded 666 may be in the new American currency design intended to combat counterfeiting. Far-right Christian Texe Marrs provides an interesting justification for such a theory:

[T]he U.S. Bureau of Engraving & printing awarded Crane & Co. a $66 million contract to supply this [special] paper to the U.S. mint. . . . [T]o accommodate orders from the U.S. government for the new paper, Crane & Co. has built a 66,000 square foot addition to its mill and is spending $6 million to upgrade its equipment. . . . Pardon me, but does anyone out there recall what the Bible has to say about that very peculiar number 6?[37]

Other prophecy buffs point to the new Multi-technology Automated Reader Cards (MARC) being used in the military for identification purposes.[38] Some have maintained that 666 can be found in "the supermarket bar codes now stamped on most products."[39] Currently, the most popular theory about the mark of the Beast involves computer microchips. In the video *Satan's System: 666*, Terry Cook confidently warns that "there is a plan to number every person on the earth by means of injecting under their skin, in either their right hand or their forehead, a microchip."[40] This notion goes hand in hand with patriot beliefs. During a shortwave radio broadcast, patriot Gary Null explained how such a device could be used:

This implanted transponder I.D. chip would replace all currency. It would replace all credit cards. It would be a permanent form of identification. You would then not have to have a driver's license or a health card or a social security card or any form of identification. This implanted microchip alone would be all you would need to conduct all commerce. . . . [E]verywhere in our society there would be scanners which, when you needed to buy something . . . your hand would go through this scanner and it would automatically send [your data] to a local computer. . . . But let's say that you were not allowed to travel. Suppose you were considered to be a political liability. You would then be challenged. You could not purchase things. It would limit your ability to purchase anything. It would limit your ability to go anywhere. You couldn't travel on planes or on trains. You would not be allowed to travel across state highways because the highways would have these scanners. And so, you would—unless you lived in a very narrow environment and didn't buy anything for yourself, and unless you lived in an underground situation—you would be constantly monitored for your entire life! In effect, you would be controlled.[41]

Nothing in Scripture, either linguistically or grammatically, indicates that the mark of the Beast in Revelation 13 is a *literal* mark on, or in, the skin. The Jews of the first century would have understood that the reference to a mark in the hand or the forehead was a *symbolic* identification "of loyalty, ownership, and heartfelt allegiance."[42] This is apparent from Exodus 13:9, which reads: "And it shall serve as a sign to you on your hand, and as a reminder on your forehead, that the law of the LORD may be in your mouth; for with a powerful hand the LORD brought you out of Egypt."

The language used here is unmistakably similar to the wording used in Revelation. In context, the Exodus verse is referring to a feast day of unleavened bread as being a symbolic way of showing commitment to God. It has nothing to do with a computer microchip. The sign on the forehead refers to one's thoughts and attitudes. The sign on the hand refers to one's activity. According to respected biblical commentators Keil and Delitzsch, the Israelites were "not only to retain the commands of God in their hearts . . . but to fulfil [sic] them with the hand, or in act and deed, and thus to show themselves in their whole bearing as the guardians and observers of the law."[43] John D. Hanna, a professor of historical theology at Dallas Theological Seminary, makes some interesting observations on this passage:

Like the Passover ([Exodus] 12:26–27), the Feast of Unleavened Bread had great educational value in the home (13:8-9). The feast was like a sign on their hand or forehead, that is, it was a continual reminder of God's mighty deliverance from Egypt.[44]

When allowing the Bible to interpret itself, it becomes clear that the mark in Revelation 13:16-18 is a *symbolic* representation of people who have turned their minds and actions over to beliefs that are against Christ (hence, anti-Christ). Revelation is addressing where a person's heartfelt allegiance lies. It has nothing to do with a literal mark, but rather a rejection of the Christian concept of God.

Patriots also erroneously believe that microchips *must* be Satan's mark because to their minds only these high-tech products could accomplish the kind of socioeconomic tracking described in Revelation. In reality, there have always been equally effective marks that could be placed on the forehead or in the hand (e.g., brands, tattoos, scars). There is no reason to suddenly believe a microchip is *the* 666 mark. Besides, an even better high-tech mark may be awaiting discovery in the twenty-fourth century. Given the many historical ends that never came, future generations will no doubt believe that their version of today's microchip (a *super*-microchip the size of a human cell rather than a grain of rice) will be the mark of the Beast.

America's Number One Prophet

The father of the modern prophecy movement, including its focus on the Antichrist and mark of the Beast, is unquestionably Hal Lindsey. His *The Late Great Planet Earth*, originally published in 1970, has been called the most popular religious book of the last twenty years.[45] It has sold twenty million copies[46] and was even made into a 1978 documentary-style film narrated by Orson Welles. Lindsey's books now line the shelves of supermarkets, drugstores and airports nationwide.

Unlike other end-time speculators, Lindsey presented prophecy in a way that appealed to everyone from average Christians to high-ranking government officials, congressmen and senators. Even Ronald Reagan "was enamored with Lindsey's *Late Great* book and mentioned during his 1980 presidential campaign that 'this may be the last generation.' "[47] Russell Chandler, an award-winning journalist and former reporter for the *Los Angeles Times*, feels Lindsey's popularity has a lot to do with packaging:

> Lindsey speaks and writes with authority and clarity in a popular style. He links biblical prophecies to current events and scientific technology—giving many the feeling of assurance that "it's all happening just as the Good Book says it would." And he sets forth uncomplicated arguments that the lives of ordinary human beings fit into God's grand plan of history.[48]

Patriots and militia members gravitate toward Lindsey's work because of his speculations about the nearness of the end. In the first edition of his *Late Great* book, for instance, he suggested that "within forty years or so of 1948" the Rapture would take place and the tribulation would begin.[49] In 1976, he told journalist Russell Chandler that the return of Christ could occur "by the end of the decade."[50] After the 1970s, Lindsey became even more convinced that the end lay just around the corner. He was so sure of the inevitable that in 1981 he published *The 1980s: Countdown to Armageddon*. Page one reads: "The decade of the 1980s could very well be the last decade of history as we know it."[51]

Such prognostications have greatly influenced patriots, especially survivalists, who are obsessed with predicting when the Antichrist will make himself known to the world. It has been reported that one of Randy Weaver's favorite books was *The Late Great Planet Earth*. The prophecy volume apparently gave Weaver all the answers he wanted regarding the coming invasion of evil forces against the

United States. [52]

Additionally, Lindsey's work has affected patriots by popularizing a newspaper style approach to interpreting prophecy. For Lindsey and his readers, nearly every world event, no matter how insignificant or far afield from theology it may be, can be inserted neatly into Scripture as fulfillment of prophecy. Forcing world events into biblical texts in such a manner can easily lead to wild speculations about the significance of microchips, the "New World Order" or gun-control legislation, which is exactly what has happened in the conservative Christian segment of the patriot movement.

Critics of Lindsey accuse him of resorting to "a mix of bad scholarship and false history" to make his preconceived ideas fit biblical texts. [53] For instance, Lindsey interprets biblical prophecies concerning Rosh, Meshech and Tubal as being references to Russia, Moscow and Tobolsk, respectively. But according to Edwin Yamauchi of Ohio's Miami University, such a position is "indefensible." *Rosh* simply means chief, or head. *Meshech* and *Tubal* were areas in what is now Turkey. [54]

Lindsey is also accused of contradicting himself in order to escape his erroneous speculation about when the end of the world will occur. Consider, for example, the obvious fact that the 1980s came and went as uneventfully as the 1970s. In response to his failed predictions, Lindsey has revised his timetables. One of these updated scenarios can be found in *Planet Earth—2000 A.D.* In this volume, Lindsey replaces 1948—the year he labeled as pivotal in *The Late Great Planet Earth*—with 1967, the year Israel won back Jerusalem through the Six-Day War:

> My recent study of Daniel 9:24–27 has convinced me that the capture of Jerusalem in 1967 may be a more prophetically significant event than the rebirth of the nation [of Israel in 1948]. [55]

Even before this latest change, Lindsey was making sure he had a few years of room for error. During a 1992 radio interview, he was asked: "At what point would you say you are wrong?" Lindsey replied, "One hundred years leeway from 1948." [56] This means that Lindsey, now in his mid-sixties, will only have to make an embarrassing admission if he lives to be nearly 120 years old.

Despite his track record, Lindsey continues to contend that "we are that generation" who will see Jesus return. "I believe you cannot miss it," he declares. "We're that generation, and I believe we're rapidly moving toward the coming of Christ." [57] In October 1995, Lindsey's latest books, *Planet Earth 2000 A.D.* and *The Final Battle*, held the number one and two spots, respectively, on *Bookstore Journal's* Bestselling Christian Paperback List of nonfiction works. [58]

It is not surprising that mainstream Christians and religiously oriented patriots continue to use Lindsey's brand of prophetic interpretation, twisting every current event into a tangled mass of Bible verses and conspiracy theories. As one prophecy buff declared in a popular conspiracy magazine, the third Seal of Revelation 6:6—which talks about an angel of the Lord not harming "the oil and the wine"—refers to George Bush sending troops against Iraq during the Gulf War.[59]

By using similarly unreliable interpretations of Scripture, many Christians continue to assert that the fall of Communism is just a ruse. The alleged Russian plan is to lull Americans into a false confidence about the world political scene. In a recent Christian magazine article entitled "The Late Great Gog and Magog," one confident believer is quoted as saying: "[N]o matter what changes have occurred on the outside . . . we know from Scripture that Russia is the Great Power of the North that will invade Israel."[60]

Misreading the Signs

The delusions articulated by Christian patriots does not mean that Christianity per se is dangerous. It does mean, however, that many religious patriots are motivated by a spiritual fervor that goes far beyond simple irritation over federal spending, gun control and taxes.

All of us are vulnerable to fears about the end of the world. In fact, a 1994 survey by the secular firm Market Facts Telenation found that fifty-nine percent of American adults believe the world will come to an end. Of this percentage, 12 percent say it will happen within "a few years," 21 percent give the earth "a few decades," and 16 percent believe the end awaits us after "a few hundred years."[61] Social scientists perceive that we "no longer need poets to tell us it could all end with a bang. . . . It now takes an active imagination not to think about human endings."[62]

There is nothing wrong with Christians looking forward to the return of their Lord and Savior. The apostles John and Paul both prayed for Jesus to come back (1 Cor 16:22; Rev 22:20). But no one has ever benefited from the disappointment and embarrassment inseparably linked to failed prophecies, predictions or suggestions about the end. Conservative New Testament scholar F. F. Bruce adamantly stated that "Holy Writ does not provide us with the means of plotting the course of future events."[63]

This may leave Christians pondering the purpose of prophecy. Jesus said, "I am telling you now before it happens, so that when it does happen you will believe that I am He" (Jn 13:19). In other words, prophecies were given in Scripture so that *after* the events were fulfilled, people could look back on the prophecy and draw encouragement from seeing that God fulfills all his plans. "Much of the detail in biblical prophecy, then, is not intended to reveal the future as much as it is intended to confirm and explicate the past, or illumine the present."[64] Historian Mark Noll gives a timely warning that church leaders should take to heart:

> The verdict of history seems clear. Great spiritual gain comes from living under the expectation of Christ's return. But wisdom and restraint are also in order. At the very least, it would be well for those in our age who predict details and dates for the End to remember how many before them have misread the signs of the times.[65]

This may be especially true for patriots, who believe the world is running out of time and see themselves at a kind of "historical cul-de-sac."[66] All of this is now manifesting itself in a sort of let's-get-our-guns-and-fight-it-out-with-the-Antichrist mentality. Disaster is sure to follow. Although the spiritual forces driving the patriot movement are significant, there are equally powerful psychological and sociological reasons why patriots—Christian and non-Christian alike—believe wild conspiracies. Those reasons will be examined next.

9

Anatomy of a Conspiracy

Attending a Patriot meeting is like having your cable-access
channel video of a PTA meeting crossed with audio from an
old Twilight Zone rerun. The people seem so sane and
regular. They are not clinically deranged, but their discourse
is paranoid, and they are awash in the crudest conspiracy
theories.
Matthew Lyons
Historian[1]

The patriot worldview is "almost a mirror image—a reverse print—of the
world that mainstream Americans see around them."[2] Members of the new
anti- government movement exist in a reality where black is white and white
is black. The nation's leaders are *really* following orders from secret higher-ups.
Law enforcement agencies designed to protect the public are *really* scheming to
enslave it. "The dominant worldview is fraudulent . . . things are not as they
seem. . . . Only the chosen few within the movement really know what is
happening and why."[3]

Patriots validate their alternate reality by pointing to what they believe are covert
operations, top secret plans and oppressive laws. Some of these were discussed in
previous pages. This chapter examines the psychological and emotional traps that
carry patriots into their sometimes wacky world of conspiracies. It is a world where
nothing happens by accident or human error; everything "is part of a systematic
effort."[4]

It All Makes Sense Now

A person's descent into the delusional realm of conspiracy theories is gradual. It
often begins with a series of small hurts, failures and frustrations. When these
setbacks are not shaken off, or when life keeps going badly, an individual may
spiral downward into cavernous regions of the mind where walls are etched with

lists of all the injustices they have suffered. Rather than resolving their grievances either by taking a critical look at themselves, or by accepting the complexities of life that have led to hardship, conspiracy-prone individuals blame their troubles on "the company," "the government" or "the system."[5] Soon "these aggrieved people fall in with others sharing the same point of view," which in turn causes even more problems:

> The group helps them to rehearse their grievances, ensuring that the wounds remain open, and exposes them to similar complaints. As a result, paranoia blossoms and spreads. . . . Members of the group bond to one another and lose contact with other people who hold different opinions. The isolation works to reinforce their views. . . . Individuals may even begin to unconsciously compete with each other to make the strongest statements.[6]

This dynamic can be seen again and again in patriot comments. One California patriot who refused to give her name to the *Daily News* for fear of government retaliation says she joined the movement after losing her house through foreclosure: "Many of us have been in the courts, and we were totally denied. Now I know why."[7] Bob Fletcher, a former spokesperson for the Militia of Montana, bluntly explains: "I'm the same as everybody else in this country. I got into this [patriot movement] because I got screwed, big time, by my government. It's a long story."[8]

Consider the plight of Michael and Kathy Chapman, who embraced conspiratorial theories when they fell on hard times in Greensboro, North Carolina. Kathy was employed at Guilford Technical Community College, but Michael could not find a job. This meant they could not pay their taxes. The IRS then garnished Kathy's salary for $1,200 in back taxes plus $1,000 in penalties. "There we were, having a hard time buying food, and the federal government wants money," Michael complains. "Of course, I didn't qualify for food stamps or welfare because of what I'd made the year before."[9]

In the midst of a topsy-turvy world that no longer makes sense, men and women of the patriot movement are taking refuge "in biblical assurances of ultimate victory and in a constitutional fundamentalism which treats the Declaration of Independence and the American Constitution as holy writ."[10] For such people, the time has passed for reasonably explaining the economy's decline, the nation's rising crime rate, governmental abuses and myriad personal problems.

"These people are not lunatics and they are not stupid," says political analyst Chip Berlet. "What they are is so stressed out for so long that the only explanation that makes sense to them anymore is to look for the simple solution that a scapegoat provides."[11] Russ Bellant, author of *Extremists in America*, feels that the conditions leading any person to such beliefs "may vary, and are often complex, but there is one key common factor: those attracted to the militias and their allied movements feel powerless."[12]

A long list of contemporary issues easily support Bellant's theory. Illegal immigration and drug trafficking, for instance, are adversely affecting many parts of the country. Patriots cannot understand why federal authorities do not deploy a garrison of soldiers along the border to seal it off.[13] We have the strongest, most advanced, best equipped fighting force in the world, yet we cannot stop illegal immigrants and criminals from crossing our borders.[14]

Patriots grow even more exasperated every time the federal government sends our fighting men to foreign locations that are of no apparent vital interest to America. There seems to be no good reason for Washington to send troops elsewhere when U.S. borders are continually being overrun by illegal aliens and drug traffickers. It makes no sense. The only possible answer is that a grand conspiracy involving a secret cabal of international elitists are bent on ruining society with crime and illegal immigrants so that U.N. peacekeepers can invade America.

It is unthinkable to patriots that Washington politicians might be refusing to close the borders because of nothing more than greed and other self-serving motives. Patriots do not stop to think, for example, that if there were no more illegals to work at rock-bottom wages, companies would be forced to hire Americans at minimum wage. Perhaps wealthy industrialists employing illegal immigrants at subminimum wages are sending a loud and clear message to Washington bureaucrats: "Keep the borders open." It is, after all, a fact of life that money talks.

I am not saying our politicians actually *are* being bribed. I am only using the argument to illustrate that America's problems do not necessarily have to be linked to a worldwide conspiracy. Alternative explanations are just as viable. Unfortunately, they are sometimes less satisfying emotionally. In the case of my hypothesis on illegal immigration, many Americans would have a difficult time comprehending how an elected representative could sell out the country for reasons no more complicated than wanting financial backing for the next campaign. Conspiracies rescue overstressed minds and emotions from the complexities of real life issues. They offer simple answers and easy targets for people's anger.

Scapegoating

According to Robert Jay Lifton, director of John Jay's Center for Violence and Human Survival in New York, the U.S. is currently experiencing a "post–Cold War confusion." Ever since the collapse of the Soviet Union and the apparent destruction of communism, there is no longer an outside enemy against which to direct frustration.[15] The pent-up anxiety has been most keenly felt by "the same socio-economic group that has embraced militias; young to middle-aged white males in rural areas."[16]

Brent L. Smith, chairman of the department of Criminal Justice at the University of Alabama, Birmingham, and author of *Terrorism in America*, explains that "worker bees in the movement tend to be much lower-educated than the general population." And with jobs for unskilled workers drying up, "they are unlikely to attain middle-class status—or much of a stake in the status quo." [17]

In response to these socioeconomic pressures, patriots have resorted to a psychological safety mechanism called scapegoating, which focuses blame on innocent parties in order to alleviate mental stress or resolve seemingly inexplicable dilemmas. It has often occurred in the U.S. during times of economic stress and is commonly associated with conspiratorial theories and paranoia, as Chip Berlet observes:

> Right-wing populist movements, even when accompanied by bizarre conspiracy theories, reflect deep divisions and grievances in the society that remain unresolved. This unresolved anger and anxiety leads some persons to begin scapegoating the problems of the society on named groups or sectors in the society. Most of the persons . . . are acting out some personal pathology, but as an act of desperation; grasping at straws to defend their economic and social status—in essence protecting hearth and home and their way of life against the furious winds of economic and social change. These are people who feel that no one is listening. While their anger and fear is frequently based on objective conditions (such as the falling buying power of the average wage earner . . .), the solutions offered by rightist demagogues point to . . . scapegoated groups of individuals as the cause of the problems. [18]

Berlet additionally notes that persons who resort to scapegoating make serious dialogue within the democratic process nearly impossible:

> Instead of engaging in a political struggle based on debate, compromise, and informed consent, persons who believe in evil conspiracies want to expose and neutralize the bad actors, not sit at the same table and negotiate. [19]

A supportive quotation for Berlet's assertion comes from patriot George Eaton, who sees only one solution to America's problems:

> When Americans are educated and informed about these schemes to force America into a One-World socialistic government, they will look at their puppet rulers as illegitimate. That realization by the people is the beginning of taking our nation back from the bankers and re-establishing Constitutional government. [20]

Political researcher and investigative reporter Daniel Junas warns that this form of emotional self-preservation can be very dangerous when coupled with the paranoia and conspiracy theories found in the patriot movement:

> The problem with conspiracy theories and a sort of conspiratorial view of the world is that . . . a person who believes in conspiracy theories tends to believe that the problems of the world are caused by a fairly, relatively, small number of people. And if you really believe that the problem is the people who are in charge, or the people who are secretly orchestrating the conspiracy, sooner or later you are likely to come to the conclusion that the solution is to kill those people, to eliminate those people, and that will somehow eliminate our problems. And that won't work. Eliminating scapegoats is not a solution to our

problem, it just leads to a continued search for scapegoats.[21]

Part of the problem is that most patriots live in regions far away from the government in Washington, D.C. They are unaware of the complex human interactions taking place among politicians, lobbyists and law enforcement personnel. Neither do they see "evidence in their daily lives of the good that government does—or of the people who do it."[22] The federal government lacks a human face. As a result, authorities are depersonalized, which makes them easy targets for conspiracy inventors.

This also heightens the possibility of violence against authorities because they have ceased to be persons with family, friends or feelings. They are merely part of an impersonal "enemy." Individuality of fellow human beings is lost. Everyone not in the "us" category is in the "them" category.[23] That is all there is to it.

In *A Call to Arms*, Mark Koernke clearly depersonalizes federal employees by describing them as foreigners. "You are dealing with internationalists," he warns. Koernke then goes a step further by making them inhuman:

What is the true motive and nature of the beast, of this creature. I will not give them the honor of calling them human beings, for I think that many of them are very alien to what we would consider human now. I look at their eyes . . . the eyes of any butchers the likes of which this planet has seen in the past.[24]

Dr. Frank M. Ochberg, a psychiatrist who has served on the National Task Force on Terrrorism, says the implications "are truly frightening."[25] After all, how difficult can it be to snuff out the life of an inhuman "alien" creature? This also is the case when it comes to viewing government officials as foreigners. According to Ochberg, advocating armed conflict is far easier psychologically if one believes these people no longer belong to the same nation: "It's rationalized as attacking an enemy—an enemy within."[26]

New-World-Order–related conspiracies stereotype and dehumanize government employees in much the same manner "as white supremacists stereotype and dehumanize religious and racial groups"[27] (see chapters eleven through twelve). Nazis did the same thing. They did not see men, women and children marching into the gas chambers of Auschwitz, Birkenau or Majdanek. Each victim had become part of a faceless, mass of nonpersons—"Jews." Such thinking is detailed with frightening clarity in a tract issued from Hitler's SS headquarters:

Just as night rises up against the day, just as light and darkness are eternal enemies, so the greatest enemy of world-dominating man is the sub-man. That creature which looks as though biologically it were of absolutely the same kind, endowed by nature with hands, feet and a sort of brain, with eyes and mouth, is nevertheless a totally different, a fearful creature. It is only an attempt at a human being, with a quasi-human face, yet in mind and spirit lower than any animal. Inside this being a cruel chaos of wild, unchecked passions; a nameless will to destruction, the most primitive lusts, the most undisguised vileness. A sub-man—nothing else! . . . Never has the sub-man granted peace, never has he permitted rest. . . . And this underworld of sub-men found its leader: the eternal Jew![28]

Today, anti-government extremists are acting out an identical mind-set. Only now the faceless, nameless mass of non-persons is composed of federal employees, law enforcement officials, judges, attorneys, environmentalists and patriot movement critics. Confirmation again comes to us from Mark Koernke, who in his 1993 videotape *America in Peril*, praised the efforts of a Branch Davidian said to have killed BATF agents with a .50 caliber rifle. "[S]he did a fine job of cutting a lot of people in two, I'm here to tell you," Koernke gloats. "I've got this funny feeling we'll do just fine."[29]

A Conspiracy Echo Chamber

Syracuse University professor Michael Barkun believes the patriot movement's cohesiveness lies in its alternative system of communication: mail order book services, computer bulletin boards, gun shows, Bible camps, pamphlets, periodicals and short-wave broadcasts knit the far right together.[30] These optional news and informational sources were born of patriot distrust for the mainstream media sources, which are allegedly little more than "rumor-gossip mills of misinformation."[31] National news services are viewed as "nothing but the official mouthpiece of the government."[32]

Militia members can no longer stand "the twisted, slanted, biased media of America who take their signals from a few private covert special interest groups bent on destroying what is left of the American way."[33] As patriot Michael Callahan, Jr. says, "We just report the news. We don't make it up. . . . All these things are factual."[34] According to Don McAlvany, the new patriot modes of communication have rendered "the socialists and New-World-Order crowd" unable to continue committing their "dastardly deeds in the darkness."[35]

Computers have become the most influential form of communication. Patriots may obtain "unbiased" news from a host of BBSs (free-standing computer databases tied to numerous phone lines) and World Wide Web pages (Internet sites where retrievable electronic files are stored), including the Motherboard of Freedom, PatriotNet, Paul RevereNet and the Patriot Archives. Twenty-eight-year-old Jeffrey Rudd, who operates the Spirit of '76 computer bulletin board system, reports that patriots are finally getting the truth about what is happening in the world:

People have bypassed the media and they're becoming their own reporters. . . . What we get is unfiltered and not slanted. I can watch something on television and get maybe a two-minute clip. But I can log onto my computer and get pages and pages of information. That's why computers and the Internet have gotten so popular.[36]

But this preferred means of news distribution has actually done little more than cause wild conspiracy theories to flourish. Patriots "rarely tap into information that might moderate their views." The computer's "cloak of anonymity further allows extreme views to fester uncensored."[37] Rudd's comment about unfiltered news in reality means unconfirmed and often untrue news.

In a 1995 interview with the Greensboro, North Carolina, *News & Record,* Clifford Stoll, author of *Silicon Snake Oil,* said "the problem with all the data flooding the new electronic media is its trustworthiness and usefulness."[38] Stoll maintains that patriots are receiving *data* rather than *information.* There is a difference:

> This information highway is actually delivering a fountain of data. We're drowning in data—which is different from information. Information has context, content, utility, timeliness, accuracy. It has a pedigree—you know who wrote it. Information has value. Data doesn't. Classically, we've had people who filtered information—reporters and editors. That's what the Internet is missing. People who will filter out the chaff.[39]

Chip Berlet agrees, stating that the world of cyberspace is "an unmediated system. . . . The person who types the fastest is the most influential. These are systems that have not yet developed social standards for a community."[40] A 1995 *Psychology Today* article correctly comments that reports of mysterious black helicopters over Montana and foreign troops training in the Rockies "buzz across the Internet unencumbered by such nuisance as confirmation."[41]

Lack of information verification on the Internet can also affect the "news" that appears in patriot literature because nearly 100 percent of patriot/militia-related computer postings eventually crosses over into patriot/militia-related printed material. Eventually, patriots end up appealing to the same "documentation" in an unbroken circle that excludes objective confirmation.

To illustrate, let us say a California patriot named Duke dials into a computer bulletin board service called FreedomNet and posts a message about sighting a convoy of what he *thinks* could have been U.N. troops heading for Camp Pendelton near San Diego. Another patriot in Ohio downloads this information and calls his militia commander, who subsequently prints the story as an "intelligence report" in their *Ready, Aim, Fire* newsletter. Only now the story reads: "Confirmed U.N. Troops Seen by California Patriot!!"

This newsletter is then circulated from patriot to patriot until it reaches a militia member in Arkansas named Martin. Now Martin thinks this is important stuff, so he posts the information on the message board of an Internet newsgroup called alt.conspiracies.UN.info. Unfortunately, Martin mistakenly thinks the story is related to a Montana rumor he heard involving something called "Operation Patriot Sweep," which is supposed to begin in California. Consequently, Martin posts his new message: "Feds Step Up Preparations For 'Operation Patriot Sweep' by Moving U.N. Convoy to San Diego."

After six weeks, the ever-conscientious Duke is surfing the Net and suddenly sees Martin's message. His heart begins to pound. *My gosh,* he thinks to himself.

That's why those U.N. troops were heading for San Diego! He spreads the word to fellow patriots, who in turn notify more patriots, and round and round the story goes, where it will stop, nobody knows.

Laird Wilcox, co-author of *Nazis, Communists, Klansmen and Others on the Fringe*, points out that once people get into conspiracy-promoting groups (e.g., the militias), they become "insulated from outside forces, they listen to themselves, and no one criticizes them. . . . You have an internal myth built up by this incestuous feedback."[42]

Who Needs Documentation?
During an interview with CNN, Ross Hullet, state commander of the Oklahoma Citizens Militia, perfectly illustrated how patriots fail to confirm most of the stories they spread. Hullet began describing America's future horrors in typical fashion: "We believe that the New World Order . . . will be enforced by foreign troops on this soil."

"Says who?" asked the CNN reporter.

"Says the United Nations," responded Hullet. "Now you have to go down and get the documents, but they're there."

The journalist then asked what any reporter worth his paycheck would have asked: "Which documents?"

At this point, Hullet was thrown off track and visibly shaken. After an extended pause, the militia commander gave a decidedly unconvincing answer: "*The* documents. They're in the library."[43]

Hullet probably had no idea what "documents" he was talking about. In fact, patriots can regularly refer only to "those documents" or "that new Senate bill" because patriot "news" stories rarely contain confirmable facts. Their reports typically come from "a source," "*one of* our people" or "*various* patriots." This is perhaps the most common propaganda tactic used by patriots to further their New World Order conspiracies.

One such story, found in the *Patriot Report*, alleges that on January 20, 1995, "a citizen" outside of Ft. Chaffee, Arkansas, "reported seeing 5 military helicopters flying in a straight line." When this unidentified patriot flipped on his shortwave radio and tuned it to the aircraft band, he heard "a clear transmission in Spanish. The one phrase he was able to understand was, 'America es captivo' [America is captive]."[44] Similar reports from unnamed patriot sources are innumerable. The following list contains only a few examples:

- "[During the Ruby Ridge siege] *a senior member* of the Red Cross support team told me that he was standing directly behind HRT agents as they loaded machine guns and heard the commitments to kill Randall, Vicki, Sara, Rachel, Elisheba, and Kevin Harris." [emphasis added][45]
- "This writer has *a friend* who personally knows *a high official* in the UN who once bragged to him that AIDS was a most 'fortuitous disease.' . . .

This writer also personally knows *a very prominent AIDS researcher* and *a very prominent U.S. surgeon* . . . both of whom believe the AIDS virus . . . [came] straight from someone's biological warfare laboratories." [emphasis added][46]

☐ "*A retired* U.S. Army Intelligence officer stated that German U.N. troops stationed here were sent back to Germany. *Their Commander* . . . confronted his superiors & asked point blank if their enemy in this training was U.S. citizens. . . . U.N. Commanders told him they were needed in the event of civil disorder, to confiscate civilian weapons. *The German Commander* [said] . . . nether he nor his men would ever take up arms against U.S. citizens. He & his unit were replaced with Russians." [emphasis added][47]

☐ "*Private citizens* in Oklahoma City were monitoring the scanner frequencies right after the explosion [and heard] that the Oklahoma Police Bomb Squad found an undetonated bomb (with military markings on the canisters) on the scene."[48]

After reading literally hundreds of such stories, I decided to check out a few of them. I picked my first patriot tale from Mark Koernke's 1993 video, *America in Peril*:

Remember the Koreans who were on top of their roofs [during the L.A. riots]? Strangely enough, the government used the video tapes that were made to track down these homeowners and they are now being prosecuted for using their weapons to defend themselves. And this is an ongoing program.[49]

This was a natural story for me to investigate because I live near Los Angeles and my mother-in-law just happens to be Korean. I contacted Mom, and she put me in touch with several individuals in the tightly-knit Korean community. No one knew of any arrests or prosecutions of Koreans in connection with the riots. I ended up speaking to Craig Coleman, the English-speaking editor of the *Korean Times* in Los Angeles. He told me that no action was taken by police against *any* of the store owners who used rifles to protect their property. Even the gun-wielding Korean man who accidentally shot and killed a Korean teenager was not prosecuted.[50]

I chose my second story from the pages of a 1995 issue of the *McAlvany Intelligence Advisor*, published by Christian alarmist Don McAlvany. Under the subheading "POLICE STATE BRIEFS," the conservative newsletter lists a story that must have planted more than one seed of fear in the Christian patriot community:

SWAT teams from several Idaho police departments participated in a practice raid on the Community Presbyterian Church in Post Falls. Captain Travis Chaney of the Kootenai County Sheriff's Department said the SWAT teams' goal is "to provide a controlled, measured response to critical incidents . . . to successfully resolve threats to public safety."[51]

McAlvany then makes an ominous editorial note that seems to be a blatant attempt to stir up paranoia: "Why would a SWAT team practice a forced armed entry of a *church*? Are Bible believers a 'threat to public safety'?" The answer to McAlvany's leading question is far less insidious than he intimates. I discovered the true story through a series of phone calls that led me to Jennifer Chapman, the secretary of the Community Presbyterian Church of Post Falls. According to Chapman, the church *donated* their old building to the police "because it had become vacant and condemned" after the congregation was blessed with a new house of worship.[52]

"There was nothing anti-Christian about it, or anything at all bad," Chapman said. She also told me that the church had received calls from people nationwide wanting information about the government's actions. Chapman made sure I got the straight story: "They were just going to tear the building down, so we let them [the police] have it to practice raids in and train their dogs to search for drugs. There's *nothing* to it."

The final story I checked out appeared in the pages of *Center for Action*, the newsletter by fifty-seven-year-old Bo Gritz, a former Green Beret who is idolized by fellow patriots. I downloaded the newsbrief from the Internet's Patriot Archives:

> The American Bar Association sent out a letter to all registered attorneys that arrived Friday, 22 October [1993]. The letter said that the ABA had met in New York City and unanimously decided to support a TOTAL BAN ON ALL FIREARMS, EXCEPT THOSE USED BY POLICE AND THE MILITARY.[53]

When I called the American Bar Association in Chicago, ABA spokesperson Tami Chozery was amused. "That is flat out not true," Chozery said. "I don't believe we've *ever* sent out a letter to 'all registered attorneys' to begin with. . . . Not all registered attorneys are members, so I'm sure we wouldn't have done that."[54] She proceeded to explain the ABA's position on gun control:

> We have a policy on gun control. . . . We have a long-standing opposition to uncontrolled use and sale of guns, and we are committed to public safety and things like that. We have adopted policy any number of times: 1965, 73, 75, 83, 91 and 93 respecting regulations. . . . Our house of delegates very rarely are unanimous, and I *know* that they are not unanimous on gun control.

Chozery and I eventually surmised that Gritz was probably referring to the 1993 policy adopted by the ABA. Chozery found the resolution in the ABA library. "The meeting *was* in New York," she said. "They got *that* right." Chozery continued:

> The resolution they're talking about was approved by voice vote, and there's no way of knowing whether it was unanimous. From other experiences, I would doubt it, but I don't know. The actual text of the resolution that was adopted [reads]: "Be it resolved that the American Bar Association supports federal, territorial and state legislation which would restrict the sale and possession of *assault weapons* to the military and law enforcement organizations."[55]

The real story, then, is that the ABA passed a resolution to support a ban only on assault weapons, not "all firearms." So much for Gritz's story.

Unconfirmed by Default

Besides using unnamed sources to effectively render their conspiratorial stories unverifiable, patriots also often cite stories that cannot be traced due to the circumstances surrounding them. This enables patriots to spread as many tall tales as they desire. For example, an article appearing in the *American's Bulletin* relates the account of a patriot named Chip Tant, who attended a gun show in Florence, South Carolina. While at the exhibition, Tant was supposedly approached by a U.N. observer who admitted that the U.N. "has been training with the CIA, FBI, ATF and other law enforcement agencies to confiscate guns in 1996, after a currency exchange."[56]

To verify this story, one would have to first locate Chip Tant. Next, one would need to find out if the gun show ever took place in Florence. An investigator would then have to verify through evidence (e.g., a ticket stub) that Chip was there. If the U.N. observer could not be located, witnesses would have to support Tant's story. Few patriots, if any, would go through all of this work. Another report by Linda Thompson presents a story with similar obstacles to verification:

> We have CONFIRMED reports of black-suited, unidentified ninjas types doing 'practice runs' in Alaska, pulling citizens over, demanding I.D., searching their cars, then letting them go, while refusing to provide i.d. themselves and holding the citizens at gun point in the process, occurring in Alaska.[57]

To corroborate this bit of news, one would have to either know someone in the far Northern regions of the continent or take a flight up to Alaska. Randy Trochmann of the Militia of Montana (MOM) provides an equally difficult story to confirm:

> [T]wo days before the [Oklahoma] explosion a military plane carrying an Assistant Secretary of Defense blew up at 40,000 feet. It was carrying documents on board about a coming bombing and was headed to Oklahoma City.[58]

Given the difficulty of confirming patriot accounts, it is not surprising that the MOM would place a qualifier in their catalog of resources:

> We, at the Militia of Montana, make no claims as to the accuracy, truth, motives and/or philosophy's [sic] advocated by any of the authors/producers contained in any of the materials offered by the Militia of Montana in this catalogue or any other listing connected with the Militia of Montana.[59]

Interestingly, MOM's own Bob Fletcher agitated patriot fears with an especially frightening account that came from one of his unnamed "intelligence" sources.

> They built a bomb during the Gulf War. . . . It's called a fuel-air bomb, and the way it works is you drop the thing and it explodes, sends out this spray of vapor—you know, tiny droplets in the air—and then, just a second or two after that, while the stuff is still in the air, a second bomb explodes: boom! . . . [I]f you have breathed in during those one or two seconds, well, when the second bomb explodes, it not only ignites the vapor in the air, it ignites the vapor in *you*, see, so you explode inside *and* out. Boom! Vaporized! You just freaking

disappear. And that's what happened during the Gulf War, my intelligence sources told me, to two hundred thousand Iraqi soldiers.[60]

To this date, it remains unconfirmed as to whether or not a weapon exists that can "vaporize" people in such a manner. The only objective evidence Fletcher has provided leaves much to be desired: "You remember those videos they showed every day? You never saw a dam—d body. Why? Cause they freaking vaporized them is why."[61] The simplistic reasoning evident here is typical of persons within the patriot movement. As Laird Wilcox points out, most militia members "are not particularly astute when it comes to critical thinking."[62]

A Closed Mind Can Make You Blind

Patriots also tend to be inconsistent in their thinking. One example of this appears in a 1995 issue of the *Free American*. Publisher Clayton Douglas complains to readers about a piece of "hate mail" he received from someone asking that the patriot publication not be circulated in their neighborhood. Douglas was especially incensed because the person writing the letter resorted to name-calling, specifically addressing Douglas as "Communist pig." Douglas responded to the letter by doing the same thing for which he had condemned his critic:

> To this poor, illiterate ass——, I have this to say. Read up (if you still can read) on just exactly what a communist is. . . . [L]ike most name-calling cowards, this ignorant fool failed to put a return address on his letter.[63]

Linda Thompson excels at using inconsistent thinking, bad logic and faulty reasoning. She claims, for instance, that the entire media is government controlled.[64] "General" Thompson pieced together this particular conspiracy after noticing that most pro-government articles, especially ones by the Associated Press, have no byline. The truth is crystal clear to her: "[E]very time there's a piece of government propaganda, it comes across the wire services with no author on it."[65] The fact is that AP articles are often printed with no byline if they are prepared by multiple reporters, or if compiled from several previously published stories written by non-AP journalists.

One of the more amusing examples of poor critical thinking involves a map of the U.S. divided into various sections that, according to MOM, coincides exactly with the NWO's plans for merging the country into global regions after U.N. troops conquer the land. Where did MOM acquire this top secret document? The scandalous blueprint was a colorful chart on the back of a 1993 Kix cereal box.[66]

Of course, not every conspiracy-related story is invented out of thin air. As Dennis Johnson, a clinical psychologist at Behavior Analysts & Consultants says, "There is almost always a kernel of truth to the false beliefs that these groups hold to."[67] Unfortunately, when a kernal of truth is planted in the fields of paranoia, the crop that springs forth bears little resemblance to reality. Sometimes misinformation is spread about so freely that believers in patriot literature cannot help but live in a much-distorted world. This is the subject of our next chapter.

10

Misinformation Specialists

I believe in what he [a patriot talk show host] says because he's done the research and surely he couldn't say it over the radio if it wasn't fact.
Dion Cole
Patriot[1]

Reports are coming in of railroad cars that are specially equipped with shackles built into the walls for "prisoner" transport. One railroad car in the Cut Bank, Montana area was loaded with handcuffs, shackles and guillotines. Sound bizarre? No, it sounds like Biblical prophecy (Revelation 20:4).
Norman N. Franz
Patriot "economist"[2]

Militia of Montana (MOM) leader John Trochmann claims to have his own intelligence network that includes federal, state and local law enforcement personnel, as well as persons in the military and on Capitol Hill. "Even old time senators" allegedly feed information to MOM that is "better than what they [the Feds] seem to have."[3]

MOM is not unique. Most patriot organizations, especially militia units, have some kind of "intelligence network." John Appelt, co-founder of Citizens for the Preservation of the Second Amendment, is quite proud of the militia movement's information gathering techniques. According to Appelt, even the government is impressed:

We have an intelligence network that people in the FBI say, "I can't believe the intelligence network you people have. It's fantastic." We have people in the Pentagon bringing out documents and giving them to us. We got people in all the service intelligence agencies bringing out stuff to us because they're patriots.[4]

But a close examination of the "intelligence" gathered by patriots indicates that these amateur sleuths need to take a few more spying lessons. Consider the rumor circulating among patriots about Senator Dianne Feinstein (D-CA), a known gun-control advocate. Patriots began labeling Feinstein a hypocrite after learning that she carried a concealed weapon. When Trochmann confronted Feinstein during his testimony before a 1995 subcommittee hearing on the militias, he received an unexpected response:

> **Mr. Trochmann:** When someone comes to destroy my family. . . . If that were ever to happen, I would defend [my family] to the last drop of blood. . . . I am told that you have a concealed weapons permit, so I guess you probably feel the same way we do.
>
> **Senator Feinstein:** I do not have a concealed weapon permit.
>
> **Mr. Trochmann:** Well, you recently had one.
>
> **Senator Feinstein:** No. I had one in the 1970s and I have not had one since then, after a terrorist incident that took place involving myself. That was the only time I had a concealed weapon permit, so I am happy to set that one straight.
>
> **Mr. Trochmann:** Well, I apologize. I will have to go back to my California informers.
>
> **Senator Feinstein:** I think you will.[5]

This dialogue accurately depicts how patriots tend to get a little bit of the truth without obtaining the whole picture. Trusted "informers" and their faulty "intelligence" have led to countless rumors. These persons who uncover various pieces of "evidence" confirming the NWO's progress often cannot even be traced. Nevertheless, their tidbits of information send fellow patriots into convulsions of paranoia. The stories, usually based on half-truths, are highly misleading.

The "Peacekeepers"
Rumors concerning an imminent U.N. invasion of America have been greatly encouraged by sightings of foreign soldiers in this country. Patriot Jim Keith declares: "The U.N. has arrived, the New World Order has arrived, and freedom may soon be a thing of the past for the people of the United States."[6] Linda Thompson claims there have been "VERIFIED REPORTS AND PHOTOGRAPHS of U.N. troops in this country in brigade strengths at numerous locations."[7]

These statements are partially correct. Foreign troops *are* being housed and trained "on American soil at various military bases across the country."[8] However, the conclusion being reached by patriots—i.e., "U.N. troops are already in place in this country, prepared to engage in 'peacekeeping' against us"[9]—is false. Under exchange agreements with foreign countries, the U.S. regularly hosts foreign troops for training purposes while our soldiers go to other countries. This exchange is designed to promote goodwill.[10] Lt. Patrick Swan, a U.S. Army spokesman in

Washington, explains:

> It is a long-standing policy to train foreign troops here and abroad. Since the
> end of the Cold War, we are training Russian troops here and in Russia to
> promote better understanding between our countries and between the two
> militaries, with the hope that we will lessen the likelihood of war.[11]

Foreign soldiers also are allowed to train in America when military exercises are
difficult to conduct in their own country. In September 1994, for instance,
approximately 180 members of the Japanese Army landed in Tacoma, Washington,
with four AH-1 attack helicopters. They came here to hold helicopter gunnery
training at the Yakima Firing Range. Lt. Col. Seiichi Takeuchi states, "In Japan,
space for such exercises is very limited. In the United States there are many
wide-open places where we can fire."[12]

Patriot hearsay about a U.N. invasion has been further instigated by sightings
of foreign armored vehicles being moved along U.S. railways and road systems.
Patriots are not imagining things. Foreign tanks and armored vehicles *are* in
America. Our military has been keeping the war machines at several military bases,
but not in preparation for a U.N. takeover. Lt. Col. Jerold Foehl, a spokesman for
Camp Grayling in Michigan, says the Russian tanks at his base are part of a
twelve-year-old program in which "captured foreign military equipment is shipped
by rail from Eglin Air Force Base in Florida for analysis by military contractors
and the training of U.S. soldiers."[13] These pieces of equipment have always traveled
on open, uncovered flatbed cars "to avoid precisely the kind of suspicions voiced
by paramilitary groups."[14] Nevertheless, patriots getting a glimpse of the vehicles
assumed they were part of a clandestine operation.

Robert M. Bryant, assistant director of the National Security Division for the
FBI, confirms that the Russian tanks "were captured by the United States Army
from the Iraqi during Desert Storm and are being used for training our own soldiers,
as well as for research and development to improve United States tanks and combat
tactics."[15]

There is an interesting postscript to this story involving the Army's code name
for these military shipments of foreign vehicles: Operation Chicken Little.[16] This
term was apparently heard by someone in the patriot movement who proceeded to
pass word along to the Militia of Montana. No one in the patriot movement seemed
to actually know the specifics of the operation, so MOM members simply printed
their own interesting theory in their *Taking Aim* newsletter:

> OPERATION CHICKEN LITTLE:. . . . [T]his could be the top-secret opera-
> tion for creating a simulated invasion of earth from space, when in actuality it
> would be from their multi-mirrored (300), laser refracting satellites that are
> now being placed in orbit, creating the ultimate optical illusion upon the
> inhabitants of the world.[17]

Often associated with the rumors about Russian tanks are stories about "foreign"
military vehicles painted with an inverted "V," which is supposedly a U.N.

symbol. It is thought that this emblem is being placed on all vehicles earmarked for a final invasion. Patriots are again mistaken. The inverted letter dates back to Operation Desert Storm, where it was used to mark equipment belonging to friendly troops. These *American* vehicles now are back in the U.S. and have been spotted on the nation's highways.[18]

Diabolical Stickers

It is especially difficult to convince a patriot that foreign troops are not preparing to attack and conquer the U.S. if that particular patriot has heard of the "bright colored reflective stickers on the backs of road signs" that observant freedom fighters have noticed. Linda Thompson claims these are "[t]roop movement markers."[19] Some patriots say the little postings are similar to those "used by our troops in World War II to provide directions."[20]

These multicolored tags allegedly are going to serve as signs for foreign troops, who may not be able to read English, but who can understand a route or location according to color-coding. Some patriots suggest "green stickers may indicate a rest area, blue may indicate a place with fresh water, brown may indicate oil and so on."[21] Others are unsure of what the labels mean, but know for certain that they are insidious: "We know there are markings on the back of street signs. What their purpose is, only the government knows."[22]

In reality, numerous people outside the government know the nature of these colored markers. Bill Shreck, a spokesman for the Michigan Department of Transportation, says the tags "are a method for identifying manufacturers of the signs and the dates they were made." Shreck began hearing rumors about the colored labels in 1994. He told the *Chicago Tribune*, "I can assure you these are not for invading troops."[23]

NWO Ninjas

A significant red flag for patriots concerns the hiring of former Asian police officers into American law enforcement ranks.[24] The *Free American* asks: "Why Royal Hong Police officers in particular? Could it be because the British control of illegal drugs, through the Royal Institute of International Affairs (the controlling agency for the Council on Foreign Relations), has always been through Hong Kong?"[25]

Linda Thompson informs us that "these guys aren't swell little patriots, they are ruthless, farm grown killers." She also reports that "Gurkha mercenaries have been spotted by intelligence workers for Mark Koernke who says they are here in this country as part of the black-suited ninja teams in Texas."[26]

The truth is not as nefarious as patriots want to believe. The importation of Asian officers is linked to a new form of heroin flooding the U.S. called China White. It comes from the "Golden Triangle" of opium poppy fields in Southeast Asia where Burma, Laos and Thailand meet. Until now, heroin has been five to ten percent pure, but China White is up to ninety percent pure and can be snorted or smoked like cocaine. It is sold in the U.S. through "secret Chinese criminal societies based in Hong Kong." [27]

The federal government faces difficult problems in its war against this particular drug. First, the Chinese criminal societies—called Triads—are highly secretive and extremely difficult to infiltrate, even more so than the Mafia crime families. Second, the Chinese community has traditionally been a closed society. This makes obtaining information about the gangs extremely difficult. Third, there is a language barrier. The Triads do not speak China's national language (Mandarin) in heroin-trafficking transactions. They speak four distinctly different dialects. [28]

Asian policemen have been hired by the U.S. to help overcome these barriers to controlling the heroin problem. FBI Director Louis Freeh clarified this during a 1994 interview with *Parade Magazine*: "Our first need is to have people who have command of the language, and we don't have that yet." [29] Freeh subsequently asked for changes in the law to allow for the use of military personnel who "know the language and the culture." [30] This is why Attorney General Janet Reno approved recruitment of Hong Kong and Taiwanese police into federal law enforcement agencies. It has nothing to do with the NWO or the U.N.

Idaho Invaded?

During the Randy Weaver standoff, patriots everywhere were sure that the U.N. invasion had begun. There were said to be 30,000 Asian troops moving throughout Idaho's mountain ranges. A number of witnesses claimed to have seen them. Countless patriots put themselves and their neighbors on red alert. Weapons were made ready and final defensive plans drawn up. The invasion was about to begin—or so they thought.

In reality, the Weaver siege occurred just after fire season, which always leaves a blanket of tiny mushrooms on the scorched forest floor. Each year, Asian restaurants and markets from New York to San Francisco send every cousin and nephew and niece out to harvest nature's delicacies. It seems that just the sight of Asians in the mostly Caucasian Northwest was enough to alarm residents.

Even patriot leader Bo Gritz admitted that this particular rumor was absurd: "There was an army out there all right, but it was an army of old men, women and children picking mushrooms for Oriental grocery stores all over America." [31]

California Terror: A Revealing Dialogue

When members of the Shasta Militia in northern California saw "soldiers" rappelling from what appeared to be a black helicopter behind a government building, they knew the end had come. They designated a militia investigator who immediately went into the structure and demanded to know what was going on. He and his followers were contemplating an attack on the site if he did not get some good answers.

"Is this the ATF?" asked the panicky militiaman.

"No," he was assured. "This is the state Bureau of Narcotic Enforcement."

"What is its connection to the United Nations?" he queried.

"None whatsoever," answered Jack Nehr, special agent in charge of the bureau's regional office in Redding.

"Then why were all those U.N. troops in the telltale blue helmets being dropped by rope from helicopters behind the building?"

Nehr explained that they were not troops, but "smoke jumpers" being trained by the California Department of Forestry and Fire Protection next door. "Here, this is a copy of our mission and my credentials," said Nehr.

But the "fact finder" was not convinced. He left, vowing that his militia might someday "retaliate" against the ATF for the Waco tragedy. He made it very clear that they would be watching, and at a moment's notice, be ready to help "defend America from a U.N. takeover."[32]

Tabloid Tricksters

Patriot paranoia is sometimes agitated by stories that seem deliberately contrived in order to cause trouble. *Spotlight*, a popular patriot tabloid, has often run pieces that are little more than complete fabrications. One such story, entitled "Salt Lake City, Utah, New FEMA Comm Center," can be found in the August 8, 1994, issue of the widely circulated newspaper. The article alleges that FEMA is "in the process of establishing a new national communications center in Salt Lake City."[33] Its subtitle reads:

More ominous developments concerning the activities of a shadowy government agency with the authority to rule the country under martial law have surfaced, this time in Salt Lake City.[34]

This story informs readers that a *Spotlight* "investigative team" staked out the area around Salt Lake International Airport for weeks, finding "what appear to be medium-[sized] tanks . . . with their guns guarding the airport."[35] A photo of a tank hidden behind a small bluff is included as proof of the military presence by the airport. The piece also reports that *Spotlight* investigators sighted infrared and laser detection systems, security fences, and National Security warning signs.

The story then quotes an unnamed source who informed *Spotlight* that the FEMA center " 'was intended to monitor 800 telephone numbers across the nation,' . . . which would include companies 'involved in mail order sale of gun components and ammunition.' " The conclusion: "It is all part of the overall plan to ultimately disarm American people, the source stated."[36]

But according to Mills Crenshaw of Salt Lake City Radio, who actually went out to the Salt Lake airport, the only military-looking folk in the area were employees from the Citadel Broadcast Co. who had "declared war" on their competitor, Simmons Broadcasting. Citadel workers had "dressed in camouflage fatigues and helmets as a publicity stunt." Crenshaw saw "no tanks of any kind" by the airport. Furthermore, Crenshaw found no bluffs near the site, which means that the tank photo *Spotlight* ran with the story was phony. There was also no new FEMA building.[37]

Soldier of Fortune (SOF) magazine has observed that *Spotlight* habitually runs "misinformed writings, convoluted reasoning and outright fabrications of fact. Any crackpot sighting, no matter how insignificant, *Spotlight* will print it, misidentified photo and all."[38] *SOF*'s heavy-worded indictment against the patriot news magazine additionally states: "*Spotlight* slithers around obvious, irrefutable facts to present a lie based on skewed half-truths."[39]

Like most supermarket tabloids, *Spotlight* also runs articles and advertisements for selected "miracle cures." Readers of the October 30, 1995 issue could order REJUVENAL, a "new natural protein" discovered by a research chemist. "THE FOUNTAIN OF YOUTH CAN BE YOURS," the ad reads. "It's a miracle compound. You can literally turn back the hands of time with this new discovery!"

Two pages later, a new wonder drug called pineogenal is offered: "NEW 'MIRACLE PILL' PROTECTS YOU FROM OVER 80 DISEASES!"[40] This marvelous little capsule—whatever it contains—supposedly will take care of nearly all physical maladies: "Imagine . . . your skin, wrinkle FREE! Your arteries unclogged! . . . Arthritis relieved! Ugly vericose veins suddenly vanishing! Cancer stopped! Ulcers gone! . . . Never catching another cold . . . all from a single 'miracle pill.' "[41]

The October 2, 1995, issue of *Spotlight* includes a special deal for six two-hour videotapes, four audiocassettes, a book, a thirty-six page "Special Document" and a two hundred sixty-one question exam that teaches how to "prevent, remove, and eliminate pain, loss of energy, and every disease known to man." The half-page sales blurb assures all takers that "WE CAN NOW STOP CANCER AND ALL OTHER DISEASES."[42]

Spotlight articles have been reprinted in countless patriot books, magazines, newsletters, brochures and newspapers across the country. The Salt Lake City tale, for example, appears in Jim Keith's *Black Helicopters Over America*. Keith writes: "An excellent investigative report by *The Spotlight* . . . has uncovered a new 'national communications center' which FEMA is putting together in Salt Lake City."[43]

A Televangelist's Warning

In late 1994, prophecy teacher and televangelist Jack Van Impe began warning his television congregation that numerous sites across the U.S. were being used by New World Order conspirators to house U.N. soldiers in preparation for a massive invasion. During the news-style show *Jack Van Impe Presents*, Van Impe claimed that "motorists had photographed trainloads of military equipment on roads and rail routes, and foreign troops of 'battalion strength' [1000 men] had been confirmed by base spokesmen at Fort Polk, LA and Fort Benning, GA."[44]

But when these assertions were investigated by reporters from the *Mobile (Alabama) Press Register*, they found Van Impe to be completely in error. "It's simply not true," said Dan Vance, deputy public affairs officer at Fort Polk. Vance explained that Fort Polk has been known to train company-sized groups of perhaps 100 foreign soldiers, but has never hosted battalion-sized elements. Fort Benning spokesman Griff Godwin said essentially the same thing, recalling that his station has trained possibly up to 200 foreign soldiers at any one time.[45]

Van Impe had previously cited the Relevance Research organization of Oakland, California as his source of information. When *Press Register* reporters attempted to track down this organization, they came up with nothing. Oakland directory assistance listed no such business in or around the Oakland area.[46] Van Impe not only refused to do a one-on-one interview with the *Press Register*, but also failed to answer a page of faxed questions, even after Van Impe Ministries executive director John Lang had informed the newspaper's reporters that Van Impe answers written questions.[47]

It is no coincidence that Van Impe's accusations sound like classic patriot movement stories. Van Impe drew his information directly from patriot/militia sources. The allegations about Ft. Polk and Ft. Benning, for instance, had already appeared in an October 1994 issue of the *Patriot Report*, a newsletter out of Arkansas.[48]

The one attempt Van Impe made to prove his assertions consisted of mimeographed sheets of paper containing pictures of trucks and other military equipment. These pictures, which he sent to the *Register*, were photos he had referred to on his television show: "They've actually taken photographs of these U.N. Army personnel in Saucier, Miss., Gulfport, Miss., in New Orleans, La., and western Texas."[49] Unfortunately, these pictures were from the same series of Militia of Montana photographs that drew widespread patriot attention when they were re-printed in *Spotlight*.[50]

All of the photos have been debunked by non-government, military experts and former soldiers who have analyzed them. For example, the photos of foreign "chemical and biological warfare" trucks in Saucier, Mississippi, actually have no offensive capabilities whatsoever. Furthermore, they are broken-down vehicles "being modified and re-exported, and the parts scrapped-out and sold locally."[51] Other photos of "Russian" tanks on flatbed cars are actually Canadian vehicles.[52]

Like many Americans, Van Impe is getting his information from patriot/militia literature. In fact, during a 1994 television program, Van Impe "mentioned the militia groups as one possible deterrent to the rising one-world government, led by the United Nations." He also predicted "that the world army eventually will play into the hands of the Antichrist spoken of in the Book of Revelation."[53]

Will the Real Patriots Please Stand Up

People caught up in conspiracy theories often miss the possibility that they themselves may at anytime fall victim to a conspiracy of manipulators who perpetuate rumors and false information for selfish gain.[54] Consider the case of Roy Schwasinger, who was arrested in early 1995 for convincing 3,000 patriots to buy a $300 "information kit" from his patriot organization We The People, based in Ft. Collins, Colorado. The kit was supposed to explain how to cash in on "a settlement fund supposedly set up by the U.S. government after it lost a $600 trillion class-action suit filed by farmers and ranchers."[55] There was no such suit or settlement.

In late 1995, Schwasinger was sentenced to nine years in prison for his role in the scam operation. Two co-defendants—Joseph Mentlick and Gary Widman—were sentenced to four years each for selling phony claims and committing fraud. Two more We The People members—forty-six-year-old Dana Dudley and forty-four-year-old Russell Landers—fled police after arrest warrants were issued against them. They traveled to Justus Township, Montana and were trapped there when the Freemen standoff with the FBI began (see chapter three).[56]

In Wisconsin, the anti-government/anti-tax Family Farm Preservation group—another patriot group—was charged by state authorities with "selling more than 1,000 phony money orders to gullible sympathizers." Patriots were told that the money orders, which sold for between $50 and $500, could be used to pay off mortgages and other debts. The money orders were worthless. Wisconsin District Attorney Gary Robert Bruno commented: "I don't know how in the world someone thought they could buy a piece of paper for $250 to pay off a $40,000 mortgage."[57]

Anti-government freedom fighters are open game for unscrupulous individuals who thrive on fear and paranoia to create riches. Patriots have already proven themselves to be trusting souls who are easily duped by anyone with a charismatic personality, impressive sounding credentials and a talent for storytelling. Several patriot leaders have already spread tall tales, especially about themselves.

Mark from Michigan

Mark Koernke is clearly the father of the patriot movement's conspiracy theories. Koernke's two 1993 videos, *America in Peril* and *A Call to Arms*, have a combined circulation of more than one million copies. According to the *Patriot Report*, he was the first person to come forward with information about the New World Order. He allegedly gathered his evidence "while serving in the U.S. Military Intelligence." His earliest lectures, which took place in the fall of 1992, contain information that is foundational to all patriot conspiracy theories:

   □ The use of foreign troops under U.N. control to police America with military power.
   □ The use of unmarked black helicopters to transport troops and/or dissident prisoners.

□ The expansion of prison camps for large numbers of patriot resistors.[58]
One of Koernke's fans, fifty-six-year-old Morris Wilson of Topeka, Kansas, turned
to Koernke's teachings in October 1995. Wilson could no longer make a living as
a floor-covering installation contractor because of taxes and regulations. He wanted
an answer to why life in America had become so difficult. Koernke's conspiratorial
theories provided the answer. Wilson remembers: "With his [Koernke's]
background in military intelligence, he has access to information that we don't
have. . . . He explained about the black helicopters."[59] Many patriots have joined
Wilson in believing Koernke because of his military background. The patriot leader
is regularly billed as an "ex-military intelligence analyst . . . in a unique position
to see firsthand how the conspirators for a one-world government have been
planning to replace our Constitution and use foreign troops to police America."[60]

Koernke himself claims to have "handled a lot of classified documents" while
in the U.S. Army as an intelligence analyst who held "a TSBI [top secret]
clearance." He further maintains that he worked as "a counter-intelligence
coordinator" and commanded the second and third brigades of "special warfare
units that train U.S. military forces in foreign warfare and tactics."[61] (A brigade
is usually composed of at least 5,000 soldiers.)

It certainly sounds as if Koernke has impressive qualifications. His military
record, however, tells a different story. Army documents I acquired through the
Freedom of Information Act indicate that Koernke served from December 22,
1977, to December 21, 1983, in the U.S. Army *Reserves*.[62] He "spent no time on
active duty analyzing intelligence."[63] Concerning his duties, Koernke was only
somewhat involved with "intelligence" as a student at the U.S. Army Intelligence
Center and Schools.[64]

Moreover, Koernke could not have commanded two brigades since the highest
rank he achieved was Specialist 5th Class.[65] Although this level of advancement,
known as E-5, is no longer even used by the Army or Army Reserves, it is
comparable to the current rank of Sergeant, also known as E-5. Such a rank is
several steps below the highest non-commissioned officer grade, which is an E-9
(Sergeant Major).

When I told Sgt. 1st Class (E-7) Larry Rapoza of the Mission Viejo, California,
U.S. Army Recruiting Station about Koernke's claims, he could not help but
chuckle, commenting: "A sergeant doesn't command a second and third Brigade."[66]

"Fairly ridiculous?" I asked.

"Yes," answered Rapoza, who then gave his impressions of what might have
occurred:

It's feasible that he [Koernke] was attached to a [reserve] division, and would
have advised a division commander, or a brigade commander, on areas of his
expertise . . . (i.e., the military-intelligence field). . . . That's feasible that he

was an advisor. To actually say he *commanded* a brigade—that he had command and control, was the final decision maker—I don't see how that's feasible. . . . I can probably put my stripes on the line and safely say that as a Spec. 5, I don't think he would have commanded—and that's the key word, "commanded"—had command and control over a brigade. He could have been an *advisor* to a brigade commander.

According to Staff Sergeant Kenneth Klenk, Commander of the Mission Viejo Recruiting Station, the lowest rank allowed to command a brigade is a full Colonel (a high-ranking commissioned officer). Klenk did not hesitate to speak in the bluntest terms possible when I asked him to give his impression of an Army Reserve Specialist 5th Class, who would make the kind of claims being made by Koernke:

> I would think that he sold you a bill of goods . . . . A 1st Cook in the Mess Hall was a Spec. 5 in charge of KP [Kitchen Patrol] and the rank doesn't vary throughout the military that much.[67]

At weekend militia conventions and nightly patriot meetings, Mark Koernke is revered as a former brigade commander and intelligence analyst for the U.S. Army. But by day, he is a janitor in a women's dormitory at the University of Michigan, "adrift in a society that does not value manual labor."[68] California State University sociologist James Wilson Gibson, notes that Koernke's life as Militiaman Mark "is far more meaningful than cleaning up a dorm."[69] (*Soldier of Fortune* observes that Koernke's occupation is "conveniently glossed over during his speaking introductions where it's simply announced that works for the University of Michigan.")[70]

Koernke spins many fantastic yarns to keep up his public image. For example, there is the dramatic account of a "face-to-face" confrontation between an unnamed patriot friend of his and NWO agents. Military Police allegedly escorted Koernke's friend to an interrogation room where he was left alone with a file on the desk. The patriot reportedly pulled the file toward him and opened it up to see a folded two-and-a-half foot by one-and-a-half foot "rap sheet" containing a "spider web of names of people to be arrested." Koernke's story ends predictably: "My name was at the top for the State of Michigan, so I can be proud. I'm number one and I don't have to try harder."[71]

For several years now, Koernke has been criss-crossing the country warning the masses of America's impending destruction and exposing the evil New World Order regime now seeking to solidify their power. In reference to his continuous and outspoken tactics, Koernke notes with a flair of humor: "Big Brother is watching [and] Little Brother has a very big mouth."[72] Few would argue with this assertion. In fact, a 1995 Time article entitled "Mark Koernke" stated that he is one of the most vocal of all the opinion leaders in the patriot movement.[73]

"General" Thompson

If Mark Koernke is the patriot movement's father, then Indiana attorney Linda

Thompson is in a sense its mother.[74] Her videotapes _Waco: The Big Lie_ and _Waco II: The Lie Continues_ have done more than any other materials to fill patriots with hatred for the government. Koernke and Thompson share an identical view of the world. At one point during 1994, she and Koernke even worked together.[75]

Who exactly is Linda D. Thompson? Her resume states that she is a forty-year-old married mother of three who served in the U.S. Army until 1978, when she was honorably discharged at the rank of Sgt. 1st Class. She adopted the title of Acting Adjutant General of the Unorganized Militia of the United States of America in March 1993, when she attempted to rally Americans to meet in Waco for a protest against the government's handling of the Davidian standoff.[76]

She claims to be a "disabled Vietnam conflict veteran." However, her military file indicates that she did not join the Army until December 19, 1974—nearly two years _after_ the January 23, 1973 Paris Peace Agreement was signed.[77] It required United States troop withdrawal from Vietnam to begin within sixty days and prohibited the United States from sending any more troops into South Vietnam.[78]

How, then, can Thompson claim to be a Vietnam veteran? Technically, a Vietnam veteran is anyone who served during that war's era, even though he or she may never have seen action. Thompson, then, is being _technically_ truthful. But anyone reading "disabled Vietnam conflict veteran" will assume that Thompson was injured in Southeast Asia. She, of course, never served in Vietnam.[79] Thompson was injured during a training exercise _in the U.S._[80] She has pieced together these facts so she can claim to be a disabled Vietnam conflict veteran.

The Indiana attorney also says she served in the Netherlands as an assistant to the U.S. Army Commanding General, NATO, Allied Forces Central Europe with a Cosmic Top Secret/Atomal security clearance. Army records again shed light on Thompson's claims. She did indeed serve in Europe, and was even an assistant to the U.S. Army Commanding General of NATO—that is, if one considers a stenographer an assistant.[81] Her U.S. Army file lists her principal duty for all years of service as: stenographer, secretary/steno, secretary/typist, and clerk typist.[82]

She additionally claims to have helped revise the NATO war plans manuals "while stationed at Allied forces Central Europe."[83] This also may be true, according to Staff Sergeant Kenneth Klenk, but only if one considers a secretary's task of typing up a document equivalent to making a revision. Klenk feels that Thompson may have "worked on" the NATO documents as a clerk typist, but could not have actually revised them because all revisions are done by Pentagon personnel and other high-ranking strategic command individuals.[84]

Concerning her domestic credentials, Thompson has stated that she is a member of the Indiana Bar Association.[85] But Thomas A. Pyrz, Executive Director of the Indiana State Bar Association, contradicts Thompson. In a letter to John Reynolds of the Free Spirit Press, Pyrz writes: "Our records reflect that Ms. Thompson is not an Association member and apparently never has been a member."[86] After word spread regarding this particular oversight on Thompson's part, she began sending out a new resume with the Indiana State Bar Association credit deleted.

Divergences from the total truth do not appear to be that unusual for Thompson, especially when it comes to stories about the Branch Davidians. One of her favorite indictments against the government involves the BATF's contention that they raided the Davidian compound because Koresh illegally owned a machine gun. Thompson has condemned the move as a petty excuse for the raid:

> Even if the Branch Davidians had a machine gun . . . if it was "illegal" it merely meant that a $200 tax had not been paid on it. All it takes to own a machine gun in this country is to pay a $200 tax and fill out a Form 4.[87]

Thompson claims she interviewed ATF spokesman Jack Killorian about this matter and that Killoran told her point blank, "It is not illegal to own a machine gun in the United States. A person who wants to own a machine gun need only pay a $200 tax and complete a registration form to legally own a machine gun."[88]

That Killorian actually said this to Thompson is highly unlikely because the laws covering machine-gun ownership contradict Killorian's alleged statement. Since mid-1986, it has been illegal for anyone (except for persons who at that time owned a machine gun) to own a fully automatic weapon. This, in fact, is exactly what Killorian told me when I interviewed him on February 22, 1994. A machine gun is "unavailable," Killorian said. "It is just patently unavailable for any machine-gun actually manufactured on or after the middle of May of 1986."[89]

Concerning the $200 tax, Killorian clarified that someone cannot pay this fee and own their own little Al Capone special. The tax exists only "for the legal transfers of machine guns that were properly registered prior to that date [1986]." Furthermore, such transfers can take place only between persons who already own a machine gun, and with "prior approval" of the federal government.[90]

If Thompson is anything, she is dedicated and serious. In preparation for the government's onslaught, she has organized a Ready Response Communications Network (RRCN) designed to relay news of importance to the patriot community. A 1994 American Justice Federation recorded telephone message states that persons wanting to join the RRCN must "pledge allegiance to the Constitution of the United States of America." Prospective members of the "ready response team" are also told one more important point: "the penalty for the knowing or intentional violation of your pledge is death!"[91]

Fletch: Intelligence Specialist

Robert Fletcher, the former "intelligence" coordinator for the Militia of Montana, says his life is "an amazing g-d— freaking story."[92] He claims to have written an unfinished autobiography that is already 750 pages long and that "the Disney people" want to make a movie from it. Fletcher maintains that he has lived through a lot:

[T]here probably isn't a single major thing that has happened in the last ten years that I haven't been right in the middle of: Iran-Contra, Ollie North . . . all of it, all of it. . . . The bull—— I've seen! Curl your freaking hair.[93]

In the world according to Fletcher, it seems that nearly all roads lead to him:

☐ He claims to have been an important investigator who supplied crucial information to Senator John Kerry and the Iran-Contra congressional investigating committee, as well as to the office of Iran-Contra independent counsel Lawrence Walsh.

☐ When Representative Henry Gonzalez, chairman of the house banking committee, needed to get to the bottom of the B.C.C.I. banking scandal, he allegedly contacted Fletcher.

☐ House Democrats investigating the "October Surprise" case—which involved charges that the 1980 Reagan-Bush campaign conspired with the Iranians to keep the American hostages until after that year's elections—allegedly turned to Fletcher, who ended up being "very much involved" in supplying "investigative research."[94]

In reality, Fletcher has never been a congressional researcher or an important asset to any government investigation. Michael Kelly, an investigative reporter for the *New Yorker*, found that Fletcher has been nothing but a Washington kibbitzer:

There have always been a lot of people like Fletcher hanging around Washington—amateur detectives pursuing stories and rumors of malfeasance and skullduggery in high places. They are the national capitol's equivalent of the types of those who loiter around the halls of every county courthouse—people with time on their hands, who have made a hobby out of knowing why the So-and-So rape case is not going to trial, and who the important drunks are, and who is doing what to whom behind closed doors.[95]

Fletcher continues to maintain that he is a Washington insider, privy to all kinds of information. A February 1995 video produced by MOM bills him as a "special investigator" who appeared as a witness in the Iran-Contra affair and served as an "investigative researcher in the Noriega hearings."[96]

Minutemen or Madmen?

Sociology professor James Wilson Gibson believes that although most militia members are psychologically healthy, many "are on the fringes of mental health."[97] Others have also sensed odd behavior and a sort of "just barely there" aura surrounding some patriots and militia members. Oklahoma Sheriff Bobby Gray of McIntosh County observes that individuals in the Unorganized Citizen Militia of Oklahoma are mostly "good people." But he adds: "[T]hey got some squirrelly ones."[98]

I must agree with Gibson and Gray. My interaction with patriots has left me feeling that some of them were not altogether stable, and yet at the same time, they were not completely *un*stable. For example, while attending a patriot meeting held by the influential patriot group The Granada Forum, I spoke with person after person who seemed absolutely unable to talk about anything but conspiracies, the New World Order or the socialist "regime" now in power.

A woman from the John Birch Society explained at lightning speed every detail outlined in the many conspiratorial books she was selling. I could not get a word in edgewise. Even as I was walking away I heard her muttering to herself about all of the conspiracies.

Then there was the sixty-five-year-old veteran of the Korean War who could communicate only with sentences containing quotations from America's Founding Fathers. My conversation with him did not last long, either.

I also overheard another patriot lecturing a newcomer about space travel, saying that it is against the Bible: "God said we don't need to be out there. It's just like in the Bible when them people was buildin' the Tower of Babel. It's all part of Satan's plan!"

Patriot Paranoia

In Reserve, New Mexico, on October 24, 1994, a U.N. flag burning celebration fueled fears that a foreign invasion was near. A local cowboy poet named Jim "Speedy" Shelton had announced to news crews that the Antichrist was already housing himself inside the United Nations building. Shelton's supporters were convinced that the end was near, and paranoia grew to a new high in the days that followed the U.N.–bashing event. A few weeks later, when ATF agents appeared in Catron County on a drug investigation, militia members "fled their homes and hid in the woods, believing that they would be routed from their homes by federal agents."[99]

A similar incident in Florida was sparked by the 1992 Los Angeles riots. When the violence began, thirty-two militia members feared a national catastrophe and martial law would ensue. They responded by retreating with their families to an encampment outside Pensacola. They remained there for three days with sentries posted and a no-campfires-at-night policy.[100]

A local cattle rancher in Washington's Okanogan County thought for sure that a U.N. invasion had begun after he stumbled across "a backwoods military camp teeming with men in fatigues." Concerned citizens showed up at Sheriff Jim Weed's office within hours. Weed assured panicked locals that it was just border patrol officials conducting joint operations with Canadian authorities. Fears eventually died down, but not before one agitated resident claimed to have actually seen Weed "getting off a U.N. helicopter at an airport wearing a blue helmet."[101]

Just about everything a patriot sees, hears or experiences can be made to fit into their conspiratorial theories. After Norm Olson of the Michigan Militia finished an interview with the *Northern Express*, he issued an serious caution to reporters: "Don't be surprised if you get calls from government agents trying to stop your story. They may try to question you about us or even wreck your printing press!" [102]

"Adjutant General" Thompson, in a refreshingly honest message to fellow patriots, recounts a story involving herself and a comrade named Ben, wherein Thompson acknowledges that she had gone a little overboard:

Did I mention the time Ben and I were out in Texas and had, over the past few weeks and in several different states, seen "folded" road signs . . . folded in the middle, in different shapes, in such a way that whatever was on the face of the signs couldn't be read, and bolted shut? Usually we saw these signs on roads where we also saw the reflective troop movement markers. So we were just sure these folded signs were some other sinister manifestation of the NWO takeover and we just HAD to get one open and find out. The day we decided to do this was Sunday. No stores that were open had bolt cutters and we didn't have any. We decided to buy, instead, a battery operated dremel tool and a cutting blade. . . . We had already checked out of our rooms and had planned to cut open one of the signs on our way out of town. . . . Stealth-like, we drive out a long distance along a country road where we had seen several of these signs. Carefully, we chose just the right spot for our clandestine investigation. One of us . . . got out of the car and began operating the dremel tool in the general direction of the sign. Suddenly, a car approaches from out of now where. Duck! Kill the headlights. The car passes. Dremel tool begins to buzz again. Another car, this time from behind us. Ben gets weeds in his teeth diving out of view. I pretend to be preoccupied with the radio. The car doesn't even slow down. The dremel tool resumes. At last, we're about to know. What are these signs? The last bolt is cut, the sign unfolds, to reveal the words: WATCH FOR WATER ON ROAD. [103]

Robert Brown, publisher of *Soldier of Fortune* magazine—which is anything but a pro-government periodical—says patriots with a "Linda Thompson mindset" are suffering from what he calls the "black-helicopter syndrome."

It's this paranoid view that there is a New World Order plot to have U.N. troops take over the United States, that large numbers of U.N. troops are conducting operations in the United States, with swarms of black helicopters swooping through the skies. What these people do is take certain pieces of information, selectively interpret them, put them together, and the whole becomes much greater than the sum [of the parts]. [104]

Unfortunately, patriots do not take criticisms well. They are absolutely convinced of their position. All information contrary to their view is dismissed as lies from deceived idiots or government agents. Those who disagree with patriots are summarily labeled as "the enemy." Such a tactic is called "demonization of opponents." This has greatly contributed to the spread of bizarre rumors by creating a powerful "us" (patriots) vs. "them" (the government, the globalists, anyone who disagrees with "us") mentality. [105]

NWO Agents Under Every Rock

In a letter to supporters, the National Rifle Association (NRA) stated they "have found no substantial evidence that 'One World' groups pose a threat to our Second Amendment Rights."[106] The *Patriot Report* responded by calling the NRA's statement "ludicrous to say the least!" The rebuttal continued to criticize the gun rights lobbying group in a classic demonization-of-opponent style of argumentation:

> The fact that the NRA would take such a position only proves that they are actually selling the gun owners out to the liberal and socialist groups who are determined to eradicate private gun ownership.[107]

Linda Thompson has used similar arguments against both non-patriot and *patriot* critics. In fact, just about anyone who questions her unsubstantiated accusations is called a government agent:

> We have seen a coordinated attack, utilizing the media, including *Soldier of Fortune*, Reed Irvine (who writes for *Soldier of Fortune*) . . . WOAI Radio in San Antonio, James Tabor (a fed psychologist), the Tom Donahue radio pro-gram, and others that have ties to the CIA and Special Forces, to discredit the Waco tape.[108]

Thompson has an entire computer file about her enemies entitled ATTACKS.ZIP, which I downloaded from her Associated Electronic News computer bulletin board:

> Larry Pratt of Gunowners [of America] has also been faxing letters warning people not to "associate" with me. . . . Also about a month ago, [there was] this clown named Kevin Schmid from Hawaii (about whom I have received information that he is an off-again/on-again paid fed-informant) . . . Tom Donahue (who is on WWCR right after me) has been trashing me for months. . . . KVI, in Seattle, two hosts, Kirby Wilbur and Mike Siegal . . . attack me regularly with false statements. . . . Ron Ingleman claimed to have "proof" the Waco tape was altered. . . . Art Bell, another radio Host, became a virtual government apologist. . . . It looks like . . . Ingleman and a couple of others (I'm working on these. . . .) were in the advance "controlled opposition/agent provocateurs" at Waco. . . . The Southern Poverty Law Center, just like the Anti-Defamation League, functions as a covert information gathering arm for the government . . . and pay "investigators" . . . to discredit people exposing the government.[109]

Herein lies the great attractions of conspiratorial theories: they cannot be disproven. Sociology professor James Aho of Idaho State University explains:

> [E]verything can be taken as evidence of a further conspiracy. . . . Everything that you do, whether its benign or malevolent, is still another sign of the conspiracy. There's no escaping it. It can never be disproven. And that must be very intellectually satisfying to a lot of people who are looking for certainty in their lives.[110]

A perfect illustration of Aho's point comes to us from Thompson. In her *Waco: The Big Lie* tape, she alleges that three BATF agents who "knew too much" about what was really happening in Waco were killed by a fellow officer. Thompson's "proof" is nothing but an out-of-focus film clip showing three agents entering a second-story window while their comrade stays outside. When this fourth agent pulls some black window masking back, the narrator asserts that the officer is throwing a grenade into the room and spraying the agents inside with machine gun fire. A chilling piece of information is then provided that suggests the unthinkable: "All three of the agents who were sent into the upstairs window were killed." [111]

But no grenade is actually seen being tossed into the room. No gun recoil is visible. No spent shell casings are seen being ejected during the murderous betrayal. Moreover, none of the agents shown going through the second-story window—Bill Buford, Walter Jordan and Keith Constantino—were killed. [112] Buford sustained gunshot wounds to both legs, Jordan received similar injuries, and Constantino suffered a broken hip, as well as extensive injuries to both his knees and legs. [113] In fact, Constantino testified at the 1994 Davidian trial and Buford shared his experiences at the 1995 congressional hearings on Waco. [114]

Thompson refutes all of this data by claiming the government is lying about who entered the room. This might be a plausible argument if it were not for John McLemore, a KWTX Channel 10 reporter who not only witnessed the shootout, but saw all three agents enter the room, exit, and safely descend from the roof. [115] How does Thompson answer McLemore? That's easy. KWTX Channel 10 is "part and parcel of the cover-up." [116]

It Never Ends

Conspiracy theories are airtight by their very nature. They deny "all the complexity and the validity of any arguments which do not fit into the scenario the conspiracy supports. Anyone who does not agree with you becomes part of the faceless enemy." [117] Even when there is no evidence whatsoever supporting a conspiracy, the sheer absence of proof is itself taken as proof of the conspiracy's effectiveness! [118]

Because conspiracies cannot be disproven, virtually any event can be used to support the theory. For instance, many patriots assert that some of the most infamous random shootings in America have been government-designed actions to facilitate stricter gun control measures. Karen Gentry, from the Southern California patriot group Guardians of American Liberty (GOAL), believes that Patrick Purdy—who murdered five children and wounded twenty-nine others in a 1989 shooting spree in Stockton, California—was set up by the government. He had been placed under "mind control," Gentry says. After all, the shooting gave the government an excuse to pass tighter weapons restrictions. [119]

The Militia of Montana claims that the much publicized December 1993 New York subway shooting of several commuters was committed by a government-controlled zombie. MOM's proof is flimsy; "[T]he individual stated in a dazed, stupor, '*I must have done something wrong.*' He was obviously a CIA pre-programmed asset. This was a pre-planned agenda to continue their efforts to **DISARM THE UNORGANIZED MILITIAS OF THE SEVERAL STATES.**"[120]

Such ideas can be traced to the 1962 movie *The Manchurian Candidate*, which is about an American soldier transformed into a human time bomb after he his subjected to experimental drug and hypnosis conditioning. This concept crept into the patriot movement through Mark Koernke, who coined the term "bio bombs" to describe those unfortunate individuals who have become Big Brother's automatons via microchips inserted into their bodies. "Whenever the feds need an atrocity to advance their agenda. . . . they trigger one of these 'bio bombs,' " Koernke reveals.[121]

Even Francisco Duran's assault on the White House with a semi-automatic assault rifle and the plane crash on the White House lawn are being blamed on federal officials. Don McAlvany asks:

Could he [Duran] have been programmed (a Manchurian candidate) for just this mission? Notice that Duran and the pilot who crash-landed on the White House lawn did no harm to government officials, but these incidents create an excuse to demand more controls.

One can only wonder if McAlvany would have been more satisfied if someone were killed or injured. Even this, however, could have been neatly inserted into a conspiracy. The unfortunate victim would no doubt have been painted by patriots as someone who "knew too much." Again, there is simply no way to disprove a conspiracy.

I Just *Know* It's True

Finally, when all excuses have been exhausted, an appeal can still be made to a standard emotional rebuttal: "Well, I still think something's not quite right." The following story is a classic example of how conspiracy theorists do not want to be confused with the facts. It originally appeared in the *Phoenix Gazzette*:

CHICAGO—Aurora has been targeted for a bizarre publicity campaign by obscure right-wing groups critical of a new city ordinance outlawing assault weapons. Just before a deadline making it illegal to own unregistered military-style weapons in Aurora, the organizations apparently faxed press releases across the nation falsely claiming that authorities plan to seize guns by force. The city, west of Chicago, on May 17 outlawed 10 of the most notorious varieties of assault weapons and required the owners of 80 other kinds to register them by Monday. As the deadline has approached, city officials have been flooded with phone calls about press releases from the Posse Comitatus of Ulysses, Pa., and the Militia of Montana in Noxon, Mont., city spokesman Scott McCleary said. "It's crazy," McCleary said. "These things are absolutely, positively 100 percent false." One of the press releases claims that on Sunday police will perform a door-to-door search for assault weapons in Aurora. "It is reported that over 200 federal agents have already amassed in the city and that the Federal Emergency Management Agency is on TOTAL STAND BY to assist in case of a civilian uprising," reads the press release from the Posse Comitatus. The information is false. The city Police Department will not conduct house-to-house searches. That would be unconstitutional without a search warrant for each address, said police spokesman Lt. Michael Gilloffo. Owners of assault weapons will be arrested only if they display them in public or use them in a crime, Gilloffo said. There are no federal agents in Aurora preparing to put down a civilian uprising, McCleary said. Aurora's anti-assault weapon legislation is similar to ordinances passed by Chicago in 1991 and Cook County in 1993. The ordinance allows owners of most assault weapons to keep them if they simply go down to the Police Department and obtain certificates of ownership. In the last three months, 23 assault weapons have been registered with Aurora police and one has been turned in, Gilloffo said. The Militia of Montana heard about Aurora's ordinance from two Aurora gun owners who called saying they were "extremely concerned" their guns would be seized, said John Trochmann, co-founder of the group. Trochmann said he faxed perhaps thousands of the press releases because he believed the constitutional rights of Aurora residents were being violated. When told by a reporter that Trochmann had his facts wrong about door-to-door searches, Trochmann insisted the city may still be planning something underhanded. "I think the city is covering up what they're really doing," Trochmann said.[122]

As of January 1996, no weapons had been confiscated in, or anywhere near, Chicago through door-to-door searches. Nonetheless, Trochmann and other patriots continue to maintain there was something "fishy" going on in Aurora.

Nothing New Under the Sun

The NWO conspiracy theories promoted by patriots are filled with countless logical and factual shortcomings. Patriot information is convoluted, twisted and impossible to verify. Their "news" is often blended with outright lies, mangled half-truths and wild extrapolations from relatively simple facts. Craig B. Hulet, a policy analyst with KC & Associates of Washington, reached a similar conclusion after investigating patriot conspiracy theories for *Soldier of Fortune*:

> Their truth and understanding are, far more often than not, just plain wrong. I could not find one instance of educational material, documentation or evidence that was not without the most egregious errors and outright fabrications. . . .
>
> Fact is, there's not one shred of evidence that anything sinister is going on.[123]

Using conspiracy theories to explain world affairs is not a new phenomenon. Numerous culprits have been blamed throughout the years for the woes of society: the Freemasons (a non-Christian fraternal men's society that has symbols, rituals and doctrines strikingly similar to occultism); the Illuminati (a defunct secretive order founded in 1776 by occultist Adam Weishaupt); and the Catholic Church.

According to patriot George Eaton, the conspiracy to take over America "is being revealed to those who have ears to hear and eyes to see."[124] Few patriots realize, however, that the basic themes underlying their beliefs can be traced "to long- standing anti-Semitic ideologies dating back to the Nineteenth Century."[125] As Kenneth Stern of the American Jewish Committee says, "the anti-government conspiracy theories that fuel this [patriot] movement are rewrites of anti-Semitic theories, but with the government replacing "Jews."[126] Part four will examine the patriot/militia movement's racist connections.

Richard Butler, founder of the Aryan Nations, preaches at his Church of Jesus Christ Christian, located in the Aryan Nation compound in Hayden Lake, Idaho.

This cartoon from a 1982 Christian Identity/Posse Comitatus newsletter illustrates the white supremacist scorn for Jews and African-Americans. According to Christian Identity ideology, Jews manipulate world events through the money supply and encourage intermarriage between whites and blacks in order to destroy the Aryan race.

Conservative Christian leader Beverly LaHaye interviewing Jeffrey Baker, a popular patriot speaker, on her national radio talk show. Baker is the author of the New World Order conspiracy-exposing book *ChequeMate: The Game of Princes*. Baker's conspiracy theories are based on the anti-Semitic forgery *The Protocols of the Learned Elders of Zion,* a copy of which rests on the table in front of him.

This snapshot, purporting to show the preinvasion shipping of Russian tanks into the heart of the U.S., was taken by an unnamed "intelligence" gatherer patriot. It has been widely distributed by and through the patriot movement by such groups as the Militia of Montana. Contra the conspiracy theories, *Soldier of Fortune* reported that the tanks were actually Canadian, not Russian.

780315	96B00	STUDENT AWAITING CLASS	CoD2dSchBnHQSchBdeUSAICSFtHUachucaAZ	-	NONE
780317	96B00	AIT STUDENT (78-509-CE)	CoD2dSchBnHQSchBdeUSAICSFtHuachucaAZ	-	NONE
780426	---	CASUAL	R TO PARENT UNIT		
770427	96810	*Intelligence Anal (USAR READY)*	*HC 70th Div (Tng) Livonia, Mich.*		
790427	96B00	*Intelligence Anal (USAR Ready)*	*C 70th Div (Tng) Livonia M.*		
200427	96B10	*Intelligence Anal (USAR Ready)*	*HHC 70th Div (Tng) Livonia Mi*		
710427	96B10	*Intelligence Anal (USAR Ready)*	*NBC 70th Div (Tng) Livonia Mi*		
321017	96B30	*Intelligence (USAR REAdy)*	*HHC 70th Div (Tng) Livonia mI*		

The following items listed in bold type are released under FOIA.

NAME Koernke, Mark Gregory

CITY/TOWN AND STATE OF LAST KNOWN ADDRESS AND THE DATE OF ADDRESS Dexter, Michigan -- November 25, 1983

SERIAL/SERVICE NUMBERS None

BRANCH OF SERVICE United States Army Reserve

DATE OF BIRTH October 28, 1957

DATES OF SERVICE December 22, 1977 to December 21, 1983
          Active duty for training - January 6, 1978 to April 29, 1978
MARITAL STATUS Married

DEPENDENTS Nancy D. Koernke (spouse), date of birth - March 29, 1957; Elizabeth A. Koernke (daughter) - December 10, 1977; Edward A. Koernke (son) -- Not available; Eric A. Koernke (son) - Not available

RANK/GRADE Specialist Fifth Class

DATE OF RANK/GRADE February 13, 1982

Two segments of Mark Koernke's military records (obtained through the Freedom of Information Act). Both parts contradict his claims to have served in the Army as an intelligence analyst and brigade commander. The top section, from the Army's "Current and Previous Assignments" log, shows that Koernke never served in the regular Army as an intelligence analyst, but only in the U.S. Army Reserves. The bottom segment reveals that Koernke's rank at the time of his discharge was Specialist Fifth Class, a rank of authority comparable to someone in charge of KP (Kitchen Patrol). Koernke thus could not have commanded two brigades (i.e., 10,000 soldiers) as he claims.

SECTION VII -- CURRENT AND PREVIOUS ASSIGNMENTS

35. SEE ITEM 28		RECORD OF ASSIGNMENTS		NON-DUTY DAYS BP YR/MO	NON-RATED DAYS EP YR/MO	☐ CONT
EFFECTIVE DATE	DUTY MOSC	PRINCIPAL DUTY	ORGANIZATION AND STATION OR OVERSEA COUNTRY			TYPE REPORT
(RES 7412-7502 Trainee	53 days PFC)					
750210	--	Enlistment	USA Rec Stn (3AW3SIAA)FtMcCln AL	--	--	--
750213	09E00	BCT	... en USWACBTBn FtMcCln AL	--	--	--
750403	71C20	Stenographer	44thMilHistDet Ft McPherson GA	--	--	--
750603	71C30	Stenographer	44thMilHistDet Ft Mc Pherson GA	7504	7512	REG
760101	71C30	Stenographer	44thMilHistDet Ft McPherson GA	7601	7608	CR
760831	71C30	Secy Steno	HQ Co USAE AFCENT SHAPE NATONeth	7609	7611	ANL
761201	71C30	Secy Steno	HQ Co USAE AFCENT SHAPE NATONeth	7612	-	-
770624	71B30	Clk Typ	HQ CO USAE AFCENT SHAPE NATO NETH			NONE
770727	71C30	Secy Typist	HQ CO USAE AFCENT SHAPE NATO NETH	7612	7706	CR
770701	71C30	Sect Typist	HQ CO USAE AFCENT SHAPE NATO NETH			
770701	71C30	Sect Typist	HQ CO USAE AFCENT SHAPE NATO NETH			
761201	71C30	Secy Steno	HQ CO USAE AFCENT SHAPE NATO NETH			
761201	71C30	Secy Steno	HqCo USAE AFCENT SHAPENATO NETH	7612	7706	CR
770624	71B30	Clk Typist	HqCo USAE AFCENT SHAPENATO NETH	-	-	None
770727	71C30	Secy Steno	HqCo USAE AFCENT SHAPENATO NETH	-	-	CR
770901	71C20	Secretary Steno	HQ CO USAE AFCENT SHAPE NATO NETH	7707	7710	CR
771101	71C20	Secretary Steno	HQ CO USAE AFCENT SHAPE NATO NETH	7711	7802	CR
780222	--	DISCHARGE	USARECCEN-FT-BENA			
6780222	--	DISCHARGE	USARECCEN FT BENJAMIN HARRISON, IN			

A section of Linda Thompson's military records (obtained through the Freedom of Information Act). This document contradicts Thompson's claim that she revised the NATO war plans manual while stationed in Europe. According to the Army's log of her "Current and Previous Assignments," Thompson's highest position—for all dates of her service—was that of a secretary/stenographer and clerk typist. NATO war plans are revised by Pentagon personnel and other individuals in high-level strategic command positions.

Patriot economist Don McAlvany, who produces the popular *McAlvany Intelligence Report*.

White supremacists/antigovernment demonstrators gather on Ruby Ridge during the 1992 seige at Randy Weaver's cabin. One protestor holds a "Death to ZOG" sign, which reflects the Christian Identity view that America is directed by the Zionist Occupational Government, the patriots' suspected Jewish-controlled puppet regime.

Patriot leader "Mark from Michigan" Koernke as he appears in his 1993 videotape *America in Peril*.

"General" Linda Thompson, as she appeared at the 1993 Branch-Davidian standoff in Waco, Texas.

Holocaust revisionist Ernst Zündel, who claims that six million Jews were not murdered during World War II. He has twice been a guest on Bo Gritz's radio talk show, which is aired over Christian radio station KDNO of Delano, California

John Trochmann, leader and cofounder of the Militia of Montana.

Likely Locations of Concentration Camps

- △ Oakdale, California
- △ Vandenberg AFB, California
- △ Fort Huachuca, Arizona
- △ Fort Chaffee, Arkansas
- △ Fort McCoy, Wisconsin
- △ Fort Drum, New York
- △ Indiantown Gap, Pennsylvania
- △ Fort A.P. Hill, Virginia
- △ Fort Benning, Georgia
- △ Eglin Air Force Base, Florida
- △ Miami, Florida

MJTF (Multi-Jurisdictional Task Force) Police Locations

- ✪ Known Facilities
- ✪ Unconfirmed

The MJTF is made up of:
1) Military-Converts National Guard Units into a National Police Force.
2) Converts all local and state police to national police.
3) Converts street gangs into law enforcement units.

The MJFT Police Mission:
1) House-to-house search and seizure of property and fire arms.
2) Separation and categorization of men, women and children as prisoners.
3) Transfer and operation of detention camps in the U.S.

These maps from Jim Keith's *Black Helicopters Over America* purportedly detail the locations of New World Order concentration camps and Multi-Jurisdictional Task Force Police locations. Keith provides no documentation for the information depicted in the maps, but they are widely accepted as factual in patriot circles.

In Brosingen (Hungary) the Jews opened the veins of a wheelwright's child and sucked his blood. (Drawing after a Polish plaque)

The centuries-old engravings on this page (and at the top of the next page) were reproduced in an anti-Semitic patriot newspaper, *Christian Vanguard,* and reflect the horrific "blood accusations" made for hundreds of years against Jews. At the top, Hungarian Jews are portrayed sucking blood from the veins of a wheelwright's child. At the bottom, other East European Jews are depicted committing a ritual murder.

The Ritual Murder at Polna Postcard of unknown origin distributed to commemorate the Ritual Murder at Konitz.

A fifteenth-century woodcut depicting the anti-Semitic legend that Jews ritually murdered St. Simon of Trent before Passover on March 23, 1475.

Four members of the Ku Klux Klan give the Nazi salute in front of a burning cross at the 1986 Aryan Nations Congress, which met in Hayden Lake, Idaho.

A 1922 "Bo Gritz for President" brochure produced when the patriot leader ran for office on the ticket of the Populist Party, a party formed mainly by white supremacists—including neo-Nazis, Christian Identity believers and the Ku Klux Klan.

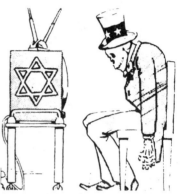

This cartoon from a neo-Nazi patriot brochure illustrates the white supremacist belief that the "Jewish-controlled" media is destroying America through biased news and corrupt programming.

PART 4

Aryan Nations

[T]he next line of leadership shall be a generation of ruthless predators that shall make past Aryan leaders and warriors seem pale in comparison. The white youth of this nation shall utilize every method and option available to them . . . and quite possible engage in the wholesale extermination of all sub-human, non-Aryan peoples. Men, women and children, without exception, without appeal, who are of non-Aryan blood shall be terminated or expelled [from America].

Twenty-five-year-old racist
Aryan Nations White Students Union[1]

I am a Nazi walking, psychopath talking Third Reich gangster. . . . Killing nig——s and Jews is what I do. . . . I like the ways, but don't think they are cruel, so when I am rolling through your hood, you spooks [blacks] better hide because you are no good, killing you off like a disease. You beg, cry, even say please, but no mercy is my middle name, killing you all because you are all the same. Ain't got no shame in my game. I kill sub-humans to get fame. So now you know what I am about. I will always take nig——s and Jews out. I broke in a house and what did I see? . . . bug-eyed bastards just staring at me. So I planted the bomb and started to run. The thing went off like a big gun. I ran down the street. Burning thoughts of Adolf Hitler were churning in my head; yet, white power I believe in is still running through my head. It is making me kill.

Sixteen-year-old racist and convicted bomber[2]

I think we're going to make this country white again. I don't want blacks hanging around. I don't think they really have any right being here. Blacks just think differently than us, and Jews are trying to take over everything.

Thirteen-year-old racist
Son of an Aryan Nations couple[3]

11

The International Jew

We have pierced the Jewish abscess. The world of the future
will be eternally grateful to us.
Adolf Hitler
1945[1]

Our future is great, but only if we deal with the Jewish
problem once and for all.
Aryan Nations
1979[2]

Patriots see world events, especially wars and economic disasters, as little more than the result of covert actions taken by a small yet powerful group of secret elitists. These sinister behind-the-scenes players are believed to be orchestrating global affairs in such a way as to make it possible for them to eventually control humanity. The origin of this outlook on history predates, by many years, the militia's misguided notions about the New World Order. Twentieth-century enemies such as black helicopters and U.N. troops are merely the latest characters in an indestructible and ever-changing myth created in 1797 by the French Jesuit Abbé Barruel, who claimed that the French Revolution (1789–1799) was started by conspirators whose legacy can be traced to the Middle Ages (c. 476–1453).

In his five-volume work *Mémoire pour servir à l'histoire du Jacobinisme* (A memoir to serve as the history of Jacobinism), Barruel blamed France's bloody revolt on the Order of Templars, a military-religious sect founded around A.D. 1118 during the Crusades (1095–1291). These sanctified knights organized to "aid and protect pilgrims on their way to the Holy Land."[3] This made them extremely popular, and they were showered with donations from pious people and gifts from royalty.

The Templars soon grew wealthy. Their influence then "spread to include the financial and banking operations of Europe."[4] They had actually become "the bankers of Europe."[5] This drew the wrath of several European royal houses and the Roman Catholic church. Especially incensed was King Philip IV, monarch of the bankrupt France, who in 1307 moved against the Templars. He was subsequently able to convince Pope Clement V to formally dissolve the order in 1312. This did not meet with the approval of the Templars, who refused to follow the papal pronouncement. They were forcefully disbanded in 1314 when 120 of their leaders were burned at the stake on charges of heresy, witchcraft and sodomy.[6]

Barruel, however, maintained that some of the knights had escaped and "pledged to abolish all monarchies, overthrow the papacy, preach unrestricted liberty to all peoples, and found a world-wide republic under its own control."[7] He further asserted that the Templars controlled the Freemasons (formed in 1717), a fraternal order based on the guild practices of medieval stonemasons. Barruel also believed that the Templars had infiltrated another group: the secretive Illuminati, founded in 1776 by Adam Weishaupt. Although this latter group was dissolved by the Bavarian government in 1786, Barruel insisted that its members had gone underground to continue pursuing their desire for world domination in conjunction with the Freemasons and Templars.

Each of these organizations supposedly contributed to the ascent of political figures who were "instrumental in overthrowing the monarchy of France." Barruel warned that "unless the conspiracy was stopped, it would grow until it ruled the world."[8] Most, if not all, of today's conspiracy theories involving the establishment of a one-world government are loosely based on Barruelian thought. It offers a framework that is easily adapted to any group. A host of scapegoats including Freemasons, Catholics and secular humanists have been vilified by persons using a Barruel-like explanation of history. Its most destructive form dates back to 1806, when Jews were first cast as the main conspirators.

"Demon" Jews

Barruel made no mention of Jews in his original theory because during the mid- to late 1700s they had no part in European politics. In fact, Jews had virtually no rights throughout this era. They could not own land, were barred from membership in the professional guilds of artisans, and lived in segregated ghettos. They had no civil protections, either, which often resulted in Jews being massacred by unruly mobs.[9]

This violent prejudice stemmed from hostilities between Christians and Jews dating back as far as the second and third centuries. Christian animosity toward the Jew was due, in part, to the idea that the Jews had handed Jesus over to the Romans for crucifixion. This, however, was only a secondary cause for Christian anger. The primary reason for conflict between the two faiths had much to do with the persecutions Christians endured under Rome's rule.

In the Roman Empire there existed licensed (legal) religions and unlicensed (illegal) religions. Any national religion could be licensed by Rome as long as that religion recognized and honored Ceasar above everything else. Judaism was the only national religion allowed to exist legally and yet not pledge allegience to any secular ruler. This agreement, originally negotiated by the Jews under Alexander the Great, was inherited by the Romans.[10]

As long as Christianity was viewed as a sect of Judaism, it was considered a legal, or licensed, religion. Romans naturally saw Christianity as part of Judaism. The main converts to Christianity were Jews. Jesus himself was a Jew. Eventually, though, the Jewish authorities made a concerted effort to inform Roman authorities that Christianity was not part of Judaism, but was an apostate sect. Christians subsequently lost their protective status and became followers of an "illegal" religion. As such, they were subject to severe persecution. This was the beginning of anti-Jewish sentiment among Christians. Conservative scholar F. F. Bruce gives a detailed analysis of this period in church history in his book *The Spreading Flame*:

[F]rom the 60s to the first century onward, Christianity was clearly recognized as a distinct religion from Judaism and after the fall of Jerusalem [A.D. 70] it consequently ranked as an illicit cult in the eyes of the law. Nor was it the sort of religion that could easily win official permission for its observance. The official recognition, according to the Jewish religion, made it possible for Jews to practice their own distinctive rights and to enjoy exemption from a variety of civil, military duties involving some contact with idolatry. But then Judaism was a religion of a distinct subject nation of the empire. Christianity was not the religion of any particular nation, nor could it invoke long established custom. It appeared to be a vulgar innovation whose religious aspect was probably a mere facade concealing something worse.[11]

Christian persecutions ended only after the Roman emperor Constantine (c. 274/280–337) converted to Christianity in 312.[12] The fledgling church received political power and was able to finally progress unimpeded. Unfortunately, early Christian leaders, in their zeal to keep believers from reverting back to Judaism, resorted to slander and insult rather than rational instruction and loving exhortation.

St. John Chrysostom (354–407), for instance, attempted to steer Antioch Christians away from Judaism by labeling the synagogue "a brothel and a theatre," "a den for unclean animals," "the temple of demons," "the cavern of devils," "a gulf and abyss of perdition."[13] Of Jews, he wrote, "[They] have all the vices of beasts and are good for nothing but slaughter. . . . They behave no better than pigs in their lewd vulgarities."[14] "They are all possessed by the devil," Chrysostom said.[15]

Inflammatory hearsay about Jews reached a peak of absurdity between the twelfth and fifteenth centuries. Jews were accused of torturing consecrated wafers of bread used by Roman Catholics during communion services.[16] Catholics, it must be remembered, believe that the bread they consume during communion has been miraculously transformed into the body of Christ, even though it still *appears* to be bread. Hence, any talk of communion wafers being "tortured" conjured up images of Christ being made to suffer again.

During Europe's darkest period, when millions were dying from the Black Death (1347–1351), the ignorant populace—unaware that the disease was being spread by fleas—blamed Jews for the devastation. Historian Morris Bishop comments:

A most woeful sequel of the plague was the persecution of the Jews. Since it is our nature to blame our misfortunes on the wickedness of others, people accused the Jews of a gigantic plot to destroy Christendom by poisoning the water supplies. . . . 200 Jews were burned alive in Strasburg. At Speyer the Jews were massacred, and their bodies were sent down the Rhine in empty wine barrels.[17]

Most offensive were the "blood accusations" that flourished in Europe between 1144 and the late 1200s. These horrendous stories accused Jews of killing Christian children and draining their blood for use in Passover meals. Other accounts of macabre murders "concluded that they occurred because Jewish men menstruated and needed to refill their blood, or because Jewish boys lost blood while being circumcised and . . . needed to replenish it."[18]

Such legends were destined to merge with Barruel's theory. And so they did, when in 1806 Barruel received a letter supposedly written by retired Italian army officer J. B. Simonini of Florence. James Ridgeway, author of the 1990 chronicle of racism in America entitled *Blood in the Face*, explains the letter's contents:

Simonini applauded Barruel for revealing the "hellish sects which are preparing the way for the Antichrist," and called his attention to the "Judaic sect," which was "the most formidable power, if one considers its great wealth and the protection it enjoys in almost all European countries." Simonini went on to tell how he stumbled onto this great conspiracy at a gathering of Piedmontese Jews in northern Italy. Pretending to be Jewish himself, Simonini said, he eavesdropped on their conversation. . . . They confided to him that Jews had not only founded the Freemasons and the Illuminati, they had even disguised themselves as Christians and become clergymen, including cardinals and bishops. Soon they hoped to have a Jew named Pope. Unwitting Christians had already granted these impostors full civil rights, allowing them to buy up land and houses to such an extent that true Christians would be dispossessed, their churches made over into synagogues, and they themselves reduced to slaves.[19]

Interestingly, "nothing whatsoever is known about this Simonini, and Barruel never managed to establish contact with him."[20] It has been theorized that the letter was a forgery produced by the French political police in an effort to turn Napoleon I (1769–1821) against Jews. The French Revolution had brought a degree of freedom to Jews in France. All repressive measures against them were repealed (1791) and they were given equal rights (1795). This, of course, did not sit well with French conservatives, who had grown accustomed to Jews being second-class citizens. Debate over the Jewish emancipation had been raging throughout all of France for many years.[21]

Despite the questionable nature of Simonini's note, Barruel circulated it and integrated its elements into his theory. Just before his death in 1820 at age 79, he "emerged as an enthusiastic believer not simply in the Masonic conspiracy but in the Jewish conspiracy as well," firmly propounding the idea that the whole of Europe "was in the grip of a vast revolutionary organization, which extended downwards into every single village of France, Spain, Italy and Germany and which was rigidly controlled by a supreme council, which in turn was controlled by Jews."[22]

Barruel's conspiracy theory, along with the various tales it spawned, gradually coalesced into a single plot line that served as a prototype for the most well-known and influential story about Jews conspiring to achieve world domination: *The Protocols of the Learned Elders of Zion*. This text describes the alleged existence of a secret cabal of Jewish schemers committed to establishing a one-world government:

> The means toward this suppose end was the fomenting of strife among Christians . . . always by encouraging moral depravity. The Jewish state that would emerge once this objective had been attained would be a despotism maintained with the help of an ubiquitous police: a society deprived of freedom but not lacking in social benefits, including full employment, to keep the masses docile.[23]

The *Protocols* continue to serve as a blueprint for most of today's conspiracy theories, including those being promoted by patriots. The anti-Semitic document holds special importance to white supremacists, who harbor a virulent hatred of Jews. According to Aryan Nations literature, it is "absolutely impossible for any Christian White man to comprehend the accelerating rot within Western Christendom, regardless of his formal education unless he has read the protocols."[24]

This is a truly extraordinary claim since the racist manuscript was exposed as a forgery more than seventy years ago. All scholars recognize the *Protocols* as "the most widespread of fabricated documents of the twentieth century" and "the greatest continuing fabrication in history to withstand the scrutiny of an age of supposedly rational thought."[25] Its checkered past is interwoven through years of political intrigue, bloody revolutions and large-scale genocide.

The French-Russian Connection

The Protocols of the Learned Elders of Zion, first published in Russia in the early 1900s, is purportedly "a verbatim record of twenty-four secret meetings of leaders of a Jewish conspiracy, who announce their determination to overthrow all states and religions, by such tricks as democracy and socialism, and to replace them with a world-wide Jewish empire."[26]

These lectures supposedly outline an operation sustained through a global network "of camouflaged agencies and organizations," which are used to control "political parties and governments, the press and public opinion, banks and economic developments . . . in pursuance of an age-old plan . . . with a single aim: establishing Jewish domination over the whole world. And this secret government is supposed to be dangerously near to achieving its aim."[27]

Countless individuals believe the *Protocols* to be a legitimate document even though English journalist Philip Graves of the *London Times* exposed it as fraudulent in 1921. Through a series of articles published in August of that year, Graves showed that large portions of the *Protocols* had been plagiarized from Parisian attorney Maurice Joly's 1864 book *Dialogue aux Enfers Entre Machiavel et Montesquieu ou la Politique de Machiavel au XIXe Siecle* (Dialogues in hell between Machiavelli and Montesquieu, or the politics of Machiavelli in the 19th century).[28]

Joly's work had nothing to do with the Jews. It was a satirical stab at Napoleon III (1808–1873). In fact, Joly was fined 300 francs and sentenced to 15 months in prison for his irreverent portrayal of the emperor.[29] How did so much of Joly's manuscript evolve into the *Protocols*? The plagiarism was the crowning act of several events that began to unfold soon after *Dialogues in Hell* gained notoriety. It all started when anti-Semites (who had no doubt been influenced by Barruel's theory and Simonini's letter) began concocting stories in which Jews articulated Machiavelli's anti-social and anti-democratic ideas.

The first Joly-inspired fable appeared in Berlin in 1868. Under the pen name Sir John Ratcliffe, Hermann Goedsche—a German journalist and former post office worker who was forced to leave the service for dishonorable conduct—produced a series of novels called *Biarritz-Rome* (1866–1868).[30] One of these volumes, entitled *To Sedan*, contained the chapter "In the Jewish Cemetery in Prague and the Council of Representatives of the Twelve Tribes of Israel."[31] It described a meeting held once every 100 years by a supreme body of Jewish leaders. The story tells of how these individuals "gathered around the grave of the most senior rabbi and issued reports on the progress of the grand plot to enslave the gentiles and take over the world."[32]

Then, in 1869, French nobleman Gougenot des Mousseax published *Le Juif, le judaisme et la judaisation des peuples chrétiens* (The Jew, Judaism and the Judaization of the Christian peoples). This accusatory volume blatantly placed Jews into Barruel's original coalition of Templar, Freemason and Illuminati conspirators. It was well received nearly everywhere.[33]

After Mousseax's book gained popularity, a new edition of Goedsche's cemetery chapter—now isolated from his novels—appeared in Russia (1872), first in a magazine, then in booklet form.[34] Years later, Goedsche cleverly transformed his tale of *several* unidentified rabbis giving *various* reports in a cemetery, into a yarn about *one* unnamed rabbi delivering a *single* speech before a Jewish congress. This latter version of the story ended up being published as "The Rabbi's Speech" and circulated in Europe as fact.[35]

By the 1870s, German extremists were declaring that all Jews were "governed by a secret international organization."[36] By 1880, belief in a Jewish world conspiracy "began to gain ground among the extreme right in France, Germany, and Russia."[37] According to historian Richard Pipes, anti-Semitism at this time received widespread acceptance in Europe "mainly in reaction to the appearance of Jews as equals in societies that had been accustomed to treating them as a pariah caste, and from disappointment that even after being emancipated, they refused to assimilate."[38]

Knowledgeable researchers agree that the *Protocols* was compiled somewhere between 1872 and 1895 (probably in the early 1890s). They seem to have been produced in response to the great turmoil taking place in Russia, which was an especially volatile arena socially, politically and economically at the time. A number of key historical events support this hypothesis.

Tsar Alexander II (1818–1881) had recently negotiated an end to the Crimean War (1853–1856), after which he abolished serfdom, which "transformed peasants into tenant farmers."[39] He then introduced limited local self-government. The nobles, of course, did not appreciate such changes. To voice their discontentment, they formed opposition groups. This was quickly followed by the Polish uprising (1863), the annexation of Central Asia (1865–1876), and the Russo-Turkish Wars (1877–1878). Tensions continued to mount until 1881, when Alexander was assassinated.

His son, Alexander III (1845–1894), succeeded him. Embittered by his father's death and surrounded by reactionary advisors, the new Tsar began undoing all that had been accomplished. He increased police powers, restricted the peasantry, tightened censorship, and enforced Russification of all minorities.[40] He made several enemies, including Alexander Ulyanov, who was subsequently executed for plotting to kill the Tsar. Ulyanov's brother, Vladimir, "vowed revenge and changed his name to Lenin."[41]

When Alexander III died from an illness in 1894, his son Nicholas II (1868–1918) took leadership of the highly unstable Russia. Only three years earlier, the devastating famine of 1891 had led to numerous conflicts between the people and the bureaucracy.[42] Moreover, Nicholas II was only twenty-six years old when he became Tsar. All of these factors served to intensify the already high level of frustration and bitterness that Russians had been feeling since the mid-1800s.

It is believed the *Protocols* was created to "demonstrate to Nicholas II the reality of the Jewish threat."[43] Someone needed to be blamed for the nation's problems, and the obvious scapegoats were the "demon" Jews, who by 1897 comprised 4.13 percent (5,189,400) of the total Russian population.[44] Although no one knows for sure exactly who penned the *Protocols*, it is fairly certain that a person, or persons, living in France manufactured the text by combining the elements of Barruel's original conspiracy theory (1806), the Simonini letter (1820), Joly's satire (1864), Goedsche's novel (1868), Mousseax's book (1869) and "The Rabbi's Speech" (post-1872). In the case of Joly's satire, large portions of it were copied word for word.[45]

Nicholas and the *Protocols*

Most historians agree that the Russian secret police (*Okhrana*) were involved in producing the *Protocols*.[46] It had always angered the secret police "that the Tsars were not sufficiently assiduous [persistent] in putting down radical conspiracies, especially Jewish ones."[47] The Okhrana could easily have fabricated the document in hopes of convincing the Tsar that Russian troubles were being caused by Jews, which would in turn justify future pogroms (organized and often officially sanctioned attacks on Jews). It has been theorized that two Paris representatives of the *Okhrana*—Orzhevsky and Ratchkovsky, head of the Tsarist police, were behind the work.[48]

Interestingly, the secret police did not give the document directly to Nicholas. They approached him through his wife, the Tsarina Alexandra. In a letter to Anna Vyrubova, Alexandra explained that while in Tobolsk she received a copy of the *Protocols* from "a friend." She read it "with interest," then recommended it to Nicholas.[49] Although Alexandra does not mention the year she recommended the *Protocols*, historians are certain that it was in Russia and available to members of the autocracy by 1895. This assertion is based in part on a 1927 affidavit by Phillip Petrovich Stepanov, the former Procurator of the Moscow Synod Office. He admits to having received a copy of the *Protocols* in 1895 from Major Alexey Sukhotin, a neighboring estate owner in the province Toula. Stepanov maintains that he had it printed for private use in 1897.[50]

The earliest known version of the *Protocols* to be released to the general public is the 1902/03 *Protocols of the Meetings of the Universal Union of Freemasons and the Elders of Zion*, which appeared in a St. Petersburg periodical.[51] Its publishers, the anti-Semitic Katzman and Kruzhevan, claimed to have received it from France.[52]

In 1903 there also appeared a religio-political work entitled *Great Things in Small Things* by Sergei Nilus, "a Russian playboy who after spending several years in France underwent a religious conversion and retired to one of Russia's leading monasteries."[53] This volume contained "religious quotations, exact predictions about the coming of the Antichrist, and symbolic drawings of stars and snakes."[54]

This first edition of Nilus' book is of little importance to our discussion. But the second edition (1905) is most relevant. It was printed by the Tsar's government printing press. Even more significant is the fact that the royal printers had combined it with the *Protocols*, entitling it *Velikoe v malom i Antikhrist, kak blizkaia politicheskaia vozmozhnost': Zapiski pravoslavnogo* (*Great things in small things and the Antichrist as an immediate political possibility: Notes of an Orthodox believer.*)

Coincidentally, 1905 was also the year Nicholas released his October 17 manifesto, which "gave the country a measure of political freedom."[55] The Tsar issued the declaration in response to a rising tide of revolutionaries. Just three days prior to its release, striking workers in St. Petersburg had vowed "to throw off the chains of centuries-old slavery."[56] The provisions of the manifesto "embodied several of the demands put forward by liberal opinion and was hardly compatible with the principle of autocracy." These compromises included the granting of fundamental civil liberties to the population, including Jews, based on principles such as "inviolability of the person, freedom of conscience, of speech, of assembly and of association."[57]

Tsarist authorities and other hard-liners were not pleased. In October, far-right leader Russkoye Sobranie reacted to the proclamation by publicly presenting another manifesto "that expressed fervent belief in the monarchy and the church and demanded special anti-Jewish laws 'in view of the Jewish hostility to Christianity.' "[58] The Tsar was apparently sympathetic to Sobranie's anti-Semitic rhetoric. Nicholas wrote in a letter to his mother that "nine-tenths of the trouble-makers were Jews."[59]

Anti-Jewish pogroms soon began under the guise of counterdemonstrations against left-wingers celebrating the manifesto. In Odessa, a pogrom claimed 300 victims; 120 were killed in Yekaterinoslav; 46 died in Kiev; and 80 in Bialystok. The terror ended in 1906 after 700 pogroms had killed and injured thousands.[60]

Anxiety in Russia abated slightly between 1906 and 1914. Then "World War I, which began in 1914, brought the situation to a head." By early 1917, "military defeats, acute civilian suffering, and government ineptness had led to food riots and strikes in Petrograd . . . and Moscow. Many soldiers refused to help put down the disorders."[61] An irreversible push was made by revolutionaries to overthrow the Tsar, and on March 15, 1917 Nicholas II abdicated his throne. The days of Imperial Russia were over.

One year later, Nicholas and Alexandra, along with their five children, Olga, 22, Tatiana, 21, Marie, 19, Anastasia, 17, and Alexis, 13, found themselves imprisoned 1,000 miles from Moscow in the railway town of Ekaterinburg, Siberia. It is here, in history's last chapter on the Romanovs, that we find the final page in the story of Nicholas and the *Protocols*.

At one point during his brief and tumultuous reign, Nicholas rejected the *Protocols* as fraudulent. This occurred after the Russian premier Piotr Arkadevich Stolypin (1862–1911) ordered two high ranking police officials named Martynov and Vasiliev to investigate the document's authenticity. The two officers concluded that the *Protocols* was a forgery. The Tsar, it is reported, "gave an order that the *Protocols* were no longer to be used, 'since it was impossible to pursue a pure aim by impure means'!"[62]

But documents penned during Nicholas' imprisonment suggest that he reversed his position on the anti-Semitic book just before his death. According to Klaudiia Bitner, who spent time with the captive family, Nicholas "blamed the 'yids' for inciting and misleading the people and causing the revolution."[63] A diary notation by Nicholas on March 27, 1918, supports Bitner's claim: "Yesterday I started to read aloud Nilus's book on the Antichrist, to which have been added the "protocols" of the Jews and Masons—very timely reading."[64] An entry in the Tsarina Alexandra's diary, under April 7, 1918, reads: "Nicholas read to us the protocols of the free masons [today]."[65]

On July 16, 1918, the Romanovs were brutally slaughtered by Bolshevik guards in the basement of the house where they were being held. All were shot, mercilessly stabbed with bayonets, and savagely bludgeoned to death. Their stripped bodies were then hacked to pieces, covered with acid, and incinerated. Their remains were buried in an unmarked communal grave nearby. When investigators later entered the prison-home, they found a copy of the *Protocols* "on a pedestal for flowers together with the first volume of Tolstoy's *War and Peace* and a Russian Bible."[66]

A Nazi Holy Book
It was not until after the Russian Revolution that the *Protocols* became widely popular in Europe. The year 1920 saw the translation and publication of one English, two American, two German, two French and two Polish editions of the forgery. The book's popularity grew primarily because of rumors that the Russian revolt had been instigated and carried out by the Jews. All of the political murders, especially of the Tsar and his family, were blamed on the Jews (even though it was Lenin, a non-Jewish Russian, who had passed the Romanovs' death sentence).[67]

In reality, Jews were hardly the new leaders of Russia. One observer recorded that Jews "were hated in both Communist and non-Communist ranks 'with a virulence difficult to describe.' "[68] Russian publicist S. S. Masloff wrote the following in 1923:

Hatred of the Jews is one of the most prominent features of contemporary Russian life; possibly even the most prominent. Jews are hated everywhere, in the north, in the south, in the east and in the west. They are detested by all social orders, by all political parties, by all nationalities and by persons of all ages.[69]

The *Protocols* were imported to Germany in 1918, where it fell into the hands of Adolf Hitler (1889–1945). By the time he came to power in 1933 there were twenty-eight editions circulating throughout the country. Hitler proceeded to have it published by the Nazi Party itself, and by 1935 the German Minister of Education had prescribed it as a basic textbook for schools.[70] In his infamous work *Mein Kampf* (1924), Hitler reveals that the *Protocols* greatly influenced his thinking:

To what extent the whole existence of this people [the Jews] is based on a continuous lie is shown incomparably by the *Protocols of the Wise Men of Zion* . . . . *[W]ith terrifying certainty they reveal the nature and activity of the Jewish people and expose their inner contexts as well as their final aims* . . . . *[O]nce this book becomes the common property of a people, the Jewish menace may be considered as broken.*[71]

Most people are painfully aware of the barbaric atrocities perpetrated by Nazi Germany against European Jews. Nazi war crimes have been catalogued in a number of historically reliable volumes such as *The Holocaust: The Fate of European Jewry; The Nazi Doctors: Medical Killings* and *the Psychology of Genocide; Shoah: An Oral History of the Holocaust;* and *Denying the Holocaust.*[72]

Although a look at Hitler's inhuman activities would provide valuable information, such a study is beyond the scope of our present discussion—the origin and spread of the conspiratorial theories currently being propagated by patriots. Consequently, our attention, if it is to remain focused on the subject at hand, must follow the path of the *Protocols*. In doing so, we are led to another anti-Semitic tome that is nearly as important as Barruel's original writings: *The International Jew*, a work published in the 1920s by a man whose name is "synonymous with American ingenuity and industriousness"—Henry Ford.[73]

Racism, American Style

Many Americans look to automobile tycoon Henry Ford (1863–1947) with great admiration. Ford was indeed a brilliant and talented man. Unfortunately, he was also the foremost advocate of anti-Semitism in the United States during the 1920s.[74] Political science professor Michael Barkun credits Ford with having produced "the first and widest American popularization of . . . the most famous anti-Semitic book of the twentieth century [the *Protocols*]."[75]

Ford's role in the growth of American anti-Semitism began just prior to the summer of 1920, when one of his representatives acquired a copy of the *Protocols* from Paquita de Shishmareff, a Russian émigré "who claimed to know all about Jewish operations in Europe."[76] Ford was easily convinced of the Jewish threat. Those close to him were not surprised by his receptivity since he had expressed anti-Semitic thoughts as early as 1915.[77] In an effort to thwart the diabolical Jewish plan, Ford printed the *Protocols* with accompanying commentary in his weekly newspaper, the *Dearborn Independent*. The series of articles, entitled "The International Jew," appeared for ninety-one consecutive weeks between May 22, 1920, and January 14, 1922. They boldly accused the Jews of utilizing communism, banking labor unions, alcohol, gambling, jazz music, newspapers and the movies to attack and weaken America, its culture and people.[78]

One would think that since the *Independent* had a circulation of 72,000 when the series began, and a circulation of 300,000 by the time it ended, Ford's desire to expose the "Jewish menace" would have been satiated.[79] But the automobile magnate was not yet through disseminating anti-Semitic beliefs. He had the inflammatory pieces of faulty journalism reprinted as a four-volume book set. It sold more than 500,000 copies and was translated into sixteen foreign languages.[80]

When asked to give his reasons for printing *The International Jew*, Ford responded by saying that he was "only trying to awake [sic] the Gentile world to an understanding of what is going on." He continued: "The Jew is a mere huckster, a trader who doesn't want to produce, but to make something out of what somebody else produces."[81] In a February 17, 1921, *New York World* interview, Ford tersely expressed his unqualified endorsement of the *Protocols*:

> The only statement I care to make about the Protocols is that they fit in with what is going on. They are sixteen years old and they have fitted [sic] the world situation up to this time. They fit it now.[82]

Through Ford's anti-Semitic publications, racism in America reached a new level. The Jewish people had become "the enemy," an evil and conniving race of power-hungry conspirators who had orchestrated every important historical event for their benefit, especially events that allegedly lowered the standards of society. Ford blamed the Jews for virtually everything:

Historical Event	The International Jew[83]
Wars	"[I]t is in the study of Jewish money-making out of war that the clues are found to most of the great abuses of which the Jews have been guilty. . . . As the unbroken program is traced through the Revolutionary War, through the Civil War, and through the Great War, the only change observable is the increasing power and profit of the Jews" (pp. 39–40).
The Russian Revolution	"The downfall of Russia was prepared by a long and deliberate program of misrepresentation of the Russian people, through the Jewish world press and Jewish diplomatic service" (p. 54).
Liquor Problems	"As soon as the Jew gained control of American liquor, we had a liquor problem with drastic consequences" (p. 145).
Social Degeneration	"It is the peculiar genius of that race to create problems of a moral character in whatever business they achieve a majority" (pp. 145–146).
Immoral Movies	"The motion picture influence of the United States, of the whole world, is exclusively under the control, moral and financial, of the Jewish manipulators of the public mind. The moral side of the movies' influence is now a world problem" (p. 157).
Jazz Music	"[W]hence come the waves . . . of musical slush that invade decent homes and set the young people of this generation imitating the drivel of morons. Popular music is a Jewish monopoly. Jazz is a Jewish creation. The mush, slush, the sly suggestion, the abandoned sensuousness of sliding notes, are of Jewish origin. . . . [G]lamorous youths mutter dirges in low monotones, voluptuous females with grossly seductive gestures moan nasal notes no real musician can recognize. . . . The general directors of the whole downward trend have been Jews" (p. 163).
Economic Problems	"The Jew . . . controls the world's finances" (p. 175).

Historical Event	*The International Jew*[83]
Media Bias	"All leading news agencies in America are Jew-controlled. . . . There have been . . . great battles which Jewry waged, successfully, to snuff out the independent Press" (pp. 217–218).

According to history professor Leonard Dinnerstein of the University of Arizona, people "from all walks of life, including college professors, illiterates, and large numbers of Christian ministers, sent money to Ford, praised him for his attacks on Jews, and requested additional materials for their own use."[84]

Ford's work was understandably praised by Hitler, who distributed *The International Jew* throughout Germany. The German leader once told an American reporter, "I regard Heinrich Ford as my inspiration."[85] It is also reported that Hitler kept a picture of Ford on the wall in his office in Munich.[86] Ford even won himself a favorable mention in *Mein Kampf*,[87] and in 1923 Hitler declared full support for Ford upon hearing that the renowned industrialist might run for president:

I wish I could send some of my shock troops to Chicago and other big American cities to help in the elections. We look to Heinrich Ford as the leader of the growing fascist movement in America. . . . We have just had his anti-Jewish articles translated and published. The book is being circulated in millions throughout Germany.[88]

In 1938, five years after Hitler seized power in Germany, Ford became the first American to receive "the highest honor the German government could grant a foreigner: the Grand Cross of the German Eagle."[89] It was presented to him on his seventy-fifth birthday. Fritz Hailer (German Counsel in Detroit) and Karl Kapp (German Counsel in Cleveland) presented the medal in Detroit, and with it, a personal greeting that had been sent by *Der Führer* himself.[90]

At the post–World War II Nuremberg trials, where high-ranking German officers and Nazi Party members were tried for their war crimes, Hitler's Youth Leader Baldur Von Shirach testified that he had become "Jew-wise" through reading *The International Jew*.[91] When asked what had made him an anti-Semite, he answered matter of factly: "Henry Ford."[92] Shirach's statement unfortunately summarized the feelings of many U.S. citizens during that period in history.

Ford had injected anti-Jewish sentiment deep into American hearts. A 1938 opinion poll found that forty-one percent of U.S. adults agreed that Jews had "too much power in the United States." (This figure rose to fifty-eight percent by 1945.) During World War II, poll takers also found that Americans viewed Jews, after the Germans and Japanese, as the greatest menace to society.[93] As a result, the 1930s and 1940s saw Jewish citizens being verbally castigated and physically attacked in America on a level reminiscent of Eastern Europe of the late 1800s.

Father Charles E. Coughlin, for instance, a Roman Catholic priest and rabid anti-Semite, fomented hours of anti-Jewish hate rhetoric over radio airwaves to millions of listeners. His organization, known as the Christian Front, "organised [sic] movements to boycott Jewish businesses . . . between 1938 and 1940, physically assaulted Jews and constantly attacked them as 'warmongers' seeking to drag the United States into war with Hitler's Germany."[94] In 1936, Coughlin began printing Social Justice, which at one point included portions of the Protocols.[95]

At this same time (c. 1938), Protestant clergyman Gerald B. Winrod published anti-Semitic diatribes in his *Defender* newsletter, which had an estimated 110,000 subscribers.[96] Winrod steadfastly insisted that his beliefs were "firmly anchored in biblical prophecy."[97] He founded the Defenders of the Christian Faith and promoted the *Protocols*, which he called "an accurate representation of Jewish plans."[98]

A few years before Winrod's rise to fame, another so-called Christian named William Pelley organized the Silver Shirts (1933), an American version of Germany's Nazi storm troopers (the Brown Shirts). Pelley's 15,000 fascist followers "emitted an unrelenting stream of propaganda against Jews controlling industry, finance and property in America."[99] In 1942, Pelley was sentenced to fifteen years in prison after being convicted under the Espionage Act for "distributing information aimed at subversion of the U.S. armed forces."[100]

These and a host of other anti-Semites leaned heavily on the words of Henry Ford, who has become nothing less than a hero to white supremacists. According to modern-day racists, Ford alerted the public to "the powerful concentration of forces organized by Jewish interests and the effects of Jewish influences in the United States from the time of the Civil War up to the uneasy years following the first world war."[101]

The engine of American anti-Semitism was clearly started by Henry Ford, and to date, no one has been able to stop it. The myth of the "demon" Jew has become a permanent fixture in the world's psyche. Today, *The International Jew* is regularly sold through racist and patriot catalogues as early "patriotic material," along with the *Protocols* and Hitler's *Mein Kampf*.[102] Norman Cohn observes, "*The International Jew* probably did more than any other work to make the *Protocols* world-famous."[103]

As of 1994, more than sixty editions of the *Protocols* had been printed in Arab countries. It is a best-seller throughout Muslim capitals in Egypt, Iran, Iraq, Libya and Syria.[104] In Saudi Arabia, King Feisal gave visiting foreign dignitaries a special artistic edition of the *Protocols* as a memento. Henry Kissinger even received a copy.[105]

Tragically, the enlightenment and sophistication of the twentieth century has somehow failed to eradicate even the most primitive stories about Jewish people. Consider the remarks of King Feisal that appeared in a 1972 edition of the Arabic weekly *al-Musawwar*. They echo loudly the whisperings of medieval Europe:

[Jews] have a certain day on which they mix the blood of non-Jews into their bread and eat it. It happened that two years ago, while I was in Paris on a visit, the police discovered five murdered children. Their blood had been drained and it turned out that some Jews had murdered them in order to take their blood and mix it with the bread that they eat on this day. This shows you what is the extent of their hatred and malice toward non-Jewish peoples.[106]

Like their racist forefathers, modern anti-Semites disseminate vicious lies born of ignorance and fear. They label Jews "the greatest warmongers in history," blame Jews for the success of the pornography industry, and accuse Jews of seeking world domination.[107] Members of the Aryan Nations, KKK and other racist groups have even continued to spread the ludicrous blood accusations prevalent in the Middle Ages.[108]

In response to this "Jewish threat," a war has been declared. Aryan nations founder Richard Butler believes the white race will soon extricate itself from the bondage of Jewry and "acknowledge that we are in a state of war individually and collectively."[109] Tom Metzger, founder of the White Aryan Resistance, puts it even more succinctly: "White man, you have the greatest reason in history to kill."[110] This mind-set has led to racist literature so virulent that the Protocols and *The International Jew* pale in comparison. This is nowhere more apparent than in the 1978 novel *The Turner Diaries* written by white supremacist William Pierce.[111]

Terrorist Bible

The Turner Diaries hit the underground racist book market in 1978 and has since become a "key piece of fiction for white supremacists and neo-Nazis."[112] It is "probably the most widely read single book among far right extremists."[113] The volume is nothing more than a 211-page cesspool of hate directed at Jews, blacks and other people of color, who are regularly knifed, shot, beaten and hanged throughout the text.

Pierce's story—set between the years 1991 and 1993—is the daily diary of Earl Turner, a rank-and-file member of The Order, an elite inner circle of militant revolutionaries who are part of a much larger terrorist group known as The Organization. This fictional diary chronicles Turner's adventures during the two years prior to the conclusion of the "Great Revolution," a guerrilla war waged against the U.S. government by white "patriots."[114] The saga begins after the government outlaws firearm ownership. Pierce summarizes the intriguing tale on the book's back cover:

[T]he patriots fight back with a campaign of sabotage and assassination. An all-out race war occurs as the struggle escalates. Turner and his comrades suffer terribly, but their ingenuity and boldness in devising and executing new methods of guerrilla warfare lead to a victory of cataclysmic intensity and worldwide scope.[115]

In agreement with the *Protocols*, the *Turner Diaries* paints Jews as the world's behind-the-scenes rulers and names "the Jewish-liberal-democratic-equalitarian plague" as the cause of society's moral decay.[116] There is, for instance, the Jewish man described as "Kappy the Kike . . . who makes his living in the White slave trade." This character sells young white girls to exclusive clubs in New York where wealthy Jews go "to satisfy strange and perverted appetites."[117]

Like Hitler's *Mein Kampf*, Pierce's novel promotes the idea that Jews are behind the mixing of races, which has led to the "decomposition of races and civilizations.[118] Turner also bemoans the state of Christianity, expressing that the "Jewish takeover of the Christian churches and corruption of the ministry are now virtually complete." He writes in his journal, "Life is uglier and uglier these days, more and more Jewish."[119]

Blacks are portrayed in a similarly negative light, appearing sporadically throughout the book as brainless sub-humans who are either raping young white girls or beating up white patriots. The book's numerous references to, and descriptions of, white girls being gang-raped by blacks indicates that Pierce may be somewhat obsessed with the idea.[120] By the end of the saga, blacks are being gunned down on sight by white revolutionaries.[121] An especially abhorrent portion of Pierce's book depicts blacks as natural-born cannibals who resort to eating defenseless whites when food grows scarce:

Blacks have solved their food shortage: cannibalism. They began by setting up barricades in one main street to stop cars driven by Whites. . . . The unfortunate Whites were dragged from their cars, taken into a nearby Black restaurant, butchered, cooked, and eaten. . . . In the cellar of one Black apartment building we found a scene of indescribable horror. . . . A group of GI's milling around the entrance were obviously distressed. . . . I pushed my way into the building [and] I recoiled from the horrible stench. . . . I descended the cellar stairs past two more GI's who were coming up. In the arms of one of them was a silently staring White child of about four, alive but apparently too weak to walk. The cellar . . . had been converted into a human slaughterhouse by the Blacks in the apartment building. The floor was slippery with half-congealed blood. There were washtubs full of stinking entrails, and others filled with severed heads. Four tiny, human haunches dangled overhead from wires. On a wooden workbench beneath one of the lanterns I saw the most terrible thing I have ever seen. It was the butchered and partially dismembered body of a teenaged girl. Her blue eyes stared emptily at the ceiling, and her long, golden hair was matted with the blood which had rushed from the gaping wound in her throat. . . . From one of the GI's outside the building I learned that parts of at least 30 children, all White, had been found in the cellar . . . . In the rear courtyard . . . was an improvised barbecue grill and a large pile of small, human bones—thoroughly gnawed.[122]

For two years, Turner and several fellow freedom fighters criss-cross the country, robbing, beating and murdering blacks and Jews along the way. Eventually, the organization successfully brings down the government as each state is systematically taken over by white revolutionary forces. Global victory, the murder of all non-whites, and "the dream of a White world" is finally achieved by 1999, a date Pierce describes as "just 110 years after the birth of the Great One" (Hitler, born in 1889). [123]

California is the first state to be "liberated." This occasion is marked by a massive rounding up and deportation of blacks. [124] Jews and "almost-White mongrels" are summarily executed after being put into "death columns" and marched "to the canyon in the foothills north of the city." [125] These glorious occasions are soon followed by the Day of the Rope, "a grim and bloody day, but an unavoidable one." [126]

The gruesome event opens with revolutionary forces sweeping through Los Angeles and surrounding neighborhoods to find race traitors—persons who had either engaged in, or encouraged, interracial relationships and racial equality programs. In ten hours, white patriots hang 55,000 to 60,000 victims, including government officials, lawyers, businessmen, TV newscasters, newspaper reporters and editors, judges, teachers, school officials, civic leaders, preachers, real estate brokers and prominent actors and actresses involved in "interracial 'love' epics:" [127]

[F]rom tens of thousands of lampposts, power poles, and trees throughout this vast metropolitan area the grisly forms hang. . . . [O]ne sees them everywhere. . . . [A]t practically every street corner I passed this evening . . . was a dangling corpse, four at every intersection. Hanging from a single overpass only about a mile from here is a group of about 30, each with an identical placard around its neck bearing the printed legend, "I betrayed my race." Two or three of that group had been decked out in academic robes before they were strung up, and the whole batch are apparently faculty members from the nearby UCLA campus. . . . In the middle of one of the unlighted blocks I saw what appeared to be a person standing on the sidewalk directly in front of me. . . . [A] beam of moonlight broke through the leaves and fell directly on the silently turning shape before me. The first thing I saw . . . was the placard with its legend in large, block letters: "I defiled my race." Above the placard leered the horribly bloated, purplish face of a young woman, her eyes wide open and bulging, her mouth agape. . . . There are many thousands of hanging female corpses like that in this city tonight, all wearing identical placards around their necks. They are the White women who were married to or living with Blacks, with Jews, or with other non-White males. There are also a number of men wearing the I-defiled-my-race placard. . . . [C]orpses with the I-betrayed-my-race placards. . . . [are those] who, for reasons of career or status or votes or whatever, helped promote or implement the System's racial program. The System had already paid them their 30 pieces of silver. Today we paid them. . . . It started at three o'clock this morning. . . . Squads of our troops with synchronized watches suddenly appeared in a thousand blocks at once, in fifty different residential neighborhoods, and every squad leader had a long list of names and addresses. . . . When the execution squads began running out of rope, we stripped several miles of wire from power poles to use in its place. We also rounded up hundreds of ladders. And we were the ones who pasted up the proclamations from Revolutionary Command in each block, warning all citizens that henceforth . . . any failure to obey the command of a soldier, will result in the summary execution of the offender. The proclamations also carry a similar warning for anyone who knowingly harbors a Jew or other non-White or who willfully provides false information to or withholds information from our police units.[128]

Similar acts of wanton violence are common throughout Pierce's diseased attempt at creating a literary work.[129] It must be noted here that white supremacists view *The Turner Diaries* as more than a fictional novel. The book is a model for their warped fantasies regarding the "white struggle" against the Jews and their non-white lackey henchmen. Even more disturbing are the unmistakable similarities between some of the beliefs, attitudes and behaviors presented in the *Diaries* and those promoted in the patriot/militia movement. This is no coincidence, but is the direct result of a crossover of concepts from the racist/white supremacist movement to the patriot movement.

Exactly how such a cross-pollinization has occured will be examined at length in chapter thirteen. For now, however, it is sufficient to show a few of the shared ideas that are so unique that they could have only originated from one source: the white supremacist movement. For example, Turner's war begins shortly after the "Cohen Act" outlaws private ownership of firearms.[130] The kind of government tracking systems patriots believe are going to be implemented by leaders of the New World Order also can be traced to the Diaries:

The Turner Diaries[131]	Patriot Radio Broadcast[132]
"Since our gasoline ration cards are magnetically coded with our social security numbers, when we stuck them into the computer . . . they would show blocked quotas—and instantaneously tell the Feds . . . where we were. . . . Every person . . . will be issued a passport . . . necessary for . . . purchasing an airline, bus, or train ticket, registering in a motel, . . . receiving any medical service. . . . No person will be able to eat a meal in a restaurant, pick up his laundry, or buy groceries without having his passport number magnetically read by a computer."	"[W]e all will be getting, in the mail, from the United States Post Office, a "U.S. identification card" for every man, woman and child. And while, at first it will be your privilege card, it will be like a social security number gradually transformed into a mandatory card, so that, as you have outlined, nobody can go anywhere, buy anything, work anywhere or do anything without having this card."

It was Pierce's book that also popularized the racist belief that our government is a Jewish-controlled puppet regime more properly called Z.O.G., or Zionist Occupational Government.[133] Z.O.G. has allegedly been "the ruling party in the United States since Franklin D. Roosevelt first became president."[134] White supremacists have since adopted this term and use it in their writings.[135] This is only one of the many ways the fictional plot line of the *Diaries* has been proclaimed as fact by patriots.

During the 1980s, the resistance tactics used by Turner's revolutionaries were given tangible expression by a small group of real-life racists led by Robert Matthews. This violent band of white supremacists decided to live out the adventures of Earl Turner by forming a terrorist organization called The Order.[136] Like Turner's Organization, Matthews' Order robbed and murdered their way across America. Their most infamous crimes, committed during 1983 and 1984, included the machine gun slaying in Denver of Jewish radio talk-show host Alan Berg, a $500,000 armored car robbery in Seattle, and the $3.6 million dollar hold-up of a Brinks armored car in Ukiah, California.[137]

By 1986, all twenty-three members of the order were behind bars and looking at lengthy prison terms. Matthews had been killed on Whidbey Island in Washington on December 9, 1984. He "held over 200 law enforcement officers at bay for more than thirty-six hours until he perished in a conflagration set off by the ammunition with which he barricaded himself."[138] In a 1989 book dedicated to Matthews, white supremacist Gary Smith writes:

We have met the monster. ZOG is not a myth. . . . Whatever Washington, D.C. may be, it's no longer the seat of *our* government. Those are not *our* politicians, nor *our* judges. . . . PRESENTLY a beast controls six choke points of American society: *Media, Economics, Demographics, Justice, Values, and Politics.* **That beast is ZOG.**[139]

The influence of Pierce's hate-filled allegory surfaced again during the Randy Weaver shootout. In an open letter to the public, Weaver wrote: "We had run smack into a ZOG New World Order ambush. . . . Samuel Hanson Weaver and Vicki Jean Weaver are Martyrs for Yah-Yashua [Lord-Jesus] and the White Race."[140]

In 1995, *The Turner Diaries* once again influenced militia violence, this time in Oklahoma City. The bombing of the Alfred P. Murrah federal building was clearly modeled after one of the missions that Earl Turner and his fellow patriots had accomplished:

Similarity	The Turner Diaries[141]	Oklahoma City Bombing[142]
Target	"FBI's national headquarters downtown"	a federal building housing FBI offices in downtown Oklahoma City

Similarity	The Turner Diaries[141]	Oklahoma City Bombing[142]
Bomb	"a little under 5,000 pounds"	slightly less than 5,000 pounds
Explosive	"ammonium nitrate fertilizer" and "[fuel] oil"	ammonium nitrate fertilizer and fuel oil
Timing	9:15 A.M.	9:02 A.M.
Vehicle	"a delivery truck"	a Ryder moving truck

Were the Oklahoma City bombers members of a newly formed Order? A comment by long-time racist Tom Metzger (White Aryan Resistance) suggests as much:

I have told people for years, at least since 1984, when The Order declared war on the central government of the United States that the government of this country—what we call the criminals—had better start listening to the dispossessed white people. . . . There was a hot war in the 1980s, and since then there's been a cold war, and now things are heating up again."[143]

Soon after the explosion, Canadian resident Rick Knight posted an Internet message entitled "KABOOM." Knight stated, "[I]t's a real injustice that White children had to be injured and killed in this attack on the ZOG's Okla. H.Q." The patriot's note then declared, "[May this] be a wake up call to the citizens of a nation which has been culpable in the bombing of children for more than fifty years."[144]

Even more significant are testimonies from persons who claim that Timothy McVeigh was extremely familiar with _The Turner Diaries_ and that he considered it to be one of his favorite books. Witnesses claim McVeigh kept the book with him while serving in the army and attempted to get others to peruse its violent contents.[145]

Interestingly, on April 19, 1995 (the day of the Oklahoma City bombing) Richard Snell, a member of the original Order, was executed for two racially motivated murders. Prior to his death in North Carolina, he made a rather cryptic comment: "Look over your shoulder; justice is coming."[146]

Hitler's Legacy
The Aryan Nations describes itself as a "GEOPOLITICAL Movement for the re-establishment of the White Aryan sovereignty over the lands of Aryan Settlement and occupation."[147] In other words, white racists want exactly what Turner's revolutionaries obtained: control over America and an eradication of all non-white races. In 1983, Aryan Nations member Gary Yarbrough explained:

We're looking for a separation of the races. Most likely it will come to force—which is the prophecy of the Bible. I am prepared to do battle if need be. The Lord will guide my bullets and deflect the bullets that are fired at me. [148] Slightly more than a year after making this statement, Yarbrough was arrested for his involvement with the murders and robberies committed by The Order. On December 30, 1985, he was sentenced to sixty years in prison to be served in three consecutive twenty-year terms. [149] Such a sacrifice is the price white supremacists are willing to pay in order to "recapture" America from the Jew and the Jew-inspired "jungle beast nig—r." [150] A force more powerful than either pure hatred or blind ignorance is giving today's white supremacists not only motivation, but courage and boldness. It is a relatively new religion called Christian Identity.

This complex mixture of Christian terminology, Hitlerian beliefs and mythology has given white supremacists a perfect reason to spew their poisonous rhetoric and commit murder. As the character Earl Turner said in his diary under the date of November 16, 1991, "We are truly the instruments of God in the fulfillment of His Grand Design." [151]

12

Christian Identity

Christian Identity is the one thing that lets the Bible make
sense.

Earl Jones
Christian Identify pastor[1]

There are no words in the English language, or any other, to
adequately describe a Jew. You cannot, hard as you may try,
insult a Jew because the very vilest and foulest things you
can think of to say about him, are nothing but pure and
unadulterated flattery in comparison to what he really is.

Thomas E. O'Brien
New Christian (Identity) Crusade Church[2]

Children are little people, little human beings, and that
means white people. . . . There's little dogs and cats and apes
and baboons and skunks and there's also little nig——s. But
they ain't children. They're just little nig——s.

Charles Conley
Christian Identity minister[3]

Religion has been used for thousands of years to mask hate and prejudice.
"Spirituality" still serves as a convenient excuse for violence and other forms
of antisocial behavior. All that is needed is a little false piety, coupled with
liberal doses of self-induced ignorance and blind devotion to "the truth." Even the
most loathsome attitudes and barbarous acts can then be attributed to "serving
God."

This holds especially true for believers in Christian Identity (also simply
referred to as Identity), a twentieth-century amalgamation of racism and pseudo-
Christian ideas. It is a complex doctrinal system that emerged in the 1940s and
reached theological maturity by the 1970s throughout the rural areas "of the West

and South—such as the Ozarks and mountain areas of the Pacific Northwest."[4] According to J. Gordon Melton, a nationally recognized chronicler of religions in America, "Identity is a religion by sociopaths, for sociopaths. It turns their sickness into virtue."[5]

Identity now claims approximately 20,000 to 30,000 adherents nationwide.[6] It is not a religious sect. Neither is it an authoritarian cult nor a mainstream denomination. It has no single leader and is not governed by a core of spiritually elite individuals. It does not even have a definitive set of beliefs that a person must embrace in order to be accepted as a follower. Identity is a social, political, and spiritual movement composed of religiously inclined racists from the ranks of the neo-Nazi community, the KKK and other white supremacist organizations.

Although their views may differ on a few peripheral issues—e.g., whether or not Hitler should be idolized, what should be done with non-whites (exportation vs. extermination), the merits of violent action as opposed to the benefits of nonviolent political activism, etc.—most Identity believers agree on five basic premises:

☐ White people (Aryans) are the Israelites of the Old Testament.
☐ The Jews are literal descendants of Satan.
☐ Adam and Eve were not, as mainstream Christianity teaches, the first people. They were the first *white* people.
☐ All non-Whites (blacks, Asians, Middle Easterners, etc.) are descendants of pre-Adamic races and make up an entirely different species than Caucasians.
☐ Armageddon, which will be a race war between whites and non-whites, is fast approaching.

Attempting to paint an easily recognizable picture of Identity's disjointed network of independent churches and self-styled leaders is extremely difficult. "Rivalries among leaders, organizational splits, and the extinction of old and the creation of new groups all make the 'mapping' of Identity a frustrating undertaking."[7] Nevertheless, its dangerous tenets and increasing popularity suggest that the public should be given at least a general overview of Identity doctrines and structure.

Moreover, many Christian Identity leaders and followers are closely affiliated with patriot movement groups and various militia spokespersons. These links between Identity racists and non-racist patriots are explored in chapter thirteen. This chapter focuses on Identity's five major doctrines: "[T]hese are beliefs that place Identity at the farthest margins of American religion, but they also suggest its potential political volatility."[8] To grasp the framework into which the "Kingdom Identity Message" fits, some background information must be provided about a nation that has drawn the attention of historians for centuries—Israel.

An Ancient People
It is historical fact that persons born of Jewish lineage are descendants of Abraham, a man who lived prior to 2100 B.C. in Ur of the Chaldees in Mesopotamia (Gen

11:31; Neh 9:7). It is acknowledged that at an unknown date Abraham moved to the land of Canaan, where he fathered two sons: Ishmael and Isaac. The younger son, Isaac, had a son whom he named Jacob. Abraham, Isaac and Jacob are referred to as the three Jewish patriarchs because they founded the Hebrew nation.

Abraham is important to Judaism and Christianity, because according to the Bible he received a divine promise that he would father a great nation (Gen 12:2). Isaac's notoriety is linked to the scriptural teaching that he was miraculously born to Abraham's wife, Sarah, when she was far beyond childbearing age (Gen 17:17; 21:5). Jacob, whose name was eventually changed to Israel, is perhaps the most well-known of the three patriarchs. From Jacob's twelve sons (Reuben, Simeon, Levi, Judah, Dan, Naphtali, Gad, Asher, Issachar, Zebulun, Joseph and Benjamin) sprang the mighty Hebrew nation that fell into Egyptian bondage.

The Hebrews originally dwelt in Egypt as honored guests, but after ten generations their population had increased so dramatically that the Egyptians feared their empire would be destroyed if the Hebrews ever chose to side with an enemy. Consequently, the Hebrews were made slaves. They were finally released from their bondage after 430 years (Ex 12:40), only to wander for forty more years throughout the desert in search of a new home. This mass exodus of approximately three million people has consistently captured the world's attention, as evidenced by the production of many books and films on the subject, not the least of which is the classic movie *The Ten Commandments.*

At the time of their emancipation, the Hebrew nation was a united group of twelve distinct tribes distinguished along familial lines stemming from ten of Jacob's sons (Reuben, Simeon, Judah, Dan, Naphtali, Gad, Asher, Issachar, Zebulun and Benjamin) and two of Joseph sons (Manasseh and Ephraim). The descendants of Levi were put in a separate category because they served as holy priests. All of Israel's descendants eventually settled in the land of Canaan, where they were known as Israelites.

Israel was initially governed by judges, but this form of rule was replaced by a succession of kings, the first of whom was Saul (reigned 1050–1010 B.C). The next Israelite king was David (reigned 1003–970 B.C.), of the well-known David and Goliath story (1 Sam 17:45-47). David's son, the legendary Solomon, governed Israel until his death in 930 B.C. (2 Sam 7; 1 Kings 10). Almost immediately after King Solomon died, the twelve tribes of Israel fell into civil war and split into two kingdoms.

Ten tribes set up a northern kingdom known as the House of Israel. The remaining tribes Benjamin, Judah and some Levites joined to form the southern kingdom, known as House of Judah. Both kingdoms were plagued by wars, invasions and internal strife for many years. Finally, in 722/21 B.C., the northern tribes were conquered by the Assyrians and carried away into captivity. The southern tribes fell to the Babylonians in approximately 586 B.C. and were sent into exile.

It is commonly known that both the Assyrians and Babylonians, after conquering a territory, removed to other areas all persons "who might be responsible for any kind of rebellion or treachery." The Assyrians (who captured the northern kingdom) put their prisoners "in small groups so that they would lose their identity and mingle with local populations." The Babylonians (who captured the southern kingdom) "transferred their captives to settlements where they could maintain their identity."[9]

Both these forms of exile were used by Assyria and Babylon against Israel and Judah respectively. As a result, the House of Judah remained in captivity as a distinct entity for seventy years. They returned to their homeland as a nation in 539 B.C., after Babylon fell to Cyrus, King of Persia, who decreed that the Israelites could return to Jerusalem (2 Chron 36:21; Jer 25:9–11).[10] The descendants of these Hebrews comprise much of the population of modern-day Israel.

Much less is known about the fate of those from the northern kingdom. It is assumed that many were assimilated into the Assyrian nation, or into the populace of surrounding countries. A majority of them may have been absorbed into the tribe of Judah. We only know with certainty that they were deported to Assyria, and settled in Halah, Habor, and the city of Medes (2 Kings 17:6). The fate of the Ten Tribes has "continued to dwell in the realm between fact and fantasy ever since."[11]

Questions about the northern kingdom's fate have produced several legends surrounding the "lost" ten tribes.[12] One such myth asserts that their descendants are the Caucasians scattered throughout earth. This concept first gained wide acceptance in Victorian England (1837–1901) when Protestants embraced the notion that they were biologically linked to Israel. Known as British-Israelism, the concept provided a doctrinal basis for Identity, which teaches that "[t]he Germanic kindred (white) peoples are the true descendants of Abraham, Isaac, and Jacob/Israel."[13]

A Man Ahead of His Time

During the mid-1600s, doomsday prophets and last days speculators were stirring hopes and fears in much the same way that today's prophecy pundits are rousing the masses. New England Puritans, who had been in America for barely one generation after fleeing religious persecution in England, were extremely confident that the end was near.[14] Cleric Michael Wigglesworth penned a 224-stanza poem, "The Day of Doom," in 1662, and it became extremely popular. Deacon William Aspinwall, of the state's General Court, predicted the world's demise "no later than 1673."[15]

End-time madness had taken hold in Europe as well, especially in England where social tensions had everyone on edge. That country's civil war from 1629 to 1649 ended with the beheading of Charles I (1600–1649). Several years of unstable rule followed under Oliver Cromwell (1599–1658). Upon Cromwell's death, his son Richard (1626–1712) ruled unsteadily and was forced to step down when Charles II returned from exile to claim the throne in 1660.

Religious upheaval continued when Charles promulgated in 1662 the Act of Uniformity, which deprived clergymen of their offices unless they accepted everything in the Anglican Prayer Book. "This act tended to throw all noncon-formists (Independents, Presbyterians, Baptists and the new Quaker sect) into a single class, called dissenters." [16]

Eschatological rumors were further fueled by a 1665 manifesto issued by the charismatic Rabbi Nathan of Gaza. It proclaimed that the Messiah had arrived. His name was Shabbetai Zevi (1626–1676).[17] The missive stirred an already widespread fascination with the fabled "lost" tribes of Israel. Wild speculations resulted:

> As the seventeenth century progressed, the belief grew that the tribes would soon reemerge into the light of history. . . . [B]y 1665 Europe was swept by reports that this reappearance by the lost tribes had already begun, although its locale was variously reported to be Persia, the Arabian Desert, and the Sahara. These reports described a vast Jewish army moving westward, prepared to smite the Turk and, if need be, to enter Europe itself in order to wreak vengeance on anti-Semitic nations. Thus in November 1665, Robert Boulter of Aberdeen published a letter describing the army and one of its vessels: "There is Sixteen hundred thousand of them together in *Arabia* and . . . there came into *Europe* Sixty Thousand more; as likewise . . . they have had Encounters with the *Turks*, and slain great numbers of them. . . . As for their Ship, . . . in the sails was this Inscription in fair Red Characters THESE ARE OF THE TEN TRIBES OF ISRAEL." A similar letter, originating on the Continent, was published in London in February 1666.[18]

Obsession with the "lost" ten tribes continued to circulate for more than a century until rumors about them reached a new high in the writings of retired English naval officer Richard Brothers (1757–1824). He began having a series of end time visions soon after an unusually loud thunderstorm hit London in January 1791.[19] Brothers maintained it was the loudest thunder that had ever been heard since man's creation, and that he had "an attending Angel to explain all the visions." [20]

He additionally declared that the thunder "was the voice of the Angel mentioned in the Eighteenth chapter of the Revelation."[21] Brothers said that London was supposed to be destroyed by 1793, but it was spared because of his intercessions. God allegedly told him: "I pardon London and all the People in it for your sake: there is no other man on earth that could stand before me to ask for so great a thing."[22]

Brothers believed his mission was twofold. First, he needed to write the chronology of the world by supernaturally revealed "knowledge." He was verbally "commanded" to do this by God. Second, as the divinely appointed leader of the dispersed Jews, it was his duty to lead them back to Palestine. He would then be revealed as "the visible Prince and Governor of the Jews."[23] Brothers further postulated that he was descended from King David, as were many Britons, although they did not know it.[24]

All of this revelation knowledge was dispensed to the public in Brothers' 1794 book, *A Revealed Knowledge of the Prophecies and Times Containing with Other Great and Remarkable Things Not Revealed to Any Other Person on Earth the Restoration of the Jews to Jerusalem by the Year M.DCC.XCVII, Under Their Revealed Prince and Prophet Wrote by Himself.* When Brothers finished this monumental work, he testified with full assurance as to its accuracy: "[A]fter it was done, the LORD GOD said to me in a vision of the Night—That is the true Age of the World."[25] Despite the purportedly divine origin of the text, its assertions linking the English with ancient Israel never became too prevalent. In fact, Brothers was declared a lunatic and institutionalized.[26]

Victorian England

Although Brothers cannot be credited with having started British-Israelism, it is certain that his thoughts influenced a number of prominent Englishmen.[27] Twenty years after Brothers' death, his British-Israel ideas finally gained some degree of recognition through the publications of Scotsman John Wilson (?–1871).

Wilson, like Brothers, claimed to have discovered the true identity of the English. In 1840, he published a series of lectures as *Our Israelitish Origins.* The book supposedly gave "evidence . . . as to the peopling of England by the race identified with Israel."[28] Unlike Brothers, Wilson believed that nearly all Northern Europeans—including the German, French, Swiss and Scandinavian—were the lost tribes of Israel.[29] Wilson's outlook on history gave birth to a growing social movement that by 1886 had established twenty-seven British-Israel associations in England.

Foremost among the exponents of the British-Israel connection was Edward Hine (1825–1891), who began looking at the issue in 1840 after hearing a speech by Wilson. Hine disagreed strenuously with Wilson, though, by maintaining that only the British were Israelites. He explained his position in *Forty-Seven Identifications of the British Nation* (1871):

> The main point of my differing with the late Mr. John Wilson, author of "Our Israelitish Origin," is, that he sought to identify all the Modern Teutonic Nations as parts of Israel. . . . I maintain that God requires the whole Ten Tribes to be consolidated in an Island Nation.[30]

Hine's popularity grew rapidly. By 1884 he was ready to sail to America and spread his message. When he arrived, he received such a warm welcome that he ended up staying in the U.S. for more than four years. Interestingly, British-Israelism had already been introduced to America. No one knows exactly how or when this occurred, but it is without question that the concepts were firmly established in the U.S. by the late 1870s.

White Religion

Although Illne's ideas were enthusiastically received, Americans tended toward Wilson's view that *all* Anglo-Saxons were of Israelite lineage, hence the term Anglo-Israelism. Both views of the "lost" tribes were embraced, especially in the early 1920s. But because British/Anglo-Israelism had no central structure, "the pattern of its diffusion depended largely on the chance acquaintance individuals made with its teachings."[31] The most notable racist to encounter British-Israelism was William J. Cameron, editor of Henry Ford's *Dearborn Independent* (printed from 1921 to 1927). As Ford's link to the media, Cameron "remained in complete charge of Henry Ford's personal press relations from the mid-1920s until the early 1940s."[32] Many believe Cameron was the actual author of *The International Jew* series.

One might ask how a British/Anglo-Israelite like Cameron could be anti-Jewish since the Jews were supposedly of Israel (the southern kingdom). This dilemma was easily solved: The southern tribes had not kept their bloodlines pure while in captivity. Hence, their subsequent generations were only half-breed Israelites. Cameron made this strong distinction between the House of Judah and the House of Israel in his view of *The Protocols of the Learned Elders of Zion*. He maintained that the Jews talked about in the *Protocols* were of the southern kingdom, while the Anglo-Saxons were the ten "lost" tribes of the northern kingdom.[33]

More precisely, then, the *Dearborn Independent's* articles were specifically about Judah-Jews, or mongrelized Israelites of the House of Judah/Southern Kingdom. This subtle distinction was never brought to the public's attention. Instead, indiscriminate anti-Semitism was allowed to rise in America as British/Anglo-Israelism flourished and evolved in ways that no one could ever have foreseen.

Changing Identities

Christian Identity took at least thirty years (1940s–1970s) to arrive at its present theological state, having gradually metamorphosed from a European belief system into a distinctively American hybrid of myth and hate. The change occurred primarily through the increasing amount of stress placed on the allegedly tainted bloodlines of Jews. American British/Anglo-Israelites initially viewed Jews as fellow kinsmen, descendants of the southern kingdom of Judah. They were acceptable, albeit as lesser members of the Israelite nation due to their ancestors' intermarriage with non-Israelites.

As time progressed, however, Jews were removed further from All-Israel, eventually being stripped entirely of any lineage to the Old Testament Israelites. "Jews" came to be regarded as savage, evil descendants of an Asiatic race of barbarians called Khazars, who lived near the Black Sea and had nothing at all to do with either the northern *or* southern kingdoms of Israel. This evolving view of the Jews from separated brethren to racial impostors was so gradual that only in hindsight can it be seen with any clarity:

Date	Statement	Doctrinal Significance
1840	"In speaking of the chosen people of God . . . we discriminate clearly between . . . Israel, or the house of Isaac, for the ten tribes; and Judah, or the Jews, for the two tribes."[34]	Jews are Israelites of the southern kingdom, and as such, are the chosen people of God along with Anglo-Saxons, who are descended from the northern kingdom of Israel.
1887	"The Jews and the Israelites are upon amicable terms. For ages the Jews have been hated. . . . Among the English they find sympathy, friends, kindness and benevolence."[35]	Jews have retained Israelite blood and are separated brethren who must be brought back into the fold of Israel under the leadership of northern European pure Israelites (Whites/Aryans).
1934	"[P]ure Jews are very few in number. . . . .[Their] originally fine, Israelitish countenance . . . [has been marred by] continuous intermarriage with the Hittites and Canaanites"[36]	There exists very few true Jews whose blood is pure enough to even be considered a legitimate descendent of the southern kingdom's House of Judah.
1944	"[T]rue Judah . . . [is undefiled by racial admixtures and are not] Idumean-Hittites, masquerading as the true seed of Abraham and seeking to expel the direct descendants of Jacob."[37]	Most people who are called Jews are actually descendants of Edomites, Hittites and Idumeans. These false Jews are trying to pass themselves off as real Jews. True Jews are only descendants of those who did not mix with other nations.
1962	"[Jews are] a 'half-breed mongrel line,' to which were added descendants of Hittites, Amorites, and Edomites. . . . [N]o Jews 'were any part of any tribe of Israel.'"[38]	No Jew has a direct link with Israelites. The people who migrated to the southern kingdom area after Judah's captivity were neither pure Israelites nor Israelites with tainted bloodlines.
1989	"[T]he Jews who are not Israelites but basically a mixed race of Turko-Finn, Mongolian tribal people from Khazaria."[39]	Jews are removed entirely out of the Near East and relegated to a mongrelized race of Asian barbarians—i.e., the Khazars.

By stages, then, the Jewish people were disassociated from their Israelite roots until it could finally be said: "The Israelites were not Jews; no Israelite was ever a Jew, and no Jew was ever an Israelite!"[40] Just when it seemed that white supremacists had run out of ways to cast aspersions on the lineage of the Jewish people, another step was taken in an effort to dislodge the Jews even further from Israel. In fact, the final move placed Jews entirely outside humanity and into the family of Satan.

Satan's Seed

As early as the mid-1940s, Identity preachers were building a new doctrine: the Serpent Seed theory. It is a fairly simple and straightforward belief: Jews are the physical descendants of a sexual union between "Mother Eve" and "the serpent" (Gen 3).[41] This serpent is variously identified as either Satan, or a demonic representative of Satan. As such, Jews are literally "Children of the Devil."[42] Most Identity believers claim the serpent was a physical manifestation of Satan himself:

> Satan (the Arch-Angel) sought to make his intrusion into the BEING OF ADAM KIND by cohabitating with Eve and incarnating himself into a physical Seed Line, hence the SEED OF THE SERPENT (Gen 3:15).[43]

In this "two seed" theory, Eve's first two sons, Cain and Abel, were only half brothers, having "THE SAME MOTHER, BUT DIFFERENT FATHERS."[44] Cain was conceived by Eve and Satan, while Abel was conceived by Eve and Adam.[45] In Identity theology, Eve's copulation with "the serpent" (Satan) was "original sin."[46] Aryan Nations founder Richard Butler writes, "[T]here are literal children of Satan in the world today . . . the descendants of Cain, who was the result of Eve's original sin."[47] Hence, the following Christian Identity belief:

> The jew [sic] has not been born who does not have an utterly EVIL nature that is easily detectable in his eye. Nevertheless, identifying these serpents conclusively will no doubt be a difficult task.[48]

Those familiar with the biblical account of Genesis will recall that Cain killed Abel. In the continuing Identity version of biblical history, Cain left the Garden of Eden after murdering his brother and fathered the Jewish race. The *Doctrinal Statement of Beliefs* published by Kingdom Identity Ministries of Harrison, Arkansas, reads: "We believe in an existing being known as the Devil or Satan and called the Serpent (Gen 3:1; Rev 12:9), who has a literal "seed" or posterity on earth (Gen 3:15) commonly called Jews today."[49] This belief is also contained in the Aryan Nations statement of beliefs:

> WE BELIEVE that there are literal children of Satan in the world today. These children are the descendants of Cain, who was a result of Eve's original sin, her physical seduction by Satan. We know that because of this sin, there is a battle and a natural enmity between the children of Satan and the Children of the Most High God. WE BELIEVE there is a battle being fought this day between the children of darkness (today known as Jews) and the children of

light (God), the Aryan race, the true Israel of the Bible.[50]

With whom did Cain produce his Satanic progeny? He allegedly intermarried into pre-Adamic races.[51] These races are usually labeled in Identity circles as either "mud people" or "beasts of the field."[52] Early Identity leader Bertrand Camparet comments: "[T]he Bible makes it unmistakably clear that we are not all descended from Adam and Eve, for there were other races on earth, already old, already numerous, when Adam was created."[53] Camparet also writes: "God had millions of the pre-Adamic Asiatic and African peoples around. . . . If these Negroes and Mongoloids were all that God wanted, he already had them."[54]

Identity leaders predictably teach that non-white races were not "all that God wanted." The Lord desired to have a "special race," and so he created Adam, who "WAS NOT THE FIRST MAN," but rather, a second type of man—the first of a "superior species."[55] He was the first white man, "the father of the White Race only."[56] Racist leader Thom Robb proclaims, "Adam and Eve were not the first people on earth, but they were the first white people."[57]

Immediately after the creation of Adam and Eve, the battle between Satan and God began. The Devil's first attack was his seduction of Eve. His second assault upon God's white children was the murder of Abel. The Adversary struck a third time when Cain began tainting the blood lines of pre-Adamic races, resulting in the creation of Jews. The fourth diabolical act occurred when the Jewish/Satanic race crucified Christ.

Since the 1920s, Satan has again been harassing God's "special" white race. His latest plot is to control the whole world through a fiendish series of moves that are inextricably tied to the Jews, as evidenced by the *Protocols*. To white supremacists, Jews are the most vile of races. Influential Christian Idenity pastor Pete Peters has gone so far as to suggest that the Jews could have been responsible for the 1995 Oklahoma bombing:

> Concerning the Oklahoma bombing . . . [W]hat ethnic group would kill inno-
> cent women and children? One group that comes to mind is Esau-Edom. Most
> have never heard of Edom because the word comes from the Bible. . . . Edom
> has the cursed Canaanite blood in them . . . and are the descendants of Esau.[58]

Esau-Edom is another term for Jews. Identity leader Charles Weisman writes: "It is the Jew's [sic] fate, as bearers of the blood and characteristics of Esau-Edom, to lack the essential attributes needed to create and build a civilization of their own. . . . Jews are repeating the life and events and roles of Esau-Edom."[59]

Although Identity followers regularly attribute murders to their Jewish enemy, the primary means through which Jews are supposedly achieving their goal of satanic world domination is much less violent, but far more effective and offensive: Jews are allegedly behind the modern acceptance of interracial marriage and integration.

Half-breeds: The Ultimate Horror

According to James Combs, Jews are behind every troublemaking movement geared to "further decay Christian-White society." One such movement has been the "racial-integration operation." Combs says there is "simply NO question about Jews being guilty."[60] He speaks for most Christian Identity followers in voicing sheer panic regarding the infiltration of other races into white America:

> There is NO example in history of a White people surviving racial merger; both
> their genetic stock and culture are destroyed. An infusion of colored "blood"
> most definitely does not result in anything other than social decline. . . .
> [S]o-called social scientists can lie to us about the splendor of race-mixing, but
> reality shows it means disaster for White-Christians (as Jews actually know it
> does). . . . Whereas the colored, by the thousands, possess much more poten-
> tial than imagined by unsuspecting Whites, they are not the White races' equal.
> . . . The elite of the colored are not remotely on par with that of the Whites.
> Even the supreme of the colored, the Japanese, are rarely anything but good
> imitators of what our gifted Whites create. Negroes and most orientals other
> than the Japanese cannot even adequately imitate the creations of Whites. Being
> able to utilize some of the Whites' technology as many blacks can do, is one
> thing; inventing comparable machinery or surpassing it is another. And the
> negroes have never shown even a faint hint of competing with our excelling
> whites in technology. Take away Whites and even the admirable Japanese will
> start a cultural and technological decline. . . . The Whites create and maintain;
> the orientals can maintain what the White create; but the blacks—when on their
> own—can neither create nor maintain. **Negroes can only destroy**. . . . [T]he
> ultimate aim [of Jews] is that Christian-Whites will be physically bred with the
> colored. Then, conclusively, we would be obliterated as a people and as the
> only barrier to Jewry's ambitions as _the_ world power.[61]

As Combs reveals, white supremacists feel that the preservation of their race is being threatened by Jews seeking to corrupt God's holy line of righteous, white children with Satan's seed, as well as with the seed of pre-Adamic "beasts":

☐ Jews seek to wipe us out as a race. . . . HOW? By mongrelizing us via
misce- genation [interbreeding] with colored races of the world, especially
the Congoloid blacks . . . "beasts of the earth" of Genesis 1:25.[62]

☐ Jews are the ones promoting multi-racial immigration and multi-culturalism.
. . . It has been the Jews' role as Esau-Edom to destroy God's order of things
by getting the white race to ignore the natural barriers of distinction between
races. The Jew thus runs to the aid and cause of the Negro and colored races
to elevate them while lowering the status of the white man. . . . Jews, who
are mongrels, desire the entire world to be mongrelized, especially the white
race.[63]

Besides social and cultural reasons, there are spiritual motives for avoiding the blood of other races. First is the obvious Satanic bloodline through Cain that white Christians must avoid at all costs. Second, interracial marriage is "one of the greatest of all sins," even when it comes to non-Jewish pre-Adamic races.[64] Third, the white race, which supposedly make up the modern descendants of Israel, is "to be above all people and . . . not to mix with them."[65] Fourth, pre-Adamic races are greatly inferior to Adamic Aryans. Combs, for example, says the "colored are manifestly such culturally-inferior peoples that a unified White people could, if desired, control them."[66]

Even moderate supremacists such as Jack Mohr and Pete Peters hold that races should not intermarry. According to Mohr, Adam was "a very special human being" and propagated a race of an entirely different order than pre-Adamic people.[67] Peters feels the same way: "[I]nterracial marriage destroys. It violates God's natural genetic law of like begetting like."[68]

Race-mixing is clearly verboten[69] to both of these moderates, who are properly termed moderates only because they deny the serpent seed doctrine, maintaining instead the classic British/Anglo-Israel position that Jews are Khazars.[70] The following comment by Peters concerning what he teaches his children about race mixing shows how strongly even the less radical racists feel about mixed marriages: "I teach them also that if they ever did such a thing—never to come around my house with their mate or their half-breed children because they've been traitors to their own sires."[71]

Former KKK Grand Dragon Louis Beam, one of the Identity movement's most flamboyant leaders, agrees: "Racial treason is the greatest crime a member of our race can commit, for from its end results there is no recovery."[72] According to David Tate of the Aryan Nations, "God loves a sinner but hates a race traitor!"[73] White supremacist Roy B. Mansker warns that "judgment will weigh heavy on the race traitors, who are allowing the alien jew [sic] to stay in power."[74] According to Richard Butler, "[O]ur greatest enemies are the race traitors in our ranks."[75]

A final reason for avoiding race mixing is found in a 1991 issue of the *Christian Patriot Crusader*, a newsletter published by Jack Mohr. Apparently, white supremacists believe that non-white males—especially blacks—are in some way "conquering" the white race every time they "defile" a white woman, who is deemed nothing less than exclusively white man's territory:

An endless succession of Jew-produced plays, films and television shows depict Black males making love to White women. . . . This change in national thinking, has made White women open game for Black males. . . . The Negro invasion of the White man's sanctuary is planned as an assault on the seat of his power and the citadel of his greatness—which has been his gene pool. When a Black man overpowers a white woman, he believes that he is exerting a form of superiority over the White race. . . . This is something every White man should remember, when he sees a colored man with a White woman. . . . The Blacks have not yet reached the place where they hang white scalps on their belts, but many are close to it, because Whites have allowed it to happen. Yet the vast majority of White people have become so befuddled by Jewish propaganda, that they believe these breaking down of barriers can go on without it ending in the destruction of their own race. . . . I am firmly convinced, from a study of history and scripture, that if the White man in America settles down to live side by side with the Black, on any terms, it is only a matter of time and not a long time—till he will cease to exist as a White man.[76]

These sentiments are echoed in the words of David Lane, a radical Identity adherent, who was convicted in 1987 for driving the getaway car used by the murderers of Denver talk-show host Alan Berg:

Anyone who supports a multi-racial religion, or state, financially, verbally, or even by passive acceptance, commits Race-treason. Such a person could just as well go out and machine gun White children, because the effect on the Race is the same—in face [sic], the machine gun would be far more humane than the future that faces White children, if we are not successful.[77]

Louis Beam, who is known for his charismatic speaking and writing, tends to express his aversion to race mixing with exceptionally high levels of emotionally evocative language:

At the mailbox I gaze with utter horror upon two young white girls with their black boyfriends. Can I not be spared this? Must I be forced to watch this horrible slow-motion, torture/obliteration of my own people? . . . Father [God], can not this biter [sic] cup be passed to another generation? Have mercy and spare me this![78]

Although hatred toward any race is offensive, America is a free country and its citizens have a constitutional right to hold whatever beliefs they choose. Unfortunately, most white supremacists are not willing to allow others this freedom. The ultimate goal of many white supremacists is nothing less than a complete takeover of America. This final plank in the foundation of Identity is built on their concepts of the "end times."

"Hail Victory!"[79]

Identity believers assert that America is the Promised Land (i.e., "the New Jerusalem") where all Israelites/whites, in fulfillment of biblical prophecy, will be gathered together just prior to Armageddon.[80] Once this is accomplished, God's "Heavenly Reich on earth" will be born.[81] The earth will subsequently be cleansed of all antichrist, Jewish, multi-racial forces in a manner described in the *Turner Diaries*.[82] Well-known Christian Identity preacher William Potter Gale told listeners of his KTTL radio program:

Yes, we're gonna cleanse our land. We're gonna do it with a sword. And we're going to do it with violence. "Oh," they say, "Reverend Gale, you're teaching violence." . . . God said you're going to do it that way, and it's about time somebody is telling you to get violent, whitey. You better start making dossiers, names, addresses, phone numbers, car license numbers, on every d—n Jew rabbi JDL [Jewish Defense League] leader in this land, and you better start doing it now. And know where he is. . . . You get these roadblock locations, where you can set up ambushes, and get it all working now.[83]

Identity pastor Thom Robb wrote similar words in his pamphlet *Interracial*: "Our nation needs to turn back to God's laws and outlaw race-mixing, with the death penalty being the judgment of doing so."[84] Robb voiced an equally chilling message at a 1986 Aryan Nations meeting:

There is a war in America today and there are two camps. One camp is in Washington, D.C., the federal government controlled by the anti-Christ Jews. . . . [T]heir goal is the destruction of our race, our faith and our people. And our goal is the destruction of them. There is no middle ground. We're not going to take any survivors, any prisoners. It's us or them."[85]

This is not to say that all non-whites will be exterminated. A few will be kept alive as slaves: "There will be only two classes—citizens and subjects."[86] Louis Beam feels white victory can be obtained only through ultimately destroying ZOG, the Zionist Occupational Government. "[T]he worst enemy on earth that White people have is ZOG—bar none," Beam says. "The real enemy is in Washington, they have done more harm to the America of my forefathers then [sic] the Russians, North Koreans, or Chinese will probably ever do."[87]

It must be remembered that white supremacists are not seeking to establish an Aryan republic out of mere free-floating prejudice. They actually believe it is their God-ordained destiny to create a white utopia, as Richard Butler makes clear in his tract *Who, What, Why, When, Where: Aryan Nations*:

WE BELIEVE that there is a day of reckoning. The usurper will be thrown out by the terrible might of Yahweh's people [God's White race] as they return to their roots and their special destiny. We know there is soon to be a day of judgment and a day when Christ's Kingdom (Government) will be established on earth as it is in heaven. [T]he saints of the Most High shall take the kingdom and possess the kingdom forever, even for ever and ever. And the kingdom and dominion and greatness of the kingdom under the whole heaven shall be given to the people of the saints of the Most High, whose kingdom is an everlasting kingdom, and all dominions shall serve and obey Him." (Daniel 2:44; 7:18; 7:27)[88]

"We're a dispossessed race now," Butler says. "If the white race is to fulfill its divine, destined purpose under scripture as God's word, it must have its own territorial imperative—a homeland of, by and for its own kind."[89] Butler has also stated, "Our mission is to conquer the earth and have dominion over it."[90]

In an open letter that appeared in the Aryan Nations publication *Calling Our Nation*, "Dale" Chesson imparted a word of encouragement to fellow Aryans that perfectly illustrates the lengths to which Identity believers are willing to go in order to recapture America :

The battles are many, large and small, but for us only VICTORY is acceptable, and VICTORY WILL BE OURS!! . . . We must remember that when one of OURS gives his life for that which we are fighting, he is not a terrorist, nor a criminal, but a warrior of the highest rank, an ARYAN WARRIOR!![91]

Identity literature clearly states that an actual war is being waged between Aryans and ZOG. White supremacists who have been imprisoned for murdering public officials and racial minorities are regularly referred to as POWs of ZOG.[92] A 1989 Aryan Nations publication actually described Robert Matthews and members of the Order as "Aryan Heroes," whose murderous exploits placed them in line after "Heroes of the Confederate States" and "Heroes of the Third Reich."[93] This attitude has given birth to a new battle cry that is repeated nationwide at KKK rallies and Identity gatherings: rahowa—RAcial HOly WAr.

A short-term goal of Identity adherents is "to see the creation of a national state for the White man, an Aryan Republic within the borders of the present occupied country [America]."[94] The chosen place of this mini-republic is the Pacific Northwest, where many white supremacists organizations (e.g., the Aryan Nations) are already situated. It is from this locale that racists plan to fight the last great battle on "the Day of the Lord." Richard Butler promises, "As His divine race, we have been commissioned to fulfill His divine purpose and plans—the restitution of all things."[95]

The hopes and dreams of all Identity believers were articulated as far back as 1980 in a small article entitled "Why Oppose the Jews." The summary statement leaves no doubt as to what white supremacists want: "Think of an America in the possession of the world's PREMIER race—the White, Aryan peoples."[96]

Identity and Militias

The conspiratorial theories upon which the patriot/militia movement is built fit very nicely into the theological framework of the Identity faith:

Every purported conspiracy and cabal, whether of international bankers, Trilateralists or the UN, can be brought within Identity's "great conspiracy"— Satan's plot to take over the world and deprive "Aryans" of their birthright, a plot that Identity believes began in the Garden of Eden and will end only at Armageddon. Plot can be nested in plot, in an ascending pyramid of conspiracies that ends with the devil himself.[97]

By propagating and encouraging such conspiracy theories within the patriot/militia movement, Identity adherents have stirred up hatred for the government, which they hope will galvanize discontented masses into a force able to topple the evil Jewish regime in power. A number of white supremacists have already worked their way in among patriots, and are influencing the thoughts and beliefs of non-racist patriots including mainstream Christians. In doing so, white supremacists have created an elaborate maze of racists and non-racists who share a similar conspiratorial worldview.[98] This issue will be explored in the next chapter.

13

Oh, What a Tangled Web

We do not believe in hatred. We do not believe in racism. If you will look over very, very carefully all the things that you have heard me say in the media and some of the others have said in the media, we have said nothing about hate. We have said nothing about racism. We have not been anti-Semitic.
Ken Adams
Michigan Militia[1]

For many years rural America has been home to militia-like organizations commonly called paramilitary units. These private armies have classically hated the government for catering politically to the nation's minorities, who have allegedly displaced whites from their proper place as this country's rightful "masters." The Silver Shirts, for instance, founded in 1933 by William Pelley, was modeled after Hitler's Brown Shirts. Pelley's force of 15,000 racists "trained openly for armed confrontation. Their field marshal Roy Zachary gained national renown in 1938 by announcing that if no one else was prepared to assassinate President Roosevelt, he'd do it himself."[2]

Next on the anti-government scene was Father Coughlin's Christian Front. In 1938, Couglin told his nationwide radio audience that the Jews, whom he labeled communists, had caused the Russian and Spanish revolutions. "He exhorted his listeners to arm, train, and organize a Christian Front against the Red Front [Jewish communists].[3] Coughlin's followers heeded his call with frightening results:

> This Christian Front was to be paramilitary, made up of platoons that would constitute a national militia. . . . The first Christian Front units assembled clandestinely in New York City. . . . [T]he next year they spread to Boston, Philadelphia, Cleveland, and other major cities in the East and Midwest. They engaged in street violence from the start, their members attacking Jewish-owned businesses and Jews in the streets. And Coughlin warned that that was only the beginning. . . . Informants reported that the Front was obtaining ammunition

from Fort Dix and other Army bases, where it was said to have the sympathy of senior military officers. It maintained a clandestine Revolutionary Council to coordinate military training and plan possible attacks. . . . Some [members] boasted about gun-running activities. One said, "Jew hunting is going to be pretty good soon, and we are practicing." Another predicted "the boys" would "dynamite Detroit, Pittsburgh, Chicago—paralyze transportation and isolate whole sections of the country. . . . A bloodbath is the only way out."[4]

The 1960s saw a resurgence of America's oldest and most successful homegrown terrorist organization—the Ku Klux Klan, which first emerged in the South between 1866 and 1868. Although the KKK was virtually destroyed as a movement when President Ulysses S. Grant oversaw the passage of the Ku-Klux Klan Act of 1871, it resurfaced with immense popularity in the 1920s. During that era, membership rose to between 1.5 million and 6 million.[5]

By the 1930s, the Klan lost most of its members due to disinterest and a rising preoccupation with the threat of war in Europe. The Klan remained an insignificant force until the 1960s, a violent decade that saw KKK membership double to 20,000 in response to President Kennedy's commitment to bringing racial equality to all Americans. The civil rights movement was subsequently faced with "the greatest surge of violent backlash since the Klan's formation after the Civil War."[6]

In many ways, the patriot/militia movement is related to these earlier groups in that today's anti-government subculture is a cumulative response to the unwanted social reforms that have occurred over the last fifty years. But to go back only as far as the 1960's cultural revolution, or the depression era, is to miss the long-standing bitterness that has been simmering for more than 100 years within the racist community.

Old Rivals

A deep-seated grudge has been held by white supremacists against the federal government ever since the Civil War. The Land of Dixie has never forgotten its humiliating defeat, as the following quotation from a 1989 issue of the neo-Nazi/Christian Identity publication, *Calling Our Nation* clearly shows:

> [T]here can be little doubt that the loser of the American 'Civil War' was the entire White Aryan Race. . . . [E]verything that has combined to strip the sovereignty of the White Aryan male centers upon the lying preachers' and politicians' destruction of the White Aryan National State in America during the period of 1861–1868.[7]

This is one reason why the Confederate flag continues to be flown in the South. It presents a subtle, yet heartfelt declaration: Our army was defeated, but our spirit was not broken. Northerners are still disdainfully referred to as Yankees by many Southerners, especially racists. Christian Identity leader James Combs makes just such a comment in a reference to blacks receiving equal employment opportunities:

> More than one White civic leader, when Federally enforced integration threat-

ened, felt confident the whole thing would "blow over." . . . [L]et them have some of our jobs and then sit back and watch the disaster. It will be so bad that even the Yankees will laugh integration out of existence.[8]

I am not saying that *all* Southerners who fly the Confederate flag, or who feel resentment over the Civil War, are racists. Many of today's Southerners who admire the Confederate forces of the 1860s are not racially prejudiced at all. Nor do they favor slavery or the subjection of any race of people. To these non-racist "rebels," bitterness toward Yankees has much more to do with simple irritation over the way the federal government handled the conflict between the states.

Having said this, it must be noted that since the post–Civil War reconstruction period, white supremacists—many of whom have Confederate sympathies—have consistently sought to disrupt integration policies. Dealing a fatal blow to the entire federal regime had been only a racist dream until the 1970s, when anti-government sentiment throughout the nation increased, especially in the farm belt. Racists saw an opportunity to drive a wedge between the Feds and a large segment of U.S. citizenry.

The Posse Comitatus, KKK, Aryan Nations and other Christian Identity–affiliated organizations blanketed America's heartland with representatives who convinced many desperate farmers that their social/economic distress was being caused by a foreign enemy who had taken over the government: Jews. Consider the following quotation from *The American Farmer: 20th Century Slave* by Identity leader James Wickstrom:

> The Jew-run banks and federal loan agencies are working hand-in-hand foreclosing on thousands of farms right now in America. They are in essence, nationalizing farms for the jews [sic], as the farmer becomes a tenant slave on the land he once owned. . . . The farmers must prepare to defend their families and land with their lives, or surrender it all.[9]

The solution white supremacists gave to their fellow Americans belied a hidden agenda: "The farmer is being backed into a wall, and he's beginning to believe there has to be an answer for all of this. *The answer is revolution*" [emphasis added].[10] This tactic worked for several years, bringing many persons with racist leanings into the Identity/anti-Semitic fold. The most advantageous time for recruitment, however, was yet to come.

From Racism to Patriotism

Long before the patriot movement, white supremacists called themselves "patriots." During the early 1980s, KKK Grand Wizard Don Black wrote a letter to "White Patriots" asking that donations be sent to David Duke's "Patriot Press."[11] An Aryan Nations newsletter circa 1982 lists the following racists as Christian "patriots":[12]

☐ *Richard Butler*, Aryan Nations founder.

☐ *Dan Gayman*, pastor of the Identity movement's Church of Israel.

❏ *Bob Miles*, a longtime Klansman and convicted felon.

In the mid-1980s, a group of white supremacists calling themselves the Arizona Patriots plotted to bomb several targets, including federal buildings in Phoenix and Los Angeles. They also hoped to "stage a mortar and machine-gun attack on IRS workers in Ogden, Utah." [13] The plan was to be financed by the cash seized from an armored car en route from casinos in Laughlin, Nevada. Fortunately, their plan was foiled by the FBI. [14]

As the 1980s progressed into the 1990s, these early "patriots" noticed that many Americans, although unaffected by the farm crisis, were beginning to also feel anger toward the government. Their unrest was due in part to frustration over federal budget battles, the national debt, unemployment, crime and unpopular gun control legislation. White supremacists realized that before them lay a vast untapped source of warriors for their long-desired overthrow of the federal government: discontented non-racists.

As previous chapters have shown, the goal of the white supremacy movement is to bring down the U.S. government so an Aryan nation can be established. Until the early 1990s, racists had neither the strength, nor the funds, to seriously destabilize the federal administration. As racist Michael Hanson stated in 1982, "we are both OUTNUMBERED AND OUTGUNNED." [15] Suddenly, however, a number of issues had arisen that could be used to swell anti-government ranks and bring about Armageddon. The plan was simple: Use millions of discontented non-racists to form a unified revolt.

To implement this plan, white supremacists joined and/or formed "patriot" groups, stirred up anti-government sentiments with hate rhetoric, spread conspiracy theories, and commited a few terrorist acts, which have in turn been blamed on the government (e. g., the Oklahoma bombing). By perpetuating an ever-maddening circle of obsessive distrust of the government, the only thing left to do was patiently wait for America to crumble from within. The strategy has only been helped by the Weaver and Waco tragedies. [16] Montana Human Rights Network president Ken Toole comments:

[W]ith the Brady Bill it was like someone poured jet fuel on the movement. Overnight we saw all this militia stuff bleed right out of the white supremacists who had been pushing the idea for years and engulf entire communities. [17]

Thus was born today's patriot/militia movement. Of course, Christian identity adherents and other racists realized that in order to stir up anti-government hate and propagate their conspiracy theories, they could not be completely honest. Any talk of a Jewish global takeover as outlined in the *Protocols* would instantly turn away non-racists, especially Judeo-Christians, who steadfastly believe that the Jewish people are descendants of Old Testament Israelites. A change of language was needed.

Consequently, Jews and blacks were relegated to a secondary "enemy" category (at least publicly) and supplanted by a new target: the federal government. White supremacists currently couch their beliefs in more acceptable terms, hiding their bigotry to "present a sanitized image to the pubic and attract new recruits." [18] The term "Jewish bankers" has been replaced with less inflammatory terms such as "International bankers" or simply "Internationalists."

A much more radical shift in identifying "the enemy" has sometimes been made if sentiments of a particular audience calls for it. As one observer says, "If you're in Eastern Idaho you're not going to see the Jewish leaders [targeted] . . . but you will see environmentalists." [19] But the ultimate scapegoats are still Jews, and they continue to be Jews, whether non-racists want to acknowledge it or not.

Wolves in Sheep's Clothing
White supremacists began changing their public image in 1986, just after members of Robert Matthews' Order were convicted for their 1983–1984 deadly crime spree. Racists started calling themselves "racialists." White supremacists became white "separatists." Cross burnings were referred to as cross "lightings." Chuck Tate, whose son David was convicted of murdering a police officer after joining the Order, admitted during a 1986 interview with the *Toronto Sun* that he and other neo-Nazis were "becoming more sophisticated about these things. . . . We're learning how to play the game." [20] A 1995 computer mail message sent to all militia's by the Texas Militia Correspondence Committee, details this strategy exactly:

> [I]t is extremely important now to reach out to the general community for their support. Get our story out before our adversaries can get theirs out. Look like respectable businessmen. Emphasize our primary purpose: to enforce the law, especially the Constitution, and that means to expose criminal wrongdoing in government and abuses of power. Forget all the rhetoric about foreign troops, New World Order, and all the rest of the stuff that sounds bizarre to ordinary Americans. Stick to the basics, and hammer it over and over: Corruption and Abuse. [21]

Testimony given by Missouri State Highway Patrol Superintendent, Fred Mills, before a 1995 Senate subcommittee, reveals that the Texas Militia's advice is being followed:

> We have had militias in Arizona . . . [as far back as] 1971, and we have seen some dramatic changes in their basic philosophies and how they basically approach things. There has been sort of the white supremacist, the racist kind of attitude in existence with many of the militia members for a long period of time. . . . And they use that in some ways to recruit individuals, but what we have noticed recently is that they have changed sort of their tune and they have been looking at what they perceive to be the overreaching of Government. . . . They have used the examples of Ruby Ridge and Waco and the Brady bill as examples of where Government is going beyond what it should be doing, and thus recruiting in perhaps more members. Now, the other members don't know

the extremist views of the fanatics themselves, so I have seen sort of a
transitioning. . . . [T]here are still the supremacist, the racist attitudes of some,
and now they are using the Government as excuses themselves.[22]

According to Bruce Hoffman—a former terrorism expert at the RAND Corporation think tank in Santa Monica, who is now based at St. Andrews University in
Scotland—the 1980s definitely saw an evolution of racist/anti-Semitic groups and
individuals:

> They were no longer just racists, anti-Semites and traditional hate groups.
> . . . They also began to bring in militant tax resisters, anti-abortion advocates,
> the anti-gun control movement, opponents of government intervention, or even
> any government above the county level. They also plugged into communities
> with particular problems, such as the Farm Belt during its economic plight.
> Since the 1980s, these radical right-wing movements have been constantly
> reinventing themselves to appeal to new and more diverse constituencies.[23]

Several patriot organizations are nothing more than fronts for white supremacists
seeking to broaden their support base and indoctrinate non-racists. Fred Mills
feels the militias are vehicles for racists "to expound their hatred and acts of
violence. . . . [M]any of them see this as an opportunity . . . to do what they want
to do."[24] The main character in *The Turner Diaries* exactly expresses what racists
have discovered: "We must convince a substantial portion of the American people
that what we are doing is both necessary and proper."[25]

Using patriotic fronts is an old tactic of extremists. Whenever Father Coughlin's
group organized in a new place, recruits would be instructed to "train and arm
under the guise of sporting or rifle clubs."[26] Today's racists have been exceptionally
effective in hiding their identity from non-racist government-haters. As of late
1995, it was estimated that forty-five militias in twenty-two states had ties to white
supremacists.[27]

Montana Senator Max Baucas commented in 1995 that since the militias have
formed in his state, there have been "anti-Semitic incidents all over." One of
Baucas's constituents informed him of some disturbing events taking place in
Ravalli County:[28]

> You see Freemen with guns in the post office, grocery store and gas stations.
> If it gets to any one of them that a person doesn't like the Freemen, they will
> call or confront a person face to face. They tell people that we are all going to
> "die like the Jews."[29]

Ted Arrington, of the political science department at University of North Carolina,
Charlotte, has studied literature from patriot organizations in his area and contends
that the movement "is made up almost entirely of alienated Whites who yearn for
their lost dominance."[30] Although this may be a slight overstatement, it cannot be
denied that many patriot/militia groups are run, supported or influenced by white
racists.

At the same time, it must be remembered that not every patriot/militia group is racist. The New Hampshire's Hillsborough County Dragoons militia "includes blacks, Latinos and Asians."[31] There is also California's Placer County Militia. Its organizer Joy Andrews says she is "personally vigilant" against racist propaganda:

> We're committed to working within the framework of the Constitution. Anyone who wants to hand out printed material at our meetings has to run it by me first. I've confiscated stuff that was racist or hate-based. That's not what we're about.[32]

Noah Chandler, a research assistant at the Atlanta-based Center for Democratic Renewal, finds that "a majority of people who join militia groups are 'innocent' recruits who feel our government is unresponsive to their concerns." He sees the militia movement as "a symptom of people who are disenfranchised and feel alienated from our quickly changing and fast-paced world."[33]

Kenneth S. Stern, of the American Jewish Committee, also admits that "racism and/or anti-Semitism is not the main organizing principle of the militias."[34] Stern is worried, though, about the strong undercurrent of racism within the patriot movement. A July 1995 report issued by the Montana Advisory Committee to the U.S. Commission on Civil Rights documented more than twenty white supremacist and hate groups in that state. The study also found that these groups focused their recruiting efforts "on economically troubled communities where people are looking for someone to blame."[35]

This is a repeat of what happened in the mid-1980s. The unseen foes are still Jews, but they have resurfaced under an amorphous, communistic New World Order, which is under the control of "international bankers." The racist influence on patriots becomes blatantly clear when comparing supremacist beliefs with patriot movement conspiracy theories. Patriots are obsessed with defeating the dreaded New World Order, not realizing they have been deceived into fighting the white supremacist's battle against the Jew.

The Jew World Order[36]

Non-racist patriots have no idea that the New World Order stories they are believing come directly from anti-Semitic conspiracy theories based on books such as the *Protocols* (see chapter seven). Militia leader Dean Compton, leader of the National Alliance of Christian Militia, declares that the New World Order promoters are simply "the rich men of the earth" and that they are "not Jews."[37] But as we have seen, the notion of an elite group of "rich men" controlling world affairs comes directly from racists who hold that "today the system of government we live under is Jewish."[38] As the Aryan Nations declares, "ZOG is for one-world government!"[39]

Compton and other non-racists may believe the conspirators are not Jews, but those who are responsible for starting NWO conspiracy theories feel otherwise. In fact, white supremacists see Compton and other non-racist patriots as part of "the Jew problem" that must eventually be solved. According to the *National*

Christian News, an Identity publication, all true patriots should not "let the phony 'Patriot' organizations tell you, 'See, the conspiracy is not Jewish!' "[40]

Although racists do not make their views known to the general patriot community, they are completely up-front with each other. To white supremacists, the federal government consists of "traitorous parasites without number in Wash-ington, D.C., who, under the thumb of world jewry [sic] are paid to pass more and more restrictive laws."[41]

These "parasites" are the same individuals being denounced as promoters of the communist New World Order. Christian Identity Pastor Pete Peters reveals the Jewish threat in a newsletter entitled *White Crime in America: Take Notice White Man*:

> Today, we do not call our false god "Baal" we call it "the government," "Uncle Sam," "the System," "The Establishment," or "Big Brother." The more recent title has been "The New World Order."[42]

Patriots are clearly falling into a covert campaign by white supremacists to turn American citizens against the government.[43] Even the Waco siege fits into this "Jew World Order" conspiracy. A message at the David Koresh Foundation site on the Internet asserts that "the raid on the Branch Davidian compound in Waco was an attempt to silence a prominent critic of 'the Jewish plan for a One World Government, and the Jewish plan for human Enslavement.' " The document says the raid was initiated by "Janet Reno, a Jew."[44]

Patriots not only borrow racist conspiracy plots, but also use terms and expressions strikingly similar to those used by white supremacists. Some patriot articles and speeches are little more than the reworked text of hate-filled racist ramblings. The word "Jew" is simply left out of the patriot literature. It is highly doubtful that such parallels, which involve unique ideas and phrases, could have evolved in complete independence of each other, as the following comparison chart shows:

White Supremacists	Patriots
"We are a conquered and occupied nation; conquered and occupied by the Jews."[45]	"America has steadily declined from the most powerful nation on earth to a corrupt, occupied nation with socialist leaders."[46]
"[W]e are 'being merged in with the USSR, so that the USSA and USSR shall be one' . . . into anti-Christ, anti-White Jewish Baal slavery."[47]	"George Orwell's 1984 has arrived in the USSA. . . . Welcome to the USSA—a branch of the New World Order."[48]
"This is an all-out war, and jews [sic] know it. They will stop at nothing in this war, and we must be alert at all times."[49]	"We are at war, right now, make no mistake about it. God bless us all. Death to the New World Order."[50]

White Supremacists	Patriots
"The most interesting development is that the Human Relations Councils have also been given emergency police powers, and they are 'deputizing' large numbers of Blacks from the welfare rolls, the way they did for the Gun Raids. . . . White reaction to the renewed activities of the Human Relations Councils and their gangs of 'deputies' will make recruiting easier for us."[51]	"An anonymous observer quoted in *Leading Edge* magazine reported that there were training maneuvers taking place near Sacramento, California . . . . [This] was part of a scheme to transport street gangs such as the Bloods, Crips, and Guardian Angels to different urban areas and to use them as storm troopers to raid private houses and to conduct searches for the confiscation of guns."[52]
"[T]he Jews constantly whine . . . over THEIR media, . . . THEIR films, magazines and book publishing houses, and THEIR (controlled) public schools."[53]	"[T]he Liberal Eastern Establishment . . . controls the reigns of power in America . . . the media, the entertainment industry, and the educational system."[54]
"ZOG is not asleep. . . . The Evil Empire will strike. . . . [I]t is an alien beast that rules this country and its sheeplike people."[55]	"What is the true motive and nature of the beast? . . . [M]any of them are very alien to what we would consider human"[56]
"Dr. [William] Pierce discusses the sellout of America's economic interests by the "New World Order" conspirators who control both political parties. . . . [T]he Israel Lobby is so great . . . [t]hey take our money . . . and, since both political parties are in their pocket, the American people don't have any choice."[57]	"That both parties [Republicans and Democrats] are controlled by the same Liberal Eastern Establishment whose goal is world government under the New World Order may be less obvious, but nevertheless is the present reality. . . . [T]he Establishment owns and controls . . . politicians in America."[58]

William Pierce, author of *The Turner Diaries*, matter of factly states that "if accuracy were the primary consideration," the coming one-world government "might be given the name Jew World Order instead of the one by which it is commonly known." Pierce believes that in order to achieve White victory, "[t]he only feasible strategy for us is to develop our own media of mass communication and then use those media to make everyone painfully aware of the true meaning of the New World Order."[59]

Communism is the ultimate enemy of patriots, which is again convenient for white supremacists, who believe "communism is Jewish."[60] Anti-Semite Jack Mohr, asserts "Communism was and is Jewish."[61] A 1993 Christian Identity newspaper notes:

> We let the JEWS con us into destroying the GOOD governments God gives us, like we did in World War Two by fighting Hitler instead of becoming his ally and helping him destroy JEWISH Communism.[62]

In the announcement for his 1992 "Rocky Mountain Rendezvous," Identity pastor Pete Peters wrote: "New information is constantly surfacing such as the Weaver incident being a New World Order operation. . . . Don't think you'll be bypassed in a Communist style purge of targeted Christian dissents [sic] that won't fit into a proposed New World Socialist Order."[63] Patriot publisher Clayton Douglas gives some advice for those who are critical of the New World Order threat: "Know Someone Who Doesn't Believe in Conspiracies? Send them a copy of the *Protocols of the Elders of Zion*. The blueprint used for the New World Order."[64]

Because white supremacist are anti-communists, they can easily infiltrate patriot meetings. At any gathering of patriots, a sizable percentage of attendees may be racists. Non-racist patriots, of course, may have no idea that some of their fellow communist-haters are thinking of Jews when shouting "Kill the Communists!" There is simply no way to tell who is, and who is not, a racist unless every person is asked if they believe the Jews are the communists.[65] This level of screening occurs nowhere in the patriot movement. Consequently, white racists have been able to mix with non-racists and spread conspiracy theories about the Jew/New World Order. The average patriot ends up believing anti-Semitic legends dressed up as anti-communist rhetoric.

In response to charges of racism in the patriot movement, militia members/ leaders have tried to downplay the significance of white supremacists in their ranks. Patriots will recognize only that there may be a few "fringe elements" trying to ride militia "coattails" for attention, or claim the movement as a whole is "in no way connected to racism."[66] But a brief look at the facts indicates that those introducing racist views to mainstream participants are some of the movement's most influential leaders.

John Trochmann: Militia of Montana (MOM)

John Trochmann's Militia of Montana is based in the small town of Noxon. He co-founded the organization with his brother David and nephew Randy. Trochmann's ties to the white supremacist community are well established and date back as far as 1990, the year he spoke at Richard Butler's Aryan Nations Congress.[67]

During an April 1995 interview with the *Missoulian*, Trochmann admitted that he had gone to the "Whites Only" Aryan Nations compound only twice.[68] In May 1995, Trochmann told reporter Lawrence Cohler of *New York Jewish Week* that he "went to the Aryan nations compound four or five times."[69]

Trochmann's racists connections began to surface publicly shortly after the 1992 Randy Weaver shooting, when he established a support group for Weaver called United Citizens for Justice (UCJ). The group's co-founders were Louis Beam, former Ku Klux Klan leader, and Chris Temple, a racist who regularly writes for *Jubilee*, an influential Identity publication that features a column by Beam.[70]

Trochmann has often tried to distance himself from racism. For example, when

Senator Dianne Feinstein asked Trochmann in June of 1995 about his white supremacist ties, he reacted with indignation. "I am sick and tired of these questions constantly," he bristled. "We have gone over it and over it and over it, and if you want to blame somebody about it, take a look at the press. . . . I already addressed that."[71]

Although MOM's leader claims virtually no link to the Aryan Nations, Aryan Nations founder Richard Butler tells a different story. In a press release, Butler adamantly maintained that Trochmann visited his compound many times. His prepared statement was often personally directed at Trochmann: "John, you even helped us write out a set of rules for our code of conduct on church property."[72] Butler is referring here to the "Aryan Nations Platform for the Aryan National State," which reads (in part):

Article I: Only Aryans (White Race) are allowed citizenship of the nation, and only citizens can: (1) vote and own property within the nation's borders. (2) conduct business, possess (keep) and bear arms. (3) hold office in government, industry or society. (4) comprise military or law enforcement personnel.

Article II: Non-citizens can live in the Republic but only under the custodianship of a citizen.

Article III: All hybrids called Jews are to be repatriated from the Republic's territory, all their wealth redistributed to restore our people.

Article IX: Abolish the current materialistic Jew-"Law Merchant" judicial system and all the "laws of men" and establish immediate return to our own God-ordained, racially inherent Anglo-Saxon, Germanic Common Law order.[73]

Butler explained his outrage in a rare interview: "[Trochmann] came over here quite often. He made six or seven trips for Bible study. . . . Why lie about the number of times here?"[74] The neo-Nazi leader is only one of many white supremacists to whom Trochmann is linked. Consider Richard Snell, who on the day of the Oklahoma bombing was executed for murdering a black police officer and a Jewish businessman. A MOM newsletter published one month prior to Snell's execution warned that his death would take place "unless we act now!!!"[75]

Before the Oklahoma bombing focused the world's critical eyes on MOM, Trochmann was quite open about his Christian Identity views. In January 1995 he told *Esquire* reporter Daniel Voll about how he wanted to yoke his beliefs to the militias:

I am following God's law. . . . Blacks, Jews, are welcome. But when America is the new Israel, they'll need to go back where they came from. . . . It's just nature's law—kind should go unto kind.[76]

In July 1995, Trochmann's ties to the white supremacist movement again surfaced when he launched a counterintelligence campaign using a "SALUTE" report form. This informational document lists the data that is to be obtained by militia members on selectively targeted "opponent" or "enemy" groups (i.e., size, activity, location, unit, time and equipment). The weekend militiamen got their forms.

Similar SALUTE reports were distributed to Aryan Nations officers in Idaho. "Recipients were instructed to gather intelligence on the locations and employees of the 'enemy': government agencies, civil rights groups and the media." [77]

Trochmann declared his "sovereignty" on January 26, 1992 via an affidavit filed at the Sanders County Courthouse in Montana. In it he declares himself a "free white Christian man" who believes in the "organic Constitution of the United States. I am not now, nor have I ever been a citizen of the United States or a resident of its subordinate territories, or a property appertaining thereto, in either a legal or factual sense." [78]

Mike Richter, a Christian Identity neighbor of Trochmann's, makes an ominous prediction about his friend: "John will be in his glory when they are attacked one of these times. He wants to be a martyr." [79]

Louis Beam: Charismatic Racist

Some observers of the racist right believe that Louis Beam is one of the most dangerous individuals in the white supremacist movement. [80] He has been a leader in the Klan as well as the Aryan Nations for many years, and continues to function as an Aryan Nations ambassador. It is widely believed that Beam will succeed the aging Richard Butler as head of the Aryan Nations.

One of Beam's most significant contributions to the white supremacist movement was his establishment of the Aryan Nations computer system, along with its "assassination point system" that young racists can pursue in their desire to be an Aryan warrior. [81] The rated points are awarded to individuals who murder politicians, law enforcement personnel, civil rights leaders, persons of a minority race, and journalists—the more important the victim, the higher the point score. [82]

Beam's influence on the militias involves the fundamental structure of the entire movement. Patriots employ what Beam calls "leaderless resistance," which is defined as numerous independent cells that operate "independently of each other, and never report to a central headquarters or a single leader for direction or instruction." [83] Beam's tactic assures the existence of a broad-based resistance that can function regardless of what measures are brought against it. Even if various members of the movement are captured or killed, the consequences are minor because "individuals and groups operate independently of each other." [84]

It is widely accepted by knowledgable observers of the patriot movement that there exists a direct link between Beam's leaderless resistance and the militia structure. [85] This link can be traced back to a four-page report included in *Special Report on the Meeting of the Christian Men Held in Estes Park, Colorado, October 23, 24, 25, 1992: Concerning the Killing of Vickie and Samuel Weaver by the United States Government*. The thirty-page booklet published by Pete Peters described the outcome of the 1992 Rocky Mountain Rendezvous that gave birth to the modern militia movement (see chapter two). Jonathan Mozzochi, executive director of the Coalition for Human Dignity in Oregon, observes that the patriot movement has perfectly mirrored Beam's instructions. Militias have "no national structure, no central command and no central leadership, either recognized from within the movement or without."[86]

According to Beam, leaderless resistance is preferable to any other form of organized rebellion for several reasons. First, it prevents effective infiltration by enemies. As the Florida State Militia's Handbook reads: "[Y]ou still have have your inner circle, and this the FBI, ATF, or other federal scumbags cannot penetrate, if you keep up your guard."[87] Second, it reduces the chance that resistance plans will be foiled. Beam's article assures readers that victory can indeed be achieved through such a tactic:

> Since the entire purpose of Leaderless Resistance is to defeat state tyranny (at least insofar as this essay is concerned), all members of phantom cells or individuals will tend to react to objective events in the same way through usual tactics of resistance. . . . [N]ewspapers, leaflets, computers, etc. . . . keep each person informed of events, allowing for a planned response that will take many variations. No one need issue an order to anyone. Those idealists truly committed to the cause of freedom will act when they feel the time is ripe, or will take their cue from others who precede them. . . . It goes almost without saying that Leaderless Resistance leads to very small or even one man cells of resistance. . . . From the point of view of tyrants and would-be potentates in the federal bureaucracy and police agencies, nothing is more desirable than that those who oppose them be UNIFIED in their command structure. . . . [T]he last thing Federal snoops would have, if they had any choice in the matter, is a thousand different small phantom cells opposing them. It is easy to see why. Such a situation is an intelligence nightmare for a Government intent upon knowing everything they possibly can about those who oppose them. . . . Leaderless Resistance presents no single opportunity for the Federals to destroy a significant portion of the Resistance.

Beam's idea can be found in a number of militia publications and BBS postings. For example, a direct quote from Beam's article in Pete Peters' Rocky Mountain Rendezvous booklet was found on the CyberspaceMinuteman BBS.[88] Another file placed in the Patriot Archives on the Internet makes a clear reference to Beam's organizational structure:

> Militias must avoid allowing any persons to become indispensable leaders, so that the Militia Movement could be suppressed by attacking its leaders. The Militia must be, to the extent possible, "leaderless" and spontaneous.[89]

It is this strategy that has allowed the patriot movement, especially the militias, to wash their hands of the Oklahoma City bombing. Although the ideologies, attitudes and beliefs rampant throughout the movement may have led to the blast, everyone can confidently, and truthfully, say: "We had nothing to do with the bombing."

Pete Peters: Christian Identity Pastor

Christian Identity preacher Pete Peters, who pastors the LaPorte, Colorado Church of Christ, is clearly the most accepted Identity figure in the patriot community. According to the racist publication *Destiny Digest*, Pastor Peters "is without doubt, America's most dynamic speaker on Kingdom Identity Covenant truth."[90] Although his ties to the patriot movement are without question, for some reason he has tried to discredit reports that he is somehow connected to the militia movement.

For example, Peters criticized a John Birch Society article accusing him and other racists of "making the rounds at militia gatherings, trying to recruit new followers and sowing their gospel of hate." The stinging criticism went on to state, "These and other dangerous demagogues are adept at grabbing the spotlight and encouraging violent confrontations and provocations."[91] Peters made an interesting response to this charge in a 1995 issue of his *Scriptures for America Newsletter*:

> Now I haven't got the slightest idea where they came up with this information seeing that I'm not aware of ever having attended one militia gathering let alone making the rounds as they report nor am I aware of being virulently racist and violent. [92]

In actuality, it was during Peters' 1992 Rocky Mountain Rendezvous that talk of forming militias was initially voiced. Additionally, Peters has indeed spoken at various patriot/militia meetings. One such event was a U.N. flag-burning ceremony held by patriots in Reserve, New Mexico on October 24, 1994.[93] Peters himself announced this appearance in a 1994 issue of his own *Scriptures for America Newsletter*. The short message about the "UNITED NATIONS DAY" celebration ended with a suggestion: "Next year on U.N. Day plan a flag burning in your county."[94] A 1995 newsletter put out by Peters also supports the contention of the Birchers. Under the heading "Tape Ministry Update," Peters advertises tape number 656:

> PASTOR PETERS SPEAKS AT A PATRIOT MEETING—Covers and includes everything from the unknown chain of cause and effect to the Bible revealed conspiracy of conspiracies to the age old symbiotic relationship to Identity itself.[95]

Peters' close connection to the militias was also revealed in the September 1994 issue of the *Ohio Kleagle*, a racist newsletter published by Ohio membership of the Knights of the Ku Klux Klan. The Internet version of this issue lists the address of Pete Peters and his Scriptures for America ministry followed by the following exhortation: "Write to this pastor to get a catalogue of 5,000 different sermons on tape. Topics include the Israel Identity message, militias, the jew [sic], race and more."[96]

Concerning Peters's claim that he is unaware "of being virulently racist and violent," he is simply redefining these terms. In his Christian Identity belief system, disparaging remarks about Jews and blacks are not racist or violent. They are simply the truth. The same may be said of another patriot leader, whose racism is only now beginning to come to light: Bo Gritz.

Bo Gritz: White Power in a Green Beret

One of the most influential leaders of the patriot/militia movement is former elite soldier Lieutenant Colonel James "Bo" Gritz, who, as the most decorated Green Beret, is said to have been the model for Rambo.[97] He is a perfect example of how cross-pollination takes place between the anti-Semitic/racist segments of the patriot movement and non-racist freedom-fighters.[98]

Evidence of Gritz's racism extends back to his 1988 bid for vice president on the Populist Party ticket with presidential candidate David Duke, a long-time racist who had previously served as Imperial Wizard of the Knights of the Ku Klux Klan. Duke "was instrumental in the Klan resurgence of the 1970s."[99]

Given Duke's background, it is no surprise that he was chosen as a candidate for the Populist Party, which was formed "as an amalgam of splinter groups including the Constitutional Party . . . various Klans, and Christian Identity groups in Indiana and Florida."[100] The base of support and leadership for the 1988 Populist campaign was "a who's who" of white supremacists, including Christian Identity leader Chris Temple; anti-Semite and tax protester M. J. "Red" Beckman; neo-nazi Harry Schmidt, who denies the Jewish Holocaust; KKK and Aryan Nations activist Kim Badynski; and Richard Flowers, who heads the highly racist Christian Patriot Association.[101]

The Duke/Gritz ticket never saw election day because Gritz "decided to withdraw in order to run (unsuccessfully) for a congressional seat."[102] But when the retired Green Beret decided to make a bid for the presidency in 1992, he returned to the Populist Party.[103] Gritz's political career fizzled again after leaving the campaign trail in order to help negotiate a surrender during the Randy Weaver siege. Gritz is credited with having successfully ended the confrontation. His mission was helped along by a letter written by Pete Peters to fellow Identity believer Randy Weaver:

> Five hundred Christian Israelites from 40 states . . . are right now praying for you. . . . [P]lease help us to help you by cooperating with Col. Gritz so that further bloodshed can be avoided. . . . You have proven your point, now allow the God of Abraham, Isaac and Jacob to prove His.[104]

In February 1993, Gritz began conducting a series of paramilitary training courses called SPIKE (Specially Prepared Individuals for Key Events). An August 1993 advertisement for SPIKE reveals that Gritz is training amateur soldiers:

> You will fire the latest Ruger semi-automatic pistols equipped with laser and red dot sights. Both street confrontation and deliberate shooting will be taught along with instinctive 'Quick Kill' skills. All guns and ammo will be furnished.[105]

Gritz's SPIKE-Delta Phase VII was billed as "fascinating excitement tailored for the whole family!" Its advertising brochure lists classes on "Close Quarters Combat" and how to "employ and defeat all methods of interrogation including Polygraph, Voice Stress Analysis . . . Hypnosis, Police and Military Interrogation, Chemical Interrogation." The main event of Phase VII was described as participation in two "fun-house" exercises set up "with 'volunteer' terrorists and 'volunteer' hostages." This brochure ends with a promise regarding one of Gritz's books: "My SPIKE SPYCRAFT manual will contain the meat and potatoes of real life James Bond operations." [106]

Although Gritz claims that he is not a racist or anti-Semite, his statements and the company he keeps indicates the opposite is true. He "has spoken at Peters' *Scriptures for America* Identity 'Bible Camps' on at least two occasions and was featured at the First National Identity-Christian Conference in North Carolina." [107]

A 1991 gathering of Klansmen, neo-Nazis and other white supremacists found Gritz sharing the podium with the likes of Terry Boyce, Imperial Wizard of the Confederate Knights of the Ku Klux Klan, as well as Christian Identity leaders Richard Hoskins and Robert Weems. [108] During a 1991 speech delivered at one of Pete Peter's Bible camps, Gritz gave a clear endorsement of Identity beliefs:

> I believe that the Christian Identity religion will continue to grow in this nation until it is able to stand self-sufficient in spite of the government. . . . I am telling you that He [God] has given us all that we need. He's given us the likes of Pete Peters. . . . the likes of the Christian Identity movement. [109]

Gritz, like other patriot leaders, endorses New World Order conspiracy theories such as an impending government takeover, the horrors of gun control and the deeds of banking elites who manipulate world affairs. In his 1992 book *Called to Serve*, Gritz ties these beliefs into classic racist and anti-Semitic conspiratorial theories regarding the Federal Reserve System: "Eight Jewish families virtually control the entire FED." [110]

It is noteworthy that Pete Peters helped finance the publication of Gritz's book. [111] Although Gritz and Peters have since had a falling out over whether homosexuals should be put to death (Peters says yes, Gritz says no), they still share the same speaking circuit. In 1994, both men spoke at a Billings, Montana, "No More Wacos" meeting called by tax-protester and anti-Semite M. J. "Red" Beckman. Members of the KKK were also in attendance. [112]

Theologically, Gritz seems closely aligned with Christian Identity. In a January 1995 newsletter, he wrote that "Cain was the SEED OF THE DEVIL. Abel was OF ADAM (Au-dawm, meaning blushing face)." [113] In this same publication, Gritz blames the Jews for virtually all that he views evil and corrupt. His rhetoric mirrors Identity hate talk:

> Who in the world is promoting abortion, pornography, pedophilia, Godless laws, adultery, New Age international banking . . . [T]here is a star war going on today between the five-points of righteousness and the six-points [Star of David] of Satan. [114]

Recently, Gritz has established Almost Heaven, a 280-acre survivalist refuge near the town of Kamiah in central Idaho. It is quickly becoming a camp for fellow whites who are fleeing the Establishment. Gritz refers to his new mini-society as a "Christian Covenant Community." Critics call the isolated settlement a heavily guarded base of operations for "patriot tax-protestors and anti-Semitic fanatics" and a haven for "anti-governmental extremists and bigots."[115]

There is no question that the latter assessment is more accurate. When Philip Weiss of *New York Times Magazine* visited residents of Almost Heaven, each one expressed Christian Identity beliefs. Dan and Barb Fuller, for example, moved to Gritz's area in order to escape the Armageddon and the antichrist bankers who are "squeezing the life out of America in preparation for the New World Order." Their source of truth is a Florida newsletter called *The Revalator*, which prints the *Protocols*.[116]

Like most white supremacist enclaves, Almost Heaven is designed to be a last retreat "for patriots in case the apocalypse they anticipate overtakes them." But Gritz's community goes a step further by functioning as a "center for a regional base of [white] power."[117] Jonathan Mozzochi, director of the Coalition for Human Dignity, says the isolated community of like-minded patriots may be "the most significant development in the white supremacist movement in the Northwest in recent years."[118]

Gritz's anti-Semitism blatantly surfaced in 1994 during his radio program "America's Town Forum," currently in broadcast on the supposedly conservative Christian station of KDNO in Bakersfield/Delano, California. His special guest on September 13, 1994, was the infamous Canadian neo-Nazi Ernst Zündel, who denies that Hitler carried out the extermination of six million Jews.[119]

Zündel first caught Canada's attention in 1984 when that country's government initiated criminal proceedings against him for publishing two books, one of which was *Did Six Million Really Die?* He was prosecuted under a Canadian law banning the willful publication and dissemination of information known to be false. A series of lengthy court battles and appeals ensued, ending in an acquittal after the Canadian Supreme Court declared the law unconstitutional. This prompted Zündel to launch a propaganda attack against the Holocaust. His self-proclaimed "game plan" is twofold:

1. "[B]ring down Jewish suffering in terms of numbers and events, both real and imagined, to what it really was, not what they say it was, what they exploit for their own political, financial and geo-political purposes."[120]

2. "[M]ake the world look at German suffering and the Allied brutality toward Germany. . . . 'The Holocaust has become an enterprise based on falsehoods and lies and they are promoting it criminally.' "[121]

Zündel, like most other Holocaust revisionists, denies that Nazi gas chambers put to death vast numbers of Jewish prisoners. During a 1994 interview for *Skeptic* magazine, Zündel was asked if he could think of a way to settle the gas chamber question once and for all. Journalist Frank Miele was shocked by the response:

Zündel offered the macabre suggestion that someone build a gas chamber according to what are alleged to be the plans, get DEGESH to supply the gas, fill it with people, gas them and see if they in fact died. Since the U.S. continues to execute people, we could also save some money in conducting such an experiment. [122]

Zündel is incensed by the Academy Award–winning movie *Schindler's List*, which he calls *Schwindler's List*. "He denounces the movie as 'socially divisive, culturally destructive, historically inaccurate, and blatantly racist, anti-German hate propaganda.'" In a fax sent to several talk shows he complained that "the policy of school teachers taking students to see this 'horror show' is 'mental child abuse' and 'mind rape' of these children." [123]

Zündel's comments on Bo Gritz's show were no less blunt. He told Gritz that a very real holocaust was the "bombing of German cities and of our neighboring towns and of the [Allied] invasion." He went on to inform Gritz, who never voiced one objection, that the Nazi death camp at Auschwitz was actually "a humanitarian center." It was "a place of orderly work, of health care for inmates . . . [and] adequate food." Zündel's description went on: "[T]hey had lectures . . . orchestras . . . sports facilities . . . they even had a swimming pool for inmates." [124]

Zündel also expressed that Hitler is "a much maligned figure in history" who "did not do the many things that they are saying about him." Gritz also failed to show any disapproval when Zündel called *Schindler's List* "the most disgusting piece of anti-German, anti-Christian hate propaganda." When Gritz finally did respond, his comments were hardly contradictory. In fact, he seemed rather pleased with Zündel:

> [T]here is a horrible, terrible, reluctance to even talk revisionist language. And I think the truth is most important, regardless of what form, how bitter it may be, how unrighteous it may seem. The truth has a resounding solidness about it that you can't find in any other Hollyweird [sic] production, no matter how fantasia-like you make it. [125]

Early in the program, Zündel made a most enlightening comment about Gritz's views. The comment seemed to surprise Gritz, who quickly changed the subject. Zündel's statement was said so quickly that most listeners probably missed it. For those able to play back a recording of the show, there is no mistaking Zündel's words. In reference to Gritz, Zündel stated: "As you can see, we are a little different in our beginnings, *but not so much in where we finally end up.*"

Observers of the far right have been troubled for years by Gritz's racism. Now new concerns are being expressed over his increasingly prophetic rhetoric about a U.N.–backed apocalypse looming on America's horizon. His words sound strikingly similar to the ramblings of David Koresh. In a July 1993 newsletter, for instance, Gritz stated: "I believe that through a system of Christian covenant communities we . . . will be sealed up against both the dragon and the Wrath of God poured out against His enemies." [126]

Such eschatological predictions, coupled with his isolated retreat of like-minded followers, may prove to be a volatile mixture. In Gritz's mind, though, it may only be fitting that he establish a kingdom of faithful white patriots. He writes: "I have been anointed with consecrated oil, and men of God have laid hands upon my head with blessings that I be a Gideon for the righteous in this time of trouble." [127]

Jack McLamb: Operation Vampire Killer

Jack McLamb is best known for his widely circulated book *Operation Vampire Killer 2000*, which is often recommended as the best primer for new members of the patriot movement. [128] The seventy-four-page exposé on the New World Order provides a concise picture of exactly how America is to be overrun by foreign troops and turned into a socialist police state. McLamb is a former Arizona police officer whose main goal is to draw law enforcement personnel into the patriot movement through his *Aid & Abet Police Newsletter*. He is the founder of Police Against the New World Order (PATNWO) and is a popular speaker at patriot functions.

McLamb clearly has racist leanings. In *Operation Vampire Killer*, he recommends and quotes approvingly from white supremacist literature. [129] During a speech given at the 1994 Seattle Preparedness Expo, he commented that interracial marriage is a violation of God's plan "and a ploy by the elitists to create a mono-colored servant class." [130] McLamb has additionally stated: "The race-mixing program was created for their [elitists] subjects. . . . Some of these Internationalists have stated over the years, . . . when all other humans are of one color, (brown), then they will be more easily managed.'" [131]

Interestingly, a close ally of McLamb's is none other than Bo Gritz. In fact, McLamb helped Gritz acquire the parcel of land on which Almost Heaven is located. [132] Pastor Pete Peters is also connected to McLamb. In 1993, Peters' *Scriptures for America Newsletter* gave *Operation Vampire Killer 2000* a rave review, declaring that the book "succinctly proves that there is an ongoing conspiracy for a one world government." [133] To Christian Identity readers of this review, the New World Order conspirators would be Jews. Along with McLamb's book, Peters has often recommended the ultimate conspiracy answerbook: *The Protocols of the Learned Elders of Zion*. [134]

Prepared to Die

The world as we know it is coming to an end for all patriots. The stage has been set. The Jews, blacks, internationalists, Russians, Chinese and other groups whom the patriots believe belong to the New World Order are poised to strike. John Trochmann, like so many others, has reached a calm resolve: "I've been so outspoken for so many years, our lives aren't worth a plugged nickle anyway, so, if it comes to it, why not give it all we've got? I'm not willing to die, but I'm willing to make the other bastard die." [135]

"When the troops come in, they'll come in such force it will be incredible," he says. "In forty-eight hours, they can have one hundred million troops here.

They'll come out of the ground! They'll come from submarines! They'll come from air drops! They'll come from everywhere!"[136]

Armageddon, the world's last great battle which will allegedly precede the Second Coming of Christ, promises to be a bloody event. But for people like Trochmann, Gritz, Peters, McLamb and other patriots, it will also be a glorious one. Perhaps this is why so many mainstream Christians have been deceived into following after the marching racist armies. Visions of God's saintly legions are all they can see. Those who profess to have the "light of truth" have become virtually blind to the darkness around them. This has resulted in myriad unholy alliances, which will be the focus of part five.

PART 5

Unholy Alliances

I do not sit with deceitful men,
Nor will I go with pretenders.
I hate the assembly of evildoers,
and I will not sit with the wicked.
I shall wash my hands in innocence,
And will go about thine altar O LORD,
That I may proclaim with the voice of thanksgiving,
And declare all Thy wonders.
King David
Psalm 26: 4–7

The one who says he is in the light and yet hates his brother
is in the darkness until now. The one who loves his brother
abides in the light and there is no cause for stumbling in
him. But the one who hates his brother is in the darkness and
walks in the darkness, and does not know where he is going
because the darkness has blinded his eyes.
St. John
1 John 2:9–11

14

Infiltration of Hate

For the time will come when they will not endure sound
doctrine; but wanting to have their ears tickled, they will
accumulate for themselves teachers in accordance to their
own desires; and will turn away their ears from the truth, and
will turn aside to myths.
St. Paul
2 Timothy 4:3-4

Although most of the secular media reports on the patriot/militia movement
have been reasonably accurate, a number of articles mistakenly have labeled
the racist and anti-Semitic elements of America's new anti-government
sub-culture as "Christian." In an August 1995 *Newsweek* piece, for instance,
Randy Weaver is described as a "Christian fundamentalist."[1] Weaver, however, is
not a Christian fundamentalist.[2]

In a report by the Bay Area Coalition for Our Reproductive Rights, Tom
Burghardt uses the term "key Christian Patriot texts" to describe Aryan Nations
literature and materials written by former KKK Grand Dragon Louis Beam.[3] Such
a statement is misleading, to say the least. Beam's materials have nothing to do
with Christianity. Nor is he a spokesman for any Christian church.

June Jordan, professor of African American studies at the University of
California, Berkeley, makes an equally unjustifiable assertion in a 1995 article for
The Progressive:

"The Aryan Nation" is the goal of the Christian Coalition. . . . Do not be
misled. There is no difference between hating "the government" and hating
"the Jews" and "the Nig—s" in the mind-mesh of the Christian-white-rights
crusade.[4]

Nothing could be further from the truth. Christianity does not accept, teach, or
condone racism in any form. Jesus said that Christians should love everyone
(Mt 19:19). The apostle James echoed these words, calling Jesus' admonition "the

royal law" (Js 2:8). Paul the apostle taught that without love for fellow human beings, everything we do is meaningless (1 Cor 13:1-13).

There clearly is an inconsistency between these teachings and the beliefs of Identity followers and other racist patriots. Why do some writers still insist on labeling racists as Christians? First, because these reporters are biased and careless. Second, because racists often call themselves Christians. True Christianity, however, opposes racism. A vast number of conservative Christians in America, and in the Christian Coalition, abhor racism/anti-Semitism. Applying the term Christian to racists and racist groups without qualification is to wrongly label an entire religious community. Equating Christianity with racism is as unfair as saying Judaism is communism.

A Christian's Perspective

True Christians have always stood against hatred and violence. Christian newspapers and magazines have regularly denounced Christian Identity and white supremacy in the strongest terms possible. For example, a March 1986 editorial that appeared in the conservative Christian magazine *Moody Monthly* called Identity a "new malevolence" that is a "threat to all Christians."[5] The Anti-Defamation League of B'nai B'rith agrees that mainstream Christianity "views Identity as twisted and warped, a perversion—not a reflection—of the faith."[6]

As far back as 1986, John Olson, executive director of the Spokane, Washington Christian Coalition, stated, "The fact that white supremacists justify their beliefs by their Christian faith should disturb us all." He added, "We who are Christian and white are the ones who ought to be at the forefront of those who oppose racial and religious hatred."[7] Many efforts have been made by Christians to combat those who would use the name Jesus as a shield for hatred and violence:

[Pastors] have rallied community opposition to the Ku Klux Klan. When the annual Christmas parade was canceled last year in Commerce, Georgia, in order to bar Klan participation, a group of local clergy invited a black Baptist pastor to speak at an alternative celebration. In Statesville, North Carolina, a group of church, business, and civic leaders drafted a resolution denouncing the Klan's "dehumanizing principles and intimidating tactics" in that community. The resolution was later adopted by area United Methodist and Presbyterian governing bodies.[8]

Many political commentators, journalists and researchers are failing to recognize that not everyone who calls himself or herself a Christian is, indeed, a Christian. The racist facet of the patriot movement consists primarily of individuals in Christian *Identity*. Consequently, many patriots, although they may *sound* Christian, are actually Identity believers outside of mainstream Christianity. Even those in the Identity movement draw a sharp distinction between themselves and "Judeo-Christians." Racists loathe Christianity's acceptance of all people regardless of color or national origin, which is a belief based on the words of Paul the apostle:

> For you are all sons of God through faith in Christ Jesus. For all of you who were baptized into Christ have clothed yourself with Christ. There is neither Jew nor Greek, there is neither slave nor free man, there is neither male nor female; for you are all one in Christ." (Gal 3:28)

Identity followers see this doctrine as nothing but a corrupting influence in the world.[9] They are also incensed over mainline Christianity's understanding that the Christian faith sprang from Judaism. One Identity brochure reads:

> It is important here to expose a fallacy, long taught by the Christian Church, that the Jews gave us Christianity. This is called the Judeo-Christian concept, embraced by Protestants and Roman Catholics, as well as Jewry, and it is a grotesque misnomer.[10]

Another racist booklet published by an Aryan Nations-affiliated church boldly declares, "The message of the Bible, as taught by most of today's churches, is not Christianity at all; but a nameless, faceless, irreligious, Satanic philosophy."[11] Identity pastor Pete Peters often has especially severe words for mainline Christian denominations and mainstream non-denominational churches:

> *Judeo*-Christianity is an effeminate religion whereas true Bible Christianity is masculine. America's decline and weakening can be attributed to the switch from a (strong, logical, masculine) Bible based Christianity to a (weak, emotional, illogical, feminine) non-Biblical *Judeo*-Christianity.[12]

Despite these distinctions between Identity patriots and Christian patriots, the two groups are often merged into one large category of "Christian patriots." In all fairness, observers of the movement are not entirely at fault for painting with such a broad brush. Christians have permitted white supremacists to link themselves to the conservative fold, which in turn has blurred the lines of distinction between racists and non-racists.

Evangelicals, fundamentalists, charismatics and Pentecostals have allowed their frustration with liberal politics to be the key factor in determining who is a friend and who is a foe. Some conservative Christians now embrace virtually anyone who shares contempt for the liberal establishment. They take no time to discover other beliefs a person may hold. Such a careless attitude is in direct disobedience to the scriptural admonition found in 1 Thessalonians 5:21: [E]xamine everything *carefully*; hold fast to that which is good; abstain from every form of evil."

It cannot be denied that there has been a lack of good judgment shown on the part of Christians. At the same time, white supremacists have made themselves extremely difficult to spot. Identity believers "do not frequently use gutter obscenities, which makes their racism and anti-Semitism less obvious."[13] White supremacists also promote causes that some Christians tend to support (e.g., school prayer, home schooling, pro-life legislation). But a close examination of racist literature reveals that their motives are far different from those espoused by mainline Christians. Consider the following white supremacist indictment against the public school system, which includes an appeal to put the Bible and prayer book in schools:

> [W]e must strive to throw off this jewish [sic] thought. We must work toward the end of these animals emasculating the minds of our children in school. We must put the Bible and prayer back in school. We have this in our Aryan Nations Academy at Hayden Lake, Idaho. I can guarantee you that no kinky-headed nig——r will ever answer the roll call there. WHITES ONLY. Back to the jungle with the animals.[14]

Although the religious rhetoric coming from racists can often sound similar to some of the views expressed by evangelicals and fundamentalists, racists invariable diverge into the realm of very un-Christian rhetoric. Note the following comments from a fifteen-year-old Ku Klux Klan Youth Corps member. She sounds exactly like a conservative Christian until midway through her speech:

> [Madalyn Murray O'Hair] banned public prayers from schools. . . . I tell you, I'm a devout Christian, I go to church and I love the Lord and I'm proud of it. You know I'd love to lead prayer in school, but I can't because of her. The only way we can stop her and all these communist nig——s out there is to join the Ku Klux Klan. . . . KKK stands for three main things . . . . Number One is God . . . . Two is for Race, which is for the *white* race—and we all know, the *right* race! . . . Number three is Country, to help make America what it once was.[15]

An appearance of conservatism has enabled white supremacists in the patriot/ militia movement to drift in and out of anti-environmentalist rallies, Christian Bible studies, tax-protester meetings and home-schooling groups. Through this constant presence of racists and their conspiratorial worldview, a significant number of mainstream Christians have unwittingly had their thinking about the "end times" and the New World Order unduly influenced by racism and racist ideologies, even though they themselves may not be racists.

Moreover, the patriot movement has become "a doctrinal free-for-all."[16] Religious views in patriot gatherings range from Christian, to Christian Identity, to full-blown Hitler worship. No questions are asked about one's spiritual beliefs as along as they espouse anti-government sentiments. This holds especially true for militias, which usually attract patriots focused on only two things: hating the government and preparing for a future war with federal authorities. Little time or energy is spent on investigating doctrinal convictions of militia members. As a result, there has been a frequent blurring of the otherwise mutually exclusive distinctions between Christianity and racism.

The individuals most responsible for this confusion are Christian leaders, who, although charged with watching over God's flock and guarding them against false teachers (Acts 20:28), have not taken the time to adequately investigate the sources from which they are gleaning information about the New World Order. These leaders and their flocks remain largely ignorant of the threat from racists.

Sadly, some evangelicals have deliberately ignored warnings from knowledge-able persons about the racist materials being used in the Christian community. According to Christian teachings, the purpose of pastors, Bible teachers and evangelists is to bring Christians into a mature faith (Eph 4:11-12), and direct believers away from fables and myths that are both meaningless and destructive (1 Tim 1:4; 4:7). In this task, many Christian leaders have failed, as the following sections clearly demonstrate.

Pat Robertson's New World Order

One of the most powerful figures in the mainstream evangelical Christian commu-nity is Pat Robertson, founder of the Christian Broadcasting Network (CBN) and host of that network's popular *700 Club* program. He also helped form the influential Christian Coalition, a political activist group seeking to re-establish a conservative foothold in the government.

The secular media began associating Robertson with patriots after the release of his 1991 book *The New World Order*, which successfully introduced conspiracy theories to a wide audience. Political researcher Daniel Junas observes that this work easily falls within the patriot movement's parameters.[17] It must be stressed that Robertson's book does not simply contain free-floating conspiracy theories, but promotes distinctive beliefs that are specifically associated with militias.

Thanks to Robertson's bestseller, which has sold more than 500,000 copies, the most extreme fringes of the patriot movement have seen their unusual conspiracy theories legitimized on a large scale in the evangelical world.[18] Also alarming is the fact that Robertson draws upon some of the very same sources used by racist patriots and white supremacists to legitimize their anti-Semitic conspiratorial worldview.

Robertson's 318-page volume is an important piece of literature in the patriot/ militia movement because it synthesizes all of the standard conspiracy texts into an easily understandable and repeatable mantra for those in the movement: the satanic New World Order will destroy America.[19] Nearly every conspiratorial plot that is *foundational* to the patriot movement is clearly and concisely promoted by Robertson:

☐ The NWO will eliminate America's national sovereignty.

☐ An elite group of godless conspirators are out to rule the world.

☐ U.N. peacekeepers will play a key role in taking over America.

☐ Computer technology and microchips fit into the NWO plan of enslavement.

☐ NWO proponents are deliberately causing the moral and spiritual breakdown of America.[20]

The influence of Robertson's book in the patriot movement can also be seen in how often it appears in patriot and militia lilterature, and how regularly it is recom-mended by patriot and racist leaders. For example, *The New World Order* was recommended by an organization called Conspiracy Nation in a posting that was made to the Internet's Patriot Archives. This particular document is a transcript of an October 28, 1994, shortwave talk radio program hosted by *Spotlight*. The sub- ject of the show was dangers of the coming New World Order.

Although many lay Christians have embraced Robertson's position, a considerable number of Christian scholars have rejected his theories. University of Pittsburgh professor Bruce Barron notes that the weakest part of Robertson's book is his conspiracy theorizing, which tends to jump from scanty evidence to bold assertions.[21]

Robertson admits that some of his speculations lack direct evidence. Nevertheless, he goes on to assert the very theories for which he has no support. On page 178, for instance, Robertson begins tracing an alleged link between Freemasonry and the "current thought processes" moving us toward a New World Order. This issue is connected to a scheme involving the secretive Illuminati, communism and American financial support of the Russian revolution.[22] The entire conspiracy is presented very matter-of-factly. But just before introducing the intriguing plot, Robertson states: "We do not know whether such a tie does exist; there is not presently any known direct evidence to support it." The only bit of documentation Robertson ultimately supplies is "one magazine source, whose data have not been verified."[23]

On page 265, Robertson makes yet another unsubstantiated assertion in reference to the assassination of President Abraham Lincoln: "There is no hard evidence to prove it, but it is my belief that John Wilkes Booth, the man who assassinated Lincoln, was in the employ of the European bankers who wanted to nip this American populist experiment in the bud."[24]

In several places, Robertson's theories appear to be updated versions of Barruel's 1797 conjectures about the French Revolution, Freemasonry, the Illuminati and the takeover of the world by a secret cabal of evil conspirators (see chapter eleven):

Weishaupt's [Illuminati founder] aims were to establish a new world order. . . . Weishaupt chose as his vehicle for infiltration and takeover the established Continental order of Freemasons. . . . Weishaupt succeeded at the international convention of Freemasons held in Wilhelmsbad, Germany, with his planned infiltration of the Continental Masonic Order and the creation of what he termed "Illuminated Freemasonry." His conspiracy was sufficiently successful from that point on to use French Freemasonry as a vehicle for placing members of the French Illuminati into key governmental positions. . . . [T]hese members set about to undermine the Bourbon dynasty of France and to prepare the way for the French Revolution. It is believed that several of the key leaders of the French Revolution were members of the Illuminati.[25]

Such speculations caused an understandable outcry from members of the Jewish community familiar with the fallout from Barruel's theory. Equally troubling were Robertson's references to "international bankers" and "European bankers" as the evil manipulators of humanity.[26] Many readers assumed that he was publishing veiled anti-Semitism. Hitler, after all, equated the "Jewish menace" with the "international world Jew" and the "international Jewish financiers in and outside Europe."[27] Furthermore, contemporary racist publications often call the New World Order conspirators either a "cabal of Jewish bankers" or "(Jewish) 'international bankers.' "[28]

Some sections of The New World Order seem to validate these charges. On page 181, for example, Robertson writes that in 1782 Jews were allowed into Freemasony. This, he points out, is the possible link between occultism and the world of high finance, which in turn has led to the godless anti-Christ plan for a New World Order.[29]

In a February 1995 issue of the New York Review of Books, journalist Michael Lind was among the first to directly accuse Robertson of spreading racially based conspiracy theories. Although Robertson never labeled his New World Order conspirators as Jews, Lind argued that "Robertson's portrayal of a world-wide conspiracy of freemasons, communists, and international bankers partook of classic anti-Semitism."[30] Lind pulled no punches in criticizing Robertson:

> Not since Father Coughlin or Henry Ford has a prominent white American so boldly and unapologetically blamed the disasters of modern world history on the machinations of international high finance in general and on a few international Jews in particular.[31]

One month later, columnist Frank Rich repeated the accusations in the New York Times.[32] Robertson fought back by sending a five-hundred-word statement to the Times, which read in part:

> I deeply regret that anyone in the Jewish community believes that my description of international bankers and use of the phrase 'European bankers' in my book refers to Jews.[33]

Robertson's letter included "sincere regrets" that his statements had been "misunderstood."[34] Some people believe Robertson meant no harm. Others feel he is simply masking his true feelings.[35] I am inclined to believe the former. Robertson has always been a firm supporter of the Jewish people and the state of Israel. Furthermore, various portions of The New World Order speak favorably of Jews, Israel and Zionism.[36]

It seems that Robertson, like so many others, has fallen for conspiracy myths that were fathered by anti-Semitism. In Robertson's version, Jews have been substituted with an assortment of unnamed international NWO bankers. Many critics remain skeptical of Robertson's innocence, though, because he—without explicitly disclaiming the racism of these sources—uses well-known anti-Semitic writers to support his theories, namely, Nesta Webster and Eustace Mullins.

Both authors have produced literature condemning Jews as the world's hidden conspirators seeking to dominate humanity. Robertson quotes Webster's 1921 book World Revolution as well as her 1924 book Secret Societies and Subversive Movements.[37] The latter volume is so blatantly anti-Semitic that it is advertised in the resource catalog of the neo-Nazi Sons of Liberty organization as a work that exposes the "Jewish founders of secret societies and their inner workings."[38]

Eustace Mullins is even more notorious for anti-Semitism and racism than Webster. His books take prominence in the aforementioned catalog, which features an endless list of hate literature including:

- *Proof of Negro Inferiority*, which "compares Negroes to gorillas";
- *Who Brought the Slaves to America*, a study "proving" that the Jews "were mainly responsible for the slave trade and bringing the blacks to America";
- *The Hitler We Loved and Why*, a pictorial exposé on why Germans loved *Der Führer*.[39]

Although Mullins is not quoted directly in *The New World Order*, Robertson's bibliography lists his book, *Secrets of the Federal Reserve* as a reliable resource. Mullins' influence is clearly seen throughout Robertson's work.[40] In fact, much of Robertson's thinking seems to have come directly from Mullins, especially regarding the Federal Reserve. Mullins directly blames the international Jewish bankers, while Robertson simply blames the international bankers.

Mullins imputes all of society's evils to the Jews, even rising medical costs and difficulties in the health care system.[41] His beliefs came from Ezra Pound, a staunch anti-Semite, who according to a 1982 *Aryan Nations Newsletter*, was "a great admirer of Adolf Hitler and Mussolini."[42] Mullins has boasted about visiting Pound "every day for three years," and that each day Pound lectured him on world history. Mullins proudly admits: "[T]hat's how I found out what I know."[43]

Mullins's view of the current threat from the New World Order is perhaps most apparent in the epilogue he wrote for the racist booklet *The World's Trouble Makers* by Bruce Brown, which is basically a restatement of the information contained in *The International Jew* by Henry Ford. Brown's one-hundred-fifty-page diatribe against the Jews even recommends the *Protocols of the Learned Elders of Zion*.[44]

Ironically, Mullins's epilogue condemns Pat Robertson by name because Robertson preaches "that we must 'love' the Jews." Mullins, in fact, actually puts Robertson into the New World Order conspiracy! According to Mullins, Robertson is a pawn of the Jews and the Christian Broadcasting Network is nothing but a Jewish-controlled vehicle through which pro-Jewish sentiments are espoused.[45] Robertson is either has chosen to ignore the pointed accusations or is unaware of Mullins's contempt for a "Jewlover" like him and a "Jew-controlled" network like CBN.

To date, Robertson has not repudiated his use of Webster or Mullins as references. Nor has he eliminated their works from subsequent printings of *The New World Order*, even though their anti-Semitism has been brought to his attention. Jerome R. Chanes, author of *Antisemitism in America*, notes that although Robertson may not be an anti-Semite, "it is certainly true that Robertson chose to fish in some very dirty waters."[46]

Chuck Missler: Friend of Patriots

Chuck Missler is the founder of Koinonia House, a conservative Christian ministry based in Coeur d'Alene, Idaho. He gained popularity with mainstream Christians primarily through his close affiliation with the California-based Calvary Chapel system of churches founded by evangelist Chuck Smith. Although Missler has had his own ministry for many years, he continues to teach regularly at Calvary Chapels nationwide.

Missler is a major bridge between Christianity and the patriot/militia movement. His *Personal Update* newsletter has carried several articles promoting New World Order conspiratorial theories. In the July 1995 issue of *Personal Update*, he suggests that the government blew up the Alfred P. Murrah building in Oklahoma City. He also condemns the government for launching "a highly orchestrated propaganda attack" against "talk radio, the pro-life movement, Constitutionalists, militias, pro-family groups, survivalists, and all forms of 'politically incorrect' views."[47]

Personal Update, like patriot publications, is brazenly anti-government. Missler believes America is no longer in a contest "between the Democrats and the Republicans but between the Constitutionalists who value our traditional heritage and the global socialists who are pursuing the dream of the New World Order. The conflict is between individual liberty and totalitarianism."[48]

Missler additionally contends that many of "the most knowledgeable" Bible commentators believe the Antichrist may be alive today. According to Missler, the demonic world leader will be even more deceitful "than the politicians who presently dominate the District of Corruption."[49] This biting reference to Washington, D.C., officials is common among patriots. An article in *Media Bypass*, a popular patriot magazine, reads: "The mindset in the 'District of Corruption' appears appalled by the resentment of 'we the people' toward the federal government."[50]

Patriot magazines are only one of the many sources from which Missler gleans his information. He claims to use "extensive contacts and private sources" to give a "behind-the-scenes perspective of the major issues."[51] Unfortunately, some of his sources are tied directly to the white supremacist movement. In the November 1995 issue of *Personal Update*, Missler not only quotes from but expresses thanks to and gives the address of the "American Patriot Fax Network . . . and 'The Spotlight.' "[52]

The American Patriot Fax Network (currently operated by Ken Varden of Las Vegas) was co-founded by Gary Hunt, a shadowy figure whose name first surfaced during the Davidian siege when he showed up in Waco claiming to hold Koresh's power of attorney. He said he had observed an allegedly "pre-arranged signal from the Branch Davidian leader—a jiggle of the compound's satellite dish."[53] Hunt was ignored by both law enforcement authorities and the courts.

According to Linda Thompson, Hunt's network began when he started faxing information to her, Ken Varden and a Florida couple named Lynda Lyon and George Sibley.[54] The network soon became connected to numerous fax "news" services run by tax protesters, white supremacists and Christian Identity believers.[55] It has since branched out to include non-racist patriots and Christians such as Missler.

A steady stream of moderate to blatantly racist/anti-Semitic materials are regularly faxed to everyone on the network.[56] It is noteworthy that approximately a year after Hunt's network began, forty-five-year-old Lynda Lyon and fifty-one-year-old George Sibley were arrested and subsequently convicted in the death of thirty-eight-year-old Alabama policeman Roger Motley.[57] The white supremacist couple shot and killed Motley in a shopping center parking lot when he approached their car.[58]

After the shooting, Lyon and Sibley "led police on a high-speed chase and held law enforcement sharpshooters at bay for more than four hours before surrendering at a road block."[59] Their vehicle contained three handguns, two semi-automatic rifles and an M-14 rifle. In the couple's Orlando home, police found a large cache of weapons, ammunition and white supremacist literature. At their Georgia "safe house," authorities seized an M-1 rifle that had been converted into a fully automatic weapon, a riot shotgun and 5,000 rounds of ammunition.[60] The day after Motley was killed, Hunt sent out the following message over his fax network:

> Many of those in the Patriot Community fully expect that a state of war will exist in this country in a relatively short period of time. George and Lynda . . . felt that this state of war existed.[61]

For several weeks, Hunt used the network to send a series of faxes about the incident. His version of the killing perfectly illustrates the danger now facing non-patriots in this country, especially those in law enforcement:

> A cop comes up to the car and they know that they have a car full of guns. . . . Without time to contemplate a better solution, they reacted as the Branch Davidians should have reacted. I know that it is politically correct to condemn George and Lynda, but I cannot, and will not. I can only fear for them and fear for our country. . . . George had been sitting in his car. . . . Lynda was making a phone call. . . . The officer refused to listen to George explain that he was under no contract as a free Citizen of Florida, to have to produce a (drivers) license in Alabama. The officer then informed George . . . that he was under arrest. George got out of his car, and then began balking. The officer reached for his gun but George was a bit quicker. George and Lynda were defending their rights as guaranteed by the Constitution, and did not allow the officer to deny them their freedom. George and Lynda's actions were to deny "law enforcement" from stealing your rights to travel freely in this country.[62]

A 1995 *Los Angeles Times* investigation found that several racist organizations belong to the American Patriot Fax Network.[63] Members who supply and receive information through the network include: Arizona Patriots, a militant Christian

Identity group; Guardians of American Liberty (GOAL), led by Stewart Webb, who from the mid-1980s and into the 1990s "made a series of threatening anti-Semitic phone calls";[64] and James Wickstrom, a Posse Comitatus leader, who in 1984 was convicted "on two counts of impersonating a public official and one count of bail jumping."[65]

Missler's use of information from the *Spotlight*, and his recommendation of it as a news source, is even more disturbing. Besides being unreliable, *Spotlight* is notorious for its racist articles and advertisements. It would be difficult for Missler to not notice the blatant anti-Semitism that is regularly featured in its pages. A survey of *Spotlight* stories from January 1994 through June 1995 reveals that the paper's main purpose is not only to propagate New World Order conspiracy theories, but also to link them to anti-Semitic ideas. The number of articles found on relevant topics are as follows:[66]

- [ ] New World Order: 75
- [ ] Anti-Israel: 50
- [ ] Concentration Camps, FEMA, black helicopters: 49
- [ ] International Jewish bankers: 40
- [ ] Anti-Black or Pro-Apartheid: 28
- [ ] Pro-militia: 26
- [ ] Foreign troops on U.S. soil: 24
- [ ] Jewish holocaust denial: 13

It is odd that Missler, who professes to be pro-Israel, would read *Spotlight*, a publication of the quasi-Nazi Liberty Lobby founded by Willis Carto, whose history of anti-Semitism dates back as far as 1960 when he edited a publication "calling for voter support for the American Nazi Party."[67] According to a 1994 article in *Covert Action Quarterly*, a widely respected investigative magazine, Carto's Liberty Lobby "is the major source of anti-Semitic propaganda in the United States."[68]

Missler seems to have fallen into a trap laid long ago by Carto. According to Louis T. Beyers, a former associate of Carto's, the Liberty Lobby's plan is to draw support from non-racists as a means of strengthening anti-government ranks: "Willis has talked to me about playing the role of a respectable conservative when his true feelings are those of a racist nationalist."[69] Beyers also maintains that Carto's ultimate aim is "to form a new power base ready to act when the country turned hard right."[70] Carto has set up a number of front organizations to pull off his scheme:

> To draw the support of those whose political beliefs might not include hatred for Jews, it [Liberty Lobby] has established an array of front groups, surrogates, and publications. These enterprises have not so much expanded the Lobby's influence as made it seem to represent a vast constituency. Among the groups sponsored by the Lobby over the past 30 years, have been (in no particular order): Americans for National Security, American Committee on Immigration

Policies, United Republicans of America, Committee for Religious Development, Friends of Rhodesian Independence, Action Associates, Youth for Wallace, National Youth Alliance, Save Our Schools, Emergency Committee to Support Victims of Political Persecution, National Taxation, Inc., and Council on Dangerous Drugs.[71]

To understand the level of anti-Semitism being promoted by the Liberty Lobby and *Spotlight*, one need only look to the philosophy of Willis Carto. In a 1955 letter to Earnest Sevier Cox, Carto boldly identified America's main enemy:

Who is calling the shots? History supplies the answer. . . . History plainly tells us who our Enemy is. Our Enemy today is the same Enemy of 50 years ago and before—and that was before Communism. . . . The Jews came first and remain Public Enemy Number One. . . . Hitler's defeat was the defeat of Europe. And America. How could we have been so blind?[72]

In a letter to the Aryan Nations, a new supporter of the racist organization expressed interest in learning more about the white supremacy movement based on a a neo-Nazi advertisement he had seen in *Spotlight*.[73] Now *Spotlight* is being advertised in Chuck Missler's *Personal Update*. This is precisely how racist conspiracy theories are gaining acceptance in mainstream Christian circles.

Don McAlvany: Intelligence Advisor?

Don McAlvany of Colorado is a valued counselor, trusted researcher and close friend of Chuck Missler.[74] He is also another conservative who has embraced the unsubstantiated conspiracy theories revolving around the New World Order, U.N. and black helicopters. He writes: "It's time for all of us to stop being passive wimps, to get angry, and to get involved—unless we prefer to live as slaves in the New World Order."[75]

Through his monthly newsletter the *McAlvany Intelligence Advisor* (*MIA*), McAlvany has churned out a significant amount of anti-government propaganda, misinformation and faulty speculation about the NWO. Due to his outspoken manner, he fancies himself "among the *Most Hated* Men in the Clinton White House." McAlvany says: "I'm on a mission to dispel the lies, misinformation and distorted statistics you get from the liberal media and from the U.S. government. And it's true. I'm not the most popular guy in Washington nor among the Clinton clan."[76]

MIA articles are perhaps best described as fear-mongering. McAlvany endlessly harps on a future wherein hundreds of thousands of patriotic, Christian Americans will be rounded up and imprisoned under false charges of "hate, environmental, financial, or gun control 'crimes.'"[77] Waco, he asserts, was a declaration of " 'open season' on non-mainstream (non-government approved) religious minorities, sects, etc."[78] McAlvany warns that many small Christian churches, communities, and groups are about to be "re-classified" as cults so the government can do away with them.[79]

A cursory reading of *MIA* reveals an excessive use of harsh language that no doubt serves to fuel the paranoia and anger of his readers. He incessantly refers to the Clinton administration as the "Clintonistas."[80] This obvious play on words refers to the brutal Sandinistas, a Marxist-Leninist political group dominating the police and army of Nicaragua.[81] McAlvany is equally scathing when referring to law enforcement agencies as the Gestapo.[82] In response to a relatively benign comment by Senator Newt Gingrich about limited government, McAlvany commented: "That statement wouldn't have sounded out of place if Hitler, Castro or Stalin had said it."[83]

In his apparent zeal to expose the coming one-world government, McAlvany has forgotten a number of scriptural admonitions, not the least of which is 1 Peter 2:13:

> Submit yourselves for the Lord's sake to every authority instituted among men, whether to the king as the supreme authority; or to governors, who are sent by him to punish those who do wrong and to commend those who do right. . . . Live as free men, but do not use your freedom as a cover-up for evil. . . . Show proper respect to everyone . . . honor the king.

By using inflammatory language, McAlvany can appeal to the farthest fringes of the political right. This is most apparent in the August 1994 edition of *MIA*. It denounces the "wicked, hedonist philosophy" being accepted by "the vast majority of American 'sheeple.' "[84] Interestingly, the word *sheeple* has previously been used exclusively in the white supremacist movement to refer to persons who meekly follow Jewish-inspired "illegal" laws. Randy Weaver used the term in reference to slaves of ZOG.[85] The violent Freemen of Montana apply the word *sheeple* to various enemies.[86] According to Michigan resident Dan Stromber, *sheeple* was also used by Oklahoma bombing suspect Terry Nichols and his brother James.[87]

Like Missler, McAlvany seems to get much of his information from anti-Semitic sources. *MIA* has quoted *Spotlight*, Bo Gritz and Eustace Mullins.[88] He has even recommended Mullins's book, *Murder by Injection*,[89] which is advertised in the neo-Nazi Sons of Liberty resource catalog.[90] McAlvany has also promoted patriot conventions featuring himself, Gritz, McLamb and Koernke.[91]

When it comes to the issue about which he, as a Christian, should be most concerned—doctrine—McAlvany is ill-informed. For example, he considers Randy Weaver "a born-again Christian," yet admits that Weaver is "kinda part of the Identity movement and they've got some kind of weirdo ideas about who is Israel and who are the Jews and so forth."[92] This definition of Weaver's doctrinal views leaves much to be desired, as does McAlvany's version of the Weaver incident.

When speaking at a 1993 Colorado Christian conference hosted by Chuck Missler, McAlvany said Weaver was asked by federal agents to spy on neighbors and tell the government which ones had guns.[93] McAlvany went on to say that Weaver would not comply because he had "a lot of Christian friends up there in the hills in Idaho."[94] Although this version of the Weaver saga is patently false, McAlvany cites it as proof of the coming persecution of Christians.

McAlvany's answer to safeguarding one's life and family against the tyrannical regime in power, and the imminent Christian persecution, is somewhat contradictory. He often appeals to God through such passages as Psalm 32:7, which reads: "You are my hiding place." He also offers spiritual encouragement: "The God of the Bible will protect, strengthen, guide and hide His people even in the midst of the storm."[95]

At the same time, McAlvany strongly urges readers in nearly every issue of *MIA* to invest in U.S. gold and silver coins.[96] Gold and silver, McAlvany says, "should be aggressively accumulated up to 35% percent of a total investment portfolio."[97] In one publication he claims that buying precious metals is an "insurance policy against the despotic, socialistic, people controlling New World Order oriented actions of their government."[98] In another newsletter, he states: "Please study the enclosed flyer on gold and call International Collectors Associates (ICA) for assistance."[99]

It is no coincidence that McAlvany recommends ICA, a gold, silver and rare coin brokerage "specializing in precious metals and other conservative investments."[100] He has been its president and owner since 1972. This makes for a lucrative, self-perpetuating circle that begins with *MIA*: (1) warn readers through *MIA* of the coming New World Order; (2) offer the only hope of survival: precious metals; (3) sell precious metals to the frightened masses; (4) use the profits to spread more NWO conspiracy theories and induce more panic; and (5) gain more gold and silver customers.

McAlvany also recommends that people move to towns with less than 15,000 inhabitants, take their children out of the public school system, and store one to two years of freeze-dried food per person, as well as "several hundred (or thousand) pounds of staple grains."[101] He declares, "If one understands the times in which we live . . . one will have at least a one-year supply of dehydrated food reserves for each member of the family."[102] This food storage advice stems from McAlvany's belief that all Bible believing Christians "may have to go 'underground' in the next 2 to 5 years."[103]

McAlvany announced his ominous speculation to 1,200 attendees of a 1993 prophecy conference sponsored by Chuck Missler.[104] For the convenience of those present, as well as for readers of *MIA*, McAlvany's ICA "offers several long-term food storage systems" containing "an assortment of easy-to-cook entrees, grains, vegetables, fruits and side dishes."[105] McAlvany's "top of the line" one-year plan, which contains three meals a day for one person, costs $2513.[106] This means McAlvany can ostensibly make more than $10,000 off of every family of four that follows his counsel.

In 1993, readers of *MIA* were given a prediction concerning the Branch Davidian trial: "Watch for disappearing BATF and/or FBI agents who know too much and don't like what they saw," McAlvany said. "[O]r for strange things happening to Branch Davidian survivors in jail."[107] The patriotic writer also recommended *Waco: The Big Lie* as "AN EXCELLENT NEW FILM ON THE WACO MASSACRE."[108]

Several years have passed. No BATF or FBI agents are missing, nothing "strange" has happened to the jailed Davidians, and Linda Thompson's video has been debunked. Nevertheless, McAlvany's *MIA* continues to propagate New World Order conspiracy theories, along with increasingly dire predictions and strategically placed exhortations to buy gold and silver coins and food storage supplies. For those interested in acquiring McAlvany's monthly *Intelligence* newsletter, subscriptions are $115 annually.

Texe Marrs: Christianity's Conspiracy-Monger

According to Texe Marrs, the world is ruled by "ten unseen men" who control the Council on Foreign Relations, Trilateral Commission, CIA, Russian KGB, British Intelligence, Freemasonry, and most of America's elected government officials.[109] "[T]here *is* a World Conspiracy by a hidden elite," Marrs contends. "All the evidence is there—mountains of evidence. No other conclusion is possible. . . . *It is for real.*"[110]

This is only the tip of the conspiratorial iceberg when it comes to Texe Marrs. There seems to be no conspiracy he does not "expose" through his Texas-based Living Truth Ministries, which supposedly is "100% patriotic and 100% pro-God."[111] He sees nearly all political/religious leaders, as well as almost every major political/religious organization, as part of "the international banking conspiracy" that is rushing us toward the establishment of a New World Order.[112]

Marrs's NWO enemy list includes, but is certainly not limited to, the Illuminati, Freemasonry, Roman Catholicism, the Pope, Billy Graham, Pat Robertson, Robert Schuller, Oliver North, Oral Roberts, Jack Van Impe, Democrats and Republicans, the U.N., the Russians, the Germans, the Turks, the Chinese, the Anti-Defamation League of B'nai B'rith and King Juan Carlos of Spain (the "Antichrist").[113]

Marrs markets his conspiracy materials through a monthly newsletter called *Flashpoint*, which he claims has a yearly budget of $700,000.[114] A six-month subscription to *Flashpoint* is given free to customers who purchase any books, tapes or videos.[115] He also advertises patriot-related resources during his *World of Prophecy* radio talk show that airs over AM, FM, and shortwave stations.

In one of his videos, Marrs exposes the federal government's plans to unleash a 208,000-man "Gestapo brigade" strike force "to assault and conquer dissenters."[116] In another tape entitled *Concentration Camps in America*, Marrs reveals the existence of NWO-related crematoriums, foreign troops, concentration camps and human tracking systems.[117] This tape also provides information on the government's "top secret, operational plan to identify, arrest, categorize, imprison, and put to death dissenters to the New World Order."[118]

Flashpoint articles are rabidly anti-government. In a 1994 issue of the newsletter, Marrs writes: "Arrogant and anti-Christian lesbians, homosexuals, and pedophile advocates now hold the reigns of political power, and the 'D.C' in Washington, D.C. has become the 'District of Corruption.' "[119] All of Marrs' materials go far beyond the usual inflammatory rhetoric and sensationalism found in the patriot movement, slipping easily into the realm of vicious yellow journalism. He is most adept at using slanderous accusations, insulting innuendoes and mean-spirited sarcasm—all in the name of God:

- "Bill Clinton is a fascist."[120]
- "Hillary and Bill [Clinton] have surrounded themselves with the most wicked and demon-possessed people imaginable."[121]
- "Has the *Inner Circle* of the Illuminati decided to put Senator Robert Dole in the oval office of the White House? Will General Colin Powell, a pro-United Nations, globalist stooge, be his vice president?"[122]
- "[H]ere are even more facts about the sexual depravity of two of Hillary's most powerful hellcats: Janet Reno and Ruth Ginsberg. . . . [N]ot only are these women immoral reprobates, but their plan is to turn our vulnerable and helpless children over to be used by depraved, hardcore pedophiles."[123]
- "[A]n evil clique of unAmerican, money-hungry greedsters and murderers has grabbed the reins of such powerful groups as the CIA, FBI, DIA, DEA, DOD, and BATF. Their circle of influence reaches into the White House and controls the halls of Congress."[124]
- "[Clinton is] a heartless, New Age occultist—an occultist who has relentlessly used the full resources of the White House to slander, defame, persecute, and kill true Christians and American patriots."[125]
- "Is President Bill Clinton a practicing Satan worshipper? . . . [Are the Clintons] demonically charged to perform hideous and barbaric acts unimaginable to decent and trusting Americans? What are the true religious beliefs of Bill and Hillary Clinton? Are they lovers of the Father of Lies—Lucifer himself? Order this exclusive Special Report. . . . [Y]ou may just conclude that Bill and Hillary Clinton are the most wicked, witchcraft-evil couple ever to reside at 1600 Pennsylvania Avenue!"[126]

In reference to the Oklahoma bombing, Marrs writes: "How disgustingly convenient, how cruelly perfect, how devilishly advantageous to the long-cherished agenda of Bill Clinton and his New World Order superiors was this monstrous firebombing and massacre in Oklahoma City!"[127] Marrs says his research of the tragedy "rips the mask off the fascist thugs who almost certainly planned and executed [it]."[128]

Given the level of Marrs's caustic anti-government rhetoric, it is not surprising that he is regularly recommended by patriots such as Jack McLamb, who, in

Operation Vampire Killer 2000, refers to Marrs's *Flashpoint* as a "very good source" for a religious perspective on the "NWO con-job."[129] Marrs has responded by having McLamb on his *Word of Prophecy* radio broadcast to talk about "how the federal authorities are trying to smear patriots."[130]

In 1994, anti-Semitic Identity Pastor Pete Peters featured in his *Scriptures for America Newsletter* a half-page advertisement for Marrs's book, *Big Sister Is Watching You*. Peters said the volume "unmasks the coven of brutally correct women who now rule over us. Hillary's regiment of hardened, militant feminists include lesbians, sex perverts, child molester advocates, Christian haters, and the most doctrinaire of communists."[131] The book struck such a positive chord with Identity believers that "Texe was a guest on Pastor Peters' Truth for the Times television program."[132]

Marrs is equally supportive of fellow patriots. He twice featured Bo Gritz on his radio broadcast to discuss a number of issues including the Randy Weaver siege, the Oklahoma bombing and the United Nations. Marrs encouraged his readers: "Be inspired as Bo unmasks the New World Order plot. . . . Don't miss this tremendous information!"[133] Another guest of Marrs's *Word of Prophecy* show has been Jim Keith, author of *Black Helicopters over America*, a book sold through Living Truth Ministries.[134]

Linda Thompson has also found a strong ally in Marrs. He has had Thompson on his radio program to discuss "her latest research and investigations," and also sells her materials through his ministry.[135] In a 1994 issue of *Flashpoint*, Marrs wrote of Thompson: "Her outstanding video, *Waco: The Big Lie*, is a powerful indictment of Big Brother/Big Sister government and its bloody assault on our constitutional liberties."[136]

This recommendation appeared less than three months after I had personally spoken to Marrs and given him information concerning Thompson's background and her faulty research. I eventually received a letter from Marrs that all but excused me of being part of the New World Order conspiracy. He not only asked me why I was criticizing Thompson and other patriots, but also inquired as to why I was choosing to excuse and whitewash the bloody horrors of the federal government.

The response was odd in that Marrs and I had not even discussed any other patiots or Christians during our telephone conversation. In fact, he raised a number of issues neither of us mentioned. Marrs then interpreted my criticisms of Thompson as railings against the victims of Big Brother. He went on to say that by voicing opposition to *Waco: The Big Lie*, I was actively seeking to cover up government atrocities through vainly and torturously smearing the character of Thompson, whom he referred to as a Christian woman.[137] As of 1996, Marrs was still recommending Linda Thompson and selling her videotapes through his ministry.[138]

Hate Begets Hate

Thanks to the above personalities, mainstream Christians have come under the influence of hate. Of this, there is no doubt. The previously discussed individuals are only a few of the many persons who have helped spread historically anti-Semitic conspiracy theories in the Christian church. Large numbers of Christians have been lulled into accepting anyone who condemns the dreaded New World Order:

☐ Speakers at the Liberty Lobby's 40th Anniversary National Convention included John Trochmann, Eustace Mullins and Ted Gunderson, who spoke on federal aggression.[139] Gunderson is featured in the Christian video *Demons: True Life Evil Forces* produced by His Majesty's Media. On this video, Gunderson voices his anti-government views by claiming that high-ranking government officials regularly have Satanists deliver children to Washington, D.C., for sex orgies.[140]

☐ Since 1993, Pastor Pete Peters has had his own television show on the influential Keystone Inspiration Network (KIN), a Pennsylvania-based conservative Christian television network.[141] Keystone's Comptroller, Rev. Clyde Campbell, has rebuffed warnings and complaints about Peters, saying: "Peters is a minister of the Gospel and he does a good job. Pete says he loves the Jews."[142] Peters says the new television exposure has brought him nationwide support.[143]

☐ Conservative radio and television broadcaster Ray Brubaker of St. Petersburg, Florida has recommended videotapes by Jack McLamb, Linda Thompson and Bo Gritz.[144]

☐ David Irving, a well-known anti-Semite who denies that six million Jews were killed under Hitler, spoke in Colorado at the Colonial Heights Presbyterian Church. His topic was "Enemies of True History."[145]

Christians have even been involved in hate-filled rallies held by violent anti-environmentalist groups. At a July 1994 Protect-Your-Constitutional-Rights rally in Silver City, New Mexico, approximately 400 patriots bashed the government and railed against the Endangered Species Act. One speaker called environmentalists "anti-human." Another commented, "[S]ome people [i.e., environmentalists]. . . . don't understand things without a punch in the nose or a bullet in the head."[146] The whole gathering was periodically punctuated by gospel music and prayers. One witness said it looked like an old-time religious revival.

The level of anti-government rhetoric within the church has become so hostile and aggressive that some Christians have grown to believe that violence is the method God wants them to use against society's problems. These individuals, who have earned the title "militant Christians," are the subject of chapter fifteen.

15
Holy Wars

Regarding the Book of Revelation, nowhere in that text can
one find a call to arms on the part of humans. Rather the
great symbolic events are brought about solely by God, His
angels and other heavenly beings. Nowhere does Revelation
call upon believers to jump-start the Armageddon. Instead, it
invites the believer to endure and persevere in faith despite
the terrible ordeals Christians suffered during Roman
persecution. And that is what believers should do.
Frank Flinn
Adjunct professor of religious studies,
Washington University (St. Louis)[1]

Michigan real estate agent Ray Southwell battled local school board officials
over his children's curricula for months. According to Southwell, Outcome Based Education and Goals 2000 lesson plans were instilling
"socialist values" in his children rather than Christian ones.[2] When repeated
attempts to change things through the system failed, Southwell surrendered to
stubborn anti-Christian educators and ceased his efforts.

The beleaguered Christian sought counsel from his pastor, Norm Olson, the
spiritual head of Calvary Baptist Church in Brutus, Michigan.[3] After discussing
the conditions of public education, as well as the state of the country, both men
decided to raise up "God's army"—the Northern Michigan Militia. The militia's
chaplain says he is confident that the paramilitary unit is of God: "I felt like the
Lord was saying that this is the army of the Lord in the United States at this
moment."[4]

Like Southwell and Olson, hundreds of Christian leaders nationwide are
advocating the formation of "Jesus-centered" militias. Some pastors are even
beginning to incorporate militant ideology into Sunday sermons in an effort to
blend church life with militia life. Members of Crossroad Baptist Church of
Pensacola, Florida keep an ASSAULT WEAPONS file in their church's library
and offer pro-gun articles at weekend services.[5] Crossroad's pastor, forty-two-year-
old Chuck   Baldwin, preaches on Sundays about Christian combat, the New

World Order and war preparations: "It's very important, if you use a firearm to try and defend yourself, that you hit your target."[6]

Baldwin is only one of many rising stars on the Christian Patriot Network. On the radio each weekday from noon to one o'clock, the Baptist pastor is "live, taking America back by storm!"[7] His programs are loaded with flag-waving, conspiracy-busting rhetoric sure to enthrall any red-blooded Christian patriot: "We're talking about citizens' militias, federal government's encroachment on individual rights, new world order, United Nations . . . gun control, it's all related." Baldwin adds, "Give us a call."[8]

Whose Army?

In "Guns and Bibles," *Christianity Today* reporters Joe Maxwell and Andrés Tapia note that even though mainstream evangelicals see themselves as being far removed from the more fanatical elements of the militias, the line between the two groups has become "frighteningly blurred."[9] Political science professor Michael Barkun feels this is due, in part, to the fact that in the patriot movement "religious symbols" have replaced doctrinal explicitness.[10] Communications professor Randy Bytwerk, a propaganda expert at Calvin College in Grand Rapids, Michigan, explains the result:

> [M]anipulation of religious symbols in militias "allows members to feel like they are still holding on to the Christian faith, but the content is no longer Christian. It sounds like they are saying the same thing."[11]

Phil Roberts, director of the Baptist Home Mission Board's Interfaith Witness Department, finds that paramilitary groups often talk about God and country, but typically put country before God:

> These groups have very little to do with religious ideology. Their's [sic] is a political point of view, not spiritual. Even though some of their members may be nominal Christians, the (military) organization often becomes their god. When a person sacrifices ethical and spiritual views to their political ideology, it can lead to fascism on the right and godless communism on the left.[12]

While some militant patriots are dedicated, albeit very confused, Christians, it must also be recognized that many militant religious zealots are about as far from Christian thought as one can get, even though they may sound amazingly similar to Christians. A vast number of patriots fall somewhere in between these two camps. Unfortunately, no one in the patriot/militia movement seems concerned with finding out exactly who is who. Maxwell and Tapia observe that for outsiders, "it can be difficult to tell the difference between orthodox Christian teachings and the militia's belief system."[13]

Most militant Christians, as well as militant non-Christians who *appear* to be Christian, embrace a closed-minded worldview that blinds them to ideas different from those espoused within their tight circle of fellow government haters. Such a narrow understanding of the world is loosely related to a third-century heresy known as Manichaeism. Manichaeism was based on a complex set of doctrines that basically centered around rigidly defined perameters of good and evil, with no gray areas.[14]

Persons with a Manichaen-style grasp of reality see everyone who disagrees with them as satanic, or part of an Antichrist conspiracy. "Conspirators become Satan worshipers, and then everything becomes clear. Absolute evil undergirds all," says Jeffrey Kaplan, an expert on religion and violence who teaches history at Arctic Sivunmun Ilisagvik College in Barrow, Alaska.[15] This kind of mind-set is apparent in the writings of Christian patriots such as Texe Marrs (see chapter fourteen).

A Manichaen worldview easily becomes dangerous if combined with militancy. For militant Manichaens, persons outside the realm of absolute good are seen as utterly evil opponents who must be destroyed. When militancy and Manichaeism are blended with apocalyptic ideas about the world's end being near, the potential for violence grows very great. This is exactly what has occurred in some of the Christian sectors of the patriot/militia movement. University of Chicago historian Martin Marty says that "this is one of the most disturbing departures from established end-times interpretation: that Christians should physically—even violently—resist the evil around them."[16]

Christian patriots have made several comments that support Marty's contention. In an interview with *Christianity Today*, for instance, Norm Olson asks: "Where do we get this idea that we are supposed to sit down and let a corrupt government get worse and worse?" Olson then gives his impression of what Scripture teaches, by stating, "Our Lord told us to contend for the faith and occupy until he comes."[17]

Olson's ideas about biblical mandates concerning militancy illustrates the Christian patriot tendency to misapply scriptural texts in support of their own agenda. Since the Bible is a key piece of literature to militant Christians, it is appropriate that we take a brief look at some of the particular ways they use the Bible to justify their behavior.

Scripture Twisters

Olson, like many other Christian patriots, abuse rather than use the Bible. In the above citation, for instance, Olson misquotes and combines two different passages of the Bible, neither of which deal with militancy, corrupt governments or a New World Order. In fact, the words "contend for the faith" were not even spoken by Jesus, as Olson implies. They were penned by another New Testament writer, Jude: "[C]ontend for the faith that was once for all entrusted to the saints" (Jude 3).

This verse, in context, is an exhortation for believers in Jesus to keep the Christian faith free from false doctrines. The passage refers to the importance of not adding to, or subracting from, "the recognized body of teaching" given by Jesus' apostles.[18] Jude is addressing the need for Christians to lovingly and intelligently defend the theological position that God's revelations to man ceased with the New Testament writings about the person of Jesus Christ. Jude's teaching forbids any further appeal to divine revelations from extrabiblical sources.[19] The text, then, is about a Christian's personal responsibility to enter into civilized debate with those who are seeking to alter the historic doctrines of Christianity. Jude's exhortation is theological, not political.

The second part of Olson's statement, "occupy until he comes," did originate with Jesus. But, again, the passage has nothing to do with Christians responding in a militant fashion to political oppression. Jesus' words, "occupy till I come," were not even spoken as straightforward directions. The phrase appears in a parable about servants who act responsibly with financial assets given to them by their master (Lk 19:13).

Olson is quoting from the old King James translation of Scripture, and in doing so, has confused himself. He seems to think that the word occupy means "to have control of " or "to have dominion over." But when the Greek texts were translated into English (1605–1625) during the days of King James I (1566–1625), the word occupy meant "to trade." This is why the word appears in a parable about a rich ruler giving money to his servants. He tells them to "occupy" (trade) and make a profit until he returns. In other words, they were to do their very best to cultivate and multiply the assets given to them by their master. For Christians, this parable is an exhortation to use to our utmost ability the gifts and talents God has given us. The verse has nothing to do with militias.

Harold Stockburger, founder of the American Patriot Federation of Tennessee, justifies Christian militancy through equally faulty appeals to Jesus' words. He cites, for example, Luke 22:36.[20] It reads: "[H]e that hath no sword, let him sell his garment and buy one." Stockburger says that "even though the Bible speaks often of not bearing the sword, there are many instances where God called his people to use their swords." He then goes on to mention a number of Old Testament passages about Israelite battles.[21]

Stockburger also uses John 18:10, the well-known passage in which Peter draws his sword during Jesus' arrest and cuts off the ear of the high priest's slave. Christ immediately heals the slave and instructs Peter to put his sword away. Stockburger puts an interesting spin on the story: "[L]ook at the verse again. It says he drew his sword. This group of men who were traveling across the countryside was armed to the teeth. . . . Peter's sword was probably the equivalent to a .357 magnum today."[22]

With regard to John 18:10, Stockburger completely ignores the fact that Jesus not only rebuked Peter for having resisted the government's actions, but actually healed the individual whom Peter had wounded. Even during his crucifixion, Jesus imparted forgiveness to his murderers (Lk 23:34). Paul the apostle makes it clear that a Christian's true "weapons" are not of this world (2 Cor 10:4-5). They are spiritual weapons of evangelism: prayer, love, service, kindness, generosity, understanding, patience. Renowned conservative Christian scholar Gleason Archer deals with these and similar passages in his valuable *Encyclopedia of Bible Difficulties*:

> The Sermon on the Mount sets forth the wholly different standard of life that characterizes a true child of God in his role as a private citizen. His conduct is governed by the holy love and kindness of God. The Christian is to come to an agreement with his adversary before they actually present their case in court (Mt 5:25). When he is smitten on one cheek, he is to turn to him the other (v. 39), rather than retaliating in kind. In general, he is not to resist evil; that is, he is not to fight back in the defense of his own personal rights. He is never to return evil for evil (Rom 12:17). By faithfully following this policy he will be "walking in the light," and that bright testimony of holy love will draw others to the light of Christ Himself (Mt 5:16). All these directives pertain to the personal conduct of the Christian as a citizen of the kingdom of God in the midst of a depraved and sin-cursed world.[23]

Stockburger's claims that Jesus' disciples were "armed to the teeth," and that Peter's sword was the equivalent of a .357 magnum, are ludicrous. Luke 22 reveals that Jesus' twelve apostles had only two swords (v. 38). Twelve men with two swords is hardly an "armed-to-the-teeth" militia. Moreover, the Greek word used in the text for "sword" is *machaira*, which describes "a short sword or dagger."[24] A dagger is certainly not comparable to the weapon of choice used by Hollywood's famous Dirty Harry.

Concerning Luke 22:36, Jesus is not advocating offensive militancy. All of the major commentaries and linguistic Bible study aids agree that he was telling his apostles to buy a sword for defensive purposes only.[25] Those wanting to apply Jesus' words in today's context must do so using the original context of self-defense, recognizing that Jesus was not advocating militant opposition to an ungodly government. Jesus told Peter "[A]ll who draw the sword shall die by the sword" (Mt 26:52). According to Jesus, persons who take up arms foolishly or commit unjustified and illegal acts of violence will eventually perish through violence.

Stockburger's appeal to Israelite battles described in the Old Testament battles also bears no relevance to taking up arms against our federal government. First, Israel was a theocracy. It functioned under the direct rule of God. Second, the Israelites were not battling their own leaders over disagreements on national policies. They were going to war with *other* hostile nations. Third, the Israelites took up arms either for the specific purpose of fighting nations in order to defend themselves or to gain possession of land.

Olson and Stockburger represent countless Christians who are misinterpreting Scripture through the lens of disdain for the government and frustration over legislation with which they disagree. An entire volume could be written refuting the erroneous interpretations of numerous biblical verses that are twisted by Christian patriots in order to justify their militancy. This preoccupation with God-sanctioned militancy is partly to blame for hundreds of violent acts that have been perpetrated by misguided zealots. The most visible expressions of this type of wayward thinking have arisen from within the ranks of what has commonly been called the pro-life movement.

Pro-Lifers Who Kill

In 1987-88, pro-life activist Randall Terry formed Operation Rescue (OR), an organization dedicated to peaceful activism against abortion. Rescuers hoped that through civil disobedience—protests on private property, blocking abortion clinic entrances—the lives of unborn children would be saved. They also hoped the publicity generated by their actions would call attention to the abortion issue, thus opening a door of public debate through which OR could better educate the populace about abortion. Terry's ultimate goal was to initiate a pro-life political force that would increase anti-abortion sentiment in America to such a degree that the Supreme Court would overturn its 1973 *Roe v. Wade* decision, which legalized abortion.

But the original intent of OR's pro-life agenda was gradually overshadowed in the minds of many onlookers as the rescue message "went unheeded by both the churches and the larger society." *Christian Century* magazine observes that "as punitive legislation increasingly forced all but the most committed of the rescue community to the sidelines, rescuers began to debate the utility of violence."[26] The level of aggression that has since been directed toward abortion providers and clinics by pro-life extremists is staggering. Since 1983 there have been 37 bombings in 33 states, 123 cases of arson, and 1,500 cases of assault, stalking, sabotage and burglary.[27]

On March 10, 1993, in Pensacola, Florida, the terrorist activities of pro-life extremists took a dramatic turn when Michael Griffin shot and killed Dr. David Gunn. Griffin reportedly shouted "Stop killing babies" as he shot Dr. Gunn four times in the back.[28] The attack did not surprise individuals who had seen "wanted" posters containing Gunn's photograph, home address, telephone number and daily schedule. The fliers were distributed at an Alabama rally sponsored by OR.[29]

In April 1994, eighty pro-life leaders met in Chicago "to hammer out a common strategy."[30] Among those in attendance was a defrocked Presbyterian minister named Paul Hill. He carried with him a "defensive action" declaration that he had signed along with thirty other pro-lifers who believed Griffin's action was "justifiable" homicide:

> We, the undersigned, declare the justice of taking all godly action necessary to defend innocent human life including the use of force. We proclaim that whatever force is legitimate to defend the life of a born child is legitimate to defend the life of an unborn child. We assert that if Michael Griffin did in fact kill David Gunn, his use of lethal force was justifiable provided it was carried out for the purpose of defending the lives of unborn children. Therefore, he ought to be acquitted of the charges against him.[31]

On July 29, 1994, forty-year-old Paul Hill acted on his beliefs by taking a 12-gauge shotgun and murdering Dr. Gunn's replacement, sixty-nine-year-old Dr. John Britton. Hill also used the firearm to kill Britton's seventy-four-year-old body-guard, James Barrett. Both Britton and Barrett were shot in the head.[32] Hill's deed was condemned by many pro-lifers throughout the country. But it cannot be denied that Hill was only doing what some persons in the pro-life movement had been advocating in philosophical terms. In fact, the year 1994 saw 400 death threats made against abortion clinic personnel.[33]

Terrorism originating from within the fringe element of the pro-life movement took another deadly turn on December 30, 1994, when John Salvi III went on a two-day shooting spree against three abortion clinics. His rampage left two dead and five wounded. Unlike past incidents of violence against doctors, Salvi's onslaught was directed at anybody in or near the clinics.

In a Brookline, Massachusetts, abortion clinic, he shot and killed twenty-five-year-old receptionist Shannon Lowery. Salvi then proceeded to spray the waiting room with gunfire from a .22-caliber semiautomatic rifle. Within ten minutes, Salvi was at the Preterm Health Service clinic less than two miles away, where he fatally shot thirty-eight-year-old receptionist Leanne Nichols. The next day he struck again, this time by spraying up to twenty-three bullets into the Norfolk, Virginia, Hillcrest Clinic.[34]

As with the Griffin and Hill attacks, Salvi's slayings were denounced by several mainstream pro-life organizations such as the National Right to Life Committee.[35] But again, there was a disturbing number of individuals who viewed Salvi as some kind of a hero. Outside his Norfolk, Virginia, jail cell, the Rev. Donald Spitz, director of Pro-Life Virginia, showed up with a bull horn and supporters. Spitz shouted "We love you! Thank you for what you did in the name of Jesus!"[36]

Others came with signs that read, "God Bless John Salvi" and "Free John Salvi, Protector of Life."[37] On March 18, 1996, Salvi was convicted of murder and sentenced to two consecutive life terms in prison with no possibility of parole, as well as an additional 18 to 20 years in prison to be served after the two life terms.[38]

Murder, Militias and Matthew Trewhella

A number of professedly Christian pro-lifers have refused to issue outright condemnations of Griffin, Hill and Salvi. Many press releases and public responses by pro-life extremists clearly reveal an undercurrent of support for those who would save babies by killing doctors. "More violence is inevitable, and it is righteous," says C. Roy McMillan, executive director of the Christian Action Group of Jackson, Mississippi. "It wouldn't bother me if every abortionist in the country today fell dead from a bullet."[39]

McMillan was a signer of Paul Hill's "defensive action declaration" supporting Griffin's murder of Gunn. Another pro-lifer who put his name on Hill's statement was Matthew Trewhella, co-founder of the California-based Missionaries to the Preborn and pastor of Mercy Seat Christian Church in Milwaukee, Wisconsin.[40] In the March 10, 1993, *Missionaries to the Preborn Newsletter*, Trewhella wrote: "[I] would not condemn someone who killed Hitler's doctors . . . neither will I condemn Michael Griffin."[41]

Trewhella is the most visible bridge between extremists in the pro-life movement and Christians in the patriot/militia movement. He has found significant allies among mainstream Christians who are outside the patriot community. Trewhella has been able to forge diverse links because he is a national committee member of Howard Phillips' U.S. Taxpayers Party (USTP), a new ultra-right political party that is drawing members from the pro-life extremist fringe, the patriot/militia movement, the mainstream pro-life movement and moderate segments of conservative Christianity.

Trewhella's militancy has been well-established by his own statements, as well as by comments of those with whom he closely works. Shortly after the near fatal shooting in Wichita, Kansas, of Dr. George Tiller by pro-lifer Shelley Shannon, Trewhella defended the action in a press release entitled, "Use of Deadly Force Is Justifiable":

> To call this a vigilante action is a misrepresentation of this situation. What we have here is one person acting in defense of other persons who are about to be killed.[42]

Gary McCullough, another leader of Missionaries to the Preborn and a close associate of Trewhella's, reflects the above sentiments in an essay entitled, "Do My Words Make Me Violent?":

> Do I mourn the death of an abortionist stopped from his gruesome trade? No, I look forward to the next time I turn on the radio and hear that an abortionist has been shot. I will rejoice in it, I will be glad someone was there to stop him before he took more innocent lives.[43]

Trewhella is extremely relevant to our study because he advocates the formation of Christian militias. The following quotation is from a May 1994 USTP convention:

> We should do what thousands of people across this nation are doing. We should be forming militias. . . . [T]here are plans of resistance being made. . . . Churches can form militia days and teach their men how to fight.[44]

He has also boasted about how his sixteen-month-old child already knows which finger is his "trigger finger." Trewhella uses this story to make an important point with supporters: "This Christmas, I want you to do the most loving thing, and I want you to buy each of your children an SKS [assault rifle] and 500 rounds of ammunition."[45]

During the aforementioned 1994 USTP convention, Trewhella revealed that his Mercy Seat Christian Church regularly holds classes for members on "the use of firearms and . . . how to be a good shot."[46] At the same convention, attendees could purchase a $1 field manual from Wisconsin's Free Militia. This manual gives explicit instructions on how to form a militia and participate in covert military actions against enemies. The language used is clearly reflective of Louis Beam's leaderless resistance and independent-cell-structure concept, but with a decidedly pro-life slant:

> Just as all life, growth, and reproduction is based on living cells, all Militia "life" is centered around its cells. The identities of cell members are known only within the cell and by their immediate superior. All basic training is done within a cell. All codes, passwords, and telephone networks are determined and held in confidence within the cell. All fortified positions are determined, prepared and concealed by the cell. All combat orders are executed by the cell as the cell sees fit within its own context. So the Free Militia IS its cells. . . . [T]here are four types or functions of cells in the Free Militia: (1) Command, (2) Combat, (3) Support, and (4) Communique. . . . Combat cells provide the patrolling and fighting capability of the Free Militia. Each cell consists of about eight able-bodied "minutemen" with its own leader, communications, rendezvous points, staging areas and standing orders. They execute the orders of their command cells and do all their own training within the combat cell itself. They are the "arms" of the Free Militia.[47]

As if the confusion were not bad enough, the pro-life movement is but another area where racists have slipped into evangelical circles. Consequently, white supremacists and anti-Semites must now be added to the mix of pro-life groups and personalities. Unlike Christian pro-lifers, however, who are concerned for *all* unborn children, racists care only about "white young women in America [who] slay their first-born child by the murderous act of ABORTION."[48]

Although pro-life racists do not care about non-white babies, this distinction is never brought out by white supremacists. Instead, racists go along with the pro-life program, attend pro-life meetings, and use Christian language—all the while sowing seeds of anger, bitterness and violence by spreading their conspiracy theories. The goal is to use non-racist pro-life forces to fight Z.O.G. since white supremacists believe abortion is a Jewish tool designed to deplete the Aryan population. That is why abortion is so terrible to white supremacists.[49] As White Aryan Resistance leader Tom Metzger declares:

> Almost all abortion doctors are Jews. Abortion makes money for Jews. Almost all abortion nurses are lesbians. Abortion gives thrills to lesbians. Abortion in Orange County [California] is promoted by the corrupt Jewish organization called Planned Parenthood. . . . Jews must be punished for this holocaust of white children.[50]

Metzger's views, which are shared by most white supremacists, have led racists to support pro-life extremists who use murder to stop abortions. After Paul Hill shot Dr. Gunn, the Florida Templar Knights of the KKK sponsored a rally in support of Hill. An Aryan Nations spokesman who voiced approval of the killing "urged racists to join the anti-abortion struggle. 'It's part of our Holy War for the pure Aryan race,' he said."[31]

It is here that the distinctions among racist pro-lifers, non-racist pro-lifers, Christian patriots, non-Christian patriots, and conservative Christians are completely blurred. What is most disturbing is that some influential evangelical leaders have actually endorsed individuals whose views are based on anti-Semitic literature. For example, Beverly LaHaye (leader of Concerned Women of America) and Pastor Chuck Smith (founder of the well-respected Calvary Chapel system of churches) have promoted works that rely on white supremacist propaganda.

The irony in all of this is that most of the evangelical leaders who appeal to works that lean on anti-Semitic literature are staunch *supporters* of Israel and the Jews. Unfortunately, such persons (e.g., LaHaye and Smith) who hold to a *non*-racist, pretribulational, premillennial view of the end times (see chapter nine), are vulnerable to anti-Semitic ideas concerning a secret cabal of conspirators seeking world domination.

One of the few differences between the New World Order conspiracy being spread by *non*-racist, pretribulational, premillennialists and the conspiracy outlined in the *Protocols* is the nature of the enemy. For racists, Jews are the conspiractors. For Christians, a myriad of conspirators—humanists, atheists, Freemasons, the Illuminati, feminists, homosexuals, liberal politicians, "international bankers," etc.—are named as tools of the Antichrist. As a result, many *non*-racist, pretribulational, premillenialists have endorsed books *proving* their preconceived ideas about the last days, not knowing that those books are relying on anti-Semitic conspiratorial theories.

The problem is only compounded when the many "patriots" who espouse conservative values and goals are thrown into the picture. The simplest way to demonstrate this chaotic mesh of criss-crossing lines is to simply list some of the many places where these widely diverse groups and individuals have overlapped:

- U.S. Taxpayers Party (USTP) National Committee member Matthew Trewhella sponsored an October 1993 rally featuring Linda Thompson. Approximately 2,500 attended.[52] Like other patriots, Trewhella insists: "We shouldn't have birth certificates or Social Security numbers . . . [or] marriage licenses."[53]

- Don McAlvany, who has also recommended Linda Thompson's work, uses his *McAlvany Intelligence Advisor* to encourage support for the USTP led by his "good friend" Howard Phillips.[54]

- Patriot Jeffrey Baker—another member of the USTP—is well-known in the patriot community for his New World Order conspiracy-exposing book *Cheque Mate: The Game of Princes*. It promotes the classic patriot conspiracies about a U.N. takeover, concentration camps and a group of secret elites bent on destroying the U.S. to achieve world dominion. When Baker appeared on the national radio program *Beverly LaHaye Live* to discuss and advertise his book, he brought with him the volume from which he drew most of his information: *The Protocols of the Learned Elders of Zion. Cheque Mate* is based on the anti-Semitic work. In fact, each chapter is built around excerpts from the *Protocols*.[55] McAlvany's materials are sold through Matthew Trewhella's Misssionaries to the Preborn ministry. One advertisement for videos by McAlvany states: "[H]ear Mr. McAlvany reveal the coming socialist and police state and give insight on how to prepare for persecution!"[56]

□ *Cheque Mate*, which is sold by Texe Marrs's Living Truth Ministries,[57] quotes from Nesta Webster.[58] Baker additionally recommends materials and resources by Jack McLamb and anti-Semite Red Beckman, who believes that the Jewish Holocaust was God's judgment on Jews.[59] Other documents Baker uses to support his arguments include *MIA* newsletters by Don McAlvany.[60]

□ One of McAlvany's staunchest allies is Chuck Missler, who regularly speaks at the Calvary Chapel system of churches led by Chuck Smith. Missler, a close friend of Smith, strongly recommends McAlvany's *MIA* newsletters, which endorses the USTP and Jeffrey Baker, who in turn introduces mainstream conservatives to the *Protocols*.

□ Chuck Smith endorses yet another New World Order conspiracy-exposing book, *En Route to Global Occupation* by Gary Kah. Smith writes: "Gary's book is an insightful look and a great analysis of the direction that the world is moving toward . . . the one-world government."[61] *En Route* leans heavily on information from anti-Semites Nesta Webster and Eustace Mullins.[62] Kah also quotes the 1937 book *Adam Weishaupt*, written by influential Christian Identity leader Gerald Winrod (see chapter eleven).[63] Winrod (1900–1957) not only published the *Protocols*, but praised Hitler for ridding Germany of "Jewish communism."[64] His Nazi extremism earned him the title "Jayhawk Nazi."[65] Gerald's son, Gordon, has continued in his father's footsteps by calling for the death of all Jews to solve America's problems.[66]

□ Beverly LaHaye also endorses *En Route to Global Occupation*. She writes: "The message of Gary Kah is a powerful reminder that we are getting closer and closer to the return of the King of Kings. . . . We are heading swiftly into a One World Government."[67]

□ Under the umbrella of the patriot movement, groups who oppose the New World Order met in November 1994 at a Burlington, Massachusetts, high school. Speakers included Sandra Martinez of Beverly LaHaye's Concerned Women for America and pro-life advocate Dr. Mildred Jefferson, founder and former officer of the National Right to Life Committee. Another speaker was Ed Brown, who runs the Constitutional Defense Militia of New Hampshire. "Brown passed out brochures offering 'Firearms Training, Combat Leadership, Close Combat, and Intelligence Measures.'" When Jefferson spoke, she tied both the National Organization of Women and

Planned Parenthood to a conspiracy of secular humanism dating back to the 1800s. Among the materials offered at the meeting were paramilitary manuals on the use of a Ruger .22-caliber rifle and primers on building bombs and incendiary devices. Other books included *Hunter*, the latest anti-Semitic novel by William Pierce, author of *The Turner Diaries*.[68]

Moderation Versus Extremism

For several years, moderate evangelicals have been encouraging Christians to restrain themselves from becoming militant, especially with regard to the abortion issue. Many well-known conservatives have even tried convincing Operation Rescue workers that their tactics would only hinder pro-life effforts and make it even more difficult to re-direct the country in a pro-life direction.[69]

Christians must begin understanding that their faith does not allow for militancy over disagreements with the government on political issues. The only time a government may be disobeyed is if that government is trying to compel a Christian to do something that is against their faith.[70] This is called the compulsion view of civil disobedience, as opposed to the promulgation view of civil disobedience. Conservative Christian scholar Dr. Norman Geisler explains:

Agreeing that abortion is contrary to the moral law of God, the promulgation view insists that a citizen has the right to engage in civil disobedience in order to oppose abortion. Here the promulgationists split into two camps: those favoring violent action (such as bombing clinics) and others favoring only non-violent disobedience (such as illegal clinic sit-ins). Compulsionists, on the other hand, believe that it is wrong to transgress the law in order to protest abortion. This is because there is a difference between a law that permits abortions and one which commands abortions. Unjust laws should be legally protested but not illegally brushed aside. It is one thing for a government to allow others to do evil, but it is another thing for them to force an individual to do evil. Only in the later case is civil disobedience justified.[71]

Unfortunately, many Christians have been unwilling to listen to the voice of moderation. They have been equally closed-minded about cautions regarding racism within the church and the bizarre nature of the conspiracy theories being touted by some Christians. On the Calvary Chapel e-mail computer list server, for instance, critics of Chuck Missler's conspiracy theories have met with harsh rebuttals from Missler supporters.[72] One such individual defended Missler by writing:

Perhaps you too quickly discount these "bizarre conspiracy theories" by accepting the standard media lines. . . . [P]ropagation of the New World Order is a fact. . . . [T]he imposition of UN will on the U.S. is a sovereignty issue with the possibility being proposed of UN "peace keeping" forces being brought into the U.S. in times of "national emergency" (yet to occur). . . . These Black Helicopters are a fact.[73]

Such a response suggests that believers in patriot conspiracy theories not only are ignorant of the facts, but are also emotionally committed to defending the views of their leaders.[74] Patriots, especially Christian patriots, need to start being more rational and analytical. Undiscerning Christians have helped create a movement that is a bizarre mish-mash of evangelicalism, Christian terminology, apocalypticism, white supremacy, anti-Semitic legends, hate-filled rhetoric and violence.

The lines of demarcation between responsible evangelicals and radical extremists should be clearly drawn. Even more importantly, the divisions between Christian and racists must be firmly re-established. If these changes do not take place, and if the current rift between patriots and the federal government remains unbridged, the patriot/militia movement is destined to bring more injury to our nation.[75]

The next several years may prove to be especially difficult since most patriots see the year 2000 as the watershed in their efforts to re-establish their concept of "freedom" in America: "[T]he Globalists have stated that the date of termination of the American way of life is the year 2000. . . . [I]t is fitting that our date to terminate—at the very least—their **plan**, is also 2000."[74] What can be done to defuse the current situation before it gets any worse? The answer to this question will be the focus of our final chapter.

16

Blessed Are the Peacemakers

We are fighting a war right now, and we're either gonna fight
to win, or we're gonna die.
Dean Compton
National Alliance of Christian Militia[1]

Rebellion is in the air and I love it!
Eustace Mullins
Anti-Semitic patriot[2]

ccording to Militia of Montana leader John Trochmann, "document after document of the New World Order plans for the total takeover of this country by the year 2000."[3] Ross Hullett, state commander of the Oklahoma Citizens Militia, agrees: "[T]he New World Order is a government, a socialistic scheme that is to be in place in this country by the year 2000."[4] A 1995 issue of the *Patriot Press* reveals that the evil forces now on a "relentless path to establishing on planet earth a super world government by the year A.D. 2000 . . . are about to make a dash to the finish line."[5] Page 148 of Jim Keith's *Black Helicopters Over America* declares the inevitable:

By the year 2000 America will be merged into a Socialist New World Order, and the world will be split into three functional divisions: European, North American, and the Pacific Rim power structure. These international blocs will be governed by the United Nations, with the U.N. Army stepping in to quell any disturbances or "quaintly archaic" nationalist sentiments. The U.N. and allied New World Order lackeys such as Bill Clinton and George Bush are, despite all their humanist rhetorical debris, clearly the frontmen for the international bankers. . . . Plans are now in full implementation for the surrender of U.S. sovereignty into the global New World Order, as envisioned by international banking and industrial controllers.[6]

Anyone suggesting to patriots that this scenario would be stopped by the U.S.

Constitution are met with emotional tirades. Clayton Douglas, publisher of the *Free American* writes: "The whole of the Constitution has been subverted and supplanted by traitorous treaties with this Globalist organization [United Nations]."[7] Patriot Nick Repac says "[M]any of us are now awakening and we know that the Constitution is suspended."[8] Some members of the Libertarian Party not only believe that the U.S. Constitution has been suspended, but feel that America is no longer a free country:

> America has already become a socialist state. . . . Laws and regulations now
> govern every aspect of your life—from what you do on the job to what you do
> in your bedroom. And police can now kill you and your family with impunity.
> Legislation already passed will soon make this country a full-blown police state,
> complete with massive federal terror squads, seizures of property from dissi-
> dents, and indefinite imprisonment without trial.[9]

Ken Adams, a Michigan Militia spokesman, alleges that his militia has sought to alleviate the tensions between patriots and the government by advocating peaceful political activism: "We are setting up programs right now to help people start registering to vote and going to the polls and getting involved in the legislation and the process that we all love."[10]

Some observers feel this statement offers a glimmer of hope. But it is difficult for me to accept the sincerity of Adams's words, since his position contradicts the standard patriot assumption that America's entire political process is corrupt. Consider the views expressed in a 1994 Militia of Montana newsletter:

> [W]hether you believe it or not; whether you know it or not; your vote has been
> stolen from you by a Cartel of Federal National Security, Bureaucrats who
> include higher-ups in the Central Intelligence Agency, political party leaders,
> Congressmen, co-opted journalists and the owners and managers of the major
> establishment news media.[11]

Don McAlvany writes: "[T]here is an unholy alliance between the Republicans and Democrats. . . . Both parties are controlled by the same Liberal Eastern Establishment whose goal is world government under the New World Order."[12] McAlvany echoes the theme of a popular patriot book entitled *Votescam: The Stealing of America*, which asserts that the government has been using computers to covertly alter election results in favor of pre-selected candidates:

> [C]omputers are covertly stealing your vote. For almost three decades the
> American vote has been subject to government-sponsored electronic theft. The
> vote has been stolen from you by a cartel of federal "national security"
> bureaucrats, who include higher-ups in the Central Intelligence Agency, politi-
> cal party leaders, Congressmen, co-opted journalists—and the owners and
> managers of the major Establishment news media, who have decided in concert
> . . . how America's votes are counted, by whom they are counted and how the
> results are verified. . . . [T]he Establishment press has actual physical control
> of the counting and dissemination of the vote, and it refuses to let the public

know how it is done. . . . [T]he theft of your vote or Votescam, is part of a . . . "collaboration" between federal officials and the news media that began shortly after the assassination of John F. Kennedy in 1963, when the "responsible" American press was persuaded by American intelligence services to hide from the American people the actual implications of the Kennedy murder.[13]
Patriots and militia members who embrace such a concept of American politics see themselves as crusaders in "a righteous war of liberation."[14] Recent events suggest that many of these freedom fighters do not see themselves waging a peaceful war.

Might Does Not Make Right

"Thousands of people are going to die if the news media doesn't wake up to the threat to our constitutional rights," warns Christian militiaman Ray Southwell of Michigan.[15] Southwell is correct about the media's need to wake up to the threat that all Americans face, but he misidentifies those who are endangering our constitutional liberties and safety. A cursory overview of some recent events is extremely revealing:

☐ Michigan Militia leader William Ordiway and his followers have repeatedly disrupted Wellston, Michigan, town meetings by "demanding that every town decision be put to a town vote—a 'show of hands' vote rather than a ballot vote." The militia disagrees with a 1993 zoning law supported by Wellston residents. Ordiway and his fellow militiamen, many of whom, like Ordiway, are not even from Wellston, claim that the zoning law is an immoral infringement of people's rights.[16]

☐ A letter to legislatures from the Constitutional Rights Federation in Hermosa Beach warns, "We consider [gun control] to be TREASON and respond accordingly. . . . We want the scalps of every anti-gun politician, bureaucrat and public employee."[17]

☐ In late 1995, sixty-year-old Willie Lampley, 50-year-old Cecelia Lampley, 56-year-old Larry Crow and fifty-three-year-old John Baird were arrested by the FBI and indicted on bomb-making charges, as well as soliciting a crime of violence. The Oklahoma group reportedly had planned to blow up the Houston Anti-Defamation League building, the Southern Poverty Law Center (an organization that tracks racist groups), abortion clinics and the U.S. Department of Health and Human Services building.[18]

Ken Toole, president of the Montana Human Rights Network, has seen numerous individuals harassed and intimidated by patriot/militia-related groups. Persons who send anti-militia/patriot letters to the editors of local newspapers have received threatening phone calls in the night. Those who have been brave enough to speak out against militias at public meetings are confronted by irate and threatening patriots.[19]

During Congressman Charles Shumer's July 11, 1995, informal forum on the militias, environmentalist Susan Schock described what she experienced for expressing pro-environmentalism positions:

Last summer, a dozen angry ranch women encircled me on the porch of the Catron County Courthouse. . . . They yelled "Why are you here?" "Go back to where you came from." "Get out of our county." "You're not welcome." . . . When I told them that I was exercising my constitutional rights, another woman put her face inches from mine and growled, "Do you want to go at it?" . . . I was targeted last April in a letter to the *Silver City Daily Press* from Ernest Cooper of Espanola, 200 miles away, who wrote "I wish to apprise (Susan) of the inherent danger of interfering in people's lives and businesses. The citizens in that quiet corner of New Mexico are, in most cases, willing to take up the use of force to ensure those rights." A regional "wise use" newspaper, the *Hatch Courier* . . . targeted me with false accusations of cattle rustling and "collusion" with the Forest Service. . . . When a photo of my home appeared in the Courier last April, my ten-year-old-daughter, Katie, asked "Won't this put us in danger, Mom?" I had to answer, "Yes, it might." As I answered her, I remembered a pickup truck skidding around the corner and a man yelling "G-d— hippie environmentalist bitch!" last winter as I walked to the door of our house where she was waiting for me alone.[20]

Martha A. Bethel, a Hamilton, Montana, city judge, has actually had a "contract" put out on her because of her attempts to uphold law and order:

My experience with these groups began in January of 1995, when one self-titled "freeman," appeared in court in response to three (3) routine traffic tickets. He described his appearance as a "special visitation," denying that the court over which I presided had any sort of jurisdiction over him. He vehemently challenged such jurisdiction, and law enforcement's authority over him, denying that he is bound in any way by the law of our state. He refused to cooperate with the initial appearance proceedings. On March 3, 1995, this defendant served me with documents demanding dismissal of the charges against him. These documents recounted a hearing held before his "common law" jurisdiction held on March 1, 1995, at which their "justices" ruled that the local courts lack jurisdiction over them. . . . They asserted that I had violated my oath of office, that the pleadings against him were a "sham pleading" and so on. The "justices" of this "common law" court demanded dismissal of the charges within ten (10) days or, as the documents stated, "lawful warrants of arrest will issue." . . . I have heard threats such as that I would be kidnapped from my home, out of my offices, or from my vehicle on the highway; that I would be tried before their "common law" court and sentenced for acts, which have been described as "treasonous." A local Justice of the Peace was told that they [sic] would be shot in the head. A deputy county attorney was warned that his house would be burned and that he would be shot in the back. Our District Judge has heard threats such as the plan to remove him from his chambers and hang him in the city park. We have done nothing but perform our official duties in compliance with the law. . . . In February I was followed home roughly 40 miles after a night court session. Several days later an unidentified caller informed me that I had been followed home . . . and to prove it gave me the location of our home. I have been harassed by dozens of phone calls, both from unidentified callers and concerned citizens warning me of what they have heard will happen to me or my home. . . . I have since that time received hate mail from across the country. On two separate occasions I had my children live with their dad for a week at a time. . . . Over the Easter weekend, law enforcement officials suggested I take the children and leave the county after they received credible information that an attempt was to be made on me or my residence. Most recently I received information from a Federal law enforcement agency that a contract has been issued for my murder.[21]

The clear message patriots are sending to non-patriots is, "Don't get in our way" and "Don't speak out publicly against us or what we want." Sadly, the tactics are working. Many financial donors to environmentalist groups now wish to remain anonymous and avoid being publicly seen with known environmentalists.[22] People who understand their views are unpopular with local patriots and militias have withdrawn from participating in the democratic decision-making process in their area.[23]

I, too, have had to weigh the consequences of speaking out about the patriot/militia movement. A number of individuals assisting me with this book requested that I not mention their names for fear of reprisals from patriot groups. This is understandable given the words of Norm Olson: "[T]here are people taking names now and people in the media will stand charges with the tyrants. Spreading news is a sacred gift of God and if you don't deliver, the people will come knocking at your door."[24]

It is no surprise that a 1995 California poll found more than two-thirds of that state's residents oppose the "formation of armed citizen militias, and more than half believe such groups pose a possible threat to society." One-third considered militias to be a "severe threat to society."[25] The role that militias play in the propagation of societal violence has been compared to a funnel:

Imagine the [militia] movement as a funnel. . . . At the widest end are arguments about gun control and government misconduct. Many people are concerned about these issues and are attracted to the movement. Once a person enters the funnel they are exposed to the conspiracy theories . . . the UN troops in the mountains, the black helicopters flying over the next ridge. Many people don't accept those ideas, and get out of the movement. Others though move deeper into the funnel learning about the shadowy figures behind the conspiracies, the Freemasons, the Illuminati, the international bankers, ultimately, the Jews. As they move deeper into the funnel they begin planning what they are going to do to confront the system, the weapons training, the bomb making, storing food and a host of other actions they can take. Finally out the far end of the funnel comes individuals who are dedicated to taking some kind of direct and confrontational action. It is a process of radicalization which leads individuals to take matters into their own hands through violent means. In this regard these organizations pose a very real threat to law enforcement and should be a concern to the entire community.[26]

"Self-styled patriots have wrapped themselves in the flag while belittling the very virtues of compassion and tolerance for which that flag stands."[27] Clearly, law-abiding Americans cannot go on living in fear of a minority of citizens. To counteract the patriot movement's threat to life, liberty and the pursuit of happiness for all persons, there are a number of steps that can be taken in various sectors of our society.

Government Reform

Kenneth Stern of the American Jewish Committee maintains that the agitation felt by patriots will definitely increase "as they see more and more things that are filtered through the lens of their conspiracy."[28] Brian Jenkins, a managing partner in the international security firm Kroll Associates, agrees that patriot paranoia "tends to feed on itself, and they become more and more worked up."[29]

I believe the government can redirect extremists away from their path of self-justifying violence by ceasing to act in ways that would be consistent with some of the patriot conspiracy theories. Federal officials can do this by addressing the *legitimate*, as opposed to the fanciful, complaints being voiced by patriots. For example, in reference to patriot beliefs that our government is not trustworthy, and that it imperils its citizens, patriot Albert Esposita comments:

> [W]e're talking about the government that experimented on its own citizens with
> . . . radiation. We're talking about the government that dropped Agent Orange
> on its soldiers and then denied it did anything wrong.[30]

It is a documented fact that thousands of Vietnam veterans who came in contact with Agent Orange, a "dioxin-laden herbicide used to defoliate Vietnam," eventually became severely ill, died or had children with birth defects.[31] Rather than reaching out to suffering veterans, the Reagan and Bush administrations "manipulated a Centers for Disease Control (CDC) study on the effects of the toxins" so the investigation would end before findings could place blame for the illnesses on the government's use of Agent Orange.[32] A year-long study (1989–1990) conducted by the Human Resources and Intergovernmental Relations Subcommittee revealed that the CDC study was "controlled and obstructed by the White House, primarily through its Agent Orange Working Group (AOWG) and the Office of Management and Budget."[33]

The radiation experiments to which Esposito is referring took place over more than fifty years during the Cold War. Apparently, the U.S. government conducted an extensive program of human radiation testing without the consent of 23,000 citizens in approximately 1,400 experiments.[34] Among those irradiated without their knowledge were "102 native Alaskans (men, women and children) and 19 U.S. Air Force and Army servicemen," who between August 1955 and February 1957 received doses of radioactive Iodine-131.[35] Participants "never were informed that they were being administered radioactive tracer elements and few of the Alaska natives understood they were participating in research." Scientists who have reviewed the 1950s research said most of the subjects "thought they were receiving medical treatment."[36]

"Dismissing or ignoring the patriot movement won't make it go away," political analyst Chip Berlet observes.[37] This is because the movement reflects the feelings of a segment of society that has grown to fear the government. If this fear can be eliminated, some of the animosity patriots feel toward the government may be lessened.

Law Enforcement Restructuring

In an article for the patriot magazine _Media Bypass_, Colorado Senator Charles Duke, a patriot sympathizer, promises that the current wave of anti-government sentiment will recede only after federal authorities change their mode of operation:

> When we see that the BATF and the FBI will clean their own ranks, when we see that violent behavior, even by government agents, will not be tolerated, when we see the elimination of the arrogance that comes from a government with unchecked control, when we see the government recognize the constitutional rights of its citizens, that is the day the criticism will stop.[38]

Ruby Ridge and Waco are but two instances in which federal law enforcement authorities have gone beyond what was necessary to accomplish their goals. The tragedies serve as reminders of how rarely top government officials are prosecuted for wrongdoing. Persons in high government positions are usually given what amounts to little more than a slap on the wrist when they make wrong—and sometimes deadly—decisions. At the same time, violent groups who threaten society should be dealt with swiftly and decisively: "[T]he Constitution does not require that a government stand by helplessly when extremist ideas, combined with an arsenal of weaponry, are used to intimidate American citizens."[39] Law enforcement needs to protect the populace from those who would use their frustration, anger and paranoia as an excuse to hurt innocent persons. Balancing the use of deadly force and diplomacy will not be an easy task for authorities. Nevertheless, it is the one with which they are faced.

Tuning Out Hate Talk

Soon after the Oklahoma City bombing, President Clinton publicly criticized numerous unnamed conservative talk radio hosts. He also commented that many individuals have used public platforms, namely, the radio airwaves, "to keep people as paranoid as possible and the rest of us all torn up and upset with each other."[40] Clinton labeled the Federal building tragedy as the kind of destruction possible when well-known personalities use hate talk to fan the flames of paranoia, bitterness and anger:

> We should be careful about the kind of language we use and the kind of incendiary talk we engage in. We never know who is listening or what impact it might have. So we need to show some restraint and discipline because of all the people in this country that might be on the edge and might be capable of doing something horrible like this.[41]

The President denounced the "loud and angry voices that inflame the public debate,"[42] and gave a final exhortation:

> [T]hose of us who do not agree with the purveyors of hatred and division, with the promoters of paranoia, . . . it is time we all stood up and spoke against that kind of reckless speech and behavior. When they talk of hatred, we must stand against them. When they talk of violence, we must stand against them. When they say things that are irresponsible, we must call them on it.[43]

Clinton was immediately castigated for daring to suggest that persons who habit-ually push the limits of free speech somehow contributed to the atmosphere of hate that led to the Murrah building explosion. In the *McAlvany Intelligence Advisor*, Don McAlvany ranted about Clinton's words, saying they were directed at "anti-liberal, anti-Clinton, free-speech conservatives who are critical of him and his policies."[44] House Speaker Newt Gingrich responded with equal indigna-tion: "It is grotesque to suggest that anybody in this country who raises legitimate questions about the size and scope of the Federal Government has any implication in this" [Oklahoma City bombing].[45] Neale Boortz, an Atlanta-based conservative talk-radio host voiced similar sentiments:

> Bill Clinton considers talk radio to be one of his biggest enemies out there. And he made the decision yesterday in Minneapolis to use this tragic event in Oklahoma as a weapon against talk radio. He wants to tie [up] every conservative or libertarian talk show host in this country. He wants to handcuff 'em to Timothy McVeigh or anybody else who might be involved in this bombing. He wants to bury these talk show hosts under the bodies of dead babies. He wants to cover 'em with the rubble and soot from Oklahoma City . . . and silence 'em. . . . In Bill Clinton's dictionary, when a conservative says something about liberal policies or philosophy, it's hate. When a liberal says something about conservative philosophy or policies, it's commentary.[46]

It is difficult to believe that these post-bombing defensive statements were anything but desperate attempts by extremists to distance themselves from the horrific event. A small sampling of the rhetoric that conservative talk-radio hosts and patriot/mi-litia leaders had spewed from their pulpits in the months prior to the bombing reveals that Clinton may have been justified in his condemnations:

□ "Don't shoot at that [the upper body of ATF agents] because they've got a vest on underneath that. Head shots. Head shots. . . . Kill the sons of bitches" (262 stations nationwide).[47]

☐ "[Gun-control activist Sarah Brady] ought to be put down. A humane shot at a veterinarian's would be an easy way to do it" (KFYI—Phoenix, AZ).[48]

☐ "Am I advocating the overthrow of this government? . . . I'm advocating a cleansing . . . an armed revolution" (KVOR—Colorado Springs, CO).[49]

☐ "The second violent American revolution is just about—I got my fingers about a fourth of an inch apart—is just about that far away. Because these people are sick and tired of a bunch of bureaucrats in Washington driving into town and telling them what they can and cannot do" (nationwide).[50]

☐ "We're not going to rest on that [lawsuit against the Brady Bill]. . . . [B]e assured that creeps like [Senator] Metzenbaum and [Senator] Kennedy are going to think that we're sitting back thinking, 'Well, the Brady law has been defeated or declared unconstitutional.' You know how these slime balls operate. The only way you're ever going to get rid of Metzenbaum is when you're finally at a point that you can stand over there, put the dirt on top of the box and say, 'I'm pretty sure he's in there.' " [51]

☐ "We are on the edge of calamity. . . . How can we change it? We stand and fight. . . . There's no sense of running cause you'll only die tired. You might as well lock and load. Eventually, coercive force is our only choice, we have either that or slavery."[52]

A feeble, and obviously contrived, attempt at downplaying the significance of these types of statements was made by the Michigan Militia's Ken Adams, who actually stated on national television that his militia was not anti-government. He also claimed it had never issued warnings about a conspiracy to replace U.S. democracy with a one-world government. Reporter Beth Hawkins of the *Detroit Metro Times* writes: "Then Adams delivered the kicker. Although the militia bills itself as a Second Amendment rights organization, he claimed that he had never made an issue of guns."[53]

Hundreds of pieces of documentation in this book clearly show that the patriot/militia is solidly built on anti-governmentalism, conspiracy theories and pro-gun advocacy. It has also been demonstrated that patriot/militia leaders, as well as "conservative" talk-radio hosts, have used an excessive amount of what Professor Phil Agre in the communication department of the University of California, San Diego, calls "[e]xtravagantly hyperbolic metaphors of mass political murder."[54]

Numerous conservatives reject such criticisms, citing the First Amendment's right to free speech. Free speech, however, cannot be exercised carte blanche. The freedom ceases with words that lead to injury and/or death. As Justice Oliver Wendell Holmes put it, "freedom of speech ends when you falsely cry 'fire' in a crowded theater."[55]

But talk radio extremists and patriot/militia leaders refuse to acknowledge that troubled and impressionable minds can withstand only so many comments about killing, beating and bombing "the enemy" before acting upon the violent rhetoric they hear. The majority of radio listeners may not pose a danger to society, but some individuals in the patriot community could hurt others after listening to endless barrages of hate talk.

Francisco Duran, for example, who sprayed the White House with gunfire in an attempt to assassinate President Clinton, was an avid listener of patriot/militia propaganda. He regularly tuned into patriot radio talk shows such as Chuck Baker's Colorado-based *On the Carpet* program (KVOR-FM). Duran's brother-in-law, Jose Gutierrez, says Duran even attended meetings of the Save America Militia.[56]

Senator Carl Levin has correctly noted that extreme hate rhetoric "contributes to an incendiary atmosphere in which an unstable individual will take the rhetoric seriously and light a match or a fuse."[57] Daniel Levitas, former director of the Atlanta-based Center for Democratic Renewal, a think-tank that tracks white supremacist organizations, explains:

> When far-right groups talk extensively about the possibility of violent confrontation, when they glorify individuals who've been involved in confrontation and when they engaged [sic] in the rhetoric that promotes violent confrontation, it's almost assured that there will be violent confrontation. . . . These far-right groups create an atmosphere that attracts the very people like (bombing suspect) Timothy McVeigh and others who are then likely to go out and commit the acts that the leaders of these groups talk about. When they take words into action, it becomes a public relations problem for the leaders and they backtrack.[58]

Persons who have come out of hate groups agree with this proposition. Ingo Hasselbach, founder of the former East Germany's first neo-Nazi political party, not only has realized the error of his ways, but admits that his messages of hate influenced untold numbers of young people toward violent acts. Hasselbach says his realization of this fact was the first step toward "rejoining the civilized world."[59]

Tragically, it took a 1992 firebombing in Germany that killed two little girls to put Hasselbach on the long road of healing introspection. It seems that American talk-radio luminaries and idolized patriot/militia leaders do not have as much courage or honesty as this former racist. What must occur before they, like Hasselbach, understand the effects that words can have on another person's actions? Hasselbach levels a stinging reproach at all who would lend their voices to the patriot/militia movement's brand of hate rhetoric:

> [T]he leaders of the Michigan militia and other such groups cannot dodge a larger moral responsibility, whether or not they are legally to blame [for the Oklahoma city bombing]. . . . [E]xtremist groups in America and Europe create a climate, through printed propaganda and computer networks, that encourages young people who might be antisocial to go over the edge and commit violent acts.[60]

Rush Limbaugh disagrees. In a brief 1995 *Newsweek* article defending free speech, the popular conservative asserted that for more than 200 years citizens "have been debating the size, scope, and role of federal government." He continued, "Now, suddenly, in 1995, it is claimed that this two-century-old argument caused the Oklahoma tragedy." Limbaugh was incensed: "The suggestion is irresponsible and vacuous; such insinuations can only have a chilling effect on legitimate discussion."[61]

Limbaugh, of course, has set up a straw man argument. The issue is not legitimate political discussion. Nor does it have anything to do with whether conservative Americans have a right to voice disagreements with liberal politicians. The issue centers on the use of irresponsible, inflammatory rhetoric, so violent in nature that it is capable of inciting some listeners to aggressive action.

Clearer Heads Will Prevail

What can the average American do to alleviate the widespread paranoia and hatred infecting our country? Political analyst Chip Berlet feels that each of us needs to reach out and try to reintegrate extremists into "rational dialogue." Paranoid conspiracy theories must be debunked "so people can have a rational discussion of how to deal with the problems and decide where we're going as a nation."[62] Berlet thinks that over a long period of time the majority of people, given enough accurate information and access to a full and open debate, will reach the right decision to preserve liberty.

Bill Wassmuth of the Northwest Coalition Against Malicious Harassment understands that before even addressing the conspiracy theories of patriots and militia members, their movement needs to be understood. Once this is done, the promoters of deceptive tactics and inflammatory rhetoric need to be held accountable "for the consequences of their words, if not in the court of law, at least in the realm of community responsibility."[63] Wassmuth continues:

> We must build up the democratic process to productively address the issues of the day rather than give in to intimidation. . . . We must continue to build a system of government that is fair and responsible, based on the principles of truth and justice, not succumbing to paranoia and conspiracy theories. We all have a role to play in the task before us.[64]

The United States has seen a great deal of anguish, bitterness, frustration and pain since the early 1990s. Ruby Ridge, Waco and Oklahoma City should never be forgotten. We must learn from these tragedies. My hope is that our country's future will be marked by governmental justice and concern for its citizens, as well as by Americans willing to use peaceful means to bring about change: "Evil is a strong force, and hate one of evil's best weapons. But love is, and always has been, stronger than hate. Good is stronger than evil. Light is more powerful than darkness. In the end, love will prevail."[65]

Notes

Introduction

[1]Timothy McVeigh, letter to editor, *Union-Sun & Journal* (Lockport, N.Y.), February 11, 1992. Quoted in David Willman, "McVeigh Lashed at Government in '92 Letters," *Los Angeles Times,* April 27, 1995, A11.

[2]Steven K. Paulson, "McVeigh, Nichols Transferred To Denver Prison," March 30, 1996 (America Online); cf. Associated Press, "Oklahoma And California Governors Honor Rescue Teams," March 7, 1996 (America Online), Richard A. Serrano and Ronald J. Ostrow, "Money Trail Details Blast Suspects' 'Lost' World," *Los Angeles Times,* October 8, 1995, A1, and Evan Thomas, "Cracking Down on Hate," *Newsweek,* May 15, 1995, 23.

[3]Terry Allen, "Professional Arab-Bashing," *Covert Action Quarterly* 53 (Summer 1995), 20–21. This article gives a detailed listing of several media stories in which government spokespersons and terrorist experts unjustly blamed Arabs for the Oklahoma bombing; cf. Jonathan Alter, "Jumping to Conclusions," *Newsweek,* May 1, 1995, 55.

[4]"Man Cleared in Attack Tells of Nasty Backlash," *Orange County Register,* April 23, 1995, 26; cf. Jeff Cohen and Norman Solomon, "Knee-Jerk Coverage of Bombing Should Not Be Forgotten," *AlterNet,* May 4, 1995, reprinted in Don Hazen, Larry Smith and Christine Triano, eds., *Militias in America 1995* (San Francisco: Institute for Alternative Journalism, 1995), 59–61, and Omied Far, Najwa Hussaini and Asma Saad, "(Un)true Lies," *YO!,* May/June 1995, reprinted in Hazen et al., *Militias in America,* 64–65.

[5]Louis Freeh, quoted in Stephen Braun and Richard A. Serrano, "'Something Big' Warned of by McVeigh, U.S. Says," *Los Angeles Times,* April 27, 1995, A12.

[6]Daniel Junas, "Angry White Guys With Guns: The Rise of the Militias," *Covert Action Quarterly* 52 (Spring 1995), 21, and Jill Smolowe, "Enemies of the State," *Time,* May 8, 1995, 61.

[7]Mark Koernke, "A Call to Arms" (Real World Productions, 1993).

[8]Linda Thompson, "Crime Briefing—Martial Law 1 of 16," BBS message #14016 (Fr: Linda Thompson, To: All), February 8, 1994, *AEN News*-FidoNet.

[9]Richard Butler. Cited in Paul Henderson, "We're Not Saluting Hitler—We're Saluting God," *Seattle Times,* April 17, 1983, 7.

[10]Erik Larson, "ATF Under Siege," *Time,* July 24, 1995, 23.

[11]Department of the Treasury. *Report of the Department of the Treasury on the Bureau of Alcohol, Tobacco, and Firearms Investigation of Vernon Wayne Howell* (Washington: U.S. Government Printing Office, 1993), 193.

[12]Norm Resnik. Cited in James Risen, "Militia Networks Boast An Alternate Take On Reality," *Los Angeles Times,* April 30, 1995, A1.

[13]Phil Agre, unpublished essay on the Oklahoma City bombing, Internet posting, April 23, 1995. Confirmed by author's January 19, 1995, telephone interview with Agre.

Part One: Sounds of Sedition

[1]James Johnson, transcripts of the United States Senate Subcommittee on Terrorism, Technology, and Government Information of the Committee on the Judiciary, "The Militia Movement in the United States," June 15, 1995, 89.

[2]Steve Hance, quoted in Susan Ladd and Stan Swofford, "Discontent Feeds Movement, Observers

Say," *News & Record* (Greensboro, N.C.), June 27, 1995, Internet edition at http://www.infi.net/nr/ extra/militias/m-discon.htm. This article is only one of a series of articles on the militias that ran from June 23 to June 27, 1995. All of the articles are available on the Internet at http://www.infi.net/nr/ extra/militias/m-index.htm

[3]Samuel Sherwood, quoted in Dan Yurman, "Militia Leader Predicts Civil War in the West (Dateline—3/12/95)," *Reports on the Militia Movement in Idaho: Visions of Blood & Fishes Swim in Political Circles,* Internet posting, November 22, 1995, AlterNet BBS gopher site, pathway begins at gopher://gopher.igc.apc.org:70/1, to Progressive Gophers folder, to AlterNet folder, to Militias in America folder, to Militia-Watch Updates folder, to "Reports on the Militia Movement in Idaho" document. Sherwood made his comment to the Associated Press on March 2 and March 10, 1995. His threatening words originally were published in the *Idaho Falls Post Register* on March 12, 1995, and subsequently reported by Yurman (E-mail adddress, dyurman@igc.apc.org.).

[4]Linda Sanders, report on *ABC World News*, November 30, 1995.

[5]Marvin McCormick, author's October 11, 1995, telephone conversation with McCormick.

Chapter 1: Rise of the Patriots

[1]*Network*, MGM Productions, 1976.

[2]Gordon Liddy, quoted in "G. Gordon Liddy Endorses Militias At Washington Rally," *San Francisco Examiner*, June 5, 1995, Internet edition at http://www.sfgate.com/examiner/index.shtml. Samuel Sherwood, leader of the United States Militia Association, made a similar comment during an interview with ABC's *Day One* on April 27, 1995. In the program segment, Sherwood stated: "These groups, as radical as their philosophy is, their only desire is to be left alone."

[3]Chi Chi Sileo, "Fringe Groups and Militias Aim to 'Restore' Constitution," *Insight on the News*, August 21, 1995, 14.

[4]Noah Chandler, quoted in Michael Taylor, "Extremists Bracing for New World Order," *San Francisco Chronicle*, April 25, 1995, Internet edition at http://www.sfgate.com/chronicle/index.shtml.

[5]James Ridgeway and Leonard Zeskind, "Revolution U.S.A.," *Village Voice*, April 25, 1995, reprinted in Hazen et al., *Militias in America 1995,* 39. In context, Ridgeway and Zeskind are referring specifically to the militia movement, but their thoughts are applicable to the patriot movement in general since both movements are often referred to as one and the same thing.

[6]Adapted from Chip Berlet, "Armed Militias, Right Wing Populism, & Scapegoating," April 24, 1995, Internet posting, AlterNet BBS gopher site, pathway begins at gopher://gopher.igc.apc.org:70/1, to Progressive Gophers folder, to AlterNet folder, to Militias in America folder, to Militias in America (1995) folder, to Chronicling the Growth of a Movement folder.

[7]Chip Berlet and Matthew Lyons, "Militia Nation," *The Progressive*, June 1995, 23.

[8]Jill Smolowe, "Enemies of the State," *Time*, May 8, 1995, 61.

[9]Mike McKinzey, quoted in Rebecca Shelton, "The New Minutemen," *Kansas City New Times*, February 22, 1995, reprinted in Hazen et al., *Militias in America 1995,* 19.

[10]Doug Fales, quoted in Lisa M. Krieger, "I Love My Country—It's the Government I Hate," *San Francisco Examiner*, May 7, 1995, Internet edition at http://www.sfgate.com/examiner/index.shtml

[11]Victoria Pope, "Notes from Underground," *U.S. News & World Report*, June 5, 1995, 25.

[12]Harold Meyerson. "State of Hatred," *LA Weekly*, April 28, 1995, reprinted in Hazen et al., *Militias in America 1995,* 58.

[13]Russ Bellant, "The Paranoid and the Paramilitary," *Detroit Metro Times*, Internet edition, Internet posting, AlterNet BBS gopher site, pathway begins at gopher://gopher.igc.apc.org:70/1, to Progressive Gophers folder, to AlterNet folder, to Militias in America folder, to Additional Articles on Militias folder.

[14]Chip Berlet, quoted in Susan Ladd and Stan Swofford, "Discontent Feeds Movement, Observers Say," *News & Record* (Greensboro, N.C.), June 27, 1995, Internet edition at http://www.infi.net/nr/extra/ militias/m-discon.htm; cf. "Women Who Love to Hate," *Mademoiselle*, August 1994, 186.

[15]Bellant, "The Paranoid."

[16]Ed Wolff, quoted in John Rothchild, "Wealth: Static Wages, Except for the Rich," *Time*, January 30, 1995, 60; cf. Meyerson, "State of Hatred," 58.

[17]Michael Elliot et al., "The West At War," *Newsweek*, July 17, 1995, 24.

[18]Elliot, 26.

[19]Elliot, 27.

[20]Meyerson, 58.

[21]James Corcoran, *Bitter Harvest* (New York: Viking, 1990), 9.

[22]Corcoran, 10.

[23]Corcoran, 9.

[24]Corcoran, 10.

[25]Corcoran, 12–13.

[26]Corcoran, 22–23.

[27]James Coates, *Armed and Dangerous* (New York: Hill and Wang, 1987; 1995 ed.), 16; cf. Corcoran, *Bitter Harvest*, 22–23.

[28]Berlet and Lyons, "Militia Nation," 24.

[29]Corcoran, *Bitter Harvest*, 8, 9.

[30]Corcoran, 9.

[31]Corcoran, 10.

[32]Corcoran, 19.

[33]McKinzey, 19.

[34]Denis Johnson, "The Militia in Me," *Esquire*, July 1995, 43.

[35]Johnson, 44.

[36]Chip Berlet, quoted in Keith Stone, "Suspicion of Government Drives Patriot Movement," *Daily News*, December 26, 1994, 16.

[37]Pope, 25.

[38]Senator Max Baucus, transcripts, "The Militia Movement," 12.

[39]Baucus, 12

[40]McKinzey, 19.

[41]Smolowe, 68.

[42]Pope, 24–25.

[43]Gary Andrew Poole, "This Land Is My Land," *Los Angeles Times Magazine*, December 3, 1995, 54.

[44]Smolowe, 68.

[45]John Andrist, quoted in Kathie Durbin, "Environmental Terrorism in Washington State," *Seattle Weekly*, January 11, 1995, reprinted in Hazen et al., *Militias in America 1995*, 35.

[46]Laird Wilcox, quoted in Wirpsa, 10.

[47]Ellen Gray, testimony before Congressman Charles Shumer's informal forum on "America under the Gun: The Militia Movement and Hate Groups in America," July 11, 1995, 2.

[48]Charles Shumway, quoted by Susan Schock in "America Under the Gun," 7.

[49]Durbin, 31.

[50]Schock, 2.

[51]Jeff DeBonis, "An Atmosphere of Lawlessness" (Public Employees for Environmental Responsibility), 1995, 2.

[52]Ken Toole, testimony in "America Under the Gun," 2.

[53]David Helvarg, *The War Against the Greens* (San Francisco: Sierra Club Books, 1994), 326. Cited in Junas, "Angry White Guys," 24.

[54]Junas, 24.

[55]Durbin, 32.

[56]Durbin, 31–32.

[57]Durbin, 31, 33.

[58]Durbin, 33, 34, 37.

[59]Durbin, 33

[60]Durbin, 33, 35.

[61]Durbin, 31.

[62]Schock, testimony in "America under the Gun," 3.

[63]Barry Siegel, "A Lone Ranger," *Los Angeles Times Magazine*, November 26, 1995, 22.

[64]Johnson, transcripts, "The Militia Movement," 111.

[65]Jon D. Hull, "The State of the Union," *Time*, January 30, 1995, 54.

[66]Bill Johnson, *MacNeil/Lehrer News Hour*, April 26, 1995.

[67]Richard Z. Chesnoff. "A New Sagebrush Revolt," *U.S. News & World*, June 5, 1995, 27.

[68]Smolowe, 69.

[69]Pope, 25.

[70]John Harrell, quoted in Robert Tomsho, "Some Militiamen See A Government Plot In Oklahoma Blast," *Wall Street Journal*, April 24, 1995, A1.

[71]Harold Sheil, *MacNeil/Lehrer News Hour*, April 26, 1995.

[72]Pope, 25.

[73]Armstrong Williams, "Clinton Attacks on Talk Radio Are Specious," *Insight on the News*, May 29, 1995, 38.

[74]Mike Williams, "Necessary to the Security of A Free State," *Soldier of Fortune*, April 1995, 49.

[75]Phillips, "The Politics of Frustration," quoted in Ladd and Swofford, "Politics Feeds Discontent."

[76]Johnson, transcripts, "The Militia Movement," 112.

Chapter 2: A Call to Arms

[1]Clayton Douglas, "Energy, Interest and Taxes: The Weapons of the Elite in Their Silent War Against the American People," *Free American*, August 1995, 3.

[2]Ross Hullett, *CNN News*, March 1, 1995.

[3]Jeffrey Miller, "Citizen Militias Drawing Concern," *Orange County Register*, April 22, 1995, 24; Keith Schneider, "Some Militia Manuals Urge Attacks," *Orange County Register*, April 29, 1995, 10; Josh Meyer, Paul Feldman and Eric Lichtblau, "Militia Members' Threats, Attacks On Officials Escalate," *Los Angeles Times*, April 27, 1995, A1.

[4]V. Krebs, quoted in Wirpsa, 10.

[5]Laird Wilcox, quoted in Wirpsa, 10.

[6]Wilcox, 10

[7]Henry McClain, quoted in Christopher John Farley, "Patriot Games," *Time*, December 19, 1994, 48.

[8]Jim Barnett, quoted in Farley, "Patriot Games," 48.

[9]Johnston, quoted in Marc Cooper, "The N.R.A. Takes Cover in the G.O.P.," *The Nation*, June 19, 1995, 882.

[10]Michael Barkun, "Militias, Christian Identity and the Radical Right," *Christian Century*, August 2–9, 1995, 738.

[11]"Fight Against Police State Escalates," *Freedom Network News*, June/July 1995, 1.

[12]Ridgeway and Zeskind, quoted in Hazen et al., *Militias in America*, 40; cf. Loretta J. Ross, "Saying it with a Gun," *The Progressive*, June 1995, 26.

[13]Pete Peters, "A Special Gathering of Christian Men is Scheduled for October 23, 24, 25, 1992" (flyer), n.d.

[14]Kenneth S. Stern, testimony in "America Under the Gun," 8–9; cf. Tom Burghardt, "Leaderless Resistance and the Oklahoma City Bombing," Internet posting, April 23, 1995, AlterNet BBS gopher site, pathway begins at gopher://gopher.igc.apc.org:70/1, to Progressive Gophers folder, to AlterNet folder, to Militias in America folder, to Additional Articles on Militias folder.

[15]Ridgeway and Zeskind, quoted in Hazen et al., *Militias in America*, 40.

[16]Williams, 48.

[17]Brown, 31.

[18]"Some Citizens Disavow Extreme-Right Views In Wake of Bombing," *Wall Street Journal*, April 24, 1995, A1; Marc Cooper, "A Visit with MOM," *The Nation*, May 22, 1995, reprinted in Hazen et al., *Militias in America 1995*, 45; Berlet and Lyons, "Militia Nation," 22; Shelton, "The New Minutemen," reprinted in Hazen et al., *Militias in America 1995*, 19.

[19]Brown, transcripts, "The Militia Movement," 31.

[20]Brown, 31

[21]Dean Compton, author's November 17, 1995, interview with Compton.

[22]Brown, transcripts, "The Militia Movement," 31.

[23]Barkun, "Militias," 738.

[24]Jon Roland, "Constitutional Militias Forming Across Nation," February 22, 1995, Internet posting,

http://www.the-spa.com/constitution/pr_5222.txt; also available in Tezcat's octopus archives, pathway starts at http://www.tezcat.com/, to Tezcat Archives, to Octopus folder, to Misc. folder, to militias.organize.

[25]Cooper, "A Visit with MOM," in Hazen et al., *Militias in America*, 45.

[26]John Snyder, quoted in Rogers Worthington, "Militias Form to Resist Feds, Gun Control," *Phoenix Gazette*, October 4, 1994, Internet edition at http://paul.spu.edu/~sinnfein/arizona.html

[27]Shelton, 19.

[28]Williams, 49.

[29]Williams, 49.

[30]Robert Higgs, *Freedom Network News*, June/July 1995, 8.

[31]Johnson, 113.

[32]John Trochmann, transcripts, "The Militia Movement," 128.

[33]Senator Arlen Specter, transcripts, "The Militia Movement," 1–2.

[34]Ken Adams, transcripts, "The Militia Movement," 84.

[35]Norm Olson, transcripts, "The Militia Movement," 126; cf. Glen Martin, "Citizens' Militias Have Taken Hold in Rural California," *San Francisco Chronicle*, April 22, 1995, Internet edition at http://www.sfgate.com/chronicle/index.shtml, and Bill Wallace, "Militia Tied to Blast Hates Gun Control," *San Francisco Chronicle*, April 22, 1995, Internet edition at http://www.sfgate.com/chronicle/index.shtml

[36]Max, quoted in Daniel Voll, "The Right to Bear Sorrow," *Esquire*, March 1995, 79.

[37]Bob Wright, *Phil Donahue*, April 25, 1995.

[38]Brown, 30.

[39]Smolowe, 62.

[40]Smolowe, 62

[41]Shelton, 20.

[42]Harold Sheil, *MacNeil/Lehrer News Hour*, April 26, 1995.

[43]Senator Herb Kohl, transcripts, "The Militia Movement," 5; cf. Senator Carl Levin, transcripts, "The Militia Movement," 16, and Desiree Cooper, "The Other Man: Mark 'From Michigan' Koernke," *Detroit Metro Times*, April 26, 1995, reprinted in Hazen et al., *Militias in America*, 50.

[44]Gary Krause, *NBC Nightly News*, April 28, 1995; cf. Senator Kohl, 5 and Senator Levin, 16–17.

[45]Quoted by Senator Kohl, 5–6. On May 15, 1995, Mullins was sentenced to a five-year prison term for violating federal firearms regulations (see Anti-Defamation League, *Beyond the Bombing: The Militia Menace Grows* [New York: Anti-Defamation League, 1995], 32).

[46]Bill Wallace, "Heated Rhetoric Set Stage for Oklahoma Blast," *San Francisco Chronicle*, May 1, 1995, A13; Internet edition at http://www.sfgate.com/chronicle/index.html; cf. Scott McLemee, "Public Enemy," *In These Times*, May 15, 1995, 19.

[47]Adams, 122.

[48]Max, 80.

[49]Williams, 50.

[50]Johnson, 123.

[51]John Bolman, *Day One*, April 27, 1995.

[52]Dan Shoemaker, quoted in McLemee, 17.

[53]Shoemaker, 17.

Chapter 3: Sovereign Citizen Rebellion

[1]Robert Scheer, "Mass Murder Isn't A Blow for Democracy," *Los Angeles Times*, April 25, 1995, B9.

[2]Samuel Sherwood, quoted in Dan Yurman, "Are These Salmon to Die For?" (Dateline—3/5/95), *Reports on the Militia Movement in Idaho: Visions of Blood & Fishes Swim in Political Circles*, Internet posting, November 22, 1995, AlterNet BBS gopher site, pathway begins at gopher://gopher.igc.apc.org:70/1, to Progressive Gophers folder, to AlterNet folder, to Militias in America folder, to Militia-Watch Updates folder, to "Reports on the Militia Movement in Idaho" document.

[3]Paul Glastris, "Patriot Games," *Washington Monthly*, June 1995, 24.

[4]Lynne Meredith, *Vultures in Eagle's Clothing* (Huntington Beach, Calif.: Prosperity Publishers, 1994, 147.

[5]Meredith, 13.

[6]Stewart Balint, quoted in Philip Weiss, "Outcasts Digging in for the Apocalypse," *Time*, May 1 1993, 49.

[7]Steve Hance, quoted in Susan Ladd and Stan Swofford, "Citizens' Revolt: Anger Aimed At Government," *News & Record* (Greensboro, N.C.), June 25, 1995, Internet edition at http://www.infi.net/nr/extra/militias/m-revolt.htm. Since this report by Ladd and Swofford was published, forty-six-year-old Hance and his two sons—James, 23, and John, 19—have become fugitives. As of April 1996, all three were wanted by authorities for assault with a deadly weapon against a law officer (see David Johnson, "FBI Standoff: The Feds Better Get In Gear," *Lewiston [Idaho] Morning Tribune*, Internet edition at http://www.lmtribune.com/stories/30916.htm).

[8]Jim LaValley, quoted in Glastris, 26.

[9]Susan Ladd and Stan Swofford. "The Law of the Land: Group Seeks County Rule," *News & Record* (Greensboro, N.C.), June 25, 1995, Internet edition at http://www.infi.net/nr/extra/militias/m-county.htm

[10]Ladd and Swofford, "The Law of the Land."

[11]*Perceptions*, May/June 1995, 17.

[12]Ladd and Swofford, "Citizens' Revolt."

[13]*Free Enterprise Society*, materials catalog no. 3, 6.

[14]Loretta J. Scott, testimony before Congressman Charles Shumer's informal forum on America under the Gun," July 11, 1995, 2.

[15]Meredith, 13.

[16]Scott, 2.

[17]Scott McLemee, "Public Enemy, *In These Times*, May 15, 1995, 15.

[18]Max Rider of the West, "Resurrection of the American Common Law Court," *American's Bulletin*, October 1995, 3.

[19]Quoted in Scott, 2.

[20]Robert Wangrud, quoted in *Clackamas County Review*, May 28–June 3, 1992. Cited in Scott, 2.

[21]*The Patriot*, January 1990, quoted in *A Season of Discontent* (Montana Human Rights Network), May 1994. Reprinted in Scott, 2.

[22]Richard McDonald, "Have You Been Hornswoggled?" *Perceptions*, May/June 1995, 20.

[23]Richard McDonald, quoted in Keith Stone, "Suspicion of Government Drives Patriot Movement," *Daily News*, December 26, 1994, 16.

[24]*The Patriot*, vol. 1 no. 5, quoted in Robert Crawford, Steven Gardiner and Jonathan Mozzochi, "Almost Heaven?" (2nd edition), *The Dignity Report*, March 1994, 4.

[25]Scott, 2; cf. *A Season of Discontent*.

[26]Stone, 16.

[27]Stone, 16.

[28]Stone, 16.

[29]*Lane County v. Oregon*, 7 Wall., at 76. Cited in *New York v. U.S.*, 112 S.Ct. 2408, at 2421.

[30]*Constitution*, Preamble.

[31]*Texas v. White*, 19 L. Ed., 227. Cited in *New York v. U.S.*, 112 S.Ct. 2408, at 2421.

[32]*Dred Scott v. Sanford*, 15 L. Ed. 691, at 701.

[33]*Lane County v. Oregon*.

[34]Alexander Hamilton, *The Federalist No. 15*. Reprinted in *The Federalist Papers* (New York: Penguin Books, 1987), Isaac Kramnick ed., 149.

[35]Peyman Mottahedeh, "State vs. U.S. Citizenship Theory Debunked," 1.

[36]Susan Ladd and Stan Swofford, "Defender on the Right," *News & Record* (Greensboro, N.C.), June 27, 1995; Internet edition at http://www.infi.net/nr/extra/militias/m-defndr.htm

[37]James A. Marcus, quoted in Glastris, 23.

[38]Marcus, 23–24.

[39]Judge Donald Teeple, quoted in Sara Rimer and James Bennet, "Rejecting the Authority of the U.S. Government, *New York Times*, April 24, 1995, A13.

[40]Glastris, 23.

[41]Terry Nichols, quoted in Rimer and Bennet, A13.

[42]*Media Bypass*, August 1995, 11.

[43]Stone, 16.

[44]Stone, 16.

[45]Stone, 16.

[46]Stone, 16.

[47]Dusty Deschamps, quoted in Marc Cooper, "A Visit with MOM," *The Nation*, May 22, 1995, reprinted in Hazen et al., *Militias in America*, 47.

[48]Peter Coppelman, quoted in Erik Larson, "Unrest in the West," *Time*, October 23, 1995, 66.

[49]Chi Chi Sileo. "Fringe Groups and Militias Aim to 'Restore' Constitution," *Insight on the News*, 15.

[50]Rogers Worthington, "Weaver Fever Hits Montana," *San Francisco Examiner*, September 24, 1995, 1995, Internet edition at http://www.sfgate.com/examiner/index.html

[51]Hance, quoted in Ladd and Swofford, "Citizens' Revolt."

[52]Karen Matthews, *ABC World News*, November 30, 1995; cf. Karen Matthews, testimony "America under the Gun," 4.

[53]Mike Tharp, "In the Shadow of Ruby Ridge," *U.S. News & World Report*, December 4, 1995, 60.

[54]Dan Yurman, "Big Trouble in Small Places: Montana Tax Protester Comes Out Shooting" (Dateline—7/18/95), *Visions of Blood & Fishes Swim in Political Circles: Reports on the Militia Movement in Idaho*, Internet posting, November 22, 1995, AlterNet BBS gopher site, pathway begins at gopher:// gopher.igc.apc.org:70/1, to Progressive Gophers folder, to AlterNet folder, to Militias in America folder, to Militia-Watch Updates folder, to "Reports on the Militia Movement in Idaho" document.

[55]Yurman, "Big Trouble."

[56]Worthington.

[57]Michael Doyle, "Anti-tax Violence Part of Wider Conspiracy?" *San Francisco Examiner*, July 12, 1995, Internet edition at http://www.sfgate.com/examiner/index.html

[58]Doyle.

[59]"Freemen Full of Hate, Short On Cash," *Mercury News Wire Services*, March 28, 1996 (America Online).

[60]Bob Anez, "Chained Freemen Yell in Arraignment" *San Jose Mercury News*, March 27, 1996, 6A (America Online), and "Armed Standoff At Montana Ranch," *Mercury News Wire Services*, March 27, 1996 (America Online).

[61]Peter Anin and Mark Hosenball, "A Showdown in Montana," *Newsweek*, April 8, 1996, 39.

[62]Anez.

[63]Jeffrey Miller, "Citizen Militias Drawing Concern," *Orange County Register*, April 22, 1995, 24.

[64]Bill Wassmuth, testimony, "America under the Gun," 2.

[65]Lynn Ludlow, "Extremists of the Manic Right," *San Francisco Examiner*, July 9, 1995, http://www.sfgate.com/examiner/index.html

[66]Robert M. Bryant, transcripts, "The Militia Movement," 27; cf. Senator Herb Kohl, transcripts, "The Militia Movement," 6.

[67]Bryant, 27. In 1978, ricin was used to assassinate a Bulgarian diplomat. The amount injected into the diplomat, equivalent to the size of a pinhead, was administered with the tip of an umbrella that punctured his hip. Instructions on how to manufacture this deadly poison are contained in *The Poor Man's James Bond*, vol. 3, which is available and often sold at patriot/militia meetings and gun shows.

[68]"Deadly Toxin," Intelligence Information, Court Documents, available from the U.S. Courthouse (St. Paul, Minn.).

[69]Wassmuth, 2.

[70]Richard Romley, transcripts, "The Militia Movement," 45.

[71]Linda Thompson, "Why We Have to Fight," BBS message #15553 (Fr: Linda Thompson, To: All), February 17, 1994, *AEN News*-FidoNet.

[72]B. Campbell, "Federal Power Abuses Spark Militias: Commentary," *Spotlight*, January 9, 1995, Internet edition in the patriot Archives, pathway starts at http://www.tezcat.com/, to Tezcat Archives, to Patriot folder, to Militia folder, to Feds_and_Militia.txt. Campbell writes: "The federal assault on the Weaver family persuaded some of us that the militia had to rise and assert itself. The federal

annihilation of the Branch Davidians persuaded the rest of us. Militia units began to form across the country. The signing of the Brady Bill revealed that all of us, not just the so-called radicals, were to be disarmed."

Part Two: Enough Is Enough
[1]Bob Worn, open letter to Senator Arlen Specter, June 16, 1995, 1–2. Reprinted in *USA Patriot Magazine*, October 1995, 39–40.

Chapter 4: The Saga of Ruby Ridge
[1]SOF Staff, "Feeding On Leftist Fears," *Soldier of Fortune*, November 1995, 54.

[2]Daniel Junas, *Militias in America: The Real Story* (Vital Film & Video, 1995).

[3]Alan W. Bock, "Weekend Warriors," *National Review*, May 29, 1995, 39.

[4]Philip Weiss, "They've Had Enough," *New York Times Magazine*, January 8, 1995, 48. The Weavers' use of a birthing shed is indicative of their involvement with Christian Idenity, which places a great deal of emphasis on the Old Testament. The Weavers apparently felt that Old Testament prohibitions against contact with menstruating women, or with women who had recently given birth, were still applicable today (see Lev. 12:1-8; 20:18).

[5]"Visions of the Mark of the Beast," *Newsweek*, August 28, 1995, 32; cf. Weiss, 48.

[6]Weiss, 48.

[7]These quotes paraphrase what was said between Weaver and Magisono. Although they are not direct quotes, they accurately represent the content of their dialogue.

[8]Department of Justice, *Department of Justice Report on Internal Review Regarding the Ruby Ridge Hostage Situation and Shooting by Law Enforcement Personnel* (Washington, D.C.: U.S. Government Printing Office, 1994), Internet edition posted by LEXIS COUNSEL CONNECT, American Lawyer Media, L.P.

[9]Vicki Weaver, letter to Z.O.G., October 16, 1990, quoted in *Atrocities At Ruby Ridge* (Star Broadcasting).

[10]Jess Walter, *Every Knee Shall Bow* (New York: Regan Books, 1995), reprinted in Jess Walter, "Every Knee Shall Bow, *Newsweek*, August 28, 1995, 31.

[11]It is impossible to construct an entirely objective version since testimony from those involved in the shootout conflict dramatically. I have done my best to present the facts without placing them in an order which would put blame on a particular individual. My version of the gun battle was compiled from several accounts: James L. Pate "Amateurs & Assassins II," *Soldier of Fortune*, January 1996, 56–61, 84–87; Tom Morganthau et al., "The Echoes of Ruby Ridge," *Newsweek*, August 28, 1995, 24–28; Gordon Witkin, "The Nightmare of Idaho's Ruby Ridge," *U.S. News & World Report*, September 11, 1995, 24, 29; Jess Walter, *Every Knee Shall Bow* (New York: Regan Books, 1995), reprinted in Jess Walter "Every Knee Shall Bow, *Newsweek*, August 28, 1995, 31; *Atrocities At Ruby Ridge* (Star Broadcasting); Department of Justice, *Department of Justice Report on Internal Review Regarding the Ruby Ridge Hostage Situation and Shooting by Law Enforcement Personnel* (Washington, D.C.: U.S. Government Printing Office, 1994), Internet edition posted by LEXIS COUNSEL CONNECT, American Lawyer Media, L.P.

[12]For an excellent appraisal of this gun battle and the subsequent government cover-up of key pieces of information regarding the Ruby Ridge siege, I recommend that readers obtain a copy of "Amateurs & Assassins II," by James L. Pate, *Soldier of Fortune*, January 1996, 56–61, 84–87.

[13]Walter, 31.

[14]Walter, 33.

[15]Tom Morganthau, "The Echoes of Ruby Ridge," *Newsweek*, August 28, 1995, 26–27.

[16]James L. Pate, "Ask Us No Questions, We'll Tell You No Lies," *Soldier of Fortune*, March 1996, 44.

[17]According to circumstantial evidence, this first shot may have actually been fired by FBI Special Agent Dale Monroe (Cf. Pate, "Ask Us No Questions," 44).

[18]Walter, 33.

[19]Walter, 33.

[20]Bo Gritz, *Atrocities At Ruby Ridge*; cf. James Bovard, *Lost Rights: The Destruction of American*

Liberty (New York: St. Martin's Press, 1994), 226.

[21]Walter, 33.

[22]Weiss, 49.

[23]Witkin, 30

[24]Weiss, 49–50.

[25]Witkin, 30.

[26]*Atrocities At Ruby Ridge.*

[27]Walter, 33.

[28]Vicki Weaver, letter to U.S. Attorney's Office, quoted in Walter, 29.

[29]Morganthau, 25.

[30]James L. Pate, "Amateurs & Assassins," *Soldier of Fortune*, December 1995, 39.

[31]Randy Weaver, quoted in Pate, "Amateurs & Assassins," 39.

[32]"The FBI Pleads Guilty," *Los Angeles Times*, October 22, 1995, M4.

[33]Witkin, 30.

[34]Morganthau, 27.

[35]Reuters, December 21, 1995.

[36]Brian Duffy. "When to Shoot," *U.S. News & World Report*, October 30, 1995, 14.

[37]Duffy, 14; cf. Morganthau, 27. Responsible critics of the government's actions at Ruby Ridge argue that this "new" federal policy on the use of deadly force is merely a restatement of the old policy that has always existed throughout law enforcement agencies. Objective observers complain that the administration's announcement of a "new" policy amounts to nothing more than a public relations ploy to deceive the average populace into believing that the government actually made some kind of substantial change in procedure due to the Weaver incident (see Pate, "Ask Us No Questions," 44).

[38]Louis Freeh, quoted in Ronald J. Ostrow, "Louis Freeh," *Los Angeles Times*, November 19, 1995, M3.

[39]"The FBI Pleads Guilty," *Los Angeles Times*, October 22, 1995, M4; cf. Pate, "Amateurs & Assassins," 40.

[40]Morganthau, 27.

[41]Morganthau, 26.

[42]Morganthau, 25.

[43]In December 1995, a U.S. Senate subcommittee issued a on the Ruby Ridge siege. The report, based on fourteen days of hearings held in September and October, found that Federal law agencies, along with Randy Weaver, were to blame for the three deaths during the incident. "Responsibility for the tragedy must begin with Randy Weaver and his unjustifiable decisions to sell illegal weapons and to refuse to appear for trial," the report by the Senate Judiciary Subcommittee on Terrorism, Technology and Government Information said. "But the chain of mistakes that led to those three deaths involves substantial failures by the very agencies of the U.S. government whose mission should be to save lives and enforce the laws." Specifically, the subcommittee found substantial fault with the performance of the Bureau of Alcohol, Tobacco and Firearms, the FBI, the U.S. Marshals Service and the Idaho U.S. Attorney's Office. It also said the ATF exaggerated the threat that Randy Weaver posed and that the U.S. attorney in Idaho failed to try ways to end the standoff peacefully after Weaver refused to come to court. The report said the FBI's rules of engagement in the siege that said agents "can and should" use deadly force against armed males were inappropriate and unconstitutional and the shot that killed Vicki Weaver should not have been fired (Reuters, December 21, 1995).

[44]Pate, "Ask Us No Questions," 44.

[45]Pate, "Ask Us No Questions," 44.

[46]Pate, "Ask Us No Questions," 44.

[47]Pate, "Ask Us No Questions," 44.

Chapter 5: Waco Revisited

[1]Don McAlvany, "The Waco Massacre: "Trial by Fire," *The McAlvany Intelligence Advisor*, July 1993, 21.

[2]"Cult Siege Trial Told of Big Arms Cache," *Los Angeles Times*, January 15, 1994, A25; cf. "Expert Says Cult Had Illegal Arms," *New York Times*, January 15, 1994, 10.

[3]Susan Ladd and Stan Swofford, "Electronic Outline: Computers Link Patriots," *News & Record*

(Greensboro, N.C.), June 26, 1995, Internet edition at http://www.infi.net/nr/extra/militias/m-electr.htm

[4]Ted Daniels, quoted in Gustav Niebuhr, "Assault on Waco Sect Fuels Extremists' Rage," *New York Times*, April 26, 1995, A12.

[5]Amo Roden, quoted in Niebuhr, "Assault on Waco."

[6]Linda Thompson, "Organization and Purpose of the American Justice Federation" (flyer), n.d.

[7]Jason Vest, "The Leader of the Fringe," *The Progressive*, June 1995, 28.

[8]Linda Thompson, "COME TO WACO SATURDAY, APRIL 3!!," BBS message #14465 (Fr: Linda Thompson, To: All), March 28, 1993, *AEN News*-FidoNet.

[9]Bechetta Jackson, "Gun Group Rallies Near Compound," *Waco Tribune-Herald*, April 4, 1993, 1C.

[10]Adam Parfry, quoted in Vest, 28.

[11]Author's 1993 interviews with several former Davidians; cf. Mark England, "Lawman: Group Tried to Deceive," *Waco Tribune-Herald*, April 14, 1988, 1C, 4C, and Mark England, "Families Gather At Trial," *Waco Tribune-Herald*, April 18, 1988, 1B.

[12]David and Debbie Bunds, author's multiple interviews with David and Debbie, March 3–June 10, 1993; cf. Alan Nelson and Sandra Gines, "Crying in the Wilderness," *Waco Tribune-Herald*, January 17, 1988, 1A, 8A, and Jeff Collins, "The Law Steps in After Strife-Torn Religious Sect's Battle," *Dallas Times-Herald*, November 24, 1987, n.p.

[13]Martin King, interview with David Koresh on television program *A Current Affair*, Nine Network Australia, January 1992.

[14]Bonnie Haldeman, author's February 28, 1993, interview with Haldeman.

[15]Bobby Howell, author's April 25, 1993, interview with Howell.

[16]Ken Carter, "Scattered Shots," *Machine Gun News*, February 1994, 19.

[17]Carter, 19.

[18]Dean Speir, "'Waco: The Big Lie' Revealed As A Hoax," *Gunweek*, January 21, 1994.

[19]James L. Pate, "Waco Whitewash Continues: Feds Find No Fault With Their Handling of Branch Davidian Standoff," *Soldier of Fortune*, February 1994, 59.

[20]Linda Thompson, "Re: HELP: Waco Video II," BBS message #1801 (Fr: Linda Thompson, To: Terry Liberty-Parker), March 30, 1994, *AEN News*-FidoNet.

[21]Phillip Arnn and Hank Kitchen, "*Waco, The Big Lie*—Rightly Named," *Watchman Expositor*, 11:4 (1994), 25. The video tape showing David Koresh with his son Cyrus was aired on national television during an ABC *Primetime Live* program. Nevertheless, *Waco II* continues to be distributed.

[22]Department of the Treasury, *Report of the Department of the Treasury on the Bureau of Alcohol, Tobacco and Firearms Investigation of Vernon Wayne Howell Also Known As David Koresh* (Washington: U.S. Government Printing Office, 1993), E-3.

[23]Linda Thompson, "Why We Have to Fight," BBS message #15553 (Fr: Linda Thompson, To: All), February 17, 1994, *AEN News*-FidoNet.

[24]Mike McNulty, "Waco: An Apparent Deviation," December 28, 1993; cf. Mark England, "Think Tank Chief Adds Fuel to Cult-Fire," *Waco Tribune-Herald*, January 16, 1994, 1A.

[25]Tom Morganthau et al., "Janet Reno Confronts Waco's Bitter Legacy," *Newsweek*, May 15, 1995, 26.

[26]"Cultists Spread Fuel Before Fire, Transcript Says," *Orange County Register*, February 15, 1994, 14; cf. "In Tapes From Sect's Compound, Members Talk About Setting Fire," *New York Times*, February 15, 1994, A15.

[27]I was able to acquire Robyn's Bible through her brother, David Bunds. Referenced pages were copied and are in my possession.

[28]Stephen Braun, "Koresh Sends Doom-Laden Letter to FBI," *Los Angeles Times*, April 11, 1993, A9.

[29]"Koresh Sends 2nd Threatening Letter," *Orange County Register*, April 13, 1993, 6.

[30]David Koresh, *Study on the Assyrians*, January 10, 1987.

[31]Scott and Jake Mabb, quoted in Sara Rimer, "Cult's Surviving Children: New Lives, New Ordeals," *New York Times*, April 27, 1993, A1.

[32]James Tabor, "Koresh Deserved It: James D. Tabor Replies," *Bible Review*, February 1994, 60.

[33]Gordon Witkin, "Raking Up the Ashes," *U.S. News & World Report*, July 24, 1995, 30; cf. "Expert Says Cult Had Illegal Arms."

[34]Ken Carter, "Branch Davidian Firearms," *Machine Gun News*, March 1994, 5.

[35]Tabor, 59–60; cf. McAlvany, 18.

[36]Kirk Lyons, "ACLU for Patriots," *Stormfront*, January 1994, Internet edition posted at *Stormfront* Home Page. *Stormfront* is a publication of Ku Klux Klan leader Don Black.

[37]"Welfare Worker Says She Was Warned Off Koresh Investigation," *Orange County Register,* October 11, 1993, 18.

[38]California authorities at one point had enough evidence to arrest Koresh for statutory rape, but by the time they arrived at his location in California, he had already fled to Texas.

[39]Melinda Beck et al., "Someone Dropped the Ball," *Newsweek*, May 17, 1993, 51; cf. author's numerous interviews with former Davidians in 1993.

[40]McAlvany, 19.

[41]Bruce Perry, quoted in Witkin, 32.

[42]Sophfronia Scott Gregory, "Children of a Lesser God," *Time*, May 17, 1993, 54; J. Michael Kennedy, "Doctors Get A Clearer Picture of How Cult Children Lived," *Los Angeles Times*, May 5, 1993, A24; Ginny Carol et al. "Children of the Cult," *Newsweek*, May 17, 1993, 48–50; "Texas Still Monitoring 12 Branch Davidian Kids," *Orange County Register*, September 28, 1993, 7; "Cult Children Tell of Abuse in Compound," *Los Angeles Times*, May 4, 1993, A16; Mark Potok, "Cult Kids' Story of Horror," *The Sacramento Bee*, May 5, 1993, A8.

[43]Carol, 49.

[44]Michelle Tom, signed affidavit.

[45]Debbie Bunds, author's June 10, 1993, interview with Bunds.

[46]Dean M. Kelley, "Waco: A Massacre and Its Aftermath," *First Things*, May 1995, 24.

[47]"TV Crewman Confirms Chat With Cultist," *Los Angeles Times*, August 29, 1993, A4; cf. "Revisiting the Tragedy in Waco," *Los Angeles Times*, April 26, 1995, B9, and Witkin, 31.

[48]Erik Larson. "How A Cascade of Errors Led ATF to Disaster at Waco," *Time*, July 24, 1995, 28–29; cf. Witkin, 30–31.

[49]Stephen Labaton, "Report On Assault On Waco Cult Contradicts Reno's Explanations," *New York Times*, October 9, 1993, A1.

[50]Douglas Frantz, "Justice Department Report Absolves FBI, Blames Koresh for 75 Waco Deaths," *Los Angeles Times*, October 9, 1993, A17; cf. Kelley, 25.

[51]Morganthau, 26.

[52]Alan Stone, quoted in Stephen Labaton, "Outside Review Criticizes F.B.I. On Raid On Cult," *New York Times*, November 16, 1993, A7.

[53]Labaton, "Outside Review," A7.

[54]Department of Justice, "Report to the Deputy Attorney on the Events at Waco, Texas," *United States Department of Justice Report on the Events at Waco, Texas February 28 to April 19, 1993*, redacted version, 294.

[55]Stephen Higgins, NBC's *Today*, March 30, 1993, quoted in Stephen Labaton, "U.S. Agency Defends Tactics in Assault On Sect," *New York Times*, March 30, 1993, A13.

[56]Morganthau, 26; cf. Tabassum Zakaria, "After the Fire, Memory Is Vivid," *Orange County Register*, April 19, 1994, 12.

[57]James Jorgenson, quoted in James Bovard, "Not So Wacko," *New Republic*, May 15, 1995, 18.

[58]Morganthau, 26.

[59]Janet Reno, quoted in Morganthau, 26.

[60]Louis Freeh, quoted in Ronald J. Ostrow, "Louis Freeh," *Los Angeles Times*, November 19, 1995, M3.

[61]Morganthau, 26.

[62]Clayton Douglas, "Energy , Interest and Taxes: The Weapons of the Elite in Their Silent War Against the American People," *The Free American*, August 1995, 3.

[63]Anti-Defamation League, *Armed & Dangerous: Militias Take Aim At The Federal Government* (New York: Anti-Defamation League, 1994), 4.

[64]Linda Thompson, "Declaration of Independence of 1994," 3.

[65]"Montana Patriots: 'We Choose to Opt Out,'" *Patriot Report*, October 1994, 4.

[66]Steve Hempfling, author's conversation with Hempfling, November 7, 1995.

Chapter 6: Guns, Government and Glory

[1]Thomas Posey "451st Day NWO Prisoner, Red Sky In the Morning America Take Warning," *American's Bulletin*, October 1995, 6.

[2]Jeffrey Miller, "Citizen Militias Drawing Concern," *Orange County Register*, April 22, 1995, 24; Keith Schneider, "Some Militia Manuals Urge Attacks," *Orange County Register*, April 29, 1995, 10; Josh Meyer, Paul Feldman and Eric Lichtblau, "Militia Members' Threats, Attacks On Officials Escalate," *Los Angeles Times*, April 27, 1995, A1.

[3]Wayne LaPierre, quoted in Gordon Witkin et al., "The Fight to Bear Arms," *U.S. News & World Report*, May 22, 1995, 29.

[4]Philip Sharp, quoted in Witkin et al., 30.

[5]Witkin et al., 30.

[6]Stephen P. Halbrook, *That Every Man Be Armed* (Oakland: The Independent Institute, 1994), 83.

[7]Sanford Levinson, "The Embarrassing Second Amendment," *The Gun Control Debate* (Buffalo: Prometheus Books, 1990), edited by Lee Nisbet, 316.

[8]ACLU Policy #47.

[9]Lee Nisbet, ed. *The Gun Control Debate* (Buffalo: Prometheus Books, 1990), 310.

[10]Ted Gest, "The Great Gun Debate: Get the Picture?" *U.S. News & World Report*, July 17, 1995, 7; "Where Gun Murders Are Most Common," *U.S. News & World Report*, November 6, 1995, 16; Michael Kramer, "Why Guns Share the Blame," *Time*, May 8, 1995, 48.

[11]Kramer, 48.

[12]Kramer, 48.

[13]Kramer, 48.

[14]Kramer, 48.

[15]Kramer, 48.

[16]Franklin E. Zimring and Gordon Hawkins. "Firearms and Assault: 'Guns Don't Kill People, People Kill People,'" *The Gun Control Debate* (Buffalo: Prometheus Books, 1990), edited by Lee Nisbet, 171.

[17]Gary Kleck, *Point Blank: Guns and Violence in America* (New York: Aldine De Gruyter, 1991), 157–158.

[18]Witkin et al., 29. Findings based on a poll of 1,000 registered voters conducted by Celinda Lake of Lake Research and Ed Goeas of The Tarrance Group, May 7–9, 1995.

[19]Jeffrey R. Snyder, "A Nation of Cowards," *The Public Interest*, Fall 1993, Internet edition posted at http:www.jim.com/jamesd/cowards.html

[20]Kleck, 398–399.

[21]Wright and P. Rossi, *Codebook for Prison Survey* (1983), quoted in Gary Kleck, "Policy Lessons from Recent Gun Control Research," in *The Gun Control Debate* (Buffalo: Prometheus Books, 1990), ed. Lee Nisbet, 154.

[22]Wright and Rossi, 154

[23]Thomas Jefferson, Proposed Virginia Constitution (1776) IT, *Papers*, I, J. Boyd ed. (New York: Putnam, 1896), 344, quoted in Wayne LaPierre, *Guns, Crime, and Freedom* (New York: Harper Collins, 1994), 7.

[24]Patrick Henry, *Debates and Other Proceedings of the Convention of Virginia*, convened at Richmond on June 2, 1788 (Petersburg, Va.: Hunter & Prentis, 1788), quoted in LaPierre, *Guns, Crime*, 16–17.

[25]James Madison. *The Federalist No. 46*. Reprinted in *The Federalist Papers* (New York: Penguin Books, 1987), Isaac Kramnick, ed., 301.

[26]Samuel Adams, quoted in Witkin et al., 32.

[27]Leonard W. Levy and Dennis J. Mahoney, *Encyclopedia of the American Constitution* (Riverside, N.J.: MacMillan, 1986), quoted in LaPierre, *Guns, Crime*, 13.

[28]Joyce Malcolm, *To Keep and Bear Arms* (Cambridge, Mass.: Harvard UNiversity Press, 1994), quoted in LaPierre, *Guns, Crime*, 14.

[29]Samuel Adams, *Writings, III* (1906), quoted in LaPierre, *Guns, Crime*, 6.

[30]George Mason, quoted in *The Debates in the Several Conventions on the Adoption of the Federal Constitution, III* (Washington, D.C.: Jonathan Elliot, 1836–45), Jonathan Elliot ed., 425–426.

[31]James Madison, *The Federalist No. 46*. Reprinted in *The Federalist Papers*, 301.

[32]LaPierre, *Guns, Crime*, 8.

[33]Akhil Amar, "The Bill of Rights as a Constitution," *100 Yale Law Journal* (1991), 1131–1166, quoted in LaPierre, *Guns, Crime,* 13.

[34]Karen L. MacNutt, *Women & Guns,* March 1995, reprinted in Hazen et al., *Militias in America,* 69.

[35]Alexander Hamilton, *The Federalist No. 28.* Reprinted in *The Federalist Papers,* 208.

[36]Daniel Levitas, testimony, "America under the Gun," 9.

[37]Frank Murray and George Archibald, "Constitution Scholars Divided Over Issues of Self-Defense," *Insight on the News,* May 29, 1995, 32.

[38]Wayne Anthony Ross, "Join A Militia—Break the Law?" *Soldier of Fortune,* April 1995, 52.

[39]Lorretta J. Ross, "Saying it with a Gun," *The Progressive,* June 1995, 26.

[40]Levitas, 5–6.

[41]Mike Williams, "Necessary to the Security of a Free State,'" *Soldier of Fortune,* April 1995, 50.

[42]John Trochmann, transcripts, "The Militia Movement," 76.

[43]Richard McDonald, quoted in Keith Stone, "Suspicion of Government Drives Patriot Movement," *Daily News,* December 26, 1994, 16. It should be noted that the elderly McDonald is not a member of any militia.

[44]MacNutt, 69.

[45]MacNutt, 70.

[46]MacNutt, 69.

[47]Trochmann, 76.

[48]Jim Faulkner, "Why There is a Need for the Militia in America," *Update, National Federal Lands Conference,* October 1994, quoted in Junas, "Angry White Guys," 25.

[49]James Johnson, transcripts, "The Militia Movement," 88, 113.

[50]Glenn Reynolds, *MacNeil/Lehrer News Hour,* April 26, 1995.

[51]Robert Leckie, *The Wars of America* (New York; Harper & Row, 1968; revised 1981), 88. This tragic episode came to be known as the Boston Massacre.

[52]Leckie, 83.

[53]Halbrook, 59.

[54]Jack Furagher, *The Encyclopedia of Colonial and Revolutionary America* (New York: Facts on File, 1990), 348.

[55]*MacNeil/Lehrer News Hour,* April 26, 1995.

[56]Susan Ladd and Stan Swofford, "Citizens' Revolt: Anger Aimed At Government," *News & Record* (Greensboro, N.C.), June 25, 1995, Internet edition at http://www.infi.net/nr/extra/militias/m-revolt.htm

[57]Susan Ladd and Stan Swofford, "Fearing for Our Country," *News & Record* (Greensboro, N.C.), June 25, 1995, Internet edition at http://www.infi.net/nr/extra/militias/m-fearing.htm

Part Three Conspiracies Unlimited

[1]Vladimir Solovyov, *Sobranie Sochineniya* (St. Pertersburg 1902–1907), vol. 5, 430–431, quoted in Walter Laqueur, *Black Hundred* (New York: Harper Collins, 1993; paperback edition), xiv–xv.

Chapter 7: Operation Enslavement

[1]Norman Cohn, quoted in Daniel Levitas, "Sleeping with the Enemy: A.D.L. and the Christian Right," *The Nation,* June 19, 1995, 888.

[2]*USA Patriot Magazine,* vol. 2 no. 2 (October, 1995), 59.

[3]Clayton Douglas, "The U.N.—Benevolent Organization or Fearful Master?" *Free American,* October 1995, 2.

[4]Douglas, 2.

[5]Terry Cook, *Satan's System: 666* (Terry Cook Productions, 1994).

[6]George Eaton, "America Is Lost Because the People are Lost," *Patriot Report,* October 1994, 2.

[7]Eaton, 2.

[8]Jim Keith, *Black Helicopters Over America: Strikeforce for the New World Order* (Lilburn, Ga.: IllumiNet Press, 1994), 145–146.

[9]*Logan's Run.* MGM Productions, 1976.

[10]P. Hewitt, letter to the editor, *American's Bulletin,* June 1995, 21.

[11]Mark Koernke, *America in Peril* (Real World Productions, 1993).

[12]George Bush, September 11, 1990, quoted in Klaus Larres, "Recycling Old Ideas," *History Today*, October 1993, 13.

[13]Michael Barkun, "Militias, Christian Identity and the Radical Right," *Christian Century*, August 2–9, 1995, 739.

[14]George Bush, ABC's *Primetime Live*, transcript #399, April 25, 1995, 22.

[15]Caspar W. Weinberger, "Commentary on Events at Home and Abroad," *Forbes*, February 15, 1993, 35.

[16]Weinberger, 35

[17]Weinberger, 35.

[18]"Another U.N. Outrage," *American's Bulletin*, June 1995, 5.

[19]*USA Patriot Magazine*, October 1995, 59.

[20]Jack McLamb, *Operation Vampire Killer 2000* (Phoenix: PATNWO, 1992), 3.

[21]Don McAlvany, "Financial & Spiritual Preparation for the '90s," Christian Conference, taped message (Vail, Colorado), August 11, 1994.

[22]Koernke.

[23]McAlvany.

[24]William L. Shirer, *The Rise and Fall of the Third Reich* (New York: Fawcett Crest, 1992), 377–378.

[25]Lee.

[26]Craig B. Hulet, "Patriots or Paranoids," *Soldier of Fortune*, August 1995, 43.

[27]Koernke.

[28]Hulet, 43.

[29]"Foreign Troops in America," *Free American*, October 1995, 3.

[30]McLamb, 32.

[31]Linda Thompson, *Waco, Another Perspective*, 4.

[32]McLamb, 32.

[33]"Another U.N. Outrage," 5.

[34]Vernon Weckner, quoted in Michael Taylor, "Extremists Bracing for New World Order," *San Francisco Chronicle*, April 25, 1995, Internet edition at http://www.sfgate.com/chronicle/index.shtml

[35]McLamb, 33.

[36]Nick Repac, "Civil Rights Task Force Representatives Meet With New Mexico Governor Johnson," *Free American*, October 1995, 11.

[37]Keith, 151.

[38]Robert Fletcher, ABC's *Primetime Live*, transcript #399, April 25, 1995, 22.

[39]*Militia of Montana Catalog* (November 1994), 14.

[40]Koernke.

[41]Susan Ladd and Stan Swofford, "Discontent Feeds Movement, Observers Say," *News & Record* (Greensboro, N.C.), June 27, 1995, Internet edition at http://www.infi.net/nr/extra/militias/m-discon.htm

[42]Chip Berlet, "Frank Donner: An Appreciation," *Covert Action Quarterly* 53 (Summer 1995), 17.

[43]Junas, "Angry White Guys," 21.

[44]Scott McLemee, "Public Enemy," *In These Times*, May 15, 1995, 16.

[45]"Sickening Stats," *Soldier of Fortune*, November 1995, 28.

[46]"Pseudo-Nazis, Pseudo-Militias," *Soldier of Fortune*, November 1995, 30.

[47]"The United Nations: Coming to Grips with a New World Order," originally published in *Der Spiegal* (Hamburg, Germany), reprinted in *World Press Review*, October 1992, 10; "U.N. May Be Harbinger of An Authentic New World Order," *National Catholic Reporter*, July 17, 1992, 28.

[48]"U.N. May Be Harbinger," 28.

[49]Reuters, "U.S. Spurns Idea of UN Taxes," January 19, 1996, text from America Online.

[50]Boutros-Boutros Ghali, "50th Anniversary of the United Nations," October 22, 1995, reprinted in *Vital Speeches of the Day*, 62:3, November 15, 1995, 66–67.

[51]Martin Sorensen, quoted in Edward Epstein, "Extremists' Bizarre Fears of U.N. Conspiracy," *San Francisco Chronicle*, May 4, 1995, Internet edition at http://www.sfgate.com/chronicle/index.shtml

[52]Keith, 110.

[53]Jack C. Plano and Milton Greensberg, *The American Political Dictionary* (Chicago: Holt, Rinehart and Winston, 1989), 473.

[54]Diane Reynolds, "FEMA and the NSC: The Rise of the National Security State," *Covert Action Information Bulletin* 33 (Winter 1990), 54.

[55]Epstein.

[56]"Martial Law and Emergency Powers," *N.F.L.C. Newsletter*, November 1994, quoted in David Helvarg, "The Anti-Enviro Connection," *The Nation*, May 22, 1995, 724.

[57]Keith, 17.

[58]Weckner, quoted in Taylor.

[59]Ken Gomes, "More Black Copters," BBS message #453 (From: Ken Gomes, To: All), July 29, 1994, *AEN News*-FidoNet.

[60]Hulet, 44.

[61]Fred Brown, "On the Trail of Black Helicopters and Implanted Chips," *Denver Post*, September 23, 1994, B1.

[62]Susan Ladd & Stan Swofford, "Fearing for Our Country," *News & Record* (Greensboro, N.C.), June 25, 1995, Internet edition at http://www.infi.net/nr/extra/militias/m-fearing.htm

[63]Hulet, 43.

[64]*Spotlight*, quoted in McLemee, 16.

[65]Thompson, 3.

[66]Don McAlvany, "America at the Crossroads: Freedom or Slavery? Part II," *McAlvany Intelligence Advisor*, October 1994, 18.

[67]Hulet, 44.

[68]Keith, 17. Keith is billed as a veteran researcher on the back cover of his book.

[69]Keith, back cover.

[70]Keith, 42–43, 48–49, 53.

[71]Keith, 21, 22, 24, 27, 31.

[72]Keith, 18, 20, 30.

[73]Keith, 42.

[74]Keith, 25.

[75]Keith, 26, 53.

[76]Keith, 17.

[77]"Black Helicopters Over America," *Soldier of Fortune*, August 1995, 45.

[78]Koernke.

[79]Mark Koernke, *A Call to Arms* (Real World Productions, 1993).

[80]James McQuaid, "Mark from Michigan," *Soldier of Fortune*, August 1995, 46.

[81]Linda Thompson, "Alert!!" n.d., 1.

[82]Quoted by Senator Carl Levin, transcripts, "The Militia Movement," 15–16.

[83]Ladd and Swofford, "Discontent."

[84]George Eaton, "EPA Refuses to Protect Citizens from Illness," *Patriot Report*, February 1995, 5.

[85]McAlvany, "Financial & Spiritual."

[86]Helvarg, 724.

[87]Linda Thompson, "NBC DRILL TIME (and I don't mean the TV network!)," BBS message #14056 (Fr: Linda Thompson, To: All), February 8, 1994, *AEN News*-FidoNet.

[88]Jill Smolowe, "Enemies of the State," *Time*, May 8, 1995, 69.

[89]Larres, 13.

[90]*The Concise Columbia Encyclopedia* (New York: Columbia University Press, 1983; 1989 second edition), 872.

[91]Larres, 14.

[92]Jennifer Morrison Taw and Robert C. Leicht, *The New World Order and Army Doctrine* (Santa Monica, Calif.: RAND, 1992), v.

[93]Taw and Leicht, ix–x.

[94]Taw and Leicht, x.

[95]Taw and Leicht, 1.

[96]George Bush, January 29, 1991, quoted in Pat Robertson, *The New World Order* (Dallas: Word, 1991), 14; cf. Eustace Mullins, *The World Order* (Staunton, Va.: Ezra Pound Institute of Civilization,

1992), 3. Mullins is a notorious anti-Semite.

Chapter 8: Antichrists & Microchips

[1]George Eaton, "America Is Lost Because the People Are Lost," *Patriot Report*, October 1994, 2.

[2]Dean Compton, lecture at the Granada Forum, November 16, 1995, and author's November 17, 1995, interview with Compton.

[3]Peter Doskoch, "The Mind of the Militias," *Psychology Today*, July/August 1995, 12.

[4]Bill Wassmuth, testimony, "America under the Gun," July 11, 1995, 1; cf. Tom Burghardt, "Leaderless Resistance and the Oklahoma City Bombing," Internet posting, April 23, 1995, AlterNet BBS gopher site, pathway begins at gopher://gopher.igc.apc.org:70/1, to Progressive Gophers folder, to AlterNet folder, to Militias in America folder, to Additional Articles on Militias folder.

[5]Compton, author's interview.

[6]Church, "Tragedy Strikes Oklahoma City," *Prophecy in the News*, May 1995, 6.

[7]Church, "Chronology of the End Time," *Prophecy in the News*, November 1994, 4.

[8]Church, "Chronology," 6.

[9]Terry Cook, *Satan's System: 666* (Terry Cook Productions, 1994).

[10]Mark Koernke, quoted in Michael Barkun, "Militias, Christian Identity and the Radical Right," *Christian Century*, August 2–9, 1995, 739.

[11]Don McAlvany, "The Waco Massacre: A Case Study on the Emerging American Police State," *McAlvany Intelligence Advisor*, July 1993, 1–2.

[12]Don McAlvany, "America at the Crossroads: Freedom of Slavery?" *McAlvany Intelligence Advisor*, August 1994, 4.

[13]Christian Civil Liberties Association, quoted in Bill Wallace, "Heated Rhetoric Set Stage for Oklahoma Blast," *San Francisco Chronicle*, May 1, 1995, A13; Internet edition at http://www.sfgate.com/ chronicle/index.shtml

[14]Gary Kah, *En Route to Global Occupation* (Lafayette, La.: Huntington House, 1991), 36–38; cf. Pat Robertson, *The New World Order* (Dallas: Word, 1991), 91.

[15]Hal Lindsey, *Apocalypse Planet Earth* (Jeremiah Films, 1990).

[16]Tim LaHaye, "Twelve Reasons Why This Could Be the Terminal Generation," *When the Trumpet Sounds* (Eugene, Oreg.: Harvest House, 1995), 437–438; cf. J. R, Church, "How Near is the Mark of the Beast," *Earth's Final Days* (Pacific Grove, Calif.: New Leaf press, 1995), 273–301.

[17]Cook.

[18]Corcoran, *Bitter Harvest*, 154.

[19]Norman Cohn, quoted in "Millenarianism," November 17, 1995, Internet article at http://www.physics.wisc.edu/~shalizi/notebooks/millenarianism.html

[20]Reuters, "Americans Believe They're in Trouble," January 20, 1996, America Online edition.

[21]*Militia of Montana Catalog* (November 1994), 5.

[22]Hal Lindsey, *The Late Great Planet Earth* (Grand Rapids: Zondervan, 1970), 113.

[23]The particulars surrounding the identification of these Antichrist candidates can be found in several works on Christian eschatological beliefs: B.J. Oropeza, *99 Reasons Why No One Knows When Christ Will Return* (Downers Grove, Ill.: InterVarsity Press, 1994); Russell Chandler, *Doomsday* (Ann Arbor: Servant, 1993); Bill Alnor, *Soothsayers of the Second Advent* (Grand Rapids: Fleming H. Revell, 1989); Robert C. Fuller, *Naming the Antichrist* (New York: Oxford University Press, 1995); and Bernard McGinn, *Antichrist* (San Francisco: Harper San Francisco, 1994). The first three books listed are written from a conservative Christian perspective. The latter two books are written from a secular point of view.

[24]Pat Robertson, *700 Club Newsletter*, February-March 1980, quoted in Fuller, 166.

[25]Alnor, 23–25.

[26]Hal Lindsey, *The 1980s: Countdown to Armageddon* (King of Prussia, Pa.: Westgate Press, 1980), 15.

[27]Dave Hunt, *Global Peace and the Rise of the Antichrist* (Eugene, Oreg.: Harvest House, 1990), 5.

[28]Saint Martin of Tours, quoted in Otto Friedrich, *The End of the World: A History* (New York: Coward, McCann and Geoghegan, 1982), 27; cf. Gary DeMar, *Last Days Madness* (Atlanta: American Vision, 1994), 196–197.

[29]Walter Laqueur, *Black Hundred* (New York: Harper Collins, 1993; paperback edition), 55.

[30]DeMar, 199.

[31]Benjamin Warfield, "Antichrist," in *Selected Shorter Writings of Benjamin B, Warfield,* vol. 1 (Nutley, N.J.: Presbyterian and Reformed, 1970), John E. Meeter, ed., 356, quoted in DeMar, 200.

[32]Oropeza, 155.

[33]Colin Deal, *Christ Returns by 1988—101 Reasons Why* (Rutherford College, N.C.: Colin Deal, 1979), 86, quoted in Fuller, 181.

[34]*Awakeners Newsletter,* 1979, 1, quoted in Alnor, 76.

[35]Joe Musser, quoted in G. R. Fischer, *The Quarterly Journal* (Personal Freedom Outreach), July-September 1989, 8. Reprinted in Oropeza, 156.

[36]Robert Mounce, "The Book of Revelation," *New International Commentary* (Grand Rapids: Eerdmans, 1977), 265, quoted in Oropeza, 158.

[37]Texe Marrs, "New Money or Beast '666' Currency," *Flashpoint,* March 1995, 2.

[38]Jennifer Ferranti, "Marine Worries ID Is Satanic," *Christianity Today,* November 13, 1995, 77; cf. Wendy Wallace, "The Four Horsemen of the Apocalypse," *Paranoia,* Spring 1995, 27.

[39]Mary Stewart Relfe. Cited in Alnor, 83.

[40]Cook.

[41]Gary Null, Radio Broadcast, WBAI-FM (99.5), reprinted as "Beyond AMERICA IN PERIL: Confirming Mark Koernke's Warnings," THE PEOPLE'S SPELLBREAKER, John DiNardo, ed., Internet posting in the Patriot Archives, pathway starts at http://www.tezcat.com/, to Tezcat Archives, to Patriot folder, to New World Order folder, to Beyond America in Peril.txt.

[42]John Hanna, "Exodus," *The Bible Knowledge Commentary: Old Testament,* eds, John F. Walvoord and Roy B. Zuck (Wheaton, Il: Victor Books, 1985), 130, quoted in Gary DeMar, "High-Tech Eschatology," *Biblical Worldview,* May 1994, 12.

[43]Keil and Delitzsch, *Biblical Commentary on the Old Testament: Pentateuch, 2:37,* quoted in DeMar, "High-Tech," 12.

[44]Hanna, 130, quoted in DeMar, "High-Tech," 12.

[45]Frank Flinn, "Government Shouldn't Fulfill Militia's Apocalyptic Prophecies," *Insight on the News,* May 29, 1995, 38.

[46]Fuller, 4.

[47]Chandler, 249.

[48]Chandler, 250.

[49]Lindsey, *The Late Great,* 54. It was this prophetic suggestion that led to the many false prophecies surrounding 1988.

[50]Chandler, 250.

[51]Lindsey, *The 1980s,* back cover.

[52]"Visions of the Mark of the Beast," *Newsweek,* August 28, 1995, 32.

[53]Tim Callahan, "The Fall of the Soviet Union & the Changing Game of Biblical Prophecy," *Skeptic,* 3:2 (1995), 92.

[54]Roy Rivenburg, "Is the End Still Near?" *Los Angeles Times,* July 30, 1992, E4.

[55]Hal Lindsey, *Planet Earth: 2000 A.D.* (Palos Verde: Western Front, Ltd., 1994), 144, quoted in Callahan, 94.

[56]Interview with Hal Lindsey on "John Stewart Live," KBRT-AM, Costa Mesa, Calif., August 4, 1992; cf. Rivenburg, E1–E2.

[57]Lindsey, *Apocalypse.*

[58]*Bookstore Journal,* October 1995, 122.

[59]Wendy Wallace, "The Four Horsemen of the Apocalypse," *Paranoia,* Spring 1995, 24.

[60]Mrs. Walker, quoted in Mike Hertenstein, "The Late Great Gog and Magog," *Cornerstone,* 20:96, n.p.

[61]Jeffery L. Sheler, "The Christmas Covenant," *U.S. News and World Report,* December 19, 1994, 64.

[62]Charles Strozier, Quoted in Sheler, 64.

[63]F. F. Bruce, quoted in D. Brent Sandy, "Did Daniel See Mussolini?" *Christianity Today,* February 8, 1993, 34.

[64]Sandy, 36.

[65]Mark Noll, "Misreading the Signs of the Times," 10–11, quoted in DeMar, *Last Days*, 21.
[66]Barkun, 730

Chapter 9: Anatomy of a Conspiracy

[1]Matthew Lyons and Chip Berlet, "Militia Nation," *The Progressive*, June 1995, 23.
[2]James Risen, "Militia Networks Boast An Alternate Take On Reality," *Los Angeles Times*, April 30, 1995, A1.
[3]Michael Barkun, "Militias, Christian Identity and the Radical Right," *Christian Century*, August 2–9, 1995, 738.
[4]Michael Barkun, quoted in Gustav Niebuhr, "Assault on Waco Sect Fuels Extremists' Rage," *New York Times*, April 26, 1995, A12.
[5]Christine Gorman, "Pssst! Calling All Paranoids," *Time*, May 8, 1995, 69.
[6]Gorman, 69.
[7]Quoted in Keith Stone, "Suspicion of Government Drives Patriot Movement," *Daily News*, December 26, 1994, 16.
[8]Michael Kelly, "The Road to Paranoia," *New Yorker*, June 19, 1995, 62.
[9]Susan Ladd and Stan Swofford, "Citizens' Revolt: Anger Aimed At Government," *News and Recorder* (Greensboro, N.C.), July 25, 1995, Internet edition at http://www.infi.net/nr/extra/militias/ m-revolt.htm
[10]Jeffrey Kaplan, "A Guide to the Radical Right," *Christian Century,* August 2–9, 1995, 741.
[11]Susan Ladd and Stan Swofford, "Discontent Feeds Movement, Observers Say," *News & Record* (Greensboro, N.C.), June 27, 1995, Internet edition at http://www.infi.net/nr/extra/militias/ m-discon.htm
[12]Russ Bellant, "The Paranoid and the Paramilitary," *Detroit Metro Times*, Internet edition at AlterNet BBS gopher site, pathway begins at gopher://gopher.igc.apc.org:70/1, to Progressive Gophers folder, to AlterNet folder, to Militias in America folder, to Additional Articles on Militias folder.
[13]Dean Compton, lecture at the Granada Forum, November 16, 1995, and author's November 17, 1995, interview with Compton.
[14]In 1995, the U.S. deported 51,600 illegal aliens. An estimated 1.5 million were turned back when caught sneaking across the border. As of January 1996, there were approximately 4 million illegal immigrants in America, and their numbers were growing by 300,000 a year. Contrary to what many patriots believe, most illegal aliens do not simply walk across the border. Smuggling illegal aliens has become "an aggressive and sophisticated industry that moves 'human cargo' by the hundreds of thousands from China, Europe and Latin America to worldwide points, including the United States" ("One-Way Tickets for Illegal Aliens," *U.S. News & World Report*, January 8, 1996, 12).
[15]Peter Doskoch, "The Mind of the Militias," *Psychology Today*, July/August 1995, 13.
[16]Doskoch, 13.
[17]Doskoch, 13.
[18]Chip Berlet, "Armed Militias, Right Wing Populism, and Scapegoating," April 24, 1995, Internet posting, AlterNet BBS gopher site, pathway begins at gopher://gopher.igc.apc.org:70/1, to Progressive Gophers folder, to AlterNet folder, to Militias in America folder, to Militias in America (1995) folder, to Chronicling the Growth of a Movement folder.
[19]Berlet.
[20]George Eaton, "300 Foreign Pilots Moving to New Mexico for Air Force Training," *Patriot Report*, February 1995, 3.
[21]Daniel Junas, *Militias in America: The Real Story* (Vital Film & Video, 1995).
[22]Margaret Thaler Singer, quoted in Doskoch, 14.
[23]Katie Hickox, "Domestic Terrorists Show 'Us vs. Them' Mentality, Expert Says," *Orange County Register*, April 22, 1995, 24.
[24]Mark Koernke, *A Call to Arms* (Real World Productions, 1993).
[25]Frank M. Ochberg, quoted in Doskoch, 14.
[26]Ochberg, 14.
[27]Kenneth S. Stern, testimony, "America under the Gun," July 11, 1995, 7.
[28]Quoted by Norman Cohn in his introduction to Herman Bernstein, *The Truth About the "Protocols of Zion"* (New York: KTAV Publishing House, 1971 edition; originally published in 1935),

xxvi–xxvii.

[29]Mark Koernke, *America in Peril* (Real World Productions 1993).

[30]Barkun, "Militias," 738.

[31]John Trochmann, transcripts, "The Militia Movement," 78.

[32]Linda Thompson, "Alert," n.d., 1.

[33]Trochmann, 78.

[34]Michael Callahan Jr, quoted in Mark Sauer and Jim Okerblom, "Patriotism or Paranoia?" *San Diego Union-Tribune*, May 4, 1995, E1.

[35]Don McAlvany, "America at the Crossroads: Freedom or Slavery Part II," *McAlvany Intelligence Advisor*, October 1994, 7.

[36]Susan Ladd and Stan Swofford. "Electronic Outline: Computers Link Patriots," *News & Record* (Greensboro, N.C.), June 26, 1995, Internet edition at http://www.infi.net/nr/extra/militias/m-electr.htm

[37]Doskoch, 14.

[38]Ladd and Swofford, "Electronic Outline."

[39]Ladd and Swofford, "Electronic Outline."

[40]Ladd and Swofford, "Electronic Outline."

[41]Doskoch, 12.

[42]Laird Wilcox, quoted in Leslie Wirpsa, "Rural Despair Feeds Militia Growth," *National Catholic Reporter*, June 30, 1995, 10.

[43]*CNN News*, March 1, 1995, 10 A.M. PST.

[44]"National News Briefs," *Patriot Report*, February 1995, 8.

[45]Bo Gritz, *Center For Action*, vol. 4 no. 6, January 1995, Internet posting in the Patriot Archives, pathway starts at http://www.tezcat.com/, to Tezcat Archives, to Patriot folder, to Militia Folder, to Gritz news.txt document.

[46]Don McAlvany, "America at the Crossroads: Freedom or Slavery?" *McAlvany Intelligence Advisor*, August 1994, 5.

[47]"News Briefs & National News," *Patriot Report*, October 1994, 6.

[48]Don McAlvany, "The Oklahoma City Tragedy," *McAlvany Intelligence Advisor*, May/June 1995, 22.

[49]Koernke, *America in Peril*.

[50]Craig Coleman, author's December 27, 1995, interview with Coleman.

[51]Don McAlvany, "POLICE STATE BRIEFS," *McAlvany Intelligence Advisor*, July 1995, 17.

[52]Jennifer Chapman, author's December 27, 1995, interview with Chapman.

[53]Bo Gritz, "America Soon to be Disarmed," *Center For Action*, vol. 3 no. 4, November 1993, Internet posting in the Patriot Archives, pathway starts at http://www.tezcat.com/, to Tezcat Archives, to Patriot folder, to Guns folder, to Bo Gritz on Disarming.txt.

[54]These comments are from my interview with Tami Chozery on January 5, 1995. Tami Chozery is a pseudonym. The woman I spoke with at the American Bar Association did not want to reveal her identity for fear of reprisal from patriots, especially militia members. Readers who want to verify Chozery's information may call the ABA in Chicago at 312-988-5000.

[55]American Bar Association, "Recommendation #10i" (1993). Tami Chozery supplied me with this information.

[56]Observer: Gun Confiscation to Begin in '96," *American's Bulletin*, October 1995, 16.

[57]Linda Thompson, "Think About It — 10," BBS message #14309 (Fr: Linda Thompson, To: All), February 9, 1994, *AEN News*-FidoNet.

[58]Randy Trochmann, quoted in Marc Cooper, "A Visit with MOM," *The Nation*, May 22, 1995, reprinted in Hazen et al., *Militias in America*, 48.

[59]*Militia of Montana Catalog* (November 1994), 2.

[60]Robert Fletcher, quoted in Kelly, 60.

[61]Fletcher, 60.

[62]Wilcox, 10.

[63]Clayton Douglas, "A Patriot's Corner," *Free American*, September 1995, 2.

[64]Linda Thompson, *Waco, Another Perspective*, p. 1.

[65]Linda Thompson, "Gurkha Mercenaries" BBS message #14051 (Fr: Linda Thompson, To: All),

February 8, 1994, *AEN News*-FidoNet; cf. Linda Thompson, "Global 2000—Population Control," BBS message #14055 (Fr: Linda Thompson, To: All), February 8, 1994, AEN News-FidoNet.

[66]Militia of Montana, *The Blue Book.* Cited in Kelly, 61; cf. Militia of Montana Information Video and Intel Update (Militia of Montana, n.d.). Cited in Junas, "Angry White Guys," 23. See also Philip Weiss, "Outcasts Digging in for the Apocalypse," *Time,* May 1, 1995, 49.

[67]Gorman, 69.

Chapter 10: Misinformation Specialists

[1]Dion Cole, *CNN Presents: Patriots & Profits,* October 29, 1995.

[2]Norman N. Franz, "One World Government," *Monetary & Economic Review,* March 1993, 13.

[3]John Trochmann, *Militias in America: The Real Story* (Vital Film & Video, 1995).

[4]John Appelt, *Militias in America: The Real Story* (Vital Film & Video, 1995).

[5]Transcripts of the United States Senate Subcommittee on Terrorism, "The Militia Movement," 120–121.

[6]Jim Keith, *Black Helicopters Over America: Strikeforce for the New World Order* (Lilburn, Ga.: IllumiNet, 1994), 144.

[7]Linda Thompson, "Think About It — 10," BBS message #14309 (Fr: Linda Thompson, To: All), February 9, 1994, *AEN News*-FidoNet.

[8]Mike Williams, "Necessary to the Security of a Free State," *Soldier of Fortune,* April 1995, 50.

[9]Linda Thompson, "Alert," n.d., 1.

[10]George de Lama, "For Militias, Invaders of U.S. Are Everywhere," *Chicago Tribune,* October 31, 1994, 1.

[11]de Lama.

[12]Kerry Webster, "Japanese Copters Pass Through Tacoma," *News-Tribune* (Tacoma, Wash.), September 14, 1994, B1.

[13]Jerold Foehl, quoted in Michael Janofsky, "Militia Plotted Assault On Military Base," *San Francisco Examiner,* June 25, 1995, Internet edition at http://www.sfgate.com/examiner/index.html

[14]Foehl.

[15]Robert M. Bryant, transcripts, "The Militia Movement," 27.

[16]Janofsky.

[17]Militia of Montana, "Report No. 7 Operations," *Taking Aim,* vol. 1 issue 7, 1994, Internet posting in the Patriot Archives, pathway starts at http://www.tezcat.com/, to Tezcat Archives, to Patriot folder.

[18]de Lama.

[19]Thompson, "Alert," 1; cf. Thompson, "Think About It."

[20]de Lama.

[21]de Lama.

[22]Michael Callahan Jr, quoted in Mark Sauer and Jim Okerblom, "Patriotism or Paranoia?" *San Diego Union-Tribune,* May 4, 1995, E1.

[23]de Lama.

[24]Don McAlvany, "Toward A Soviet America: Strangling Americans' Freedom And Constitution," *McAlvany Intelligence Advisor,* March 1994, 12.

[25]"Foreign Police, Why?" *Free American,* September 1995, 15.

[26]Linda Thompson, "Gurkha Mercenaries," BBS message #14051 (Fr: Linda Thompson, To: All), February 8, 1994, *AEN News*-FidoNet; cf. J.B. Campbell, "Federal Power Abuses Spark Militias: Commentary," Spotlight, January 9, 1995, Internet edition in the patriot Archives, pathway starts at pathway starts at http://www.tezcat.com/, to Tezcat Archives, to Patriot folder, to Militia folder, to Feds and Militia.txt.

[27]Peter Maas, "The Menace of China White," *Parade Magazine,* September 18, 1994, 4.

[28]Maas, 6.

[29]Louis Freeh, quoted in Maas, 6.

[30]Freeh, 6.

[31]Bo Gritz, quoted in "On the Moderate Fringe," *Time,* June 26, 1995, 62.

[32]George Skelton, "There is No Easy Answer On Militias," *Los Angeles Times,* April 27, 1995, A3. Two months after this incident, authorities received a phone tip about some militia members who

were planning to bomb the Redding office, still believing it was the ATF. Although no arrests were made, a raid was made on the home of the patriot "fact-finder." Documents seized included extremist/paramilitary literature and manuals on explosives/booby traps. Authorities also found assault weapons and a supply of gun powder large enough to build a bomb. None of the material was illegal. Consequently, no charges were filed.

[33]Craig B. Hulet, "All the News That's Fit to Invent," *Soldier of Fortune,* August 1995, 57.

[34]Mike Blair, "Salt Lake City, Utah, New FEMA Comm Center," *Spotlight,* August 8, 1994, quoted in Hulet, 57.

[35]Blair, Quoted in Hulet, 57.

[36]Blair, quoted in Hulet, 57.

[37]Hulet, 57.

[38]Hulet, 60.

[39]Hulet, 59.

[40]*Spotlight,* October 30, 1995, B-9.

[41]*Spotlight,* October 30, 1995, B-11.

[42]*Spotlight,* October 2, 1995, 15.

[43]Keith, *Black Helicopters Over America,* 109.

[44]Dave Helms, "Massive Plot?: Some Truth, Wild Theories," *Mobile Press Register* (Mobile, Alabama), 1A.

[45]Helms, 4A.

[46]Helms, 4A.

[47]Helms, 4A.

[48]"News Briefs & National Shorts," *Patriot Report,* October 1994, 7.

[49]Jack Van Impe, quoted in Helms, 4A.

[50]Hulet, 61; cf. Helms, 1A, 4A.

[51]Hulet, 61.

[52]Hulet, 56, 58.

[53]Helms, 4A.

[54]Russ Bellant, "The Paranoid and the Paramilitary," *Detroit Metro Times,* Internet edition at AlterNet BBS gopher site, pathway begins at gopher://gopher.igc.apc.org:70/1, to Progressive Gophers folder, to AlterNet folder, to Militias in America folder, to Additional Articles on Militias folder.

[55]"Suckers of the Far Right," *Time,* May 29, 1995, 12.

[56]Charlie Brennan, "We the People Fugitives in Standoff," *Rocky Mountain News,* March 28, 1996, 6A.

[57]"Suckers," 12.

[58]"Michigan Issues Warrant for Mark Koernke," *Patriot Report,* October 1994, 3.

[59]Morris Wilson, quoted in James Risen, "Militia Networks Boast An Alternate Take On Reality," *Los Angeles Times,* April 30, 1995, A30.

[60]George Eaton, "Mark Koernke Draws Crowds Across U.S.," *Patriot Report,* February 1995, 3.

[61]Mark Koernke, *America in Peril* (Real World Productions, 1993).

[62]Department of the Army, "Current and Previous Assignments," Mark Koernke, Section VII.

[63]James McQuaid, "Mark From Michigan," *Soldier of Fortune,* August 1995, 46.

[64]Department of the Army, "Current and Previous Assignments," Mark Koernke, Section VII.

[65]Department of the Army, Personnel Information on Mark Koernke.

[66]Larry Rapoza, author's January 5, 1995, interview with Rapoza.

[67]Kenneth Klenk, author's February 12, 1996, interview with Klenk. Commissioned officers begin their ranking at O-1 (Second Lieutenant). A full Colonel is an O-6 grade.

[68]Desiree Cooper, "The Other Man: Mark 'From Michigan' Koernke," *Detroit Metro Times,* April 26, 1995, reprinted in Hazen et al., *Militias in America,* 49.

[69]Peter Doskoch, "The Mind of the Militias," *Psychology Today* (July/August 1995), 13.

[70]James McQuaid, "Mark From Michigan," *Soldier of Fortune,* August 1995, 46.

[71]Koernke.

[72]Mark Koernke, *A Call to Arms* (Real World Productions, 1993).

[73]David Van Biema, "Mark Koernke," *Time,* June 26, 1995, 57.

[74]Jeffrey Kaplan, "A Guide to the Radical Right," *Christian Century,* August 2–9, 1995, 741.

[75]Linda Thompson, "02/Nwo Recap," BBS message #14009 (Fr: Linda Thompson, To: All), February 8, 1994, *AEN News*-FidoNet.

[76]Thompson, Linda, "ALERT," BBS message #14290 (Fr: Linda Thompson, To: All), March 27, 1994, *AEN News*-FidoNet; cf. R. Joseph Gelarden, "Lawyer Urges Nation to Join Against Feds At Waco Site," *Indianapolis Star,* March 31, 93, p. E1.

[77]Department of the Army, "SPECIAL ORDER NUMBER 249 EXTRACT," 19 December 1974.

[78]Phillip B. Davidson, *Vietnam At War: The History 1946–1975* (Novato, Calif.: Presidio Press, 1988), 730; cf. Arnold R. Isaacs, *Without Honor: Defeat in Vietnam and Cambodia* (Baltimore: John Hopkins University Press, 1983), 123.

[79]Department of the Army, Special Orders, February 10, 1975, 1; cf. Department of the Army, Personnel Qualification Record, Part 2, Section II-Current and Previous Assignments, #35.

[80]Report on Channel 6 news (Indianapolis, Ind.), July 4, 1994.

[81]Department of the Army, Personnel Qualification.

[82]Department of the Army, Personnel Qualification.

[83]Linda Thompson, ATTACKS.ZIP file, *AEN News*-Fidonet BBS.

[84]Klenk.

[85]Linda Thompson. Curriculum Vitae.

[86]Thomas A. Pyrz, letter from Thomas A. Pyrz to Mr. John Reynolds, August 16, 1994.

[87]Linda Thompson, *Waco, Another Perspective,* 4.

[88]Linda Thompson, "Waco: The Big Lie," *Jubilee* 6:2 (September/October 1993), online edition posted in *AEN News* Files as JUBWACO.ZIP.

[89]Jack Killorian, author's February 22, 1994, interview with Killorian.

[90]Killorian.

[91]American Justice Federation recorded telephone message, February 18, 1994.

[92]Bob Fletcher, quoted in Michael Kelly, "The Road to Paranoia," *New Yorker,* June 19, 1995, 62.

[93]Fletcher, quoted in Kelly, 62.

[94]Kelly, 68.

[95]Kelly, 69.

[96]*Invasion & Betrayal* (Militia of Montana, 1995).

[97]Doskoch, 13.

[98]Robert Tomsho, "Some Militiamen See A Government Plot In Oklahoma Blast," *Wall Street Journal,* April 24, 1995, A1.

[99]Susan Schock, testimony, "America under the Gun," 5.

[100]Daniel Voll, "The Right to Bear Sorrow," *Esquire,* March 1995, 79.

[101]Jill Smolowe, "Enemies of the State," *Time,* May 8, 1995, 69.

[102]Robert Downes and George Foster, "On the Front Lines With Northern Michigan's Militia," Northern Express (Traverse City, Mich.), August 22, 1994, reprinted in Hazen et al., *Militias in America,* 15.

[103]Linda Thompson, "Re: On the Lighter Side . . ." BBS message #6235 (Fr: Sam Kerns, To: All), April 23, 1994, AEN Chat-FidoNet.

[104]Bob Brown, quoted in Jason Vest, "The Leader of the Fringe," *The Progressive,* June 1995, 29.

[105]Katie Hickox, "Domestic Terrorists Show 'Us vs. Them' Mentality, Expert Says," *Orange County Register,* April 22, 1995, 24.

[106]National Rifle Association. Internet posting in the Patriot Archives, pathway starts at http://www.tezcat.com/, to Tezcat Archives, to Patriot folder, to Guns folder, to NRA_and_Militias.txt.

[107]"NRA: NWO Crowd Not After Guns" Patriot Report, October 1994, 4.

[108]Linda Thompson, "Why We Have To Fight," BBS message #15553 (Fr: Linda Thompson, To: All), February 17, 1994, *AEN News*-FidoNet.

[109]Linda Thompson, ATTACKS.ZIP, downloaded from AEN Files archive on August 31, 1994.

[110]James Aho, *MacNeil/Lehrer News Hour,* April 26, 1995.

[111]Linda Thompson, *Waco, The Big Lie.*

[112]Government Printing Office, *Report of the Department of the Treasury on the Bureau of Alcohol, Tobacco and Firearms Investigation of Vernon Wayne Howell Also Known As David Koresh,* 100.

[113]Investigation of Vernon Wayne Howell, 102–103.

[114]Phillip Arnn and Hank Kitchen, "Waco, The Big Lie—Rightly Named," *Watchman Expositor* 11:4 (1994), 24.

[115]Arnn and Kitchen, 23.

[116]Linda Thompson, "Re: HELP: Waco video II," BBS message #1801 (Fr: Linda Thompson, To: Terry Liberty-Parker), March 30, 1994, *AEN News*-FidoNet.

[117]Ken Toole, testimony, "America under the Gun," 2.

[118]Frank Donner, *The Age of Surveillance: The Aims & Methods of America's Political Intelligence System* (New York: Alfred Knopf, 1980), 14. Cited in Chip Berlet, "Frank Donner: An Appreciation," *Covert Action Quarterly* 53 (Summer 1995), 19.

[119]Josh Meyer, Paul Feldman and Eric Lichtblau, "Militia Members' Threats, Attack on Officials Escalate," *Los Angeles Times,* April 27, 1995, A1.

[120]*Militia of Montana Catalog* (November 1994), 9.

[121]McQuaid, "Mark from Michigan," 46.

[122]Tom Pelton, "Pro-Gun Groups' False Rumors Have City On Defense," *Phoenix Gazette,* August 12, 1994, CL18 (final section, classified page), Internet edition.

[123]Craig B. Hulet, "Patriots or Paranoids?" *Soldier of Fortune,* August 1995, 85.

[124]George Eaton, "Old Invasion Plans Parallel Globalist Agenda," *Patriot Report,* February 1995, 7.

[125]Matthew Lyons and Chip Berlet , "Militia Nation," *The Progressive,* June 1995, 23.

[126]Kenneth S. Stern, testimony, "America under the Gun," 10–11.

Part Four Aryan Nations

[1]Greg Withrow, quoted in B.J. Del Conte and Lee Lamothe, "The Good Dies Young," *Toronto Sun,* April 23, 1986, 32.

[2]Name Withheld, quoted in Richard M. Romley, transcripts, "The Militia Movement," 55-56.

[3]Blu Dorr, quoted in Del Conte and Lamothe, 32.

Chapter 11: The International Jew

[1]Adolf Hitler, quoted by Norman Cohn, introduction to Herman Bernstein, *The Truth About the "Protocols of Zion"* (New York: KTAV Publishing House, 1971 edition; originally published in 1935), xxviii.

[2]David Scoffins, "A Lesson From History—Or—How Britain Ceased to Be A Christian Country," *Aryan Nations* 25, 10.

[3]D. Douglas, ed., *The New International Dictionary of the Christian Church* (Grand Rapids, Mich.: Zondervan, 1974; 1978 edition), 956.

[4]Douglas, 956.

[5]*Concise Columbia Electronic Encyclopedia,* 1994, America Online edition.

[6]Douglas, 956. Both Philip IV and Pope Clement V benefited from the destruction of the Templars. Philip's debts to the Templars were eradicated, and nearly all of the possessions of the Templars were transferred to the pope.

[7]Cohn, xv.

[8]James Ridgeway, *Blood in the Face* (New York: Thunder's Mouth Press, 1990), 28.

[9]Walter Laqueur, *Black Hundred* (New York: Harper Collins, 1993; paperback edition), 38.

[10]Gretchen Passantino, author's February 15, 1996 interview with Passantino. Gretchen Passantino is a well-known and highly respected conservative Christian author and researcher who specializes in the areas of cults, world religions and philosophy.

[11]F. F. Bruce, *The Spreading Flame* (Grand Rapids: Eerdman's, 1958), 164.

[12]Morris Bishop, *The Middle Ages* (Boston: Houghton Mifflin, 1968; 1987 edition), 10.

[13]Walter A. Elwell, *Evangelical Dictionary of Theology* (Grand Rapids: Baker Book House, 1984; 1989 edition), 61 and Cohn, xi.

[14]St. Chrysostom, quoted in Leonard Dinnerstein, *Anti-Semitism in America* (New York: Oxford University Press, 1994), xx.

[15]St. Chrysostom, quoted in Elwell, 61.

[16]John George and Laird Wilcox, *Nazis, Communists, Klansmen, and Others on the Fringe* (Buffalo, N.Y.: Prometheus Books, 1992), 442.

[17]Bishop, 308, 310.

[18]Dinnerstein, xxiii; cf. Douglas, 50.

[19]Ridgeway, 28, 29.

[20]Cohn, xvii.

[21]Douglas, 50.

[22]Cohn, xvii–xviii.

[23]Richard Pipes, *Russia Under the Bolshevik Regime* (New York: Vintage Press, 1995), 255.

[24]Hillman Holcomb, "Christian Technocracy," *Aryan Nations* 25, 25.

[25]George and Wilcox, 442, and Ridgeway, 32–33.

[26]Otto Friedrich, *Before the Deluge* (New York: Harper Perennial, 1972; 1995 edition), 95–96.

[27]Cohn, xii.

[28]This work is given an 1864 date in Bernstein's *The Truth About the "Protocols of Zion*, xxix.

[29]George and Wilcox, 442.

[30]The spelling of Goedsche's pseudonym appears variously as Ratcliffe, Ratcliff and Retcliffe. The name Goedsche occasionally appears as Goedzsche.

[31]Bernstein, 21; cf. Laqueur, 32.

[32]Ridgeway, 32.

[33]Laqueur, 34.

[34]Bernstein, 22. A copy of the 1872 Russian edition of Goedsche's cemetery story is stored in the Russian Department of the Library of Congress, Washington, D.C.

[35]Bernstein, 32.

[36]Pipes, 255.

[37]Laqueur, 34–35.

[38]Pipes, 255.

[39]Gerard and Patricia Del Re, *History's Last Stand* (New York: Avon Books, 1993), 92.

[40]*Concise Columbia Encyclopedia,* America Online ed.

[41]Del Re, 92.

[42]Sheila Fitzpatrick, *The Russian Revolution* (New York: Oxford University Press, 1984; 1994 edition), 32.

[43]Paul Johnson, *A History of the Jews* (New York: Harper Perennial, 1987), 455.

[44]Robert S. Wistrich, *Antisemitism: The Longest Hatred* (New York: Schocken Books, 1991), 171.

[45]Fry, *Water Flowing Eastward* (Paris: 1933), quoted in Bernstein, 37.

[46]Marc Ferro, *Nicholas II: Last of the Tsars* (New York: Oxford University Press, 1994), 100; cf. Pipes, 255 and Friedrich, 95.

[47]Johnson, 455. In 1934, a libel suit was brought by Rev. A. Levy of Port Elizabeth, South Africa, against three anti-Semites who had been spreading slander based on the *Protocols*. The court ruled in favor of the plaintiff, stating: "The Protocols are an impudent forgery, obviously for the purpose of anti-Jewish propaganda."

[48]Laqueur, 35. During a trial in Berne, Switzerland, Vladimir Bourtsev—the eminent historian of the Russian Revolution—testified as an expert witness. He told the court that General Globotchov had informed him that it was indeed General Ratchkovsky and his agents who had fabricated the *Protocols* (see Bernstein, 69).

[49]Alexandra Romanov, letter from Alexandra to Anna Vyrubova, March 20, 1918, currently stored at Beinecke Rare Book and Manuscript Library, Yale University, Romanov Collection, container I, quoted in Mark D. Steinberg and Vladmir M. Khrustalev, *The Fall of the Romanovs* (New Haven, Conn.: Yale University Press, 1995), 244.

[50]Phillip Petrovich Stepanov, affidavit of April 17, 1927, reprinted in Bernstein, 39–40.

[51]Pipes, 255; cf. Laqueur, 35. The date of this first version of the *Protocols* is given in various scholarly works as either 1902 or 1903. I have not been able to determine to my satisfaction which year is accurate. Consequently, I have chosen to give both dates. A plausible explanation is that the text was first issued in 1902, but did not gain wide circulation until 1903. Another explanation is that it began to be printed in 1902 in a series of articles that extended into 1903.

[52]Herbert H. Goldberg, "The 'Protocols of the Elders of Zion' Unmasked!," *Hashivah* 17:2 (1994), 2. It was Kruzhevan who instigated the Kishinev, Bessarabia, pogrom in which 50 Jews were murdered, almost 500 wounded, and 1,300 homes destroyed.

[53]Laqueur, 35. The title of Nilus' Russian text may also be translated as *The Big in the Small*.

[54]Laqueur, 35.

[55]Laqueur, 18.

[56]Ferro, 93.

[57]Ferro, 93–94.

[58]Laqueur, 18.

[59]Ferro, 101.

[60]Laqueur, 21.

[61]Concise Columbia Encyclopedia, America Online ed.

[62]*Protokoly tsionskikh mudretsov* (Paris, 1938; reprinted in Moscow, 1991), 106–107, quoted in Laqueur, 27.

[63]Klavdiia Bitner testimony, August 4, 1918, in *Gibel' tsarkoi sem'i*, 422, quoted in Steinberg and Khrustalev, 404.

[64]Tsar Nicholas II, diary, August 2, 1917, quoted in Steinberg and Khrustalev, 241.

[65]Tsarina Alexandra, personal diary, April 7, 1918, quoted in *Chicago Daily News*, June 23, 1920, 2. Reprinted in Pipes, 257.

[66]Nametkin, "Report of the Examination of the Ipat'ev House, August 2–8, 1918: Documents of the Investigation into the Death of Nicholas II" [Sokolov Archive], Houghton Library, Harvard University, vol. 1, doc. 9. Quoted in Steinberg and Khrustalev, 244.

[67]Cohn, ix.

[68]A. Mackenzie, *The Russian Crucifixion* (London: n.p., n.d.), 125, quoted in Pipes, 101.

[69]S. Masloff, *Russia After Four Years of Revolution* (London/Paris: n.p., 1923), 148, quoted in Pipes, 101.

[70]Cohn, ix.

[71]Adolf Hitler, *Mein Kampf*, trans. Ralph Manheim (Boston: Houghton Mifflin, 1971), 307–308.

[72]Leni Yahil, *The Holocaust: The Fate of European Jewry, 1932–1945* (New York: Oxford University Press, 1991); Robert Jay Lifton, *The Nazi Doctors: Medical Killings and the Psychology of Genocide* (New York: Basic Books, 1986); Claude Lanzmann, *Shoah: An Oral History of the Holocaust* (New York: Pantheon, 1985); Deborah E. Lipstadt, *Denying the Holocaust* (New York: The Free Press, 1993).

[73]Lipstadt, *Denying the Holocaust*, 37.

[74]Wistrich, 118.

[75]Michael Barkun, *Religion and the Racist Right* (Chapel Hill, N.C.: University of North Carolina Press, 1994), 34.

[76]Ridgeway, 38–39.

[77]Dinnerstein, 81

[78]Lipstadt, 37.

[79]Dinnerstein, 81. By 1924, the *Dearborn Independent* had a circulation of 700,000, "only 50,000 fewer than that of the largest daily newspaper at that time, New York City's *Daily News*."

[80]Lipstadt, 37.

[81]Dinnerstein, 81.

[82]Henry Ford, quoted in foreword to G. F. Green, ed., reprint of *The International Jew* (London: 1948; abridged edition), 4.

[83]Green, 17–218.

[84]Dinnerstein, 82.

[85]Albert Lee, *Henry Ford and the Jews* (New York: Stein and Day, 1980) 47, quoted in Dinnerstein, 83.

[86]Ridgeway, 43; cf. Dinnerstein, 83.

[87]Hitler, *Mein Kampf*, 639

[88]Adolf Hitler, quoted in Ridgeway, 43.

[89]Dinnerstein, 83.

[90]Dinnerstein, 83; cf. Ridgeway, 42–43.

[91]Green, 7.

[92]Joseph E. Persico, *Nuremberg: Infamy on Trial* (New York: Penguin Books, 1994), 254.

[93]Wistrich, 120.

[94]Wistrich, 115.

[95]George and Wilcox, 37.

[96]Wistrich, 115

[97]Ridgeway, 46.

[98]George and Wilcox, 35.

[99]Wistrich, 115–116

[100]Ridgeway, 46.

[101]Green, 4.

[102]Aryan Nations catalog, n.d.; cf. *1995 Sons of Liberty Book and Video Cassette List*, 1995, 23. Racist publications often pay tribute to Henry Ford for having done so much to spread the word about the Jewish conspiracy (see "Communism is Jewish," *Calling Our Nation* 33, 26).

[103]Norman Cohn, quoted in Ridgeway, 43.

[104]George and Wilcox, 442.

[105]Wistrich, 233; cf. Goldberg, 2–3. On January 29, 1974, King Feisal presented an anthology of anti-Semitic writings including the *Protocols* to French journalists accompanying the visiting French Foreign Minister.

[106]King Feisal, "'Fu'ad al-Sayyid, 'al-Malik Faysal Yatahaddath 'an'," *al-Musawwar* 24, August 4, 1972, 13, quoted in Wistrich, 207.

[107]*Sons of Liberty*, 31; cf. James Combs, *Who's Who in the World Zionist Conspiracy*, 58–59 and Bruce H. Brown, *The World's Trouble Makers* (Metairie, La.: Sons of Liberty, 1985), 12–16.

[108]Bob Hallstrom, "Oprah, the Jews and Ritual Murder," *Calling Our Nation* 61, 22–24 and "Jewish Murder Plan Against Gentile Humanity Exposed," *Christian Vanguard*, February 1976, 3-15.

[109]Richard Butler, "Of the State of War," *Aryan Nations* 25, 4.

[110]Tom Metzger, quoted in "The Far Right Is Upon Us," *The Progressive*, June 1995, 10.

[111]Pierce, a great admirer of Henry Ford's, highly recommends *The International Jew*. Pierce devoted his entire shortwave radio program of September 25, 1993, to "The Wisdom of Henry Ford." The transcripts of this show are available at William Pierce's National Alliance Internet Page, http://www.natvan.com/.

[112]Kenneth S. Stern, testimony, "America under the Gun," 3.

[113]Irwin Suall, quoted in Peter Applebome, "Bombing Foretold in 'Bible' for Extremists," *New York Times*, April 26, 1995, A14.

[114]William Pierce, *The Turner Diaries* (Hillsboro, W. Va.: National Vanguard Books, 1978; second edition, 1995 printing), iii.

[115]Pierce, back cover.

[116]Pierce, 42.

[117]Pierce, 84–85

[118]Pierce, 29.

[119]Pierce, 64.

[120]Pierce, 24, 91, 92, 114, 147, 152, 179. 187, 205.

[121]Pierce, 145.

[122]Pierce, 150–152

[123]Pierce, 210.

[124]Pierce, 149–150.

[125]Pierce, 158, 162.

[126]Pierce, 160, 163.

[127]Pierce, 162, 163.

[128]Pierce, 160–163.

[129]The following excerpts are but a few examples of the kind of gratuitous violence that permeates Pierce's *The Turner Diaries*. These instances represent the less offensive material: "[Henry] leaped onto Berman's back, seized him by the hair, and cut his throat from ear to ear in one, swift motion" (p. 10); "[Our group] ambushed the Cook County sheriff outside his home and blew his head off with a shotgun" (p. 16); "Then came the great Houston bombings . . . which left more than 4,000 persons dead" (p. 94); "[T]he Organization hit the Israeli Embassy in Washington this afternoon. . .

[T]here must have been more than 300 people in the embassy when our 4.2 inch mortars began raining TNT and phosphorous onto their heads" (p. 118).

[130]Pierce, 1.

[131]Pierce, 8, 23–24.

[132]Frye, Radio Broadcast, WBAI-FM (99.5), reprinted as "Beyond AMERICA IN PERIL: Confirming Mark Koernke's Warnings," THE PEOPLE'S SPELLBREAKER, John DiNardo, ed., Internet posting in the Patriot Archives, pathway starts at http://www.tezcat.com/, to Tezcat Archives, to Patriot folder, to New World Order folder, to Beyond America in Peril.txt.

[133]Philip Jenkins, "Home-Grown Terror," *American Heritage*, September 1995, 44

[134]Louis Beam, "Skinheads," *The Seditionist*, reprinted in *Calling Our Nation* 60, 27.

[135]"Is America Worth Saving," *Aryan Nations* 25, 6; cf. Louis Beam, *The Seditionist*, issue 1 (Winter 1988), 1.

[136]It is noteworthy that *The Turner Diaries* also features a small group of racist revolutionaries called The Order. Turner eventually joins this group, which is the elite core of the broader Organization.

[137]Anti-Defamation League, *Extremism on the Right* (New York: Anti-Defamation League, 1988), 51–52.

[138]Anti-Defamation League, 52.

[139]Gary Smith, *Land of the ZOG* (Boring, Oreg.: CPA Book Publisher, 1989), 76.

[140]Randy Weaver, open letter to the public given to Jackie Brown, quoted in Philip Weiss, "They've Had Enough," *New York Times Magazine*, January 8, 1995, 49.

[141]Pierce, 30, 35, 35–36, 38.

[142]Jack Nelson, "Book Called 'Blueprint for Revolution,'" *Los Angeles Times*, April 23, 1995, A30; cf. Applebome, A14 and Richard A. Serrano and Melissa Healy, "McVeigh's Trail Combed for Clues," *Los Angeles Times*, April 30, 1995, A1.

[143]Tom Metzger, quoted in Peter Applebome, "Anger of Radical Right Erupting More," *Orange County Register*, April 23, 1995, 26.

[144]Rick Knight, quoted in Joe Chidley, "Spreading Hate on the Internet," *MacLean's*, May 8, 1995, 37; cf. David Futrelle, "Cyberhate," *In These Times*, May 15, 1995, 17.

[145]Dave Dilly, *CNN Presents: Patriots & Profits*, October 29, 1995.

[146]Peter Applebome, "Radical Rights' Fury Boiling Over," *New York Times*, April 23, 1995, A13.

[147]"Aryan Nations Theopolitical Platform," n.d.

[148]Gary Yarbrough, quoted in Paul Henderson, "We're Not Saluting Hitler–We're Saluting God," *Seattle Times*, April 17, 1983, 10.

[149]Anti-Defamation League, 53.

[150]Roy B. Mansker, "The Cry for Justice Grows Louder," *Calling Our Nation* 34, 2.

[151]Pierce, 71.

Chapter 12: Christian Identity

[1]Earl Jones, letter to Tom McIver, January 15, 1995, 2.

[2]Thomas E. O'Brien, *Verboten* (Metairie, La.: New Christian Crusade Church, 1974; 1987 reprint entitled *Proof: God's Chosen Are White Adamic Christians, "Verboten"*), 76.

[3]Charles Conley, quoted in James Ridgeway, *Blood in the Face* (New York: Thunder's Mouth Press, 1990), 70. This comment was made at a Klan rally during the 1960s in response to public outrage over the KKK bombing of the Sixteenth Street Baptist Church in Birmingham, where four young black girls where killed. Conley argued that nobody should be upset because black children were not really human children.

[4]Michael Barkun, "Militias, Christian Identity and the Radical Right,'" *Christian Century*, August 2–9, 1995, 740.

[5]Gordon Melton, quoted in James Coates, *Armed and Dangerous* (New York: Hill and Wang, 1987; 1995 edition), 92.

[6]Larry Witham, "Apocalypse Eventually," *Insight on the News*, May 29, 1995, 33; cf. Barkun, 740. The Center for Democratic Renewal and the Southern Poverty Law Center—two racist monitoring organizations—estimate that the militant white racist movement, of which Christian Identity is a part, includes about 23,000 to 25,000 "hard-core" members. There are possibly an additional 150,000 sympathizers who buy movment literature, send contributions to movement groups, or attend rallys. Another 450,000 may not actually purchase movement literature but do read it. See Raphael S. Ezekiel, *The Racist Mind* (New York: Viking, 1995), xxi.

[7]Michael Barkun, *Religion and the Racist Right* (Chapel Hill, N.C.: University of North Carolina

Press, 1994), xi.

[8] Barkun, *Religion*, ix

[9] *The Eerdmans Bible Commentary* (Grand Rapids: William B. Eerdmans, 1970; 1987 third edition), 361

[10] J. D. Douglas and Merrill C. Tenney, eds., *The New International Dictionary of the Bible* (Grand Rapids: Zondervan, 1987), 194–195.

[11] Sarah Harel-Hoshen, catalog to Bath Hatefutsoth exhibition (1991), reprinted on CD-Rom, *Beyond the Sambatyon: The Myth of the Ten Lost Tribes of Israel* (Creative Multi-Media, 1994).

[12] Several tribes and nations throughout the world claim to be descended from the "lost" ten tribes of Israel. Interestingly, each group does seem to have numerous religious traditions/beliefs and social customs indicating that at some point in their history they may have, at the very least, been influenced by Isrealites. Among the many groups of people who trace their lineage back to Israel are: the black Lembas people of South Africa, Zimbabwe and Mozambique; the Mountain Jews of the Caucasia region in Daghestan, Azerbaijan and Armenia; the Pathans of Afghanistan; the Ben Menashe (Manasseh) of North East India; and the Chiang-Min population who live in the mountain ranges on the Chinese-Tibetan border. Even some Japanese people claim that residents of Japan are descended from Israel (see *Beyond the Sambatyon: The Myth of the Ten Lost Tribes of Israel* [Creative Multi-Media, 1994]).

[13] Pete Peters, "Frequently Asked Questions and Answers on Isreal-Identity," Internet posting at Scriptures for America, http://ra.nilenet.com/!tmw/, to Library, to Israel-Identity FAQ, to Question 5.

[14] The Pilgrims landed on America's shores in 1620 at Plymouth Rock.

[15] Russell Chandler, *Doomsday* (Ann Arbor, Mich.: Servant, 1993), 71.

[16] *Comptons Electronic Online Encyclopedia,* 1994, America Online edition.

[17] *Beyond the Sambatyon.*

[18] Barkun, *Religion*, 5

[19] Richard Brothers, *A Knowledge of the Prophecies and Times* (Yorlck's Head, England: Francis & Robert Bailey, 1794), 43.

[20] Brothers, 41.

[21] Brothers, 40.

[22] Brothers, 44.

[23] Brothers, iii, 39, 51.

[24] Brothers, 43.

[25] Brothers, iii.

[26] Barkun, *Religion*, 6.

[27] James Hastings, ed., *Encyclopedia of Religion and Ethics* (New York: Charles Scribner & Sons), 482.

[28] John Wilson, *Our Israelitish Origin* (London: James Nisbet & Co., 1840; 1843 edition), 114.

[29] Wilson, 80.

[30] Edward Hine, *Forty-Seven Identification of the British Nation* (London: S. W. Partridge & Co., 1871), v.

[31] Barkun, *Religion*, 20.

[32] Barkun, *Religion*, 31.

[33] William J. Cameron, quoted in Barkun, *Religion*, 39.

[34] Wilson, 52.

[35] M. Eshelman, *Two Sticks; or, The Lost Tribes of Israel Discovered: The Jew and the Isrealite Not the Same* (Mount Morris, Il: Brethren Publishing Company, 1887), 261, quoted in Barkun, *Religion*, 122–123.

[36] George R. Riffert, "Judah—The Jews and the Bible in a False Light," *Destiny* 9 (October 1938), 13, quoted in Barkun, *Religion*, 127.

[37] F. Parker, *A Short History of Esau-Edom in Jewry*, 2d ed. (London: Covenant Publishing Co., 1949), 25, 35, 36, 38, 39, 43, quoted in Barkun, *Religion*, 128.

[38] Bertrand L. Camparet, *Israel's Fingerprints: Who are the Jews? Was Jesus Christ a Jew? An Identification of the True Israel by Biblical and Historical Sources* (Flagstaff, Ariz.: Patriot Associates Publishers, 1962), 23, 24, 29–30, 34, quoted in Barkun, *Religion*, 130.

[39]Bob Hallstrom, "Oprah, the Jews and Ritual Murder," *Calling Our Nation* 61, 22.

[40]"Subversion," *Calling Our Nation* 15, 7.

[41]James E. Wise, *The Seed of the Serpent* (Harrison, Ark.: Kingdom Identity Ministries, n.d.,), 7, 8.

[42]*Sons of Liberty Book and Video Cassette List*, 33.

[43]Charles Lee Mange, *The Two Seeds of Genesis 3:15* (Nevada, Mo.: Wake Up America, n.d.), 6.

[44]"Seed of the Serpent," *Morning Watch Chapel*, n.d., 7.

[45]Robert Miles, "Cain and Abel," *Beyond the Bars . . . The Stars*, July-Agust 1985, C.

[46]The "Serpent Seed" doctrine does not assert that Eve had intercourse with a snake. Identity teaches that the term "serpent" is figurative language for a physical manifestation of Satan in the form of a man-like being (see Bertrand Camparet, *Adam was not the First "Man"* [flyer]), 2.

[47]Richard Butler, quoted in Brad Knickerbocker, "Followers See Validation for their Views in the Bible," *Christian Science Monitor*, April 20, 1995, 10.

[48]Michael L. Hansen, "The Aryan Art of War," *Calling our Nation* 34, 8.

[49]*Doctrinal Statement of Beliefs* (Harrison, Ark.: Kingdom Identity Ministries, n.d.), 6.

[50]Richard Butler, *Who, What, Why, When, Where: Aryan Nations* (tract), 3.

[51]Pete Peters, "Frequently Asked Questions and Answers on Isreal-Identity," Internet posting at Scriptures for America, http://ra.nilenet.com/!tmw/, to Library, to Israel-Identity FAQ, to Question 11.

[52]*Aryan Nations Newsletter* 35, 1.

[53]Camparet, 2.

[54]Bertrand Camparet, *The Cain-Satanic Seed Line* (Hayden Lake, Idaho: Aryan Nations, n.d.,), 5.

[55]The American Institute of Theology, *Correspondence Bible Course* (Newhall, Calif.: The American Institute of Theology, 1970; 1981 edition), 16, and O'Brien, 3.

[56]Butler, *Who, What, Why*, 3.

[57]Thom Robb, *Interracial* (Harrison, Ark.: Message of Old Publications, n.d.), 4; cf. Pete Peters, "Frequently Asked Questions and Answers on Isreal-Identity," Internet posting at Scriptures for America, http://ra.nilenet.com/!tmw/, to Library, to Israel-Identity FAQ, to Question 11.

[58]Pete Peters, "Concerning the Oklahoma Bombing," *Scriptures for America* 2 (1995), 2; (This issue is available from Internet posting at Scriptures for America, http://ra.nilenet.com/!tmw/.)

[59]Charles Weisman, *Who is Esau-Edom* (Burnsville, Minn.: Weisman Publications, 1991), 26.

[60]James Combs, *Tolerance: Jewry's War on Whites* (Boring, Oreg.: Christian Patriot Association, n.d.), 10, 11.

[61]Combs, 14–17.

[62]"Why Oppose the Jews," *Calling Our Nation* 15, 6.

[63]Charles Weisman, 108–109.

[64]"Last Days of ZOG," *Calling Our Nation* 59, 25; cf. Robb, 7.

[65]Robb, 5.

[66]Combs, 3.

[67]Jack Mohr, "Kingdom Identity: Part I," *Christian Patriot Crusader*, 7:4 (December 1991), 4, 5.

[68]Pete Peters, *A Scriptural Understanding of the Race Issue* (LaPorte, Colo.: Scriptures for America, 1990), 15.

[69]O'Brien, 47–52. This is a German term that means absolutely forbidden. O'Brien's booklet accurately sums up the views of Mohr and Peters.

[70]Jack Mohr, *Seed of Satan: Literal or Figurative?* (tract); cf. *Who Are You and Why Are You Here* (Bay St. Louis, Miss.: America Awake, n.d.), 5, and letter from Jack Mohr to Apologetics, May, 28, 1990, 8. See Pete Peters, "Frequently Asked Questions," Question 5.

[71]Pete Peters, "Inter-Racial Marriage," part 1, cassette 170, (La Porte, Colo.: Scriptures for America), quoted in Viola Larson, "Identity: A Christian Religion for White Racists," *Christian Research Journal* (Fall 1992), 25; cf. Pete Peters, *A Scriptural Understanding*, 15.

[72]Louis Beam, *Aryan Nations* 25, 17.

[73]David Tate, "WHY?" *Aryan Nations* 25, 12. Tate is currently serving a life sentence for machine-gunning to death thirty-one-year-old Missouri State Trooper Jimmie Linegar in 1985.

[74]Roy B. Mansker, "The Jews Have A Plan," *Calling Our Nation* 33, 4.

[75]Richard Butler, letter to an Aryan Kinsman, *Aryan Nations* 25, 20.

[76]William Gayley Simpson, "The Everlasting Truth About Race," *Christian Patriot Crusader*, 7:4

(December 1991), 19–20.

[77]David Lane, "Migration," *Calling Our Nation* 59, 9. In 1985, Lane was convicted of racketeering and conspiracy to launch a race war against Blacks and Jews in order to establish a White nation. He was sentenced to forty years in prison. He was also convicted in 1987 for his role in the Alan Berg murder and sentenced to additional 150 years. He continues to contribute articles and letters to various white supremacist publications, especially those distributed by Richard Butler's Aryan Nations.

[78]Louis Beam, *The Seditionist*, issue 1 (Winter 1988), 4.

[79]The phrase "Hail Victory" is commonly used by white supremacists to express of their committment to, and confidence in, defeating the Jewish enemy. It is used in racist literature, and is often shouted as a battlecry after an extended speech or at public rallies (Cf. Mansker, 34).

[80]Jack Mohr, *I Believe*, (tract), 6.

[81]Richard Butler, Quoted in Doug Vaughan, "Terror on the Right: The Nazi and Klan Resurgence," *Utne Reader*, August/September 1985, 48. Butler believes that "Ameri" means "heavenly" and "rica" stands for "reich," meaning kingdom; hence, his belief that "America" is God's "heavenly kingdom" (Cf. "America," [Lake Hayden, Idaho: Aryan Nations, n.d., 1]).

[82]David Tate, "Spring Cleaning," *The Way*, May-July 1989, 10.

[83]Willam Potter Gale, 1983, quoted in Coates, 96–97.

[84]Robb, 7

[85]Thom Robb, quoted in Bill Walker, "Warriors in the Fight Against Racial Equality," *Minneapolis Star-Tribune*, July 22, 1986, 9A; cf. Coates, 80–81.

[86]Butler, quoted in Vaughan, 48.

[87]Beam, *Seditionist*, 8.

[88]Butler, *Who, What, Why*, 4.

[89]Butler, quoted in "Terror on the Right," 47.

[90]Butler, quoted in Knickerbocker, 10.

[91]"Dale" Chesson, "To All Aryan Brothers and Sisters," *Calling Our Nation* 34, 9.

[92]Randy Duey, "An Open Letter to the Movement," *Beyond the Bars . . . The Stars*, March-April 1986, F; cf. L. Chesson, 9.

[93]"God's Natural Law or Jewry's Unnatural Law?" *Calling Our Nation* 59, 35.

[94]Beam, *Seditionist*, 2; cf. Butler, letter to an Aryan Kinsman, 20.

[95]Butler, *Who, What, Why*, 4.

[96]"Why Oppose," 6.

[97]Barkun, "Militias," 740.

[98]Barkun, "Militias," 740.

Chapter 13: Oh, What a Tangled Web

[1]Ken Adams, transcripts, "The Militia Movement," 85.

[2]Philip Jenkins, "Home-Grown Terror," *American Heritage*, September 1995, 40.

[3]Jenkins, 40.

[4]Jenkins, 40, 42.

[5]John George and Laird Wilcox, *Nazis, Communists, Klansmen, and Others on the Fringe* (Buffalo: Prometheus, 1992), 21, 30.

[6]James Ridgeway, *Blood in the Face* (New York: Thunder's Mouth Press, 1990), 68.

[7]"Bedford Forrest and His Critter Company," *Calling Our Nation* 59, 2.

[8]James Combs, *Tolerance: Jewry's War On Whites* (Boring Oreg.: Christian Patriot Association, n.d.), 15.

[9]James Wickstrom, "The American Farmer: 20th Century Slave." Quoted in Corcoran, *Bitter Harvest*, 30.

[10]Richard Butler, quoted in Corcoran, *Bitter Harvest*, 35.

[11]Don Black, "The Ku Klux Klan Has A Plan" (flyer), c. early 1980s.

[12]David Scoffins, "Choose You This Day Whom You Will Serve," *Calling Our Nation* 29, 30. Bob Miles served six years in prison for "conspiring to violate civil rights and possession of explosives for the bombings of ten empty school buses used for integration purposes in Pontiac, Michigan." (see George and Wilcox, 370.) Miles was also "convicted of an attack on a Willow Run, Michigan,

school principal, who was tarred and feathered." (see Ridgeway, 85)

[13]Evan Thomas et al. "The Plot," *Newsweek*, May 8, 1995, 33; cf. Robin Wright and Josh Meyer, "Tradition-Rooted 'Patriot' Groups Strive to Curtail Modern 'Tyranny,'" *Los Angeles Times*, April 24, 1995, A12.

[14]Several conspirators involved in this case were sentenced to lengthy jail terms.

[15]Michael L. Hansen, "The Aryan Art of War," *Calling Our Nation* 34, 6.

[16]James Risen, "Militia Networks Boast An Alternate Take On Reality," *Los Angeles Times*, April 30, 1995, A1.

[17]Ken Toole, quoted in Marc Cooper, "A Visit with MOM," *The Nation*, May 22, 1995, reprinted in Hazen et al., *Militias in America*, 46.

[18]Loretta J. Ross, testimony, "America under the Gun," 1.

[19]David Helvarg, quoted in Kathie Durbin, "Environmental Terrorism in Washington State," *Seattle Weekly*, January 11, 1995, reprinted in Hazen et al., *Militias in America*, 36.

[20]Chuck Tate, quoted in B. J. Del Conte, "White Supremacists Eye the Mainstream," *Toronto Sun*, July 21, 1986, 24.

[21]John Roland, "Rumored March 25 Arrests," newsgroup message #180430, March 24, 1995, posted to talk.politics.guns.

[22]Fred Mills, transcripts, "The Militia Movement," 72.

[23]Wright and Meyer, A12.

[24]Mills, 70.

[25]William Pierce, *The Turner Diaries* (Hillsboro, W. Va.: National Vanguard Books, 1978; 1995 second edition), 49.

[26]Jenkins. 40.

[27]Peter Doskoch, "The Mind of the Militias," *Psychology Today*, July/August 1995, 70.

[28]Senator Max Baucus, transcripts, "The Militia Movement," 10.

[29]Baucus, 10.

[30]Susan Ladd and Stan Swofford. "Discontent Feeds Movement, Observers Say," *News & Record* (Greensboro, N.C.), June 27, 1995, Internet edition at http://www.infi.net/nr/extra/militias/m-discon.htm

[31]Jill Smolowe, "Enemies of the State," *Time*, May 8, 1995, 62.

[32]Glen Martin, "Citizens' Militias Have Taken Hold in California," *San Francisco Chronicle*, April 22, 1995, A9.

[33]Noah Chandler, quoted in Leslie Wirpsa. "Rural Despair Feeds Militia Growth," *National Catholic Reporter*, June 30, 1995, 10.

[34]Kenneth S. Stern, testimony, "America under the Gun," 4–5.

[35]Durbin, 36.

[36]"THE JEW WORLD ORDER, JEWS OF THE WORLD: Let My People Go!," Internet postings at the Banned Web Page, http://www.gsu.edu/~hisjwbx/, to Table of Contents, #1; cf. *1995 Sons of Liberty Book and Video Cassette List*, 33.

[37]Dean Compton, author's November 17, 1995 interview with Compton.

[38]Scoffins, 29.

[39]Clermont, "Reflections on the Twentieth Century," *Calling Our Nations* 61, 14.

[40]"The Jewish Bible," *National Christian News* 31, 41.

[41]Richard Butler, letter to an Aryan Kinsman, *Aryan Nations* 25, 20.

[42]Pete Peters, *White Crime in America*, n.d., 5.

[43]The blending of the white supremacist movment and the patriot movement is unmistakable on the Internet, where patriot/militia material and white supremacist literature overlap regularly. At one WWW page known as the 1st Banned Web Page (http://www.gsu.edu/~hisjwbx/), numerous links are given to hard-core racists Pages such as those run by Skinheads, the KKK and Identity sites. Also included is a listing of national militia units with the message: "JOIN THE MILITIA: PREVENT TYRANNY."

[44]David Futrelle, "Cyberhate," *In These Times*, May 15, 1995, 17.

[45]Gordon Kahl, quoted in Corcoran, *Bitter Harvest*, 152–153.

[46]George Eaton, "America Is Lost Because the People Are Lost," *Patriot Report*, October 1994, 2.

[47]Richard Butler, "Do We Love to Have It So," *Calling Our Nation* 60, editorial page.

[48]Don McAlvany, "Financial & Spiritual Preparation for the '90s," Christian Conference, taped message (Vail, Colorado), August 11, 1994; cf. Don McAlvany, "The Fourth Reich: Toward An American Police State," *McAlvany Intelligence Advisor*, January 1995, reprinted in *NEXUS New Times Magazine*, 2:13.

[49]Robert C. Mansker, letter to the editor, *Calling Our Nation* 33, 33.

[50]Linda Thompson, "Sept. 19 Militia Assembly Canceled 9 of 9 pages," BBS message #18672 (Fr: Linda Thompson, To: All), August 9, 1994, *AEN Local*-FidoNet.

[51]Pierce, 68–69.

[52]Jim Keith, *Black Helicopters Over America* (Lilburn, Ga.: IllumiNet Press, 1994), 77; In *America in Peril*, Mark Koernke makes a similar assertion: "[A] full agreement has been signed in Los Angeles, and both the Bloods and the Crips are now being trained, equipped, and uniformed by, with, federal funding through California. . . . Their mission is to be the forefront, the master forces, to come through the door."

[53]"Why Oppose the Jews," *Calling Our Nation* 15, 6.

[54]McAlvany, "As the New World Order Rolls On: The Plunge Toward the Black Hole," *McAlvany Intelligence Advisor*, December 1994, 2.

[55]Louis Beam, *The Seditionist*, issue 1 (Winter 1988), 4.

[56]Mark Koernke, *A Call to Arms* (Real World Productions, 1993); cf. *America in Peril*.

[57]William Pierce, "American Dissident Voices New Tapes List" (Updated 2d August, 1993), Internet posting at National Alliance Home Page, http://www.natvan.com/, to American Dissident Voices, to New Tapes List and "Israel: Facing the Facts," American Dissident Voices (taped radio program), October 23 , 1993, Internet edition at National Alliance Home Page, http://www.natvan.com/, to American Dissident Voices, to document named.

[58]McAlvany, "As the New World," 17.

[59]William Pierce, "'Free' Trade, and the Deindustrialization of America, *National Vanguard Magazine*, Internet edition at National Alliance Home Page, http://www.natvan.com/NATVAN/NATVANDIR. HTML

[60]Glenn Miller, "Grand Dragon Miller," *White Patriot* 56, 10; cf. "Is America Worth Saving," *Aryan Nations* 25, 7.

[61]Jack Mohr, letter to Apologetics Ministry, May 28, 1990, 2.

[62]"The Jewish Bible," *National Christian News*, 1993, #31, 40.

[63]Pete Peters, "A Special Gathering of Christian Men is Scheduled for October 23, 24, 25, 1992" (flyer).

[64]Clayton R. Douglas, *Free American*, quoted in Anti-Defamation League, *Beyond the Bombing: The Militia Menace Grows* (New York: Anti-Defamation League, 1994), 26.

[65]*The International Jew* reads: "Communism all over the world, not in Russia only, is Jewish" (see Henry Ford, reprint of *The International Jew* [London:1948; abridged edition], G.F. Green ed., 135).

[66]Ken Adams, transcripts, "The Militia Movement," 86.

[67]Loretta J. Ross, testimony, "America under the Gun," 3; cf. Kenneth S. Stern, testimony, "America under the Gun," 6.

[68]Michael Janofsky, "White Supremacists Hold Hate Fest," *San Francisco Examiner*, July 23, 1995, Internet edition at http://www.sfgate.com/examiner/index.html; cf. Stern, 6.

[69]John Trochmann, quoted in Stern, 6.

[70]Junas, "Angry White Guys," 23; cf. Keith Schneider, "Bomb Echoes Extremists' Tactics, *New York Times*, April 26, 1995, A14.

[71]John Trochmann, transcripts, "The Militia Movement," 129.

[72]Richard Butler, quoted in Stern, 7.

[73]"Aryan Nations Platform for the Aryan National State," n.d., 1–2; cf. Ross.

[74]Richard Butler, quoted in Stern, 7.

[75]"Groups Attach Significance to Date of April 19," *Orange County Register*, April 22, 1995, 24.

[76]John Trochmann, quoted in Daniel Voll, "At Home with M.O.M.," *Esquire*, July 1995, 48. Trochmann has since abandoned the moral/theological aspects of Christian Identity. According to his close friend Mike Richter, Trochmann reportedly "doesn't believe in Jesus anymore" (Mike Richter, quoted in Voll, 52). Evidence for this comes from a second visit to MOM's Montana enclave

by *Esquire* reporter David Voll. During that visit he was treated by Trochmann and other MOM members to a show at the Playground Lounge—a premier strip joint in Great Falls, Montana. The *Esquire* reporter was left with an unforgettable memory: "Within twenty minutes of taking a front-row seat at the dance stage, during an amazing two-girl act that features whipped cream, the co-founder of the Militia of Montana is leaning forward into the ample breasts of a young stripper who slowly teases a dollar bill from his teeth. He sits back down, grinning, whipped cream smeared on his face. We stay for a couple of hours, and my cowboy hat ends up on the head of a naked woman named Charyne."

[77]"Prominent Militia Networks Launch Counter-Intelligence Campaign," *Klanwatch*, 80, October 1995, 2.

[78]John Trochmann, quoted in Stern, 6.

[79]Voll, 52.

[80]Johnny Lee Clary, author's November 20, 1995, interview with Clary. Johnny Lee is the former Imperial Wizard of the White Knights of the Ku Klux Klan. He ceased his racist activities after becoming a conservative Christian. He has since appeared on a number of television talk shows including Geraldo Rivera and the Sally Jesse Raphael Show.

[81]"Today's Anti-Government Extremists Foreshadowed by 1980s Revolutionaries," *Klanwatch Intelligence Report*, 80, October 1995, 7.

[82]Anti-Defamation League, *Extremism on the Right* (New York: Anti-Defamation League, 1988), 67.

[83]Louis Beam, "Leaderless Resistance," *Special Report On The Meeting of the Christian Men Held in Estes Park, Colorado, October 23, 24, 25, 1992: Concerning the Killing of Vickie and Samuel Weaver By the United States Government* (LaPorte, Colo.: Scriptures for America, 1992), 22.

[84]Beam, "Leaderless," 22.

[85]It is widely acknowledged by well-informed observers of the patriot movement that the militia structure did not form independent of Beam's "leaderless resistance" teachings. The direct link between Beam's views and the militia movement has been documented and discussed in numerous publications: Keith Schneider, "Bomb Echoes Extremists' Tactics," *New York Times*, April 26, 1995, 4; James Ridgeway and Leonard Zeskind, "Revolution U.S.A.," *Village Voice*, April 25, 1995, reprinted in Hazen et al., *Militias in America*, 41-42; Scott McLemee, "Public Enemy," *In These Times*, May 15, 1995, 19.

[86]Smolowe, 64.

[87]Quoted in Anti-Defamation Lague, *Armed & Dangerous: Militias Take Aim* (New York: Anti-Defamation League, 1994), 7.

[88]Tom Burghardt, "Leaderless Resistance and the Oklahoma City Bombing," Internet posting, April 23, 1995, AlterNet BBS gopher site, pathway begins at gopher://gopher.igc.apc.org:70/1, to Progressive Gophers folder, to AlterNet folder, to Militias in America folder, to Additional Articles on Militias folder.

[89]"Militia Day Proclamation," Internet posting in the Patriot Archives, pathway starts at http://www.tezcat.com/, to Tezcat Archives, to Patriot folder, to Militia folder, to Militia Day.txt.

[90]*Destiny Digest*, 3:9 (September 1992), 17.

[91]*New American*, 2:3, (February 6, 1995), quoted in Pete Peters, "Personal From the Editor's Pen, *Scriptures for America Newsletter* (1995), Internet posting at Scriptures for America, http://ra.nile-net.com/!tmw/.

[92]Peters, "Personal From the Editors Pen."

[93]Robin S. Cox, "Americans Burn U.N. Flag," *Christian Israel Fellowship* (flyer), n.d.

[94]"October 24, 1994 was UNITED NATIONS DAY," *Scriptures for America Newsletter* (1994), 10.

[95]"Tape Ministry Update," *Scriptures for America Newsletter* (1995), 10.

[96]*Ohio Kleagle*, September 1994, Internet editio at http://www.cris.com/~Chrident/Kleagle1.html. The term "Kleagle" is a KKK word used to describe someone who is "an organizer."

[97]"Bo Gritz for President Brochure," c. 1991/92. Gritz has been awarded 62 valor citations; cf. Michael Barkun, *Religion and the Racist Right* (Chapel Hill: University of North Carolina Press, 1994), 211.

[98]Joseph P. Shapiro, "An Epidemic of Fear and Loathing," *U.S. News and World Report*, May 8, 1995, 38.

[99]Anti-Defamation League, 84. Duke achieved national recognition in 1989 when he won a seat on

the Louisiana State Legislature as a Republican. He narrowly lost a 1990 U.S. Senate seat held by J. Bennett Johnston. The former Klan leader is no longer involved in electoral politics.

[100]Ridgeway, 129. Political researcher Daniel Junas defines the Populist Party as "an electoral amalgam of neo-Nazis, the Ku Klux Klan, and other racist and anti-Semitic organizations" (see Junas, 23).

[101]Robert Crawford, Steven Gardiner and Jonathan Mozzochi. "Almost Heaven?" *The Dignity Report* (2nd edition), March 1994, 2.

[102]Barkun, 211.

[103]"Bo Gritz for President Brochure," c. 1991/92.

[104]Pete Peters, letter to Randy Weaver, c/o Bo Gritz. Reprinted in "Special Message from Pastor Peter J. Peters," September 1992, 2.

[105]Bo Gritz, *Center for Action*, September 1993, 4, quoted in Crawford, Gardiner and Mozzochi, 3.

[106]"Spike VII Schedule," April 1995.

[107]"Racist Identity Sect Fuels Nationwide Extremist Movement," *Klanwatch*, 79 (August 1995), 5; cf. Mike O'Keefe, "White Hot," *Westword* (Denver), July 12–18, 1989, 20.

[108]"Racist Identity," 5.

[109]Bo Gritz, quoted in Ross, 4.

[110]Ross, *Testimony*, p. 4. Cf. Crawford, Gardiner, and Mozzoci, "Almost Heaven," p. 5.

[111]Bo Gritz, *Called to Serve*, 609, quoted in Jonathan Mozzochi, testimony, "America under the Gun," 1; cf. Ross, 4. Several accounts confirm that Gritz has publicly acknowledged Peters' financial help (see "Front Man for Fascism?: Bo Gritz and the Racist Populist Party," March 1992, 5. This essay is published by People Against Racist Terror, P.O. Box 1990, Burbank, Calif. 91507, 818-509-3435).

[112]Ross, 4.

[113]Bo Gritz, *Center for Action*, January 1994, quoted in Crawford, Gardiner and Mozzochi, 4.

[114]Gritz, *Center*, January 1994, quoted Crawford, Gardiner and Mozzochi, 5.

[115]Crawford, Gardiner and Mozzochi, 1.

[116]Philip Weiss, "They've Had Enough," *New York Times Magazine*, January 8, 1995, 26.

[117]Crawford, Gardiner and Mozzochi, 1.

[118]Jonathan Mozzochi, quoted in Dan Yurman, "Is Idaho a State of Hate or is it Just Confused," (Dateline—5/9/95), *Samizdat: Militia News From Idaho*, Internet posting, December 9, 1995, AlterNet BBS gopher site, pathway begins at gopher://gopher.igc.apc.org:70/1, to Progressive Gophers folder, to AlterNet folder, to Militias in America folder, to Resources folder, to Econet Western Lands Gopher folder, to The Western Lands Gopher Library Archive, to 13-Jan-96 Samizdat: Militia News from Idaho.

[119]During this particular program, Gritz also mentioned that he had previously allowed Aryan Nations founder Richard Butler on the show as a guest in order to talk about the formation of his white supremacist Church of Jesus Christ, Christian/Aryan Nations in Hayden Lake, Idaho.

[120]Zündel says that no more than 300,000 Jews were murdered under the Nazis.

[121]Ernst Zündel, quoted in Frank Miele, "Giving the Devil His Due," *Skeptic* 2:4 (1994), 65.

[122]Miele, 65.

[123]"The Banning of Schindler's List," *Skeptic* 2:4 (1994), 67.

[124]Ernst Zündel, "America's Town Forum," hosted by Bo Gritz, September 13, 1994, KDNO.

[125]Bo Gritz, "America's Town Forum," hosted by Bo Gritz, September 13, 1994, KDNO

[126]*Center for Action*, July 1993, 3, quoted in Crawford, Gardiner and Mozzochi, 3.

[127]Bo Gritz, *Center for Action*, January 1995, 2, quoted Crawford, Gardiner and Mozzochi, 5.

[128]Koernke, *America*.

[129]McLamb, 41, 72.

[130]Jack McLamb, quoted in Ross, 5.

[131]McLamb, *Operation Vampire*, 34.

[132]Crawford, Gardiner and Mozzochi, 1.

[133]Earl Jones, book review of "*Operation Vampire Killer 2000*," *Scriptures for America Newsletter*, 1 (1993), 4.

[134]Pete Peters, *Strength of a Hero and the Warrior's Song* (LaPorte, Colo.: Scriptures for America, 1989; 1994 edition), 2; cf. Pete Peters, "Concerning the Oklahoma Bombing," *Scriptures for America Newsletter* 2 (1995), 8.

[135]Michael Kelly, "The Road to Paranoia," *New Yorker*, June 19, 1995, 74.

[136]Kelly, 74.

Chapter 14: Infiltration of Hate

[1]Tom Morganthau, "The Echoes of Ruby Ridge," *Newsweek*, August 28, 1995, 26.

[2]At the time of the 1992 Ruby Ridge shootings, Weaver and his familiy held to Christian Identity (see chapters four and twelve). However, recent interviews with Weaver suggest that he has disavowed his theological/spiritual beliefs while continuing to hold on to his racist/white supremacist views.

[3]Tom Burghardt, "Leaderless Resistance and the Oklahoma City Bombing," Internet posting, April 23, 1995, AlterNet BBS gopher site, pathway begins at gopher://gopher.igc.apc.org:70/1, to Progressive Gophers folder, to AlterNet folder, to Militias in America folder, to Additional Articles on Militias folder.

[4]June Jordan, "In the Land of White Supremacy," *The Progressive*, June 1995, 21.

[5]"The View That Draws Gunpoint," *Moody Monthly*, March 1986, 7.

[6]Anti-Defamation League, "Religion as Bigotry: The Identity Church Movement," *Special Edition*, October 1991, 2.

[7]John Olson, quoted in Eva Stimson, "White Supremacists take on Trappings of Religion," *Christianity Today*, August 8, 1986, 31.

[8]Stimson, 31.

[9]Chisum, "Beware the Deceivers!!!" *Destiny Digest*, May 1990, 1.

[10]*The Servant People* (Merrimac, Mass.: Destiny Publishers, n.d.), 15.

[11]Thomas E. O'Brien, *Verboten* (Metairie, La.: New Christian Crusade Church, 1974; 1987 reprint entitled *Proof: God's Chosen Are White Adamic Christians, "Verboten"*), 1.

[12]Pete Peters, *Strength of a Hero and the Warrior's Song* (LaPorte, Colo.: Scriptures for America, 1989; 1994 edition), 2.

[13]Loretta J. Ross, testimony, "America under the Gun," 1.

[14]Richard Butler, *Aryan Nations* 25, 18.

[15]Cheryl Hoffman (pseudonym), quoted in Verne Becker, "The Counterfeit Christianity of the Ku Klux Klan," *Christianity Today*, April 20, 1984, 32.

[16]Scott McLemee, "Public Enemy," *In These Times*, May 15, 1995, 15.

[17]Junas, "Angry White Guys," 21.

[18]Skipp Porteous, "Militia Madness," *Freedom Writer*, June 1995, Internet edition at http://www.berkshire.net/~ifas/fw/9506/militia.html; cf. McLemee, 16.

[19]Russ Bellant, "The Paranoid and the Paramilitary," *Detroit Metro Times*, Internet edition, Internet posting, AlterNet BBS gopher site, pathway begins at gopher://gopher.igc.apc.org:70/1, to Progressive Gophers folder, to AlterNet folder, to Militias in America folder, to Additional Articles on Militias folder.

[20]Pat Robertson, *The New World Order* (Dallas: Word, 1991), 6, 208, 215, 221.

[21]Bruce Barron, "A Summary Critique: The New World Order," *Christian Research Journal*, 15:3 (Winter 1993), 45.

[22]Robertson, 178.

[23]Robertson, 178.

[24]Robertson, 265.

[25]Robertson, 67–68.

[26]Robertson, 117, 265.

[27]Adolf Hitler. *Mein Kampf* (Germany: Verlag Frz. Eher Nachf, GmbH, 1925; reprinted Boston: Houghton Mifflin, 1971), transl. Ralph Manheim, 311, 465; cf. Adolf Hitler, January 30, 1939, Reichstag Speech, reprinted in Norman H. Baynes, ed., *The Speeches of Adolf Hitler*, vol. 1, 740-741, quoted in Wistrich, *Antisemitism* (New York: Schocken Books, 1991), 74.

[28]Bruce Brown, *The World's Trouble Makers* (Metairie, La.: Sons of Liberty, 1985), 7, and James Combs, *Who's Who in the World Zionist Conspiracy* (n.p., n.d.), 14.

[29]Robertson, 181.

[30]Jerome R. Chanes. *Antisemitism in America Today* (New York: Birch Lane Press, 1995) 299; cf. Michael Lind, *New York Review of Books*, February 2, 1995, 21–25.

[31]Lind, quoted in Daniel Levitas, "A.D.L. and the Christian Right," *The Nation*, June 19, 1995, 886.

[32]Levitas, 886. Cf. Gustav Niebuhr, "Pat Robertson Says He Intended No Anti-Semitism in Book He

Wrote Four Years Ago" *New York Times,* March 4, 1995, 10.

[33]Pat Robertson, letter to *New York Times,* March 4, 1995, 10.

[34]Jerome R. Chanes. *Antisemitism in America Today* (New York; Birch Lane Press, 1995) 299. Cf. Robertson.

[35]Anthony Lewis, "The Crackpot Factor," *New York Times,* April 14, 1995, A15.

[36]Robertson, *New World Order,* 54, 74,

[37]Robertson, 71,180.

[38]*1995 Sons of Liberty Book and Video Cassette List,* 7.

[39]*1995 Sons of Liberty Book and Video Cassette List,* 6, 21, 22.

[40]Robertson, 272.

[41]Eustace Mullins, *Murder by Injection.* Advertised in *1995 Sons of Liberty Book and Video Cassette List,* 15.

[42]Manfred Roeder, *Teutonic Unity* 44, 3.

[43]Eustace Mullins, Radio Free America interview, October 28, 1994, hosted by Tom Valentine, transcripts posted on the Internet at http://lablinks.com/sumeria/politics/eustace.html

[44]Brown, 12.

[45]Eustace Mullins, epilogue in Brown, 145–146.

[46]Jerome R. Chanes. *Antisemitism in America Today* (New York: Birch Lane Press, 1995), 299.

[47]Chuck Missler, "Clear and Present Danger," *Personal Update,* July 1995, 6–9.

[48]Missler, 8.

[49]Chuck Missler, "The Genealogy of the Antichrist," *Personal Update,* September 1995, 9.

[50]Jim Thomas, "From the Publisher," *Media Bypass,* August 1995, 4.

[51]Chuck Missler, "K-Rations," *Personal Update,* November 1993, 15.

[52]Chuck Missler, "Constitution a Crime," *Personal Update,* November 1995, 3.

[53]"Patriot Fax Network Links Militant Anti-Government Extremists Nationwide," *Klanwatch* 70 (December 1993), 3.

[54]Linda Thompson, "Gary Hunt: Traitor Exposed," HUNT.ZIP *AEN News*-FidoNet document, Part 4 of 9 Parts.

[55]"Patriot Fax," 1.

[56]"Patriot Fax," 2.

[57]Lyon and Sibley were sentenced to death in Alabama. As of February 1996, their executions were pending an appeal.

[58]"Patriot Fax," 1.

[59]"Patriot Fax," 2.

[60]"Patriot Fax," 2.

[61]Gary Hunt, quoted in "Patriot Fax," 3.

[62]Gary Hunt, series of faxes between October 2, 1993, and October 25, 1993, quoted in "Patriot Fax," 2–4.

[63]Robin Wright and Josh Meyer, "Tradition-Rooted 'Patriot' Groups Strive to Curtail Modern 'Tyranny,'" *Los Angeles Times,* April 24, 1995, A12.

[64]Anti-Defamation League, *Armed and Dangerous: Militias Take Aim at the Federal Government* (New York: Anti-Defamation League, 1994), 6.

[65]John George and Laird Wilcox, *Nazis, Communists, Klansmen, and Others on the Fringe* (Buffalo: Prometheus Books, 1992), 372.

[66]Ross, 6.

[67]Russ Bellant, *Old Nazis, the New Right, and the Republican Party* (Boston: South End Press, 1988; 1991 edition), 38.

[68]Scott McLemee, "Spotlight on the Liberty Lobby," *Covert Action Quarterly* 50 (Fall 1994), 24.

[69]Louis T. Beyers, quoted in McLemee, *Spotlight,* 24.

[70]McLemee, *Spotlight,* 24.

[71]McLemee, *Spotlight,* 24.

[72]Willis Carto, letter to Earnest Sevier Cox. Reprinted in C. H. Simonds, "The Strange Story of Willis Carto—His Fronts, His Friends, His Philosophy, His Lobby for 'Patriotism'" *National Review,* September 10, 1971, 979, quoted in McLemee, *Spotlight,* 25.

[73]L., letter to the editor, *Calling Our Nation* 33, 31.

[74]Missler, "Clear," 9. Missler often cites McAlvany's research in his *Personal Update* articles (see Chuck Missler, "Magog Update," *Personal Update*, October 1993, 3).

[75]Don McAlvany, "Toward A Soviet America: Strangling Americans' Freedom and Constitution," *McAlvany Intelligence Advisor*, March 1994, 26.

[76]Don McAlvany, "The $10 Trillion Paper Pyramid Cover-Up," 1993, 4.

[77]Don McAlvany, "The Fourth Reich: Toward An American Police State," *McAlvany Intelligence Advisor*, January 1993. Reprinted in NEXUS *New Times Magazine*, vol. 2 no. 13.

[78]Don McAlvany, "The Waco Massacre: "A Case Study on the Emerging American Police State," *McAlvany Intelligence Advisor*, July 1993, 21.

[79]McAlvany, "The Waco," 21.

[80]Don McAlvany, "Terminating the U.S. Constitution: The Conference of States," April 1995, 3, 23, 27; cf. McAlvany, "The Waco," 21, 28.

[81]*Concise Columbia Encyclopedia*, America Online edition.

[82]McAlvany, "Terminating," 3.

[83]Don McAlvany, "Political Briefs," *McAlvany Intelligence Advisor*, February 1995, 19. The statement by Newt Gingrich to which McAlvany responded is as follows: "I'm for limited government, but a very strong limited government."

[84]Don McAlvany, "America At the Crossroads: Freedom or Slavery?" *McAlvany Intelligence Advisor*, August 1994, 1, 2.

[85]Philip Weiss, "They've Had Enough," *New York Times Magazine*, January 8, 1995, 48.

[86]Max Rider of the West, "Resurrection of the American Common Law Court," *American's Bulletin* 14:10 (October 1995), 1.

[87]Sara Rimer and James Bennet, "Rejecting the Authority of the U.S. Government," *New York Times*, April 24, 1995, A13.

[88]McAlvany, "America," 7; "The Waco," 13, 16; and Don McAlvany, "Greater Self-Sufficiency for Troubled Times: Getting Out of Harms Way," *McAlvany Intelligence Advisor*, September, 1993, 10.

[89]McAlvany, "Greater Self-Sufficiency," 10.

[90]*1995 Sons of Liberty Book and Video Cassette List*, 15.

[91]McAlvany, "Greater Self-Sufficiency," 28; cf. Don McAlvany, "The NAFTA Nightmare: As Mexico and Canada Plunge Toward Collapse," *McAlvany Intelligence Advisor*, February 1995, 20 and *Preparedness Expo '95* Catalog, November 3, 4, & 5, 1995.

[92]Don McAlvany, Christian Conference, taped message (Vail, Colorado), "Coming Persecution of Christians," August 27, 1993.

[93]Chuck Missler highly recommends Don McAlvany and his newsletter. Missler writes: "Don's newsletter is the *McAlvany Intelligence Advisor*. We subscribe to numerous newsletters to complement our own sources, but this one is *essential!* Don's is a 'must read.' We strongly urge everyone to contact Don for a free sample issue" (Chuck Missler, "Vail Conference," *Personal Update*, October 1993, 8).

[94]McAlvany, Christian Conference.

[95]McAlvany, "The Waco," 28.

[96]Don McAlvany, "Reflections on America on a Quiet Summer Day," *McAlvany Intelligence Advisor*, July, 1995, 20; cf. McAlvany, "America at the Crossroads," 28.

[97]McAlvany, "Conclusion and Recommendation," *McAlvany Intelligence Advisor*, August 1993, 11.

[98]McAlvany, "Conclusion and Recommendation," 12.

[99]McAlvany, "The Waco," 28.

[100]McAlvany, "Conclusion and Recommendation," 19.

[101]McAlvany. "Toward A Soviet America," 26.

[102]Don McAlvany, "Toward Medical Self-Sufficiency: Understanding Alternate Medicine," *McAlvany Intelligence Advisor*, August 1995, 28.

[103]Missler, "Vail Conference," 8.

[104]Missler, "Vail Conference," 7.

[105]Don McAlvany, "Precious Metals in Uncertain Times: The Lull Before the Store," *McAlvany Intelligence Advisor*, September 1995, 13.

[106]Rex Turner (ICA), author's February 14, 1995, interview with Turner.

[107]McAlvany, "The Waco," 21.

[108]McAlvany, "Conclusion and Recommendation," 19.

[109]Texe Marrs, flyer advertisement for *Circle of Intrigue*, n.d.

[110]Texe Marrs, "Dark Majesty: Unmasking the Secret Brotherhood," *Flashpoint*, Special Edition, n.d., 1.

[111]Texe Marrs, mass mailing appeal letter, n.d., 1.

[112]Texe Marrs, "Campaign '92," *Flashpoint*, Special Edition, n.d., 3.

[113]Marrs, "Dark Majesty," 1; Texe Marrs, "The Masonic Plan for America," *Flashpoint*, January 1995, 1–2; Texe Marrs, "The Treaty From Hell," *Flashpoint*, May 1995, 2; Texe Marrs, "The Pope Over Jerusalem," *Flashpoint*, May 1995, 5; Texe Marrs, "All Fall Down: The Plot to Crown the Pope the Prince of Peace," flyer advertisement for *All Fall Down*, n.d.; Texe Marrs, "The United Nations Plot," *Flashpoint*, September 1993, 4; Texe Marrs, "Foreign Occupation Troops in America," *Flashpoint*, December 1994, 3; Texe Marrs, "Are Christian Leaders Anti-Semitic, Neo-Nazi Bigots?" *Flashpoint*, September 1994, 1–2; Texe Marrs, "Pope Meets With ADL Henchmen," *Flashpoint*, April 1995, 1–2; Texe Marrs, advertisement for *The Antichrist King—Juan Carlos, Flashpoint*, January 1995, 5 (Marrs has never stated that he personally believes the Antichrist is Juan Carlos. Nevertheless, he sells the book *The Antichrist King—Juan Carlos* by Charles Taylor, who does name the Spanish monarch as the devil's beast.)

[114]Texe Marrs, mass mailing appeal letter, 1995.

[115]Marrs, appeal letter.

[116]Texe Marrs, "What's Ahead for 1996–1999," *Flashpoint*, February 1996, 6.

[117]Texe Marrs, "New Videos Document Power of Bible Prophecy," video advertisement flyer, n.d.

[118]Texe Marrs, "Concentration Camps in America," *Flashpoint*, September 1994, 5.

[119]Texe Marrs, "A Slime Pit of Sexual Depravity," *Flashpoint*, January 1994, 1.

[120]Texe Marrs, "Fascist Terror Stalking America," *Flashpoint*, June 1995, 2.

[121]Texe Marrs, "A Slime Pit," 1.

[122]Texe Marrs, "What's Ahead," 6.

[123]Texe Marrs, "A Slime Pit," 1.

[124]Texe Marrs, "The Bloodstained Hands of Big Brother Government," *Flashpoint*, June 1995, 6.

[125]Texe Marrs, "Who Slaughtered the Innocents in Oklahoma City," flyer advertisement for *Fascist Terror Stalking America*, n.d.

[126]Texe Marrs, "Illuminata: The Secret New Age Occultism of Bill and Hillary Clinton," *Flashpoint*, April 1995, 5.

[127]Texe Marrs, "Fascist Terror," 2.

[128]Texe Marrs, "Who Slaughtered the Innocents."

[129]Jack McLamb, *Operation Vampire Killer 2000* (Phoenix: PATNWO, 1992), 38.

[130]Texe Marrs, "*Word of Prophecy* Tapes Available," *Flashpoint*, April 1996, 4.

[131]Pete Peters, "Book Review: Big Sister is Watching You," *Scriptures for America Newsletter* 4 (1994), 8.

[132]Peters, 8.

[133]Texe Marrs, "The Bo Gritz Tapes," advertisement for taped broadcasts of Marrs and Gritz, n.d.

[134]Texe Marrs, *Flashpoint*, May 1995, 4–5.

[135]Texe Marrs, "World of Prophecy Tapes Available," *Flashpoint*, January 1995, 4.

[136]Texe Marrs, "The People's Right to Form a Militia," *Flashpoint*, August 1994, 1.

[137]Texe Marrs, letter to the author, June 27, 1994, 2–3.

[138]Texe Marrs, "America Under Siege," flyer advertisement for *America Under Siege*, n.d.

[139]"CONFAB Draws National Coverage," *Spotlight*, September 18, 1995, 12.

[140]*Demons: True Life Evil Forces* (His Majesty's Media, 1995).

[141]Pete Peters, "Concerning our Television Debut," *Scriptures for America Newsletter,* 4 (1993), 5.

[142]Skipp Porteous, "Anti-Semitism: Its Prevalence Within the Christian Right," *Freedom Writer*, May 1994, Internet edition posted at http://www.berkshire.net/~ifas/fw/9405/antisemitism.html

[143]Prior to getting his own program on KIN, Peters was a guest on the network's very popular show *Keystone on the Line* (October 19, 1993). This broadcast reached the entire American continent, as well as Hawaii and the Virgin Islands. Host Jerry Jacobs used the program to praise and recommend Peters's book *America the Conquered*. According to Peters, this one show brought new responses from forty states. (see Peters, "Concerning our Television Debut," 5).

[144]Ray Brubaker, mass mailing letter, c. 1993, 4.

[145]"New from the Video Department," *Scriptures for America Newsletter*, 3 (1995), 10.

[146]Susan Schock, testimony, "America under the Gun," 5.

Chapter 15: Holy Wars

[1]Frank Flinn, "Government Shouldn't Fulfill Militia's Apocalyptic Prophecies," *Insight on the News*, May 29, 1995, 39.

[2]Beth Hawkins, "Patriot Games," *Detroit Metro Times*, October 12, 1994, reprinted in Hazen et al., *Militias in America*, 9.

[3]Norm Olson was removed as pastor of Calvary Baptist Church and leader of the Northern Michigan Militia after publicly accusing the Japanese government of committing the Oklahoma City bombing.

[4]Marc Cooper, "From the Horses Mouth," *The Nation*, April 22, 1995, reprinted in Hazen et al., *Militias in America*, 48.

[5]Chuck Baldwin, quoted in Daniel Voll, "The Right to Bear Sorrow," *Esquire*, March 1995, 80.

[6]Baldwin, quoted in Voll, 80.

[7]Baldwin, quoted in Voll, 80.

[8]Baldwin, quoted in Voll, 80.

[9]Joe Maxwell and Andrés Tapia, "Guns and Bibles, *Christianity Today*, June 19, 1995, 34.

[10]Michael Barkun, quoted in Maxwell and Tapia, 34.

[11]Jeffrey Kaplan, quoted in Maxwell and Tapia, 36.

[12]Phil Roberts, quoted in Martin King, "Michigan Militia Leader Not A Southern Baptist," *Christianity Today*, April 24, 1995, America Online edition.

[13]Maxwell and Tapia, 34–35.

[14]Walter A. Elwell, *Evangelical Dictionary of Theology* (Grand Rapids: Baker, 1984), 683.

[15]Jeffrey Kaplan, quoted in Maxwell and Tapia, 36.

[16]Martin Marty, quoted in Maxwell and Tapia, 36.

[17]Norm Olson, quoted in Maxwell and Tapia, 36.

[18]Donald Guthrie, ed., *The Eerdman's Bible Commentary* (Grand Rapids, Eerdman's, 1970; third edition), 1275

[19]Charles F. Pfeiffer and Everett F. Harrison, ed., *The Wycliffe Bible Commentary* (Chicago: Moody Press, 1962), 1488.

[20]Harold Stockburger, "Taking A Stand," *Patriot Press*, July 1995, 8.

[21]Stockburger, 8.

[22]Stockburger, 8.

[23]Gleason Archer, *Encyclopedia of Bible Difficulties* (Grand Rapids: Zondervan, 1982), 341.

[24]Vine, *An Expository Dictionary of New Testament Words*, reprinted in *Vine's Complete Expository Dictionary of Old and New Testament Words* (Nashville: Thomas Nelson, 1985), 613.

[25]Norman Geisler and Thomas Howe, *When Critics Ask* (Wheaton, Ill.: Victor Books, 1992), 361; cf. A.T. Robertson, *Word Pictures in the New Testament* (Grand Rapids: Baker Book House, 1930; reprint edition), vol. 2, 271.

[26]Jeffrey Kaplan, "A Guide to the Radical Right, *Christian Century*, August 2–9, 1995, 744.

[27]Bureau of Alcohol, Tobacco, and Firearms statistics. Cited in Tom Burghardt, "Neo-Nazis Salute the Anti-Abortion Zealots," *Covert Action Quarterly* 52, 26. It must be remembered that these figures only represent *reported* instances of violent and illegal acts. Not every crime can be conclusively linked to pro-life extremists. In fact, many of these crimes remain unsolved. Consequently, it is unsubstantiated theory that all of the crimes were committed by pro-life extremists.

[28]Timothy Egan, "Anti-Abortion Violence: Is it a Conspiracy?" *San Francisco Examiner*, June 18, 1995, Internet edition at http://www.outright.com/pritch/abor.html

[29]Susan Headden, "Free (To Kill) Speech," *U.S. News & World Report*, November 6, 1995, 12. Operation Rescue organizers maintain that they did not intend for their "wanted" posters to incite Gunn's murder. The desired effect of the posters was to bring public "shame" Dr. Gunn, and by doing so, bring him to a point where he would choose to stop providing abortions. It is not my intention to suggest that OR leaders wanted Gunn to be murdered, or that they produced the flyers in an effort to facilitate that event.

[30]Douglas Frantz, "The Rhetoric of Terror," *Time*, March 27, 1995, 49.

[31]"Defensive Action," 1994, Internet version at http://www.cais.net/agm/main/statemen.html. The names of those who signed this statement are as follows: Mike Bray (Pastor, Reformation Lutheran Church—Bowie, Maryland), C. Roy McMillan (Executive Director, Christian Action Group—Jackson, Mississippi), Andrew Burnett (Director, Advocates for Life Ministries—Portland, Oregon), Cathy Ramey (Associate Editor, Life Advocate Magazine—Portland, Oregon), Matt Trewhella (Pastor, Mercy Seat Christian Church—Milwaukee, Wisconsin), Paul J. Hill (Director, Defensive Action—Pensacola, Florida), Paul deParrie (Author of Numerous Titles—Portland, Oregon), Regina Dinwiddie (Christian Pro-Life Activist & Producer of Rescue Radio—Missouri and Kansas), Michael Dodds (Leader of Wichita Rescue Movement—Wichita, Kansas), Henry Felisone (Director, Queens Pro-Life Group—Queens, New York), Tony Piso (Pastor, Evangelical Mission Church—Forest Hill, New York), Jacob Miller (Evangelist, Assembly of Yahweh & Pro-Life Activist—Tampa, Florida), Dan Bray (Director, Defenders of the Defenders of Life—Bowie, Maryland), David Crane (Director, Rescue Virginia—Norfolk, Virginia), Donald Spitz (Evangelist & Assistant Director for Rescue Virginia—Norfolk, Virginia), Michael Jarecki (Ret. Pastor, Saint Mary's Church—Brushton, New York), Bill Koehler (Director of Project Awareness—North Bergen, New Jersey), Kenneth Arndt (Director, New Hampshire Rescue—Windham, New Hampshire) Dave Leach (Editor, _Prayer and Action Weekly News_—Des Moines, Iowa), Mike Walker (Leader in National Assoc. of Planned Parenthood Fighters—Alabama), Thomas Carleton (Catholic Priest—Presently Incarcerated in Billerica, Massachusetts), Valerie Zyskowski (Member of Leadership Committee, Rescue Pittsburgh—Pittsburgh, Pennsylvania), Joseph F. O'Hara (Director, Wyoming Valley Rescue Group—Pennsylvania), David Graham (Attorney at Law—Olathe, Kansas), David Trosch (Catholic Priest, Publisher Justifiable Homicide Cartoon & President Life Enterprises Unlimited—Mobile, Alabama), Dawn Stover (Assistant Director, Advocates for Life Ministries—Portland, Oregon), Mike Meyer (Chairman, Tri-State Rescue Committee—Cincinnati, Ohio), David Craig (Former Presbyterian Pastor—Hope, Indiana) John Brockhoeft (author of "The Brockhoeft Report"—incarcerated in Burlington, Kentucky), Mary Beddingfield (Executive Committee, No Place to Hide Campaign—Pittsburgh, Pennsylvania), Donna Bray (Co-Founder, Defenders of the Defenders of Life—Bowie, Maryland).

[32]John W. Kennedy, "Florida Shootings Stifle Pro-Lifers," _Christianity Today_, September 12, 1994, America Online edition.

[33]Burghardt, 26. It must be remembered that this figure only represents _reported_ instances of death threats. Not every threat can be conclusively linked to pro-life extremists. In fact, many of these threats have never been traced to a particular individual. Consequently, it is unsubstantiated theory that all of threats were committed by pro-life extremists.

[34]Michael D. Lemonick, "An Armed Fanatic Raises the Stakes," _Time_, January 9, 1995, 34.

[35]Stephen Hedges, David Bowermaster and Susan Headden, "Abortion: Who's Behind the Violence?" _U.S. News and World Report_, November 14, 1994, 50.

[36]Donald Spitz, quoted in Jill Smolowe, "Fear in the Land," _Time_, January 16, 1995, 35.

[37]Smolowe, 34–35; cf. James Risen, "Abortion Foes Rally for Shooting Suspect," _Los Angeles Times_, January, 2, 1995, A15.

[38]John Ellement, "Jury Convicts Salvi in Clinic Murders," _Rocky Mountain News_, Maarch 19, 1996, 3A; cf. Michael Matza, "Salvi Guilty in Deaths of 2 at Abortion Clinics," _Philadelphia Inquirer_, March 19, 1996, A1.

[39]Roy McMillan, quoted in Frantz, 48.

[40]Missionaries to the Preborn was founded in Milwaukee in 1990, but its headquarters moved to California in 1995.

[41]Matthew Trewhella, _Missionaries to the Preborn Newsletter_, March 10, 1993. Quoted in John Goetz, "Missionaries' Leader Calls for Militias," _Front Lines Research_ 1:2 (August 1994), 3.

[42]Matthew Trewhella, _Defensive Action Press Release_, quoted in Goetz, 3–4.

[43]Gary McCullough, "Do My Words Make Me Violent," Internet posting at http://www.cais.com/agm/ domyword.html

[44]Matthew Trewhella, USTP Convention, videotape, May 27–29, 1994.

[45]Matthew Trewhella, USTP Convention; cf. Melinda Liu, "Inside the Anti-Abortion Underground," _Newsweek_, August 29, 1994, 28.

[46]Trewhella, USTP Convention.

[47]*Field Manual of the Free Militia,* reprint ed. (Great Barrington, Mass.: Riverwalk Press, 1996), 78, 80.

[48]John C. Inquest. "The Tenth Egyptian Plague Hits America: ABORTION," *Aryan Nations* 25, 22.

[49]Beth Heick. Cited in "Who to Hate: Anatomy of a Female Racist," *Mademoiselle,* August 1994, 136.

[50]Tom Metzger, quoted in Burghardt, 27.

[51]Burghardt, 27.

[52]Bill Dunham, "Bureau of Alcohol, Tobacco and Firearms Intelligence Statement," October 26, 1994, ATF tactical Intelligence Branch, Washington, D.C., Internet posting at ftp://tezcat.com/patriot.

[53]Trewhella, USTP Convention.

[54]Don McAlvany, "As the New World Order Rolls On: The Plunge Toward the Black Hole," *McAlvany Intelligence Advisor,* December 1994, 18, 23; cf. Don McAlvany, "Conclusion and Recommendation," *McAlvany Intelligence Advisor,* August 1993, 19 and Don McAlvany, "Election '96: The Establishment Fix is Almost In," *McAlvany Intelligence Advisor,* October 1995, 21.

[55]Missionaries to the Preborn flyer, n.d.

[56]Jeffrey Baker, *Cheque Mate: The Game of Princes* (Springdale, Pa.: Whitaker House, 1993), 47–53, 62, 69, 70, 79, 134, 141-142, 150–151, 154, 157–164, 243.

[57]Texe Marrs, advertisement flyer for *Cheque Mate: The Game of Princes,* n.d.

[58]Baker, 51.

[59]Baker, 331, 334. In his 1984 book *The Church Deceived,* Red Beckman identifies the Jews as the Antichrist Church controlling public schools, Christian churches and the government. According to Beckman, this Jewish race "was not a victim during World War II because they were getting their just reward for their evil choices." The Jews, according to Beckman, were slaughtered by Hitler as a means of divine judgment (see M. J. "Red" Beckman, *The Church Deceived* [Billings, Mont.: Common Sense Press, 1984], 42–43).

[60]Baker, 50

[61]Chuck Smith, quoted in endorsements flyer, received from Gary Kah Ministries, 1.

[62]Gary Kah, *En Route to Global Occupation* (Lafayette, La.: Huntington House, 1991), 25, 26, 61, 62, 100, 102, 104, 108, 109, 117.

[63]Kah, 117.

[64]Leonard Dinnerstein, *Antisemitism in America* (New York: Oxford University Press, 1994), 112.

[65]John George and Laird Wilcox, *Nazis, Communists, Klansmen, and Others on the Fringe* (Buffalo: Prometheus Books, 1992), 206.

[66]Anti-Defamation League, *Extremism on the Right* (New York: Anti-Defamation League, 1988), 175.

[67]Beverly LaHaye, quoted in endorsements flyer, received from Gary Kah Ministries, 1.

[68]Chip Berlet, "Armed Militias, Right Wing Populism, & Scapegoating," April 24, 1995, Internet posting, AlterNet BBS gopher site, pathway begins at gopher://gopher.igc.apc.org:70/1, to Progressive Gophers folder, to AlterNet folder, to Militias in America folder, to Militias in America (1995) folder, to Chronicling the Growth of a Movement folder.

[69]See Bob Vernon, "Operation Rescue: A Policeman's Perspective," *Masterpiece* (a publication of Grace Community Church in Van Nuys, California), March/April, 1991, 16–19.

[70]Pro-lifers who participate in civil disobedience contend that they are allowed to break the law by God because the government is directly forbidding them to defend the defenseless. In other words, the government is trying to stop them from obeying God, who has commanded that Christian defend those who cannot defend themselves.

[71]Norman Geisler, *Civil Disobedience: When Is It Right?* (Lynchburg, Va.: Quest Productions, 1990), 5–6. To request a copy of this excellent booklet write to Dr. Norman Geisler, Southern Evangelical Seminary, 5801 Pineville-Matthews Rd., Charlotte, NC 28226, ph. 704-543-9475.

[72]In an E-mail message to me dated March 4, 1996, Roger Stuart sent the following information regarding this listserver: It is hosted by Eric Nelson (elnelson@netcom.com). The moderator is George Hillman (geo316@cris.com). The computer generated instructions were controlled by Netcom. Whether it is "officially" run by Calvary Chapel Ministries, remains unclear, but a subscriber must list which Calvary Chapel he or she attends in order to get on the BBS. Also, the instructions read: "Commercial, controversial and non Calvary Chapel related messages can lead to cancellation of your subscription." This means that only Calvary Chapel related discussions are only

allowed.

[73]Clay Pryor, "Re: Hidden Messages in the Torah," BBS message (Fr: Clay Pryor To: calvary-list-serv@netcom.com), February 14, 1996.

[74]In the Clay Pryor message defending Chuck Missler, Pryor even backed Missler's recommendation of Linda Thompson's Waco videos. Pryor's computer posting became irate when rebutting the charge that Missler has pulled from some highly questionable sources in the fanatical militia groups, as well as from some anti-Semitic and racist segments of the patriot movement. Pryor's response is as follows: "Now you have gone too far in your stereotyping. How do you define a fanatic? I have heard the definition of a fanatic as 'someone who loves God more than you do.' Perhaps these people love our country (and it's original God) more than you do. As for 'racist and white supremacists,' sure there are some people with these beliefs associated with the militia movement (as in any organization or movement or affiliation . . . perhaps even in your own congregation), however, most are rooted out and eliminated from any formal militia groups. . . . That's why your 'sensational' portrayal of these groups (in alignment with media portrayals) is commonly accepted by people who do not look into the Government abuses that have caused these groups to come into existence. That is exactly what the anti-Constitution Clinton administration wants you to think about these issues. They would love nothing more than to 'crack down' on these 'terrorist' groups and institute 'law and order' in this country."

[75]Don McAlvany, "Election '96," 20–21.

[76]Jack McLamb, _Operation Vampire Killer 2000_ (Phoenix, Ariz.: PATNWO, 1992), 5.

Chapter 16: Blessed are the Peacemakers

[1]Dean Compton, lecture at the Granada Forum, November 16, 1995.

[2]Eustace Mullins, quoted in Dan Yurman, "Wilderness Gathering Sets the Stage for Change from Talk to Action," (Dateline—Post Falls, Idaho 4/17/95), _Samizdat: Militia News From Idaho_, Internet posting, December 9, 1995, AlterNet BBS gopher site, pathway begins at gopher://gopher.igc.apc.org:70/1, to Progressive Gophers folder, to AlterNet folder, to Militias in America folder, to Resources folder, to Econet Western Lands Gopher folder, to The Western Lands Gopher Library Archive, to 13-Jan-96 Samizdat: Militia News from Idaho. Mullins made this statement when he was the featured speaker at a Northwest Liberty Network Seminar in Idaho.

[3]John Trochmann, transcripts of ABC's _Primetime Live_, transcript #399, April 25, 1995, 25.

[4]Ross Hullett, _CNN News_, March 1, 1995; cf. Don McAlvany, "Terminating the U.S. Constitution: The Conference of States," _McAlvany Intelligence Advisor_, April 1995, 20.

[5]_Patriot Press_, October 1995, 2.

[6]Jim Keith, _Black Helicopters Over America: Strikeforce for the New World Order_ (Lilburn, Ga.: IllumiNet Press, 1994), 148–149.

[7]Clayton Douglas, "The U.N.—Benevolent Organization or Fearful Master?" _Free American_, October 1995, 2.

[8]Nick Repac, "Civil Rights Task Force Representatives Meet With New Mexico Governor Johnson," _Free American_, October 1995, 11.

[9]"Fight Against Police State Escalates," _Freedom Network News_, June/July 1995, 1.

[10]Ken Adams, transcripts, "The Militia Movement," 85.

[11]Militia of Montana, _Taking Aim_, vol. 1 issue 7, 1994, Internet posting in the Patriot Archives, pathway starts at http://www.tezcat.com/, to Tezcat Archives.

[12]Don McAlvany, "As the New World Order Rolls On: The Plunge Toward the Black Hole," _McAlvany Intelligence Advisor_, December 1994, 17; cf. Don McAlvany, "Conclusion," _McAlvany Intelligence Advisor_, June 1994, 15.

[13]James M. Collier and Kenneth F. Collier, _Votescam: The Stealing of America_ (New York: Victoria House, 1992), 1–3.

[14]Norm Olson, quoted in Robert Downes and George Foster, "On the Front Lines with Northern Michigan's Militia," _Northern Express_ (Traverse City, Michigan), August 22, 1994, reprinted in Hazen et al., _Militias in America_, 14.

[15]Ray Southwell, quoted in Downes and Foster, 14.

[16]"Wise Use Update" January 1996, Internet AlterNet BBS gopher site, pathway begins at gopher://gopher.igc.apc.org:70/1, to Progressive Gophers folder, to AlterNet folder, to Militias in America

folder, to Resources folder, to Econonet Western Lands Gopher folder, to The Western Lands Gopher folder, to Wise Use Update 1/96.

[17]George Skelton, "There is No Easy Answer on Militias," *Los Angeles Times*, April 27, 1995, A3.

[18]Rogers Worthington, "U.S. Indicts Alleged Bombmaker," *Chicago Tribune*, November 21, 1995, 14.

[19]Ken Toole, testimony, "America under the Gun," 3.

[20]Susan Schock, testimony, "America under the Gun," 3–4.

[21]Martha Bethel, testimony, "America under the Gun," 1–3.

[22]Schock, 4.

[23]Toole, 3.

[24]Norm Olson, quoted in Downes and Foster, 14.

[25]Bill Wallace, "Citizen Militias Worry Californians," *San Francisco Chronicle*, May 31, 1995, A6. This was a statewide poll of 504 adults with an accurate to within 4.5 percentage points.

[26]Toole, 2–3.

[27]"This Modern World," reprinted in Hazen et al., *Militias in America,* 58.

[28]Wallace, "Heated Rhetoric," A13.

[29]Wallace, A13

[30]Susan Ladd and Stan Swofford, "Fearing for Our Country," *News & Record* (Greensboro, N.C.), June 25, 1995, Internet edition at http://www.infi.net/nr/extra/militias/m-fearing.htm

[31]Namika, "Agent Orange: The Dirty Legal War at Home," *Covert Action Quarterly* 43, 26.

[32]Committee on Government Operations, "The Agent Orange Coverup: A Case of Flawed Science and Political Manipulation," House Report (H. Rep.), 101–672, quoted in Namika, 26.

[33]Namika, 26.

[34]Glenn Alcalay, "Damage Control On Human Radiation Experiments," *Covert Action Quarterly* 52, 46.

[35]Joseph Heberta, "Scientific Panel Rips Alaska Radiation Experiments 1/31/96," Associated Press, America Online edition.

[36]Heberta.

[37]Ladd and Swofford, "Discontent Feeds Movement, Observers Say," *News & Record* (Greensboro, N.C.), June 27, 1995, Internet edition at http://www.infi.net/nr/extra/militias/m-discon.htm

[38]Charles R. Duke, "Physician Heal Thyself," *Media Bypass*, August 1995, 32.

[39]Herb Kohl, transcripts, "The Militia Movement," 7.

[40]Quoted in "Clinton Continues Attack on Hate Speech as Hunt for Bombing Suspect Intensifies," *Wall Street Journal*, April 25, 1994, A5.

[41]Bill Clinton, *60 Minutes*, April 23, 1995, quoted in Louis Freedberg, "GOP Accused of Fanning Flames of Extremism/Anti-government Rhetoric Blamed," April 24, 1995, *San Francisco Chronicle*, A6.

[42]Bill Clinton, April 24, 1995, quoted in Don McAlvany, "The Oklahoma City Tragedy: Implications for Free Speech, Political Dissent, and Liberty in America (A Clear and Present Danger)," *McAlvany Intelligence Advisor*, May/June 1995, 5.

[43]"Clinton Continues Attack," *Wall Street Journal,* A5.

[44]McAlvany, "The Oklahoma City," 5

[45]Newt Gingrich, quoted in Peter Applebome, "Radical Rights' Fury Boiling Over," *New York Times*, April 23, 1995, A13.

[46]Neale Boortz, *Phil Donahue*, April 25, 1995.

[47]Gordon Liddy, August 26, 1994, quoted in Jeff Cohen and Norman Solomon, "Guns, Ammo, Threats, and Talk Radio," *Alternet*, February 17, 1995, reprinted in Hazen et al., *Militias in America,* 63; cf. *Indianapolis News*, September 2, 1994.

[48]Bob Mohan, quoted in Cohen and Solomon, 63.

[49]Chuck Baker, September 6, 1994, quoted in Leslie Jorgensen, "Media Advisory: Right-Wing Talk Radio Supports Militia Movement," *Extra!*, April 21, 1995, Internet edition at http://paul.spu.edu/~sinnfein/fair.html; cf. Cohen and Solomon, 62.

[50]Rush Limbaugh, quoted in Robert Wright, "Did Newt Do It?" *The New Republic*, May 15, 1995, 45.

[51]Chuck Baker, quoted in Leslie Jorgensen. Cf. Cohen and Solomon, 62.

[52]Mark Koernke, *A Call to Arms* (Real World Productions, 1993).

[53]Beth Hawkins, "Damage Control," *Detroit Metro Times*, April 26, 1995, reprinted in Hazen et al., *Militias in America*, 51.

[54]Phil Agre, unpublished essay on the Oklahoma City bombing, Internet posting, April 23, 1995. Confirmed by author's January 19, 1995, telephone interview with Agre.

[55]Oliver Wendell Holmes, quoted by Senator Arlen Specter, transcripts, "The Militia Movement," 4.

[56]Leslie Jorgensen and Sherry Keene-Osborne, "Under the Gun," *Westword*, December 14, 1994, reprinted in Hazen et al., *Militias in America*, 22–26.

[57]Carl Levin, transcripts, "The Militia Movement," 16.

[58]Daniel Levitas, quoted in Hawkins, "Damage Control," 51.

[59]Ingo Hasselbach, "Extremism: A Global Network," *New York Times*, April 24, 1995, A19.

[60]Hasselbach, A19.

[61]Rush Limbaugh, "Blame the Bombers—Only," *Newsweek*, May 8, 1995, 39.

[62]Ladd and Swofford, "Discontent."

[63]Bill Wassmuth, testimony, "America under the Gun," 5.

[64]Wassmuth, 5.

[65]John Perkins, "He's My Brother," *Cornerstone* 25:108 (1995), 43. John Perkins is an African-American Christian who was a leader in the civil rights movement of the 1960s. His moving story about being nearly beaten to death by Mississippi highway patrolmen appears in this 1995 issue of *Cornerstone*. To request a copy of the article or magazine, write to: *Cornerstone*, 939 W. Wilson Ave., Chicago, Ill. 60640, 312-561-2450.

Bibliography

The following bibliography does not include all of the documentation cited. This is a selected bibliography of those materials that I feel are most important to those who wish to further study the patriot/militia movement or white supremacy. Moreover, I do not endorse all of the resources listed herein. They are provided for research purposes only.

Non-Patriot, Non-Militia Materials
Books: Politics, Law, Government, Social Issues

Anti-Defamation League. *The Religious Right: The Assault on Pluralism in America.* New York: Anti-Defamation League, 1994.

Arendt, Hannah. *Totalitarianism.* New York: Harcourt Brace Jovanovich, 1951; 1968 edition.

Berlet, Chip, ed. *Eyes Right.* Boston: South End Press, 1995.

Bishop, Morris. *The Middle Ages.* Boston: Houghton Mifflin, 1968; 1987 edition.

Bovard, James. *Lost Rights: The Destruction of American Liberty.* New York: St. Martin's Press, 1994.

Bradford, M. E. *Original Intentions.* Athens, Ga.: University of Georgia Press, 1993.

Carson, Clarence B. *Basic American Government.* Wadley, Ala.: American Textbook Committee, 1993.

Carsten, F. L. *The Rise of Fascism.* Berkeley: University of California Press, 1967; 1980 second edition.

Cheles, Luciano, Ronnie Ferguson and Michalina Vaughan, eds. *Neo-Fascism in Europe.* London: Longman, 1991.

Clanton, Gene. *Populism.* Boston: Twayne, 1991.

Columbia University. *The Concise Columbia Encyclopedia.* New York: Columbia University Press, 1983; 1989 edition.

Cornell, James. *The Great International Disaster Book.* New York: Pocket Books, 1976; 1979 edition.

Criley, Richard. *The FBI v. The First Amendment.* Los Angeles: The First Amendment Foundation, 1990.

Del Re, Gerard and Patricia. *History's Last Stand.* New York: Avon Books, 1993.

Department of Justice, "Report to the Deputy Attorney on the Events at Waco, Texas," *United States Department of Justice Report on the Events at Waco, Texas February 28 to April 19, 1993,* redacted version.

Department of the Treasury. *Report of the Department of the Treasury on the Bureau of Alcohol, Tobacco and Firearms Investigation of Vernon Wayne Howell Also Known As David Koresh.* Washington: U.S. Government Printing Office, 1993.

Diamond, Sara. *Spiritual Warfare: The Politics of the Christian Right.* Boston: South End Press, 1989.

Eigen, Lewis D., and Jonathan P. Siegel. *The MacMillan Dictionary of Political Quotations.* New York: MacMillan, 1993.

Ferro, Marc. *Nicholas II: Last of the Tsars.* New York: Oxford University Press, 1994,

Fitzpatrick, Sheila. *The Russian Revolution.* New York: Oxford University Press, 1984; 1994 edition.

Fresia, Jerry. *Towrad an American Revolution.* Boston: South End Press, 1988.

Friedrich, Otto. *Before the Deluge.* New York: Harper Perrenial, 1972; 1995 edition.

Fuller, Robert C. *Naming the Antichrist.* New York: Oxford University Press, 1995.

Furagher, Jack. *The Encyclopedia of Colonial and Revolutionary America.* New York: Facts on File, 1990, p. 348.

Gary Kleck, *Point Blank: Guns and Violence in America.* New York: Aldine de Gruyter, 1991.

Gittfried, Paul, and Thomas Fleming. *The Conservative Movement.* Boston: Twayne, 1988.

Gross, Martin L. *A Call For Revolution.* New York: Ballantine, 1993.

Halbrook, Stephen P. *That Every Man Be Armed.* Oakland: The Independent Institute, 1994.

Johnson, Paul. *A History of the Jews.* New York: Harper Perennial, 1987.

Kennedy, Paul. *The Rise and Fall of Great Powers.* New York: Vintage Books, 1989.

Kramnick, Isaac ed. *The Federalist Papers.* New York: Penguin Books, 1987.

LaPierre, Wayne. *Guns, Crime, and Freedom.* New York: Harper Perennial, 1994.

Laqueur, William. *Black Hundred: The Rise of the Extreme Right in Russia.* New York: Harper Collins, 1993.

Leckie, Robert. *The Wars of America.* New York; Harper & Row, 1968; revised 1981.

MacKay, Charles. *Extraordinary Popular Delusions & the Madness of Crowds.* New York: Crown Trade Paperback, 1980.

Mason, Alpheus Thomas, and Donald Grier Stephenson, Jr. *American Constitutional Law.* Englewood Cliffs, N.J.: Prentice Hall, 1990.

Massie, Robert K. *The Romanovs: The Final Chapter.* New York: Random House, 1995.

McGinn, Bernard. *Antichrist.* San Francisco: Harper San Francisco, 1994.

Miller, Nathan. *Stealing From America.* New York: Paragon, 1976; 1992 edition.

Nisbet, Lee, ed. *The Gun Control Debate.* Buffalo: Prometheus, 1990.

Padover, Paul K. *The Living U.S. Constitution.* New York: Mentor Books, 1953; 1983 revised edition.

Plano, Jack C., and Milton Greensberg, *The American Political Dictionary.* Chicago: Holt, Rinehart and Winston, 1989, 473.

Samples, Ken, Erwin deCastro, Richard Abanes and Robert Lyle. *Prophets of the Apocalypse: David Koresh and Other American Messiahs.* Grand Rapids: Baker Book House, 1994.

Schultz, Bud, and Ruth Schultz. *It Did Happen Here: Recollections of Political Repression in America.* Berkeley: University of California Press, 1989.

Siegel, Jonathan P. *The MacMillan Dictionary of Political Quotations.* New York: MacMillan, 1993, p. 135.

Sowell, Thomas. *A Conflict of Visions: Ideological Origins of Political Struggles.* New York: William Morrow, 1987.

Steinberg, Mark D., and Vladmir M. Khrustalev, *The Fall of the Romanovs.* New Haven, Conn.: Yale University Press, 1995

Stoessinger, John G. *The United Nations & the Superpowers.* New York: Random House, 1965; 1977 edition.

Taw, Jennifer Morrison, and Robert C. Leicht. *The New World Order and Army Doctrine.* Santa Monica, Calif.: RAND, 1992.

Van den Haag, Ernest, and John P. Conrad. *The U.N.: In or Out?.* New York: Plenum Press, 1987.

Vankin, Jonathan, and John Whalen. *Fifty Greatest Conspiracies of All Time.* New York: Citadel Press, 1995.

Books: Racism, White Supremacy, Anti-Semitism, Patriot/Militia

Anti-Defamation League. *Armed and Dangerous: Militias Take Aim at the Federal Government.* New York: Anti-Defamation League, 1994.

————. *Beyond the Bombing: The Militia Menace Grows.* New York: Anti-Defamation League, 1995.

————. *Extremism and the Right.* New York: Anti-Defamation League, 1988.

Barkun, Michael. *Religion and the Racist Right.* Chapel Hill, N.C.: University of North Carolina, 1994.

Bellant, Russ. *Old Nazis, the New Right and the Republican Party.* Boston: South End Press, 1988; 1991 edition.

Bernstein, Herman. *The Truth About the Protocols of Zion.* New York: KTAV Publishing House, 1935; 1971 edition.

Chalmers, David M. *Hooded Americanism: The History of the Ku Klux Klan.* Durham: Duke University Press, 1987.

Chanes, Jerome R. *Antisemitism in America Today.* New York: Birch Lane Press, 1995

Coates, James. *Armed and Dangerous.* New York: Hill and Wang, 1985; 1995 edition.

Corcoran, James. *Bitter Harvest.* New York: Viking, 1990.

Dinnerstein, Leonard. *Antisemitism in America.* New York: Oxford University Press, 1994.

Division of Church and Society of the National Council of Churches of Christ in the USA. *The "Christian Identity" Movement.* n.c.: National Council of Churches of Christ in the USA, n.d.

Ezekiel, Raphael S. *The Racist Mind.* New York: Viking, 1995.

Flynn, Kevin, and Gary Gerhardt. *The Silent Brotherhood: Inside America's Racist Underground.* New York: The Free Press, 1989.

George, John, and Laird Wilcox. *Nazis, Communists, Klansmen and Others on the Fringe.* Buffalo: Prometheus Books, 1992.

Hockenos, Paul. *Free to Hate.* New York: Routledge, 1993.

Lanzmann, Claude. *Shoah: An Oral History of the Holocaust.* New York: Pantheon Books, 1987.

Lifton, Robert Jay. *The Nazi Doctors: Medical Killings and the Psychology of Genocide.* New York: Basic Books, 1986.

Lipstadt, Deborah. *Denying the Holocaust.* New York: The Free Press, 1993.

Persico, Joseph E. *Nuremberg: Infamy on Trial.* New York: Penguin Books, 1994

Ridgeway, James. *Blood in the Face.* New York: Thunder's Mouth Press, 1990.

Wistrich, Robert S. *Antisemitism.* New York: Schocken Books, 1991.

Yahil, Leni. *The Holocaust: The Fate of European Jewry, 1932–1945.* New York: Oxford University Press, 1990.

Books: Christianity, Eschatology, Church History, Bible Study Aids

Alnor, William M. *Soothsayers of the Second Advent.* Old Tappan, N.J.: Revell, 1989.

Archer, Gleason. *Encyclopedia of Bible Difficulties.* Grand Rapids: Zondervan, 1982.

Bruce, F. F. *The Spreading Flame.* Grand Rapids: Eerdman's, 1958.

Chandler, Russell. *Doomsday.* Ann Arbor: Servant, 1993.

Clouse, Robert G., ed. *The Meaning of the Millennium: Four Views.* Downers Grove: InterVarsity Press, 1977.

DeMar, Gary. *Last Days Madness.* Atlanta: America Vision, Inc., 1994.

Donald Guthrie, ed., *The Eerdman's Bible Commentary.* Grand Rapids, Eerdman's, 1970; third edition.

Douglas, J. D., and Merril C. Tenney, eds., *The New International Dictionary of the Bible.* Grand Rapids: Zondervan, 1987.

Douglas, J. D. *The New International Dictionary of the Christian Church.* Grand Rapids: Zondervan, 1974; 1978 edition.

Elwell, Walter A., ed. *Evangelical Dictionary of Theology.* Grand Rapids: Baker Book House, 1984.

Geisler, Norman. *Civil Disobedience: When is it Right?.* Lynchburg, Va.: Quest Productions, 1990.

Geisler, Norman, and Thomas Howe. *When Critics Ask.* Wheaton, Ill.: Victor Books, 1992.

Geisler, Norman, and William E. Nix. *A General Introduction to the Bible.* Chicago: Moody Press, 1968; 1986 edition.

Grenz, Stanley J. *The Millennial Maze.* Downers Grove: InterVarsity Press, 1992.

Hastings, James, ed. *Encyclopedia of Religion and Ethics.* New York: Charles Scribner & Sons.

Hunt, Dave. *A Cup of Trembling.* Eugene, Oreg.: Harvest House, 1995.

——. *Global Peace and the Rise of Antichrist.* Eugene, Oreg.: Harvest House, 1990.

——. *How Close Are We?* Eugene, Oreg.: Harvest House, 1993.

Ice, Thomas, and Timothy Demy, eds. *When the Trumpet Sounds.* Eugene, Oreg.: Harvest House, 1995.

James, William T., ed. *Storming Toward Armageddon: Essays in Apocalypse.* Green Forest, Ark.: New Leaf Press, 1992; 1994 printing.

——. *The Triumphant Return of Christ: Essays in Apocalypse II.* Green Forest, Ark.: New Leaf Press, 1993.

——. *Earth's Final Days: Essays in Apocalypse III.* Green Forest, Ark.: New Leaf Press, 1995.

Jonsson, Carl Olof, and Wolfgang Herbst. *The Sign of the Last Days—When?.* Atlanta, Ga.: Commentary Press, 1987, p. 147.

Lewis, David Allen. *Prophecy 2000.* Green Forest, Ark.: New Leaf Press, 1990.

Lightner, Robert P. *The Last Days Handbook.* Nashville: Thomas Nelson, 1990.

Lindsey, Hal. *The 1980s: Countdown to Armageddon.* New York: Bantam, 1980; 1981 edition.
————. *The Late Great Planet Earth.* Grand Rapids: Zondervan, 1970.
————. *The Rapture.* New York: Bantam, 1983.
————. *There's A New World Coming.* Eugene, Oreg.: Harvest House, 1973; 1984 edition.
————. *There's A New World Coming.* Santa Ana, Calif.: Vision House, 1973.
Lutzer, Edwin W. *Hitler's Cross.* Chicago: Moody, 1995.
Oropeza, B .J. *99 Reasons Why No One Knows When Christ Will Return.* Downers Grove, Ill.: InterVarsity Press, 1994.
Pfeiffer, Charles F., and Everett F. Harrison, ed., *The Wycliffe Bible Commentary.* Chicago: Moody Press, 1962.
Richards, Lawrence O. *Expository Dictionary of Bible Words.* Grand Rapids: Zondervan, 1985; 1991 edition.
Robertson, A. T. *Word Pictures in the New Testament,* "The Gospel According to Luke," Grand Rapids: Baker Book House, 1930.
Robertson, Pat. *The New World Order.* Dallas: Word, 1991.
Vine, W. E. *An Expository Dictionary of New Testament Words,* reprinted in *Vine's Complete Expository Dictionary of Old and New Testament Words.* Nashville: Thomas Nelson, 1985.
Walvoord, John F. *The Nations in Prophecy.* Grand Rapids, Mich.: Zondervan/Academie, 1988.

Magazines, Newspapers, Journals
"Citizen Militias Drawing Concern," Orange County Register, April 22, 1995, 24.
"Cult Children Tell of Abuse in Compound," *Los Angeles Times*, May 4, 1993, A16.
"Cult Siege Trial Told of Big Arms Cache," *Los Angeles Times*, January 15, 1994, A25.
"Cultists Spread Fuel Before Fire, Transcript Says," *Orange County Register*, February 15, 1994, 14.
"Defeating Terrorists Without Defeating the Constitution," *Los Angeles Times*, April 26, 1995, B8.
"Groups Attach Significance to Date of April 19," *Orange County Register*, April 22, 1995, 24.
"In Tapes From Sect's Compound, Members Talk About Setting Fire," *New York Times*, February 15, 1994, A15.
"Man Cleared in Attack Tells of Nasty Backlash," *Orange County Register*, April 23, 1995, 26.
"Notebook," New Republic, May 15, 1995, 10.
"Oklahoma City's Lingering Question: Why?" *U.S. News & World Report*, August 21, 1995, 10.
"On the Moderate Fringe," *Time*, June 26, 1995, 62.
"One-Way Tickets for Illegal Aliens," *U.S. News & World Report*, January 8, 1996, 12.
"Patriot Fax Network Links Militant Anti-government Extremists Nationwide," *Klanwatch* 70 (December 1993), 1–4.
"Pseudo-Nazis, Pseudo-Militias," *Soldier of Fortune*, November 1995, 30.
"Radio Preacher Foresees Doom Soon," *U.S. News & World Report*, Dec. 19, 1994, 71.
"Revisiting the Tragedy in Waco," *Los Angeles Times*, April 26, 1995, B9.
"Sickening Stats," *Soldier of Fortune*, November 1995, 28.
"Some Citizens Disavow Extreme-Right Views In Wake of Bombing," *Wall Street Journal*, April 24, 1995, A1, A5.
"Suckers of the Far Right," *Time*, May 29, 1995, 12.
"Texas Still Monitoring 12 Branch Davidian Kids," *Orange County Register*, September 28, 1993, 7.
"The Far Right Is Upon Us," *The Progressive*, June 1995, 8–10.
"The FBI Pleads Guilty," *Los Angeles Times*, October 22, 1995, M4.
"The Law Still Under Fire," *U.S. News & World Report*, August 15, 1994, 35.
"The Rise of the Militias," Orange County Register, April 22, 1995, 24.
"The United Nations: Coming to Grips with a New World Order," originally published in *Der Spiegel* (Hamburg, Germany), reprinted in *World Press Review*, October 1992, 9–10.
"The View That Draws Gunpoint," *Moody*, March 1986, 7.
"TV Crewman Confirms Chat With Cultist," *Los Angeles Times*, August 29, 1993, A4.
"U.N. May Be Harbinger of An Authentic New World Order," *National Catholic Reporter*, July 17, 1992, 28.
"Visions of the Mark of the Beast," *Newsweek*, August 28, 1995, 32.
"Where Gun Murders Are Most Common," *U.S. News & World Report*, November 6, 1995, 16.

"Who to Hate: Anatomy of a Female Racist," *Mademoiselle*, August 1994, 135–137, 186.

Abanes, Richard. "Controversy Still Smolders A Year After Waco Disaster," *Christian Research Journal*, Spring/Summer, 1994, 5–6, 41.

Alcalay, Glenn. "Damage Control On Human Radiation Experiments," *Covert Action Quarterly* 52, 46–47.

Allen, Terry. "Professional Arab-Bashing," *Covert Action Quarterly* 53 (Summer 1995), 20–21.

Alter, Jonathan. "Jumping to Conclusions," *Newsweek*, May 1, 1995, 55.

————. "Toxic Speech," *Newsweek*, May 8, 1995, 44–46.

Applebome, Peter. "Anger of Radical Right Erupting More," *Orange County Register*, April 23, 1995, 26.

————. "Bombing Foretold in 'Bible' for Extremists," New York Times, April 26, 1995, A14.

————. "Radical Rights' Fury Boiling Over," *New York Times*, April 23, 1995, A13.

Armbrister, Trevor. "The Man Who Beat the IRS," *Reader's Digest*, July 1994, 65–69.

Arnn, Phillip, and Hank Kitchen, "*Waco, The Big Lie*—Rightly Named," *Watchman Expositor*, 11:4 (1994), 23–26.

Barkun, Michael. "Militias, Christian Identity and the Radical Right," *Christian Century*, August 2–9, 1995, 738–740.

Barone, Michael. "A Brief History of Zealotry in America," *U.S. News & World Report*, May 8, 1995, 44–45.

Barron, Bruce. "A Summary Critique: The New World Order," *Christian Research Journal*, 15:3 (Winter 1993), 43–45.

Beck, Melinda, et al. "Someone Dropped the Ball," *Newsweek*, May 17, 1993, 51.

Becker, Verne. "The Counterfeit Christianity of the Ku Klux Klan," *Christianity Today*, April 20, 1984, 30–35.

Bellafante, Gina. "Waco: The Flame Still Burns," Time, May 1, 1995, 47.

Berlet, Chip. "Frank Donner: An Appreciation," *Covert Action Quarterly* 53 (Summer 1995), 17–19.

————. "Voices of Hope," *The Progressive*, June 1995, 25.

Berlet, Chip, and Matthew Lyons. "Militia Nation," *The Progressive*, June 1995, 22–25.

Blumenthal, Sidney. "Her Own Private Idaho," *New Yorker*, July 10, 1995, 27–33.

Bock, Alan W. "Weekend Warriors," *National Review*, May 29, 1995, 39–42.

Bovard, James. "Not So Wacko," *New American*, May 15, 1995, 18.

Braun, Stephen, and Richard A. Serrano, "'Something Big' Warned of by McVeigh, U.S. Says," *Los Angeles Times*, April 27, 1995, A1, A12.

Braun, Stephen. "Koresh Sends Doom-Laden Letter to FBI," *Los Angeles Times*, April 11, 1993, A9.

Briggs, David. "Broadcaster Sees World's Sign-Off," *Orange County Register*, July 15, 1994, 6.

Brown, Fred. "On the Trail of Black Helicopters and Implanted Chips," *Denver Post*, September 23, 1994, B1.

Burghardt, Tom. "Neo-Nazis Salute Anti-Abortion Zealots," Covert Action Quarterly 52 (Spring 1995), 26–31.

Callahan, Tim. "The Fall of the Soviet Union & the Changing Game of Biblical Prophecy," *Skeptic* 3:2 (1995), 92–97.

Carol, Ginny, et al. "Children of the Cult," *Newsweek*, May 17, 1993, 48–50.

Carter, Ken. "Branch Davidian Firearms," *Machine Gun News*, March 1994, 5.

Carter, Ken. "Scattered Shots," *Machine Gun News*, February 1994, 18–19.

Chesnoff, Richard Z. "A New Sagebrush Revolt," *U.S. News & World*, June 5, 1995, 26–27.

Chidley, Joe. "Spreading Hate on the Internet," *MacLean's*, May 8, 1995, 37.

Chotzinoff, Robin. "Do the White Thing," *Westword*, July 12–18, 1989, 12, 20.

Cohen, Jeff, and Norman Solomon, "Guns, Ammo, Threats, and Talk Radio," *AlterNet*, February 17, 1995. Reprinted in Don Hazen, Larry Smith and Christine Triano, eds., *Militias in America 1995*. San Francisco: Institute for Alternative Journalism, 1995, pp. 62–63.

————. "Knee-Jerk Coverage of Bombing Should Not Be Forgotten," *AlterNet*, May 4, 1995. Reprinted in Don Hazen, Larry Smith and Christine Triano, eds., *Militias in America 1995*. San Francisco: Institute for Alternative Journalism, 1995, 59–61.

Cooper, Desiree. "The Other Man: Mark 'From Michigan' Koernke," *Detroit Metro Times*, April 26,

1995, reprinted in Don Hazen, Larry Smith and Christine Triano, eds. *Militias in America 1995.* San Franclsco. Institute for Alternative Journalism, 1995, 49–55.

Cooper, Marc. "A Visit with MOM," *The Nation,* May 22, 1995, reprinted in Don Hazen, Larry Smith and Christine Triano, eds. *Militias in America 1995.* San Francisco: Institute for Alternative Journalism, 1995, 44–48.

————. "From the Horses Mouth," *The Nation,* April 22, 1995, reprinted in Don Hazen, Larry Smith and Christine Triano, eds. *Militias in America 1995.* San Francisco: Institute for Alternative Journalism, 1995, p. 48.

————. "The N.R.A. Takes Cover in the G.O.P.," *The Nation,* June 19, 1995, 877–878, 880–882.

Corry, John. "Meeting the Enemy," American Spectator, July 1995, 48–49.

Crawford, Robert, Steven Gardiner and Jonathan Mozzochi. "Almost Heaven?" (2nd edition), *The Dignity Report,* March 1994.

Cushman, Erik. "Crime and Punishment, Missoula Independent, March 23, 1995, reprinted in Don Hazen, Larry Smith and Christine Triano, eds. *Militias in America 1995.* San Francisco: Institute for Alternative Journalism, 1995, 16–18.

de Lama, George "For Militias, Invaders of U.S. Are Everywhere, *Chicago Tribune,* October 31, 1994, 1.

Del Conte, B. J. "Gospel of Hate, *Toronto Sun,* July 20, 1986, 37.

————. "Liberation of Canada," *Toronto Sun,* July 22, 1986, 26.

————. "White Supremacists Eye the Mainstream," *Toronto Sun,* July 21, 1986, 24.

Del Conte, B. J., and Lee Lamothe. "The Good Dies Young," *Toronto Sun,* April 23, 1986, 32.

DeMar, Gary. "High-Tech Eschatology," *Biblical Worldview,* May 1994, 9–12.

Doskoch, Peter. "The Mind of the Militias," *Psychology Today,* July/August 1995, 12–14, 70.

Downes, Robert, and George Foster, "On the Front Lines With Northern Michigan's Militia," *Northern Express* (Traverse City, Mich.), August 22, 1994, reprinted in Don Hazen, Larry Smith and Christine Triano, eds. *Militias in America 1995.* San Francisco: Institute for Alternative Journalism, 1995, 13–15.

Duffy, Brian. "Ruby Ridge Redux," *U.S. News & World Report,* August 21, 1995, 10.

————. "When to Shoot," *U.S. News & World Report,* October 30, 1995, 14.

Durbin, Kathie. "Environmental Terrorism in Washington State," *Seattle Weekly,* January 11, 1995, reprinted in Don Hazen, Larry Smith and Christine Triano, eds. *Militias in America 1995.* San Francisco: Institute for Alternative Journalism, 1995, 31–38.

Egan, Timothy. "New Idaho Community Raises Neighbors' Fears," *New York Times,* October 5, 1994, A10.

Elliot, Michael et al., "The West At War," *Newsweek,* July 17, 1995, 24–28.

England, Mark. "Families Gather At Trial," *Waco Tribune-Herald,* April 18, 1988, 1B, 10B.

————. "Lawman: Group Tried to Deceive," *Waco Tribune-Herald,* April 14, 1988, 1C, 4C.

————. "Think Tank Chief Adds Fuel to Cult-Fire," *Waco Tribune-Herald,* January 16, 1994, 1A.

Ensign, Ted. "Gulf War Syndrome: Guinea Pigs & Disposable GIs," *Covert Action Quarterly* 43, 19–25.

————. "The Militia-U.S. Military Connection," *Covert Action Quarterly* 53 (Summer 1995), 13–16.

Far, Omied, Najwa Hussaini and Asma Saad, "(Un)true Lies," *YO!,* May/June 1995. Reprinted in Don Hazen, Larry Smith and Christine Triano, eds., *Militias in America 1995.* San Francisco: Institute for Alternative Journalism, 1995, 64–65.

Farley, Christopher John. "A Fire Sale of Firepower," *Time,* May 15, 1995, 44.

————. "America's Bomb Culture," *Time,* May 8, 1995, 56.

————. "Patriot Games," *Time,* December 19, 1994, 48–49.

Ferranti, Jennifer. "Marine Worries ID Is Satanic," *Christianity Today,* November 13, 1995, 77.

Fineman, Howard. "Friendly Fire," Newsweek, May 8, 1995, 36–38.

————. "We're Not Running Now," *Newseek,* May 29, 1995, 42.

Flinn, Frank. "Government Shouldn't Fulfill Militia's Apocalyptic Prophecies," *Insight on the News,* May 29, 1995, 38–39.

Frantz, Douglas. "Justice Dept. Report Absolves FBI, Blames Koresh for 75 Waco Deaths," Los

Angeles Times, October 9, 1993, A17

————. "The Rhetoric of Terror," *Time*, March 27, 1995, 48–51.

Futrelle, David. "Cyberhate," *In These Times*, May 15, 1995, 17.

Gest, Ted. "The Great Gun Debate: Get the Picture?" *U.S. News & World Report*, July 17, 1995, 7.

Gest, Ted. "The Gun Lobby," U.S. News & World Report, May 22, 1995, 37–38.

Glastris, Paul. "Patriot Games," *Washington Monthly*, June 1995, 23–26.

Goldberg, Herbert H. "The 'Protocols of the Elders of Zion' Unmasked!," *Hashivah* 17:2 (1994), 1–6.

Gorman, Christine. "Pssst! Calling All Paranoids," *Time*, May 8, 1995, 69.

Gregory, Sophfronia Scott. "Children of a Lesser God," *Time*, May 17, 1993, 54.

Harmon, Amy. "Hate-Group Use of Cyberspace Protested," *Los Angeles Times*, December 14, 1994, A3.

Hasselbach, Ingo. "Extremism: A Global Network," *New York Times*, April 24, 1995, A19.

Hawkins, Beth. "Patriot Games," *Detroit Metro Times*, October 12, 1994, reprinted in Don Hazen, Larry Smith and Christine Triano, eds. *Militias in America 1995*. San Francisco: Institute for Alternative Journalism, 1995, 7–12.

Headden, Susan. "Free (To Kill) Speech," *U.S. News & World Report*, November 6, 1995, 12.

————. "Taking the Fight to Court," *U.S. News and World Report*, November 14, 1994, 67.

Healy, Melissa. "Slower Approach to Anti-Terrorism Laws Urged," *Los Angeles Times,* May 1, 1995, A14.

Heard, Alex. "The Road to Oklahoma City," *New Republic*, May 15, 1995, 15–20.

Hedges, Stephen, David Bowermaster and Susan Headden, "Abortion: Who's Behind the Violence?" *U.S. News and World Report*, November 14, 1994, 50–55, 57–58, 67.

Heller, Scott. "Home-Grown Extremism," *Chronicle of Higher Education*, May 12, 1995, A10–A11, A18.

Helms, Dave. "Massive Plot?: Some Truth, Wild Theories," *Mobile (Alabama) Press Register*, 1A, 4A.

Helvarg, David. "The Anti-Enviro Connection," *The Nation*, May 22, 1995, 722, 724.

Henderson, Paul. "We're Not Saluting Hitler–We're Saluting God," *Seattle Times*, April 17, 1983, 6–15.

Hertenstein, Mike. "End of History?—Not Yet," *Cornerstone* 20:96, 5–6

Hickox, Katie "Domestic Terrorists Show 'Us vs. Them' Mentality, Expert Says," *Orange County Register*, April 22, 1995, 24.

Hinds, Michael deCourcy. "Arson Team Says Members of Cult Started Fatal Fire," *New York Times*, April 27, 1993, A9.

Hulet, Craig B. "All the News That's Fit to Invent," *Soldier of Fortune*, August 1995, 56–61, 78–80.

————. "Black Helicopters Over America," *Soldier of Fortune*, August 1995, 45.

————. "Patriots or Paranoids," *Soldier of Fortune*, August 1995, 43–46, 84–85.

Hull, Jon D. "The State of the Union," *Time*, January 30, 1995, 53–57, 60.

Jenkins, Philip. "Home-Grown Terror," *American Heritage*, September 1995, 38–40, 42, 44–46.

Johnson, Denis. "The Militia in Me," *Esquire*, July 1995, 38, 40–41, 43–45.

Johnson, George. "5 Rules Frame Plot-Theory Paranoia," *Orange County Register*, April 30, 1995, 1, 20.

Johnson, Kevin. "Indictment: Hatred Fueled Blast," *USA Today*, August 8, 1995, 3A.

Jordan, June. "In the Land of White Supremacy," *The Progressive*, June 1995, 21.

Jorgensen, Leslie, and Sherry Keene-Osborne, " Under the Gun," *Westword,* December 14, 1994, reprinted in Don Hazen, Larry Smith and Christine Triano, eds. *Militias in America 1995*. San Francisco: Institute for Alternative Journalism, 1995, 22–26.

Junas, Daniel. "Angry White Guys with Guns: The Rise of the Militias," *Covert Action Quarterly* 52 (Spring 1995), 20–25.

Kaplan, Jeffrey. "A Guide to the Radical Right," *Christian Century,* August 2–9, 1995, 741–744.

Kelley, Dean M. "Waco: A Massacre and Its Aftermath," *First Things*, May 1995, 22–37.

Kelly, Michael. "The Road to Paranoia," *New Yorker*, June 19, 1995, 60–63, 66–70, 72–75. .

Kennedy, J. Michael. "Doctors Get A Clearer Picture of How Cult Children Lived," *Los Angeles Times*, May 5, 1993, A24.

Kennedy, John W. "Pro-Life Movement Struggles for Viability," *Christianity Today*, November 8, 1993, 40–42, 44.

King, Patricia. "Bo Gritz Builds His 'Heaven,'" *Newsweek*, September 5, 1994, 37.

King, Wayne. "Uncovering Links Among Right-Wingers," (Orange County) *Register*, June 11, 1983, A1, A2.

Knickerbocker, Brad. "Followers See Validation for their Views in the Bible," *Christian Science Monitor*, April 20, 1995, 10.

————. "White Separatists Plot 'Pure' Society," *Christian Science Monitor*, 1, 10–11.

Kramer, Michael. "Why Guns Share the Blame," *Time*, May 8, 1995, 48.

Labaton, Stephen. "Outside Review Criticizes F.B.I. On Raid On Cult," *New York Times*, November 16, 1993, A7.

————. "Report On Assault On Waco Cult Contradicts Reno's Explanations," *New York Times*, October 9, 1993, 1, 10,

————. "U.S. Agency Defends Tactics in Assault On Sect," *New York Times*, March 30, 1993, A13.

Lacayo, Richard. "How Safe is Safe?" *Time*, May 1, 1995, 68–72.

Lacitis, Erik. "Church At War," *Seattle Times*, September 17, 1985, F1, F8.

Larres, Klaus. "Recycling Old Ideas," *History Today*, October 1993, 13–16.

Larson, Erik. "ATF Under Siege," *Time*, July 24, 1995, 20–29.

————. "How A Cascade of Errors Led ATF to Disaster in Waco," *Time*, July 24, 1995, 28–29.

————. "Unrest in the West," *Time*, October 23, 1995, 52–56, 63–65.

Larson, Viola. "Identity: A Christian Religion for White Racists," *Christian Research Journal* (Fall 1992), 20–28.

Lemonick, Michael D. "An Armed Fanatic Raises the Stakes," *Time*, January 9, 1995, 34–35.

Levitas, Daniel. "A.D.L. and the Christian Right," *The Nation*, June 19, 1995, 882, 884, 886, 888.

Limbaugh, Rush. "Blame the Bombers—Only," *Newsweek*, May 8, 1995, 39.

Maas, Peter. "The Menace of China White," *Parade Magazine*, September 18, 1994, 4–6.

MacNutt, Karen L. *Women & Guns*, March 1995, reprinted in Don Hazen, Larry Smith and Christine Triano, eds. *Militias in America 1995*. San Francisco: Institute for Alternative Journalism, 1995, 69–70.

Maxwell, Joe, and Andrs Tapia, "Guns and Bibles, *Christianity Today*, June 19, 1995, 34–37, 45.

McDonald, Marci. "The Enemy Within," *Maclean's*, May 8, 1995, 34–38.

McLemee, Scott. "Public Enemy," *In These Times*, May 15, 1995, 14–19.

————. "Spotlight on the Liberty Lobby," *Covert Action Quarterly* 50 (Fall 1994), 23–32.

McQuaid, James. "Linda From La La Land," *Soldier of Fortune*, August 1995, 47.

————. "Mark from Michigan," *Soldier of Fortune*, August 1995, 46.

Meyer, Josh, Paul Feldman and Eric Lichtblau, "Militia Members' Threats, Attacks On Officials Escalate," *Los Angeles Times*, April 27, 1995, A1, A13.

Meyerson, Harold. "State of Hatred," *LA Weekly*, April 28, 1995, reprinted in Don Hazen, Larry Smith and Christine Triano, eds. *Militias in America 1995*. San Francisco: Institute for Alternative Journalism, 1995, 57–58.

Miele, Frank. "Giving the Devil His Due," *Skeptic* 2:4 (1994), 58–70.

Miller, Jeffrey. "Citizen Militias Drawing Concern," *Orange County Register*, April 22, 1995, 24.

Miller, Wynn. "Right-Wing Militants Mix Political Fantasy, Violence," *Christian Science Monitor,* April 26, 1995, n.p.

Mollins, Carl. "At Home With A Racist Guru," *Maclean's*, May 8, 1995, 42–43

Morganthau, Tom, et al., "Janet Reno Confronts Waco's Bitter Legacy," *Newsweek*, May 15, 1995, 26.

————. "The Echoes of Ruby Ridge," *Newsweek*, August 28, 1995, 24–28.

————. "The View From the Right," *Newsweek*, May 1, 1995, 36–39.

Namika, A. "Agent Orange: The Dirty Legal War at Home," *Covert Action Quarterly* 43, 26–28.

Naylor, David. "Oaths and Fists Fly As Archrivals Meet," *Toronto Sun,* September 22, 1986, 4.

Nelson, Alan, and Sandra Gines, "Crying in the Wilderness," *Waco Tribune-Herald*, January 17, 1988, 1A, 8A

Nelson, Jack. "Book Called 'Blueprint for Revolution,'" *Los Angeles Times*, April 23, 1995, A30.

Nethaway, Rowland. "How Government Lies Help Fuel Paranoia," *Orange County Register,* April 27, 1995, 9.

Niebuhr, Gustav. "Assault on Waco Sect Fuels Extremists' Rage, *New York Times,* April 26, 1995, A12.

O'Keefe, Mike. "Church Versus State," *Westword,* July 12–18, 1989, 18.

————. "White Makes Right," *Westword,* July 12–18, 1989, 10, 13–114, 18.

Ostrow, Ronald J. "Louis Freeh," *Los Angeles Times,* November 19, 1995, M3.

Pate, James L. "Amateurs & Assassins," *Soldier of Fortune,* December 1995, 38–43, 77.

————. "Ask Us No Questions, We'll Tell You No Lies," *Soldier of Fortune,* March 1996, 44–45, 85.

Pate, James L. "Executions or Mercy Killings?" *Soldier of Fortune,* March 1994, 62–65, 84–87.

————. "Nothing Accomplished," *Soldier of Fortune,* November 1995, 36–39.

————. "Truth Behind New World Order Combat Arms Survey," *Soldier of Fortune,* September 1995, 62–64, 78–80.

Perkins, John. "He's My Brother," *Cornerstone* 25 issue 108, 41–43.

Poole, Gary Andrew. "Hold It: This Is My Land," *Los Angeles Times Magazine,* December 3, 1995, 28–30, 32, 54–58.

Pope, Victoria. "Notes from Underground," *U.S. News & World Report,* June 5, 1995, 24–27.

Potok, Mark. "Cult Kids' Story of Horror," *The Sacramento Bee,* May 5, 1993, A8.

Quittner, Joshua. "Home Pages for Hate," *Time,* January 22, 1996, 69.

Reynolds, Diane. "FEMA and the NSC: The Rise of the National Security State," *Covert Action Information Bulletin* 33 (Winter 1990), 54–58.

Ridgeway, James, and Leonard Zeskind. "Militias: After the Bombing," *Village Voice,* April 25, 1995, reprinted in Don Hazen, Larry Smith and Christine Triano, eds. *Militias in America 1995.* San Francisco: Institute for Alternative Journalism, 1995, 39–43.

Rimer, Sara. "Cult's Surviving Children: New Lives, New Ordeals," *New York Times,* April 27, 1993, A1, A9.

Rimer, Sara, and James Bennet, "Rejecting the Authority of the U.S. Government," *New York Times,* April 24, 1995, A13.

Risen, James. "Abortion Foes Rally for Shooting Suspect," Los Angeles Times, January 2, 1995, A15.

Rivenburg, Roy. "Is the End Still Near?" *Los Angeles Times,* July 30, 1992, E1–E2, E4–E5.

Ross, Loretta. "Saying It With A Gun," *The Progressive,* June 1995, 26–27.

Ross, Wayne Anthony. "Join A Militia—Break the Law?" *Soldier of Fortune,* April 1995, 52–53.

Rothchild, John. "Wealth: Static Wages Except for the Rich," *Time,* January 30, 1995, 60–63.

Saavedra, Tony. "Suspicion & Fear," Orange County Register, April 23, 1995, 26.

Sandy, D. Brent. "Did Daniel See Mussolini?" *Christianity Today,* February 8, 1993, 34–36.

Sauer, Mark, and Jim Okerblom, "Patriotism or Paranoia?" *San Diego Union-Tribune,* May 4, 1995, E1.

Savage, David. "Rule Changes Limit FBI's Infiltration of Extremists," *Los Angeles Times,* April 22, 1995, A19.

Scheer, Robert. "Mass Murder Isn't A Blow for Democracy," *Los Angeles Times,* April 25, 1995, B9.

Schneider, Keith. "Bomb Echoes Extremists' Tactics," *New York Times,* April 26, 1995, A14.

————. "Some Militia Manuals Urge Attacks," *Orange County Register,* April 29, 1995, 10.

Serrano, Richard A., and Ronald J. Ostrow, "Money Trail Details Blast Suspects' 'Lost' World," *Los Angeles Times,* October 8, 1995, A1, A22, A24.

Serrano, Richard, and James Risen. "Terrorism," *Los Angeles Times,* April 22, 1995, A1, A21, A30.

Serrano, Richard, and Melissa Healy. "McVeigh's Trail Combed for Clues, *Los Angeles Times,* April 30, 1995, A1, A31.

Shannon, Elaine. "Crime: Safer Streets, Yet Greater Fear," *Time,* January 30, 1995, 63, 66–67.

Shapiro, Joseph P. "An Epidemic of Fear and Loathing," *U.S. News & World Report,* May 8, 1995, 37–41.

Sheler, Jeffery L. "The Christmas Covenant," *U.S. News and World Report,* December 19, 1994, 62–64, 66–67, 69, 70–71.

Shelton, Rebecca. "The New Minutemen," *Kansas City New Times*, February 22, 1995, reprinted in Don Hamon, Larry Smith and Christine Trinno, eds. *Militias in America 1995*. San Francisco: Institute for Alternative Journalism, 1995, 19–22.

Shermer, Michael. "Proving the Holocaust," *Skeptic* 2:4 (1994),32–57.

Siegal, Barry. "A Lone Ranger," *Los Angeles Times Magazine*, November 26, 1995, 20–22,24–25, 37–38, 40.

Sileo, Chi Chi. "Fringe Groups and Militias Aim to 'Restore' Constitution," *Insight*, August 21, 1995,_14–15.

Skelton, George. "There is No Easy Answer On Militias," *Los Angeles Times*, April 27, 1995, A3.

Smolowe, Jill. "Enemies of the State," *Time*, May 8, 1995, 58–64, 66, 68–69.

————. "Fear in the Land," *Time*, January 16, 1995, 34–36.

Speir, Dean. "'Waco: The Big Lie' Revealed As A Hoax," *Gunweek*, January 21, 1994, n.p.

Spencer, William David. "Does Anyone Really Know What Time It Is?" *Christianity Today*, July 17, 1995, 29.

Staples, David. "Extremist Would Deport Jews and Bar Non-White Immigrants," *Ottawa (Canada) Citizen*, August 29, 1987, A20.

Stimson, Eva. "White Supremacists take on Trappings of Religion," *Christianity Today*, August 8, 1986, 30–31.

Stone, Keith. "Suspicion of Government Drives Patriot Movement," *Daily News*, December 26, 1994, 1, 16.

Stout, David. "Is Silencing the Far Right Censorship?" *Orange County Register*, April 30, 1995, 18.

Sussman, Vic. "Hate, Murder and Mayhem On the Net," *U.S. News & World Report*, May 22, 1995, 62.

Tabor, James. "Koresh Deserved It: James D. Tabor Replies," *Bible Review*, February 1994, 59–60.

Tharp, Mike. "In the Shadow of Ruby Ridge," *U.S. News & World Report*, December 4, 1995, 59–60.

Tharp, Mike. "The Rise of the Citizen Militia," *U.S. News & World Report*, August 15, 1994, 34–35.

Thomas, Evan, et. al, "Inside the Plot," *Newsweek*, June 5, 1995, 24, 26–27.

————. "The Dead, The Plot," *Newsweek*, May 8, 1995, 27–34.

Tomsho, Robert. "Some Militiamen See A Government Plot In Oklahoma Blast," *Wall Street Journal*, April 24, 1995, A1, A4.

Vaughan, Doug. "Terror on the Right: The Nazi and Klan Resurgence," *Utne Reader*, August/September 1985, 44–57.

Vernon, Bob. "Operation Rescue: A Policeman's Perspective," *Masterpiece*, March/April, 1991, 16, 18.

Vest, Jason. "Leader of the Fringe," *The Progressive*, June 1995, 28–29.

Voll, Daniel. "At Home With M.O.M.," *Esquire*, July 1995, 46–49.

————. "The Right to Bear Sorrow," *Esquire*, March 1995, 75–82.

Vollers, Maryanne. "The White Woman From Hell," *Esquire*, July 1995, 50–52.

Walker, Bill. "Warriors in the Fight Against Racial Equality," *Minneapolis Star-Tribune*, July 22, 1986, 9A.

Walter, Jess. "Every Knee Shall Bow," *Newsweek*, August 28, 1995, 29–33.

Webster, Kerry. "Japanese Copters Pass Through Tacoma," *News-Tribune* (Tacoma), September 14, 1994, B1.

Weinberger, Caspar W. "Commentary on Events at Home and Abroad," *Forbes*, February 15, 1993, 35.

Weiss, Philip. "Outcasts Digging In For the Apocalypse," Time, May 1, 1995, 48–49.

————. "They've Had Enough," *New York Times Magazine*, January 8, 1995, 26, 29, 31–32, 38, 44, 48–52.

Wieseltier, Leon. "Gog, Magog, Agog," *New Republic*, May 15, 1995, 46.

Williams, Mike. "Necessary to the Security of A Free State," *Soldier of Fortune*, April 1995, 48–53, 81–82.

Willman, David. "Far Right Sees Waco, Idaho Cases As Harbingers," *Los Angeles Times*, April 24, 1995, A16.

Willman, David. "McVeigh Lashed at Government in '92 Letters," *Los Angeles Times*, April 27, 1995, A11.

Wirpsa, Leslie. "Rural Despair Feeds Militia Growth," *National Catholic Reporter*, June 30, 1995, 10.

Witham, Larry. "Apocalypse Eventually," *Insight on the News*, May 29, 1995, 33.

Witkin, Gordon, et al., "The Fight to Bear Arms," *U.S. News & World Report*, May 22, 1995, 29–30, 32, 34, 36–37.

Witkin, Gordon. "One Man's Story," *U.S. News & World Report*, September 18, 1995, 22.

Witkin, Gordon. "Raking Up the Ashes," *U.S. News & World Report*, July 24, 1995, 30–33.

Witkin, Gordon. "The Nightmare of Idaho's Ruby Ridge," *U.S. News & World Report*, September 11, 1995, 24, 29.

Wood, Chris. "'Aryan of the Year,'" *Maclean's*, May 8, 1995, 39.

Worthington, Rogers. "U.S. Indicts Alleged Bombmaker," *Chicago Tribune*, November 21, 1995, 14.

Wright, Robert. "Chaos Theory," *New Republic*, July 10, 1995, 6.

Wright, Robert. "Did Newt Do It?" New Republic, May 15, 1995, 4, 45.

Wright, Robin, and Josh Meyer, "Tradition-Rooted 'Patriot' Groups Strive to Curtail Modern 'Tyranny,'" *Los Angeles Times*, April 24, 1995, A12.

Zakaria, Tabassum. "After the Fire, Memory Is Vivid," *Orange County Register*, April 19, 1994, 12.

Zoba, Wendy Murray. "Future Tense," *Christianity Today*, October, 2, 1995, 19–23.

Internet/BBS postings

"G. Gordon Liddy Endorses Militias At Washington Rally," *San Francisco Examiner*, June 5, 1995, Internet edition at http://www.sfgate.com/examiner/index.shtml

"Wise Use Update" January 1996, Internet AlterNet BBS gopher site, pathway begins at gopher://gopher.igc.apc.org:70/1, to Progressive Gophers folder, to AlterNet folder, to Militias in America folder, to Resources folder, to Econonet Western Lands Gopher folder, to The Western Lands Gopher folder, to Wise Use Update 1/96.

Bellant, Russ. "The Paranoid and the Paramilitary," *Detroit Metro Times*, Internet edition, Internet posting, AlterNet BBS gopher site, pathway begins at gopher://gopher.igc.apc.org:70/1, to Progressive Gophers folder, to AlterNet folder, to Militias in America folder, to Additional Articles on Militias folder.

Burghardt, Tom. "Leaderless Resistance and the Oklahoma City Bombing," Internet posting, April 23, 1995, AlterNet BBS gopher site, pathway begins at gopher://gopher.igc.apc.org:70/1, to Progressive Gophers folder, to AlterNet folder, to Militias in America folder, to Additional Articles on Militias folder.

Berlet, Chip. "Armed Militias, Right Wing Populism, & Scapegoating," April 24, 1995, Internet posting, AlterNet BBS gopher site, pathway begins at gopher://gopher.igc.apc.org:70/1, to Progressive Gophers folder, to AlterNet folder, to Militias in America folder, to Militias in America (1995) folder, to Chronicling the Growth of a Movement folder.

Department of Justice, Department of Justice Report on Internal Review Regarding the Ruby Ridge Hostage Situation and Shooting by Law Enforcement Personnel. Washington, D.C.: U.S. Government Printing Office, 1994, Internet edition posted by LEXIS COUNSEL CONNECT, American Lawyer Media, L.P.

Doyle, Michael. "Anti-tax Violence Part of Wider Conspiracy?" *San Francisco Examiner*, July 12, 1995, Internet edition at http://www.sfgate.com/examiner/index.shtml

Egan, Timothy. "Anti-Abortion Violence: Is it a Conspiracy?" *San Francisco Examiner*, June 18, 1995, Internet edition at http://www.outright.com/pritch/abor.html

Epstein, Edward. "Extremists' Bizarre Fears of U.N. Conspiracy," *San Francisco Chronicle*, May 4, 1995, Internet edition at http://www.sfgate.com/chronicle/index.shtml

Heberta, H. Joseph. "Scientific Panel Rips Alaska Radiation Experiments 1/31/96," Associated Press, America Online edition.

Janofsky, Michael. "Militia Plotted Assault On Military Base," *San Francisco Examiner*, June 25, 1995, Internet edition at http://www.sfgate.com/examiner/index.shtml

————. "White Supremacists Hold Hate Fest," *San Francisco Examiner*, July 23, 1995, Internet edition at http://www.sfgate.com/examiner/index.shtml

Jorgensen, Leslie. "Media Advisory: Right-Wing Talk Radio Supports Militia Movement," *Extra!*, April 21, 1995, Internet edition at http://paul.spu.edu/~sinnfein/fair.html

Kennedy, John W. "Florida Shootings Stifle Pro-lifers," *Christianity Today*, September 12, 1994, America Online edition.

King, Martin. "Michigan Militia Leader Not A Southern Baptist," *Christianity Today*, April 14, 1995, America Online edition.

Krieger, Lisa M. "I Love My Country—It's the Government I Hate," *San Francisco Examiner*, May 7, 1995, Internet edition at http://www.sfgate.com/examiner/index.shtml

Ladd, Susan, and Stan Swofford. "A Patriot and Militia Sampler," *News & Record*. Greensboro, N.C., June 25, 1995, Internet edition at http://www.infi.net/nr/extra/militias/m-samplr.htm

————. "Citizen's Revolt: Anger Aimed At Government," *News & Record*. Greensboro, N.C., June 25, 1995, Internet edition at http://www.infi.net/nr/extra/militias/m-revolt.htm

————. "Citizens for the Reinstatement of Constitutional Government," *News & Record*. Greensboro, N.C., June 25, 1995, Internet edition at http://www.infi.net/nr/extra/militias/m-crcg.htm

————. "Defender on the Right," *News & Record*. Greensboro, N.C., June 26, 1995, Internet edition at http://www.infi.net/nr/extra/militias/m-defndr.htm

————. "Discontent Feeds Movement, Observers Say," *News & Record*. Greensboro. N.C., June 27, 1995, Internet edition at http://www.infi.net/nr/extra/militias/m-discon.htm

————. "Electronic Outlet: Computers Link Patriots," *News & Record*. Greensboro, N.C., June 26, 1995, Internet edition at http://www.infi.net/nr/extra/militias/m-electr.htm

————. "Fearing For Our Country," *News & Record*. Greensboro, N.C., June 25, 1995, Internet edition at http://www.infi.net/nr/extra/militias/m-fearing.htm

————. "Officers Can Do Little About Militias," *News & Record*. Greensboro, N.C., June 25, 1995, Internet edition at http://www.infi.net/nr/extra/militias/m-oficrs.htm

————. "On on the Brink of Doom," *News & Record*. Greensboro, N.C., June 26, 1995, Internet edition at http://www.infi.net/nr/extra/militias/m-brink.htm

————. "The Law of the Land: Group Seeks County Rule," *News & Record*. Greensboro, N.C., June 25, 1995, Internet edition at http://www.infi.net/nr/extra/militias/m-county.htm

————. "The Patriot Movement," *News & Record*. Greensboro, N.C., June 25, 1995, Internet edition at http://www.infi.net/nr/extra/militias/m-movemt.htm

Ludlow, Lynn. "Extremists of the Manic Right," *San Francisco Examiner*, July 9, 1995, http://www.sfgate.com/examiner/index.shtml

Martin, Glen. "Citizens' Militias Have Taken Hold in Rural California," *San Francisco Chronicle*, April 22, 1995, Internet edition at http://www.sfgate.com/chronicle/index.shtml

National Rifle Association. Internet posting in the Patriot Archives, pathway starts at http://www.tezcat.com/, to Tezcat Archives, to Patriot folder, to Guns folder, to NRA_and_Militias.txt.

Porteous, Skipp. "Anti-Semitism: Its Prevalence Withiin the Christian Right," *Freedom Writer*, May 1994, Internet edition posted at http://www.berkshire.net/~ifas/fw/9405/antisemitism.html

————. "Militia Madness," *Freedom Writer*, June 1995, Internet edition at http://www.berkshire.net/~ifas/fw/9506/militia.html

Reuters, "Americans Believe They're in Trouble," January 20, 1996, text from America Online.

————. "U.S. Spurns Idea of UN Taxes," January 19, 1996, text from America Online.

Snyder, Jeffrey R. "A Nation of Cowards," *The Public Interest*, Fall 1993, Internet edition posted at http:www.jim.com/jamesd/cowards.html

Taylor, Michael. "Extremists Bracing for New World Order," *San Francisco Chronicle*, April 25, 1995, Internet edition at http://www.sfgate.com/chronicle/index.shtml

Wallace, Bill. "Heated Rhetoric Set Stage for Oklahoma Blast," *San Francisco Chronicle*, May 1, 1995, Internet edition at http://www.sfgate.com/chronicle/index.shtml

————. "Militia Tied to Blast Hates Gun Control," *San Francisco Chronicle*, April 22, 1995, Internet edition at http://www.sfgate.com/chronicle/index.shtml

————. "Citizen Militias Worry Californians," *San Francisco Chronicle*, May 31, 1995, Internet version at http://www.sfgate.com/chronicle/index.shtml

Worthington, Rogers. "Weaver Fever Hits Montana," *San Francisco Examiner*, September 24, 1995, 1995, Internet edition at http://www.sfgate.com/examiner/index.shtml

Yurman, Dan. "Are These Salmon to Die For?" (Dateline—3/5/95), *Reports on the Militia Movement in Idaho: Visions of Blood & Fishes Swim in Political Circles,* Internet posting, November 22, 1995, AlterNet BBS gopher site, pathway begins at gopher://gopher.igc.apc.org:70/1, to Progressive Gophers folder, to AlterNet folder, to Militias in America folder, to Militia-Watch Updates folder, to "Reports on the Militia Movement in Idaho" document.

————. "Big Trouble in Small Places: Montana Tax Protester Comes Out Shooting" (Dateline—7/18/95), *Reports on the Militia Movement in Idaho: Visions of Blood & Fishes Swim in Political Circles,* Internet posting, November 22, 1995, AlterNet BBS gopher site, pathway begins at gopher://gopher.igc.apc.org:70/1, to Progressive Gophers folder, to AlterNet folder, to Militias in America folder, to Militia-Watch Updates folder, to "Reports on the Militia Movement in Idaho."

————. "Is Idaho a State of Hate or is it Just Confused," (Dateline—5/9/95), *Samizdat: Militia News From Idaho,* Internet posting, December 9, 1995, AlterNet BBS gopher site, pathway begins at gopher://gopher.igc.apc.org:70/1, to Progressive Gophers folder, to AlterNet folder, to Militias in America folder, to Resources folder, to Econet Western Lands Gopher folder, to The Western Lands Gopher Library Archive, to 13-Jan-96 Samizdat: Militia News from Idaho.

————. "Militia Leader Predicts Civil War in the West" (Dateline—3/12/95), *Reports on the Militia Movement in Idaho: Visions of Blood & Fishes Swim in Political Circles,* Internet posting, November 22, 1995, AlterNet BBS gopher site, pathway begins at gopher://gopher.igc.apc.org:70/1, to Progressive Gophers folder, to AlterNet folder, to Militias in America folder, to Militia-Watch Updates folder, to "Reports on the Militia Movement in Idaho."

Television/Videos/Movies/CD-Roms

60 Minutes, 4/23/95
ABC World News, 11/30/95
ABC World News, 11/30/95.
ABC's *Day One,* 4/27/95
ABC's *Primetime Live,* 4/25/95
Beyond the Sambatyon: The Myth of the Ten Lost Tribes of Israel. Creative Multi-Media, 1994.
Channel 6 News. Indianapolis, Ind., 4/4/94.
CNN News, 3/1/95.
CNN Presents: Patriots & Profits, 10/2995.
Logan's Run, (MGM, 1976).
MacNeil/Lehrer News Hour, 4/26/95.
Militias in America: The Real Story. Vital Film & Video, 1995.
NBC Nightly News, 4/28/95
Network. MGM, 1976.
Phil Donahue, 4/25/95.

Testimony Transcripts

Testimony before Congressman Charles Shumer's informal forum on "America Under the Gun: The Militia Movement and Hate Groups in America," July 11, 1995.
Transcripts of the United States Senate Subcommittee on Terrorism, Technology, and Government Information of the Committee on the Judiciary, "The Militia Movement in the United States," June 15, 1995.

Patriot/Militia/Racist/White Supremacist Materials
Books: Patriot/Militia Literature

Baker, Jeffrey. *Cheque Mate: The Game of Princes.* Springdale, Pa.: Whitaker House, 1993.
Collier, James M., and Kenneth F. Collier. *Votescam: The Stealing of America.* New York: Victoria House, 1992.
Grigg, William Norman. *Freedom on the Altar.* Appleton, Wis.: American Opinion Publishing, Inc., 1995.
Kah, Gary. *En Route to Global Occupation.* Lafayette, La.: Huntington House, 1991.
Keith, Jim. *Black Helicopters Over America: Strikeforce for the New World Order.* Lilburn, Ga.: IllumiNet Press, 1994.

McLamb, Jack. *Operation Vampire Killer 2000.* Phoenix, Ariz.: PATNWO, 1992.
Meredith, Lynne. *Vultures in Eagle's Clothing.* Huntington Beach, Calif.: We the People, 1994
Rosenstiel, Scott. *Sovereignty Introduction Manual.* Toluca Lake, Calif.: Scott Rosenstiel, 1995.
————. *The Complete Book of Sovereign Citizenship.* Toluca Lake, Calif.: Scott Rosenstiel, 1995.

Books: Racist, White Supremacist, Anti-Semitic, Christian Identity, Anglo-British Israelism
American Institute of Theology, *Correspondence Bible Course.* Newhall, Calif.: American Institute
    of Theology, 1970; 1981 edition.
Anonymous. *The Protocols of the Learned Elders of Zion* (1934 edition), transl. from the Russian by
    Victor E. Marsden.
Armstrong, Herbert W. *The United States and Britain in Prophecy.* USA: Worldwide Church of God,
    1967; 1980 edition.
Brothers, Richard. *A Revealed Knowledge of the Prophecies and Times Containing with Other Great
    and Remarkable Things Not Revealed to Any Other Person On Earth the Restoration of the Jews
    To Jerusalem by the Year M.DCC.XCVII, Under Their Revealed Prince and Prophet Wrote By
    Himself.* England: Francis & Robert Bailey, 1794.
Brown, Bruce. *The World's Trouble Makers.* Metairie, La.: Sons of Liberty, 1985.
Capt, E. Raymond. *Missing Links Discovered in Assyrian Tablets.* Thousand Oaks, Calif.: Artisan
    Sales, 1985.
Hasskarl, G. C. H. *"The Missing Link;" or The Negro's Ethnological Status.* Chambersburg, Pa.: The
    Democratic News, 1898.
Hine, Edward. *Forty-Seven Identifications of the British Nation with the Lost Tribes of Israel.* London:
    S. W. Partridge & Co., 1871.
Hitler, Adolf. *Mein Kampf.* Germany: Verlag Frz. Eher Nachf, GmbH, 1925; reprinted Boston:
    Houghton Mifflin, 1971, transl. Ralph Manheim.
Mullins, Eustace. *The Curse of Canaan.* Staunton, Va.: Revelation Books, 1987.
————. *The World Order.* Staunton, Va.: Ezra Pound Institute of Civilization, 1992.
Nations of Europe. London: James Nisbet & Co., 1840.
Pierce, William (aka Andrew Macdonald). *Hunter.* Hillsboro, W. Va.: National Vanguard Books, 1989;
    1994 2nd printing.
————. *The Turner Diaries.* Hillsboro, W. Va.: National Vanguard Books, 1978; 1980 edition.
Smith, Gary. *Land of ZOG.* Portland, Oreg.: Vuepoint, 1989.
Weisman, Charles A. *The Origin of Race and Civilization.* Burnsville, Minn.: Weisman Publications,
    1990.
————. Who is Esau-Edom? Burnsville, Minn.: Weisman Publications, 1991; 1992 edition.
Wilson, J. *Our Israelitish Origin: Lectures on Ancient Israel, and the Israelitish Origins of the Modern
    Nations of Europe.* London: James Nisbet and Co., 1840; 1843 edition.
Winchell, Alexander. *Preadamites; or a Demonstration of the Existence of Men Before Adam.* Chicago:
    S. C. Griggs & Co., 1880.

**Pamphlets, Tracts, Flyers, Brochures, Booklets, Videotapes, Audiocassettes, Periodicals: Pa-
triot/Militia, Christian, and Christian Patriot**
Atrocities At Ruby Ridge. Star Broadcasting.
Church, J. R. *Prophecy in the News.* November 1994, April 1995, May 1995, June 1995, January
    1996.
Cook, Terry. *Satan's System: 666.* Terry Cook Productions, 1994.
Demons: True Life Evil Forces. His Majesty's Media, 1995
Free American: August 1995, September 1995, October 1995.
Free Enterprise Society, Materials Catalogue, no. 3.
Freedom Network News, June/July 1995.
Koernke, Mark. *A Call to Arms.* Real World Productions, 1993.
Koernke, Mark. *America in Peril.* Real World Productions, 1993.
Lindsey, Hal. *Apocalypse Planet Earth.* Jeremiah Films, 1990.
Marrs, Texe. *Flashpoint:* Special Edition, n.d., September 1993, January 1994, August 1994,
    September 1994, October 1994, November 1994, December 1994, January 1995, February 1995,

March 1995, April 1995, May 1995, June 1995, July 1995, August 1995, February 1996

McAlvany, Don. "Financial & Spiritual Preparation for the '90s," Christian Conference, taped message (Vail, Colorado), August 11, 1994.

McAlvany, Don. Christian Conference, taped message (Vail, Colorado), "Coming Persecution of Christians," August 27, 1993.

McAlvany, Don. *McAlvany Intelligence Advisor*: January 1993, July 1993, August 1993, September 1993, March 1994, June 1994, August 1994, October 1994, November 1994, December 1994, January 1995, February 1995, March 1995, April 1995, May/June 1995, July 1995, August 1995, September 1995, October 1995.

Media Bypass, August 1995

Militia of Montana. *Invasion & Betrayal*. Militia of Montana, 1995.

Militia of Montana. *Militia of Montana Catalogue*, November 1994.

Missler, Chuck. *Personal Update*: October 1993, November 1993, January 1994, July 1995, August 1995, September 1995, November 1995.

Monetary & Economic Review, March 1993.

Mottahedeh, Peyman. "State vs. U.S. Citizenship Theory Debunked."

Paranoia, Fall 1994, Spring 1995.

Patriot Press: July 1995, August 1995, October 1995, November 1995.

Patriot Report: October 1994, February 1995

Perceptions, May/June 1995.

Thompson, Linda. "Alert!!."

————. "Declaration of Independence of 1994."

————. "Organization and Purpose of the American Justice Federation."

————. *Waco, Another Perspective*.

Trewhella, Matthew. *Defensive Action Press Release*. Missionaries to the Preborn.

————. *Missionaries to the Preborn Newsletter*, March 1994.

USA Patriot Magazine, October 1995

USTP Convention, videotape, May 27–29, 1994.

Pamphlets, Tracts, Flyers, Brochures, Booklets, Videotapes, Audiocassettes, Periodicals: Racist, White Supremacist, Anti-Semitic, Christian Identity, Anglo-British Israelism

American's Bulletin, June 1995, October 1995.

Beam, Louis. "Leaderless Resistance," *Special Report On The Meeting of the Christian Men Held in Estes Park, Colorado, October 23, 24, 25, 1992: Concerning the Killing of Vickie and Samuel Weaver By the United States Government*. LaPorte, Colo.: Scriptures for America, 1992, p. 22.

————. *The Seditionist*, issue 1 (Winter 1988).

Beckman, M. J. "Red" *The Church Deceived*. Billings, Mont.: Common Sense Press, 1984.

Butler, Richard. "Aryan Nations Platform for the Aryan National State," n.d.

————. "Aryan Nations Theopolitical Platform," n.d.

————. *Calling Our Nation*: no. 15, no. 29, no. 32, no. 33, no. 34, no. 59, no. 59, no. 60, no. 61.

————. *Who, What, Why, When, Where: Aryan Nations*. Hayden Lake, Idaho: Aryan Nations, n.d.

————. *The Protocols of the Learned Elders of Zion: An Outline*. Hayden Lake, Idaho: Aryan Nations, n.d.

Capt, E. Raymond. *Marks of Israel*.

CDL Report: issue 49, issue 112, issue 126.

Christian Defense League. *Patriot Review*: April/May 1991, April 1992

Christian Vanguard, February 1976.

Combs, James. *Tolerance: Jewry's War On Whites*.

————. *Who's Who in the World Zionist Conspiracy*.

Dickey, C. R. *The Bible and Segregation*. Merrimac, Mass.: Destiny Publishers, 1958.

Emry, Sheldon. *The Marks of Israel*. Phoenix, Ariz.: Lord's Covenant Church, 1980.

————. *The Old Jerusalem Is Not*. Phoenix, Ariz.: Lord's Covenant Church America's Promise, n.d.

Gale, William Potter. *Identity: Racial and National.* Mariposa, Calif.; Ministry of Christ Church, n.d.
————. *The Faith of Our Fathers.* Mariposa, Calif.: Ministry of Christ Church, 1963.
Kingdom-Identity Ministries. *Doctrinal Statement of Beliefs.* Harrison, Ark.: Kingdom-Identity Ministries.
Mange, Charles Lee. *The Two Seeds of Genesis 3:15.* Nevada, Mo.: Wake Up America, 1977; 1982 edition.
Mohr, Jack. *Christian Patriot Crusader* 7:4 (December 1991).
————. *Exploding the "Chosen People" Myth.* Bay St. Louis, Miss.: Jack Mohr, n.d.
————. *I Believe.* Bay St. Louis, Miss.: Jack Mohr, n.d.
————. *Seed of Satan: Literal or Figurative?* Bay St. Louis, Miss.: Jack Mohr, n.d.
————. *Who Are You and Why Are You Here?.* Bay St. Louis, Miss.: Jack Mohr, n.d.
Odeneal, W. Clyde. *Segregation: Sin or Sensible?.* Merrimac, Mass.: Destiny Publishers, 1958.
Peters, Pete. "A Special Gathering of Christian Men is Scheduled for October 23, 24, 25, 1992."
————. *A Scriptural Understanding of the Race Issue.* LaPorte, Colo.: Scriptures for America, 1990.
————. *Scriptures for America Newsletter:* vol. 3 (1992) 4 (1993) 4 (1994) 5 (1994) 2 (1995) 3 (1995)
————. Special Report on the Meeting of the Christian Men Held in Estes Park, Colorado, October 23, 24, 25, 1992: Concerning the Killing of Vickie and Samuel Weaver by the United States Government. LaPorte, Colo.: Scriptures for America, 1992.
————. *Strength of A Hero and the Warrior's Song.* LaPorte, Colo.: Scriptures for America, 1989; 1994 edition.
————. *The Real Hate Group.* LaPorte, Colo.: Scriptures for America, n.d.
————. White Crime in America, n.d.
Polk, Keen. *"Everything After Its Kind".* Bellflower, Calif.: Keen Polk, n.d.
Robb, Thomas. *Interracial.* Harrison, Ark.: Message of Old Publications, n.d.
Ross, Malcolm. *Christianity vs Judeo-Christianity.* Canada: Stronghold Publishing Co., 1987; 1990 edition.
Spotlight: June 5, 1995, August 14, 1995, September 18, 1995, September 25, 1995, October 2, 1995, October 30, 1995.
Swift, Wesley A. *Were All the People on the Earth Drowned in the Flood?.* Lake Hayden, Calif.: Aryan Nations, n.d.; original sermon delivered 1962.
————. *In the Beginning...God.* Lake Hayden, Idaho: Aryan Nations, n.d.; original sermon delivered 1967.
O'Brien, Thomas E. *"Verboten".* Metairie, La.: New Christian Crusade Church, 1974; 1987 reprint entitled *Proof: God's Chosen Are White Adamic Christians, "Verboten".*
Mullins, Eustace. *Marching Through Georgia.* transcript of lecture in pamplet form, available from Sons of Liberty.
————. *Jewish War Against the Christian World.* transcript of lecture in pamplet form, available from Sons of Liberty.
Thomas, J. Llewellyn. *Objections to British Israel Teaching Examined.* London: Covenant Publishing, 1951.
Wise, James E. *The Seed of the Serpent.* Harrison, Ark.: Kingdom-Identity Ministries, n.d.

Internet/ BBS Postings: Racist, White Supremacist, Anti-Semitic, Christian Identity, Anglo-British Israelism, Patriot/Militia, Christian, and Christian Patriot
"Report No. 7 Operations," *Taking Aim* 1 issue 7, 1994, Internet posting in the Patriot Archives, pathway starts at http://www.tezcat.com/, to Tezcat Archives, to Patriot folder.
"THE JEW WORLD ORDER, JEWS OF THE WORLD: Let My People Go!," Internet postings at the Banned Wed Page, http://www.gsu.edu/~hisjwbx/, to Table of Contents, #1.
Campbell, J. B. "Federal Power Abuses Spark Militias: Commentary," *Spotlight,* January 9, 1995, Internet edition in the patriot Archives, pathway starts at pathway starts at http://www.tezcat.com/, to Tezcat Archives, to Patriot folder, to Militia folder, to Feds_and_Militia.txt.
Gomes, Ken. "More Black Copters," BBS message #453 (From: Ken Gomes, To: All), July 29, 1994, *AEN News*-FidoNet.

Gritz, Bo. "America Soon to be Disarmed," *Center For Action* 3:4, November 1993, Internet posting in the Patriot Archives, pathway starts at http://www.tezcat.com/, to Tezcat Archives, to Patriot folder, to Guns folder, to Bo_Gritz_on_Disarming.txt.

—————. *Center For Action* 4:6, January 1995, Internet posting in the Patriot Archives, pathway starts at http://www.tezcat.com/, to Tezcat Archives, to Patriot folder, to Militia Folder, to Gritz_news.txt document.

Kerns, Sam "On the Lighter Side," BBS message #5869 (Fr: Sam Kerns, To: All). April 21, 1994, *AEN Chat*-FidoNet.

Null, Gary and T. C. Fry. Radio Broadcast, WBAI-FM (99.5), reprinted as "Beyond AMERICA IN PERIL: Confirming Mark Koernke's Warnings," THE PEOPLE'S SPELLBREAKER, John DiNardo, ed., Internet posting in the Patriot Archives, pathway starts at http://www.tezcat.com/, to Tezcat Archives, to Patriot folder, to New World Order folder, to Beyond_America_in_Peril.txt.

Peters, Pete. "Concerning the Oklahoma Bombing," *Scriptures for America* II (1995), 2; available from Internet posting at Scriptures for America, http://ra.nilenet.com/!tmw/.

—————. "Frequently Asked Questions and Answers on Isreal-Identity," Internet posting at Scriptures for America, http://ra.nilenet.com/!tmw/, to Library, to Israel-Identity FAQ, to Question 5.

—————. "Frequently Asked Questions and Answers on Isreal-Identity," Internet posting at Scriptures for America, http://ra.nilenet.com/!tmw/, to Library, to Israel-Identity FAQ, to Question 11.

—————. *America the Conquered* advertisement, Scriptures for America, Internet posting at http://ra.nilenet.com/!tmw/.

Pierce, William. "The Wisdom of Henry Ford." The transcripts of this show are available at William Pierce's National Alliance Internet Page, http://www.natvan.com/.

Roland, John. "Rumored March 25 Arrests," newsgroup message #180430, March 24, 1995, posted to talk.politics.guns.

—————. "Constitutional Militias Forming Across Nation," February 22, 1995, Internet posting, http://www.the-spa.com/constitution/pr_5222.txt; also available in Tezcat's octopus archives, pathway starts at http://www.tezcat.com/, to Tezcat Archives, to Octopus folder, to Misc. folder, to militias.organize.

Thompson, Linda. "Ala.ERT," BBS message #14290 (Fr: Linda Thompson, To: All), March 27, 1994, *AEN News*-FidoNet

—————. "02/Nwo Recap," BBS message #14009 (Fr: Linda Thompson, To: All), February 8, 1994, *AEN News*-FidoNet.

—————. "COME TO WACO SATURDAY, APRIL 3!!," BBS message #14465 (Fr: Linda Thompson, To: All), March 28, 1993, *AEN News*-FidoNet.

—————. "Crime Briefing—Martial Law 1 of 16," BBS message #14016 (Fr: Linda Thompson, To: All), February 8, 1994, AEN News-FidoNet.

—————. "Gary Hunt: Traitor Exposed," *AEN News*-FidoNet document, Part 4 of 9 Parts.

—————. "Gurkha Mercenaries" BBS message #14051 (Fr: Linda Thompson, To: All), February 8, 1994, *AEN News*-FidoNet; Cf. Linda Thompson, "Global 2000—Population Control," BBS message #14055 (Fr: Linda Thompson, To: All), February 8, 1994, *AEN News*-FidoNet.

—————. "NBC DRILL TIME (and I don't mean the TV network!)," BBS message #14056 (Fr: Linda Thompson, To: All), February 8, 1994, *AEN News*-FidoNet.

—————. "Re: HELP: Waco Video II," BBS message #1801 (Fr: Linda Thompson, To: Terry Liberty-Parker), March 30, 1994, *AEN News*-FidoNet.

—————. "Re: On the Lighter Side ....," BBS message #6235 (Fr: Sam Kerns, To: All), April 23, 1994, *AEN Chat*-FidoNet.

—————. "Sept. 19 Militia Assembly Canceled 9 of 9 pages," BBS message #18672 (Fr: Linda Thompson, To: All), August 9, 1994, *AEN Local*-FidoNet.

—————. "Think About It — 10," BBS message #14309 (Fr: Linda Thompson, To: All), February 9, 1994, *AEN News*-FidoNet.

—————. "Why We Have to Fight," BBS message #15553 (Fr: Linda Thompson, To: All), February 17, 1994, *AEN News*-FidoNet.

—————. ATTACKS.ZIP, downloaded from AEN Files archive on August 31, 1994.

Index